International Practices

3 2044 070 085 766

EDITED BY EMANUEL ADLER AND VINCENT POULIOT

It is in and through practices – deeds that embody shared intersubjective knowledge – that social life is organized, that subjectivities are constituted, and that history unfolds. One can think of dozens of different practices (from balancing to banking or network-ing) which constitute the social fabric of world politics. As an entry point to the study of world politics, the concept of practice accommodates a variety of perspectives in a coherent yet flexible fashion and opens the door to much-needed interdisciplinary research in International Relations. Thanks to the practice lens, the book organizes a productive dialogue among leading scholars from different theoretical traditions and whose works span various subfields ranging from International Law and Humanitarianism to nuclear deterrence and the United Nations. *International Practices* crystallizes the authors' past research on international practices into a common effort to turn the study of practice into a novel research program in International Relations.

EMANUEL ADLER is the Andrea and Charles Bronfman Chair of Israeli Studies in the Department of Political Science at the University of Toronto and editor of *International Organization*. Professor Adler also currently holds an honorary Professorship at the University of Copenhagen and is a member of the European Academy of Sciences.

VINCENT POULIOT is Assistant Professor in the Department of Political Science at McGill University and Associate Director of the Centre for International Peace and Security Studies (CIPSS). His research interests lie at the intersection of practice theory and the global governance of international security.

Cambridge Studies in International Relations: 119

International Practices

EDITORS
Christian Reus-Smit
Nicholas J. Wheeler

EDITORIAL BOARD
Stuart Croft, James Der Derian, Martha Finnemore, Lene Hansen,
Robert Keohane, Rachel Kerr, Jan Aart Scholte, Peter Vale,
Kees Van Der Pijl, Jutta Weldes, Jennifer Welsh, William Wohlforth

Cambridge Studies in International Relations is a joint initiative of
Cambridge University Press and the British International Studies
Association (BISA). The series will include a wide range of material, from
undergraduate textbooks and surveys to research-based monographs and
collaborative volumes. The aim of the series is to publish the best new
scholarship in International Studies from Europe, North America and the
rest of the world.

Cambridge Studies in International Relations

International Practices

EDITED BY

EMANUEL ADLER AND VINCENT POULIOT

CAMBRIDGE
UNIVERSITY PRESS

JZ
1242
.I5755
2011

CAMBRIDGE UNIVERSITY PRESS
Cambridge, New York, Melbourne, Madrid, Cape Town,
Singapore, São Paulo, Delhi, Tokyo, Mexico City

Cambridge University Press
The Edinburgh Building, Cambridge CB2 8RU, UK

Published in the United States of America by Cambridge University Press, New York

www.cambridge.org
Information on this title: www.cambridge.org/9780521281171

© Cambridge University Press 2011

This publication is in copyright. Subject to statutory exception
and to the provisions of relevant collective licensing agreements,
no reproduction of any part may take place without the written
permission of Cambridge University Press.

First published 2011

Printed in the United Kingdom at the University Press, Cambridge

A catalog record for this publication is available from the British Library

Library of Congress Cataloging in Publication data
International practices / edited by Emanuel Adler and Vincent Pouliot.
p.   cm.
Includes index.
ISBN 978-0-521-28117-1 (pbk.) – ISBN 978-1-107-01043-7 (hardback)
1. International relations.   2. World politics.   3. Diplomacy.   I. Adler, Emanuel.
II. Pouliot, Vincent, 1979–   III. Title.
JZ1242.I5755   2011
327.1–dc22
2011005725

ISBN 978-1-107-01043-7 Hardback
ISBN 978-0-521-28117-1 Paperback

Cambridge University Press has no responsibility for the persistence or
accuracy of URLs for external or third-party internet websites referred to
in this publication, and does not guarantee that any content on such
websites is, or will remain, accurate or appropriate.

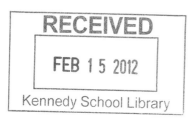
RECEIVED

FEB 1 5 2012

Kennedy School Library

Contents

Figure

Note on the contributors

RITA ABRAHAMSEN is Associate Professor in the School of International Development and Global Studies and in the Graduate School of Public and International Affairs at the University of Ottawa

EMANUEL ADLER is the Andrea and Charles Bronfman Chair of Israeli Studies in the Department of Political Science at the University of Toronto

JANICE BIALLY MATTERN is Associate Professor in the Department of Political Science at the National University of Singapore

JUTTA BRUNNÉE is Professor of Law at the University of Toronto and holds the Metcalf Chair in Environmental Law

ARJUN CHOWDHURY is Assistant Professor in the Department of Political Science at the University of British Columbia

RAYMOND D. DUVALL is Morse–Alumni Professor and Chair of the Department of Political Science at the University of Minnesota

LENE HANSEN is Professor in the Department of Political Science at the University of Copenhagen

FRIEDRICH KRATOCHWIL is Professor of International Relations in the Department of Political and Social Sciences at the European University Institute in Florence and international scholar at Kyung Hee University, Seoul

RICHARD LITTLE is Professor Emeritus in the School of Sociology, Politics and International Studies at the University of Bristol

PATRICK M. MORGAN is Professor in the Political Science Department and holder of the Tierney Chair in Global Peace and Conflict Studies at the University of California, Irvine

IVER B. NEUMANN is Professor and Research Director at the Norwegian Institute of International Affairs

VINCENT POULIOT is Assistant Professor in the Department of Political Science at McGill University and Associate Director of the Centre for International Peace and Security Studies (CIPSS)

NORRIN M. RIPSMAN is Professor in the Department of Political Science at Concordia University

OLE JACOB SENDING is Senior Researcher and Head of the Centre for Global Governance at the Norwegian Institute of International Affairs

JANICE GROSS STEIN is the Belzberg Professor of Conflict Management in the Department of Political Science and the Director of the Munk School of Global Affairs at the University of Toronto

STEPHEN J. TOOPE is the President and Vice-Chancellor of the University of British Columbia

ERIK VOETEN is Peter F. Krogh Associate Professor of Geopolitics and Justice in World Affairs in the Edmund A. Walsh School of Foreign Service and Government Department at Georgetown University

MICHAEL C. WILLIAMS is Professor in the Graduate School of Public and International Affairs at the University of Ottawa

Acronyms and abbreviations

AHA	Africa Humanitarian Action
AIDMI	All India Disaster Mitigation Institute
ALNAP	Active Learning Network for Accountability and Performance
ANC	African National Congress
ARRP	Advanced Reform and Restructuring Program (World Bank)
CAS	Country Assistance Strategy (World Bank)
CBDR	common but differentiated responsibilities
CCID	Cape Town Central City Improvement District
CIA	Central Intelligence Agency
CID	City Improvement District (Cape Town)
CIPSS	Centre for International Peace and Security Studies
CPIA	Country Policy and Institutional Assessment (World Bank)
CPR	Country Performance Rating (World Bank)
CPSU	Communist Party of the Soviet Union
DEC	Development Economics Vice Presidency (World Bank)
DEC	Disaster Emergencies Committee
ECHO	European Community Humanitarian Organization
ED	Executive Director (World Bank)
EMU	Economic and Monetary Union
ERD	evaluation reports database (ALNAP)
G4S	Group4Securicor
GATS	General Agreement on Trade in Services
GATT	General Agreement on Tariffs and Trade
GDP	gross domestic product
GICHD	Geneva International Centre for Humanitarian Demining
GNI	gross national income
HAP-I	Humanitarian Accountability Partnership International
IBRD	International Bank for Reconstruction and Development (World Bank)
ICCPR	International Covenant on Civil and Political Rights

ICISS	International Commission on Intervention and State Sovereignty
ICJ	International Court of Justice
ICVA	International Council of Voluntary Agencies
IDA	International Development Association (World Bank)
IISD	International Institute for Sustainable Development
IMF	International Monetary Fund
IO	international organization
IOs	international organizations
IPCC	Intergovernmental Panel on Climate Change
IR	International Relations
IRC	International Rescue Committee
IRQMS	Islamic Relief's Quality Management System
JCS	Joint Chiefs of Staff
MIRV	Multiple Independently Targeted Re-entry Vehicle
MSF	Médecins sans Frontières
NATO	North Atlantic Treaty Organization
NGO	non-governmental organization
NSC	National Security Council
OAU	Organization of African Unity
OPCS	Operations Policy and Country Services (World Bank)
PBA	Performance Based Allocation System (World Bank)
PPP	public–private partnership
PSC	private security company
R&D	research and development
ROK	Republic of Korea
SAPS	South African Police Service
SCHR	Southern Center for Human Rights
SSHRC	Social Sciences and Humanities Research Council of Canada
SSU	Strategic Surveillance Unit (Cape Town)
TRIPS	Trade-Related Aspects of Intellectual Property Rights
UDHR	Universal Declaration of Human Rights
UN	United Nations
UNDP	United Nations Development Programme
UNFCCC	United Nations Framework Convention on Climate Change
UNGA	United Nations General Assembly
UNIFIL	United Nations Interim Force in Lebanon
VCLT	Vienna Convention on the Law of Treaties
WMD	weapons of mass destruction
WTO	World Trade Organization

PART I

Practices in International Relations and social theory

1 | International practices: introduction and framework

EMANUEL ADLER AND VINCENT POULIOT[*]

In this book, we invite students of International Relations (IR) to approach world politics through the lens of its manifold practices. By focusing on what practitioners do, we zoom in on the quotidian unfolding of international life, from multilateral diplomacy to finance trading through environmental negotiations. We analyze the ongoing accomplishments that, put together, constitute the "big picture" that is variously described by existing IR theories. Of course, practices have long been a prime object of analysis in the IR discipline. Building on the "practice turn"[1] that has recently been taken in social theory, we develop and systematize an interparadigmatic research program that takes competent performances as its main entry point in the study of world politics. Our claim is not that practice offers the universal, grand theory or totalizing ontology of everything social. Instead, taking international practices seriously spells out the many faces of world politics, including power and security, trade and finance, strategy, institutions and organizations, resources, knowledge and discourse, etc. in action, as part of a "doing" in and on the world.

The study of international practices has gained significant momentum recently. In IR, among the first scholars to draw attention to practices were the poststructuralists who, building on the path-breaking works of Michel Foucault, among others, revisited world politics as a set of textual practices.[2] One of the key insights brought to IR by poststructuralism is precisely that the complex pictures of world politics are made up of a myriad of everyday

[*] The authors would like to thank Steven Bernstein, Lilach Gilady, Lene Hansen, Matthew Hoffmann, Markus Kornprobst, Frédéric Mérand, Iver Neumann, Ole Jacob Sending, Wendy Wong, Ruben Zaiotti, and two anonymous reviewers, for very useful comments on earlier versions of this chapter. Conference participants in Toronto were also instrumental in improving the text. We also acknowledge the financial support of the Social Sciences and Humanities Research Council of Canada (SSHRC); the Connaught Fund, the Munk School of Global Affairs, the Centre for International Studies (in particular, Louis Pauly and Tina Lagopoulos), and the Faculty of Arts and Sciences (in particular, Dean Meric Gertler) at the University of Toronto; as well as the Centre for International Peace and Security Studies (CIPSS) at McGill University and Université de Montréal. Finally, we extend our gratitude to Virginia DiGaetano and James McKee for their research assistance; and to Patricia Greve whose unsurpassed contribution made the book possible every step of the way.
[1] Schatzki, Knorr Cetina, and von Savigny, 2001.   [2] Der Derian and Shapiro, 1989.

practices that too often go overlooked in scholarly research.[3] At about the same time, a number of IR scholars inspired by the works of prominent social theorists such as Pierre Bourdieu started to put matters of practice at the center of their analyses.[4] Coming from the emerging constructivist corner, growing interest in "deeds"[5] and "practical reasoning"[6] also contributed to establish international practices as valid objects of analysis in the discipline. That said, the recent turn to practice in IR came only at the turn of the millennium when, building on a similar intellectual movement in social theory, Neumann advocated "returning practice to the linguistic turn."[7] Since then, a rapidly increasing number of scholars have joined the fray.[8]

This is not to say, of course, that before the mid-1980s the matter of international practices had been wholly ignored in the IR discipline. In fact, we contend that there is nothing arcane or even paradigm-specific in the study of international practices: most existing frameworks are at least indirectly concerned with them – though not always mindfully. For example, classical realists like Kissinger used to devote most of their energy on practices such as diplomacy and balancing.[9] Similarly, what the English School calls "the institutions of international society" – Bull's balance of power, international law, diplomacy, great-power management, and war – certainly comes quite close to our focus on socially organized and meaningful activities.[10] On the rationalist side, we show elsewhere that Schelling's theory of bargaining foretold, in very productive ways, many of the themes central to a practice framework.[11] As for liberals, one could argue, perhaps stretching a little, that what Keohane and Nye were looking for in their seminal *Power and Interdependence* is patterns of cooperative practices in dealing with monetary or environmental issues.[12] Overall, given their often implicitly acknowledged prominence as objects of analysis, the time is ripe for a coordinated, self-conscious, and theoretically informed scrutiny of international practices.

This book will purport to demonstrate that the momentum that the study of international practices has gained recently amounts to a research opportunity across paradigmatic divides. Whatever one's specific theoretical perspective, we

---

[3] See, for example, Der Derian, 1987; and Doty, 1996.

[4] See Ashley, 1987; Bigo 1996; Guzzini, 2000; Hopf, 2002 and 2010; Huysmans, 2002; and Keck and Sikkink, 1998, 34–36.

[5] Onuf, 1989.   [6] Kratochwil, 1989. See also Reus-Smit, 1999.   [7] Neumann, 2002.

[8] See, for example, Adler, 2005 and 2008; Adler-Nissen, 2008; Brunnée and Toope, 2010; Büger and Gadinger, 2007; Gheciu, 2005; Katzenstein, 2010; Koivisto and Dunne, 2010; Krebs and Jackson, 2007; Krotz, 2007; Leander, 2005; Mérand, 2008; Mitzen, 2006; Pouliot, 2008, 2010a, and 2010b; Seabrooke and Tsingou, 2009; Villumsen, Forthcoming; Wiener, 2008; and Williams, 2007. On pragmatism in IR, see Friedrichs and Kratochwil, 2009; Haas and Haas, 2002; Hellmann, 2009; and Kratochwil, 2007.

[9] Kissinger, 1973.   [10] Bull, 1995.

[11] See Adler and Pouliot, 2011; and Schelling, 1980.   [12] Keohane and Nye, 2001.

claim, as soon as one looks into practices it becomes difficult, and even impossible, to ignore structures (or agency), ideas (or matter), rationality (or practicality), stability (or change): one becomes ontologically compelled to reach beyond traditional levels and units of analysis. By implication, there is no such thing as *the* theory of practice but a variety of theories focused on practices. In fact, an IR practice-oriented theoretical approach comprises a fairly vast array of analytical frameworks that privilege practice as the key entry point to the study of world politics. This is why the concept of international practices can supply a particularly fertile ground for making interparadigmatic conversations possible. Thus, instead of interparadigmatic competition, subsumption, synthesis, or even complementarity, we believe that the concept of practice promises cross-fertilization – the engine of social scientific refinement.

In this introduction, we argue that a focus on international practices promises four key advances for the IR discipline. First, by focusing on practices in IR we can understand both IR theory and international politics better or differently. In other words, world politics can be understood as structured by practices, which give meaning to international action, make possible strategic interaction, and are reproduced, changed, and reinforced by international action and interaction. This focus helps broaden the ontology of world politics, serves as the basis for a new research program around which debates in IR theory can be structured, and can be used as a unit of analysis that transcends traditional understandings of "levels of analysis." Second, the concept of practice supplies a "focal point" making interparadigmatic conversations possible. Starting from the assumption that dialogue is a key driver of theoretical advancement, we develop a modular framework that allows scholars with different theoretical preferences to talk to, as opposed to across, each other. Our definition of practice is sufficiently flexible to accommodate a variety of perspectives. Third, a practice-oriented approach promises to avoid many of the traditional dichotomies in social and IR theory. We show how the notion spans divides between stability and change, agency and structure, as well as ideas and matter. As a result, a number of new possibilities for cross-fertilization emerge among competing IR paradigms. Finally, putting practice at the center of IR theory opens an exciting and innovative research agenda. We illustrate how our framework revisits central concepts of our discipline, including power, history, strategy, and others, and we suggest a few new research questions and puzzles that derive from our focus on international practices. In order to structure our interparadigmatic dialogue, in this introduction we also devise a theoretical framework centered on the transformative dynamics of practices. We conceptualize practice as either *explanans* or *explanandum* and inventory the many ways in which socially meaningful and organized performances interact with the natural and social environments. In order to operationalize this framework, we also discuss methodological issues, including levels of aggregation, and encourage pluralism in the study of international practices. But first, we define the central notion of this book.

Practices

Practices are competent performances. More precisely, practices are socially meaningful patterns of action which, in being performed more or less competently, simultaneously embody, act out, and possibly reify background knowledge and discourse in and on the material world. Practices, such as marking a linear territorial boundary, deterring with nuclear weapons, or finance trading, are not merely descriptive "arrows" that connect structure to agency and back, but rather the dynamic material and ideational processes that enable structures to be stable or to evolve, and agents to reproduce or transform structures. We shall explore the social-theoretical implications of this definition in the second part of the chapter. Here our objectives are, first, to differentiate between behavior, action, and practice, and, second, to unpack the notion of practice by looking into its main conceptual elements.

In common parlance, the concepts of behavior, action, and practice are often used interchangeably. Conceptually, however, they are not the same. An easy way to grasp their differences is to conceive of these notions as a gradation: actions are a specific type of behaviors, and practices are a particular kind of action.[13] In a nutshell, the concept of behavior evokes the material dimension of doing, as a deed performed in and on the world; then the notion of action adds an ideational layer, emphasizing the meaningfulness of the deed at both the subjective and intersubjective levels; and, finally, the term "practice" tacks another layer on to the edifice – or, better put, makes it hang together as one coherent structure, by pointing out the patterned nature of deeds in socially organized contexts. The distinction between behavior and action is the easiest to grasp: action is behavior imbued with meaning. Running in the streets aimlessly is mere behavior, running after a thief is an action endowed with meaning. Practices, however, are patterned actions that are embedded in particular organized contexts and, as such, are articulated into specific types of action and are socially developed through learning and training.[14] Action is always a constitutive part of any practice, yet the reverse is not necessarily true. Action is specific and located in time; practices are general classes of action which, although situated in a social context, are not limited to any specific enacting. Police squads chasing down a criminal gang is a practice, because it is socially structured and reiterated. Similarly, an American carrier entering the Strait of Hormuz is an

---

[13] Cook and Brown, 1999, 387. As these authors illustrate: "In the simplest case, if Vance's knee jerks, that is behavior. When Vance raps his knee with a physician's hammer to check his reflexes, it is behavior that has meaning, and thus is what we call action. If his physician raps his knee as part of an exam, it is practice. This is because the meaning of her action comes from the organized contexts of her training and ongoing work in medicine (where it can draw on, contribute to, and be evaluated in the work of others in her field)."

[14] Corradi, Gherardi, and Verzelloni, 2010. Consequently, a focus on practice, as opposed to action, is more encompassing than Weber's *Verstehen* or Schütz's subjective hermeneutics.

action endowed with social meaning. The same action, however, when embedded in an organizational context, repeated over time and space, constituted by knowledge about the exploitation of potential force, and articulated as part of a complex set of other social performances, which may require learning and training, is part and parcel of the practice of coercive diplomacy.

By *international* practices, we denote socially organized activities that pertain to world politics, broadly construed. In so defining the scope of our volume, we do not take a position in the many definitional debates that rage in the discipline, such as those between comparative vs. international politics, or global governance vs. international relations. Instead, we argue that one of the key epistemological consequences of taking international practices seriously precisely is to bring those scholarly debates "down" to the ground of world politics in order to empirically scrutinize the processes whereby certain competent performances produce effects of a world political nature. Put differently, the scope of analysis – global, international, transnational, regional, organizational, substate, local, etc. – is itself a matter of practice: defining what counts as an international practice and what does not is best left with practitioners themselves in their actual performance of world politics.

Let us now unpack the notion of practice. First, a practice is a *performance*[15] – that is, a process of doing something. Contrary to entities or substances, which can be grasped in a reified way, practices have no existence other than in their unfolding or process.[16] The performance of practice goes with, and constitutes, the flow of history. As a form of action, practice differs from preferences or beliefs, which it expresses, and from discourse or institutions, which it instantiates. Second, practice tends to be *patterned*, in that it generally exhibits certain regularities over time and space. In a way reminiscent of routine, practices are repeated, or at least reproduce similar behaviors with regular meanings. These patterns, as we explained above, are part of a socially organized context, which not only gives them meaning, but also structures interaction. This is not to say that practice is strictly iterative, however, as there is always wiggle room for agency even in repetition.[17] As a general rule, though, iteration is a key characteristic of practices – and the condition of possibility for their social existence.

Third, practice is more or less *competent* in a socially meaningful and recognizable way. The structured dimension of practice stems not only from repetition but also, and in fact primarily, from the fact that groups of individuals tend to interpret its performance along similar standards.[18] Social recognition is thus a fundamental aspect of practice: its (in)competence is never inherent but attributed in and through social relations. The notion of performance implies that of a public, of an audience able to appraise the practice. As Barnes notes, contrary to

---

[15] See Goffman, 1959; and Butler, 1990.   [16] Jackson and Nexon, 1999.
[17] De Certeau, 1990. See Goffman, 1959; and Turner, 1994 for a critique.
[18] Goffman, 1959.

habit, which is performed on an individual scale (and is apprehended as such), a practice can be done correctly or incorrectly.[19] The ascription of (in)competence is an eminently complex social process: for instance, in some contexts incompetent practice might be more "successful" in bringing results than virtuoso performance. Fourth, practice rests on *background knowledge*, which it embodies, enacts, and reifies all at once. Knowledge not only precedes practice as do intentions, beliefs, etc. In addition, intersubjectivity is bound up in the performance and can only be expressed as such.[20] Background knowledge is practical; it is oriented toward action and, as such, it often resembles skill much more than the type of knowledge that can be brandished or represented, such as norms or ideas.[21]

Finally, practice weaves together the *discursive and material* worlds. Without language, communication, and discourse, people could not tell the difference between behavior and practice. Not only is language the conduit of meaning, which turns practices into the location and engine of social action, but it is itself an enactment or doing in the form of "discursive practices."[22] By nature, practices represent the world in specific ways: they implicitly make the claim that "this is how things are."[23] At the same time, practices are mediated by material artifacts.[24] Practice typically is enacted in and on the world, and thus can change the physical environment as well as the ideas that individually and collectively people hold about the world.

As an illustration, take the practice of international summitry – G8 annual summits, for example. These meetings of state officials constitute an international practice insofar as they conform to the five dimensions that we have just laid out. First, G8 summits are performances: they consist of a number of actions and processes that unfold in real time, from the welcoming ceremony to the joint press conference through the official photography. Second, these performances are patterned from one year to the next. Although each meeting boasts its own particularities, there is much regularity in their staging, including the pecking order or the mixture of formal and informal discussions. Third, participating state officials generally exhibit a variable degree of competence as they attend the summit. The media and populations typically recognize the meaning of a clip featuring the British prime minister casually joking with the US president, for example. Fourth, much of the performance rests on a form of background knowledge that is bound up in practices. For instance, there is a very specific and skillful way for state officials to subtly take a little distance from the consensus forged for the official communiqué. Fifth, and finally, G8 summits are both ideational and material. Participants spend a lot of time publicly and privately talking about their meetings in order to represent preferences and

---

[19] Barnes, 2001.   [20] See Wittgenstein, 1958; and Taylor, 1985.   [21] Bourdieu, 1990.
[22] Foucault, 1980.   [23] Swidler, 2001.   [24] See Reckwitz, 2002; and Latour, 2005.

policies. To do so, they make use of a variety of materials – conference rooms, ceremonial artifacts, the internet, note exchanges with Sherpas, etc.

Conceptually, any given practice can be appraised through different levels of aggregation. For example, the practice of international summitry is an aggregate of several competent performances, including formal dining, press conference delivery, bilateral work meetings, etc. We suggest that the identification of the most appropriate level of aggregation should be based on two criteria. First, the research puzzle: should it deal with international summitry, then it is more appropriate to conceive of G8 summits as one aggregate practice; a study into intergovernmental rites, however, may want to zoom in at a lower level. Second, the practical experience of performers helps decide what the most appropriate level of aggregation is. In the case at hand, should state officials act out G8 summits as one whole, then it is a relevant starting point. Sherpas, however, may conceive of the informal multilateral meetings as "where the action is." Methodologically speaking, sense-making and situated-ness are particularly important aspects of the study of international practices.

We find Hansen's distinction, in Chapter 11 of this volume, between specific and general practices[25] compelling for thinking about practice aggregation and constellation of practices. We will say much more about constellations of practice in this chapter's fourth section. Right now, suffice it to say that the importance of Hansen's distinction lies in the notion that specific practices often may be asserted as though they belong to general practices, whereas "uncontested specific 'routine' practices" may be crucial for the reproduction of general practices. Methodologically, this distinction may require us to examine prominent specific practices, asking "which general practices they mobilize and whether a specific practice's claim to a general category of practice is stable or not."[26] In the G8 case, for instance, it would be important to inquire about the extent to which joint press conferences may play a role in the reproduction of multilateral diplomacy, and whether changes in conference procedures may be indicative of changes in more general patterns of such diplomacy.

The study of international practices also faces the issue of corporate practices – that is, practices that are performed by collectives in unison. In world politics, most practices belong to this type: war, for example, is a socially meaningful pattern of action which, in being performed more or less competently, simultaneously embodies, reifies and acts out background knowledge and discourse in and on the material world. In a very important sense, G8 summits are performed not only by singular heads of state but also by large teams of representatives. In fact, because of the background knowledge that is necessarily bound up in it, practice is always a "collective accomplishment."[27] Consequently, we explain corporate practices as being both structured and acted out by communities of practice, and by the diffusion of background knowledge across agents in these

---

[25] Hansen, Chapter 11 in this volume.   [26] *Ibid.*   [27] Barnes, 2001.

communities, which similarly disposes them to act in coordination. For example, through country-to-country discussions held at different levels (heads of state, Sherpas, political advisors, expert groups, etc.), a given country mission seeks to grasp, in a very coordinated fashion, what the position of a foreign capital is on a particular issue and how flexible it could be. Such corporate practices are not the action of one corporate agent (a state) but that of a community of representatives whose members enter in patterned relations, within an organized social context, thanks to similar background dispositions.

Fostering interparadigmatic conversations in IR

Bringing practice to the forefront of IR theory intends not to promote a new "ism" but to serve existing "isms." As such, it is justified because being the "gluon" of IR – the ontological entity that cuts across paradigms under different names but with a related substance – practice may help promote the development of a common language despite theoretical divides.

Gluons are elementary particles that "glue" the quarks together and mediate or carry the strong or nuclear force. The more separated the quarks are from each other, the stronger the force. We use this powerful metaphor to emphasize practice's role as "glue," not only at the ontological, but also at the epistemological, level. Mediating between the material and meaningful, and between structure and process, practice may be considered the ontological core concept that amalgamates the constitutive parts of social international life. And, in spite of the fact that when it comes to epistemology, scholars from different IR theory traditions often talk across, rather than to, each other, the concept of practice partly helps draw disciplinary boundaries and bind different communities into a single discipline. While we do believe in the benefits of a healthy dose of competition in intellectual refinement, we are also convinced that open dialogue is a necessary companion. Putting practice at the center of IR theory is not meant to discourage researchers to establish the value of their respective paradigms; instead, it provides a conceptual structure to reflexively and critically appraise one's own theoretical assumptions in relation to others. Practice, we propose, can "glue" students of world politics together in spite of their metatheoretical differences.

Whether one speaks of balancing, human rights protection, deterrence, or finance trading, these practices have traditionally been theorized in isolation from one another in IR. Some are seen as the preserve of neorealism because of their materiality, whereas others allegedly fall on the constructivist turf by virtue of their symbolic nature. All too often, practices that belong to world economic processes are studied separately from those of international security, and reciprocally. Moreover, a lack of dialogue between practice approaches at the micro- and macro-levels promotes inward-looking theorizing and lack of cross-fertilization. Systemic theories conceive of practice as the functional consequence of structural dynamics;[28] rational choice theory is interested in one specific type of international practices – those associated with cost-benefit calculations,[29] and other individualistic approaches often overlook the social contexts that make practices more than psychological processes.[30] That kind of pigeonholing is indeed untenable from a practice perspective, and this book seeks to illuminate the commonality of international practices. In so doing, a focus on practice promises a new dialogue of ideas in order to better understand the pressing matters of world politics. The diplomatic practice, for instance, in many ways upholds the contemporary international society, informs its past and future evolution, and helps explain the choices and policies defended by its actors. Our discipline can only benefit from a theoretical crossfire at the dozens of different practices that constitute the social fabric of world politics.

The concept of practice, therefore, has unparalleled potential in providing a conceptual intersection around which IR theories may cluster. As an entry point to the study of world politics, it accommodates, and speaks to, a variety of perspectives in a coherent yet flexible fashion. Over the last few years, calls for bridge-building, analytical eclecticism, and synthesis have abounded in the fragmented discipline of IR.[31] To many, the advancement of knowledge derives from cumulation. This book takes a different tack on interparadigmatic debates in IR. Instead of combining different theoretical perspectives into one single framework, the objective is for a variety of perspectives to meet around a *conceptual focal point* while retaining their distinctiveness. Bringing practice to the forefront leads not to synthesis but to dialogue.[32] Around the notion of practice, this book organizes and structures a conversation among theorists associated with neoclassical realism, rational choice institutionalism, the English School, constructivism, and poststructuralism. Since there is no such thing as a unified practice approach in social theory, we believe this pluralism to be particularly conducive to much-needed interparadigmatic dialogue in IR. Our goal is conversation, not conversion, so as to overcome what Buzan and Little rightly criticize as "theoretical atomisation" in our discipline.[33]

In addition, the different contributors tackle a number of empirical issues that could benefit from a cross-topical investigation. The notion of practice also opens the door to interdisciplinary research in IR. Subfields like security studies, international political economy, and global governance too often become watertight compartments with no flows of knowledge transfers. Against this tendency, this book gathers scholars coming from different subfields in IR and seeks to throw theoretical bridges across empirical issues. Practices associated

[28] See, for example, Waltz, 1979.   [29] See, for example, Fearon, 1996.
[30] See, for example, Goldstein and Keohane, 1993.
[31] See, for example, Wendt, 1999; Moravcsik, 2003; Katzenstein and Sil, 2008; and Zürn and Checkel, 2005.
[32] See Hellman, 2003; and Neumann, 2003.   [33] Buzan and Little, 2001.

with international political economy, such as banking, share a common ontology with high-politics practices such as balancing. New emerging practices of transnational networking, prompted by processes of globalization, also belong to the same practical world and should be studied as such.

As the next section develops, one important reason why dialogue across paradigms via a focus on practice is a real possibility is the concept's broader ontology, which blends material and ideational factors, as well as structure and agency, into social doing. Actually, a practice-oriented framework offers an elaborated conceptual apparatus in IR theory for breaking the Cartesian dualism between materials and ideas. It does so not by denying their individual or combined importance and effects, but by theorizing the social world in such a way that material reality and ideas' ontological traction depends on practical meaningful social action. Practices' broader ontology also combines structure and agents into social doing. One of the greatest strengths of zooming in on international practices, therefore, is being able to explain how the world is governed at particular points in time as well as the transformation of the agents themselves.

Finally, taking practices as a theoretical focal point has value added for individual IR theoretical perspectives, as we shall illustrate in more depth below. For rationalism, the main value added may consist in taking reflexive strategic choice as a pervasive practice in contemporary politics and in drawing attention to the background knowledge that makes rationality possible. The most important value-added contribution of putting the concept of practice at the forefront of constructivism, on the other hand, may consist in grounding both material and ideational factors in the unfolding of social and political life. Whatever one's theoretical perspective, it is in and through practices that world politics takes shape: structures (material and intersubjective), agency and subjectivity, relations of power, rationality and rules, resources, institutions and order, knowledge, morality, interests, as well as reproduction and transformation – that is, history itself.

Overcoming dichotomies in social theory

The "practice turn in social theory," which inspires this volume, builds on earlier philosophers as diverse as Marx, Dewey, Heidegger, Wittgenstein, Merleau-Ponty, and Foucault.[34] In the second half of the twentieth century, a number of high-profile sociologists further developed practice theory in the study of social life: for instance, Mead's[35] and Goffman's[36] symbolic interac-

---

[34] For a philosophical *tour d'horizon*, see among others, Bernstein, 1971; Schatzki, 1996; Taylor, 1993; Toulmin, 2001; and Turner, 1994.

[35] Mead, 1934.   [36] Goffman, 1959.

tionism, Garfinkel's ethnomethodology,[37] Bourdieu's theory of practice,[38] and Giddens' structuration theory[39] are all part of the fray. No doubt, these authors did not always see eye to eye and their social theories retain crucial differences. Ultimately, however, their frameworks are united in their prioritization of practices. As practice theory makes headway in several disciplines including sociology, anthropology, cultural studies, management, philosophy, and history of science, etc. a "practice turn in social theory" has been proclaimed.[40]

The promise that a practice framework holds in surmounting conventional divides in social theory is particularly striking. A practice framework not only transcends, but also synthesizes, three different approaches to culture that have characterized recent strands in social theory.[41] At first, culture was conceptualized as a set of ideas carried in individuals' heads. In this mentalist version, akin to psychology, the mind is the site of the social. In IR theory, this cultural approach relies on social and cognitive psychology to explain foreign policy by means of individuals' "ideas" and beliefs.[42] Subsequently, heavily influenced by postmodernism and poststructuralism, according to which culture exists outside of agents in chains of signs and symbols, culture took a turn to language and an understanding of meanings as located in discourse. In IR theory, this turn led to critical and poststructuralist readings of IR "texts."[43] The third approach to culture, characteristic of constructivism, places meanings as part of the intersubjective structures that emerge out of social interaction. A constructivist perspective in IR theory converged "around an ontology that depicts the social world as intersubjectively and collectively meaningful structures and processes,"[44] and around reflexive agents who reproduce and change social structures.[45] As one step further in the theorization of culture, practice theory is an invitation to build on these three strands of social theory and conceive of the social as bundles of ideas and matter that are linguistically, materially, and intersubjectively mediated in the form of practices. Culture, in other words, is not only in people's minds, discourse, and interactions; it is also in the very performance of practices.[46] From that perspective, practices not only organize the world – they are also the raw materials that comprise it. Thanks to this ontology, the concept of practice promises to move beyond a number of entrenched dichotomies in social theorizing.

First, practices are both *material* and *meaningful*. In fact, practice theory helps close the traditional divide between ideas and matter. On the one hand, practices are material insofar as they are doings enacted in and on the world. Practices engage with the environment and its artifacts, whether natural,

---

[37] Garfinkel, 1967.   [38] Bourdieu, 1977.   [39] Giddens, 1984.
[40] Schatzki, Knorr Cetina, and von Savigny, 2001.   [41] Reckwitz, 2002.
[42] See Jervis, 1976; and Goldstein and Keohane, 1993.
[43] Der Derian and Shapiro, 1989.   [44] Adler, 2002, 100.   [45] Wendt, 1999.
[46] Swidler, 1986.

cultural, or political. In addition, many practices often involve the use of "things" as indispensably as that of minds or speech. In Latour's action-network theory, for instance, material objects, agents, and meanings interact continually.[47] In IR, the intersubjective structure of nuclear deterrence is sustained by the existence of thousands of warheads; and the opposite is also true.[48] The practice of finance trading, to take another example, requires not just human beings and their physical faculties and actions, but also computers and other technologies that help institutionalize background knowledge as finance trading, and that allow people to perform their performances competently. In addition, practice typically does something in the world, and thus can change the physical world as well as the ideas that individually and collectively people hold about it. Contrary to thinking or reflecting about the world in a contemplative fashion, practices are directed toward the material world and thus exist only embodied in materials. Practices also are bodily in the sense that their enactment involves corporeal parts other than the brain.[49] At the same time, practices also are shot through with meaning – they are "culture in action."[50] A deed performed in a social setting cannot be said to have an immanent meaning encapsulated in its materiality. Through social interaction, people attribute meanings to their activities and build on these to further interact. In order for practices to make sense, then, practitioners must establish (contest, negotiate, communicate) their significance.[51]

As a performance in and on the world, practice leans on language in two senses, weak and strong. In a weak sense, language sustains intersubjectivity and thus links agency, structure, and process in socially meaningful ways. Without language, communication, and discourse, people could not tell the difference between behavior and practice.[52] The constitution of competent performance, in other words, is fundamentally epistemic, insofar as accounts of lived practices are textually constituted.[53] In its strong sense, not only is language the conduit of meaning, which turns practices into the location and engine of social action, but it is also and primarily an enactment or doing.[54] Discursive practices, thus, are socially meaningful speech acts, according to which saying is doing.[55] Although practices still rely on knowledge and embody material objects, in a discursive strong sense, the competence of routinely doing something socially meaningful often relies on discourse. It is thus relevant to conceive of discourse as practice and to understand practice as discourse.

---

[47] Latour, 2005.   [48] Pouliot, 2010b.
[49] See Bourdieu, 1990; and Polanyi, 1983.   [50] Swidler, 1986.
[51] As Tilly notes, for example: "Reason giving has consequences both because it proposes a definition for the relationship and because it justifies the practices of one party toward the other. Reasons, relationships, and practices align." Tilly, 2006, 48.
[52] Rorty, 1982.   [53] Thanks to Lene Hansen for this formulation.   [54] Foucault, 1980.
[55] Searle, 1969.

Second, practices are both *individual (agential)* and *structural*.[56] When "disaggregated," practices are ultimately performed by individual social beings and thus they clearly are what human agency is about. Collectively, however, we understand practices as structured and acted out by communities of practice, and by the diffusion of background knowledge across agents in these communities, which similarly disposes them to act in coordination. Practices are agential, however, not only because they are performed by individuals and communities of practice, but also because they frame actors who, thanks to this framing, know who they are and how to act in an adequate and socially recognizable way.[57] Because social structure does not cohere on its own,[58] agency means the human capacity of doing things that could be done differently.[59] Recursively, in and through practice agents lock in structural meaning in time and space. Agency also means doing things for reasons, many of which are structurally supplied, some of which, however, result from human creativity and experimentation. Practices enable agency, namely, they translate structural background intersubjective knowledge into intentional acts and endow them with social meaning. Structure, in turn, shows up in practices in the form of standards of competence that are socially recognized. There is, then, a normative or rule-like dimension to practice, which is bound up in its application. While performed by individual human beings, practices are possessions of collectives insofar as their meanings belong to communities of practice. "Suspended" between structures and agency, practices are simultaneously enacted (agency) and inserted within a social context or political order (structure). The advantage of taking practices as the main site of the social, thus, lies in enabling a superior formulation of the agent–structure conundrum, where agency and structure jointly constitute and enable practices. By implication, the methodological "bracketing" that is sometimes advocated in IR – begin with agents (or structures), and then look at the other side of the co-constitution equation[60] – can only take us some distance in understanding world politics.

Third, from a practice perspective, knowledge is not only located "behind" practice, in the form of intentions, beliefs, reasons, goals, etc. Knowledge is also "bound up" in the very execution of the practice. For the seasoned practitioner, knowledge does not precede practice but is "enclosed" in its execution.[61] Of course, people reflexively think about their practices. Not only does practice not trump reflexivity, judgment, and expectations, which are core features of social life, but it actually depends on individuals' reflexive normative and instrumental judgments to remain effectively institutionalized. Strategic practice, for example, reflects political judgments, whose ground is not only empirical but

---

[56] See Bourdieu, 1977; and Giddens, 1984.
[57] See Rasche and Chia, 2009, 719; and Goffman, 1977.   [58] Sewell, 1992.
[59] Giddens, 1984, 9.   [60] See, for example, Legro, 1996 on the "cooperation two-step."
[61] Ryle, 1984.

also practical.[62] Thus, to confirm that something is indeed what it is through repeated rituals of practice[63] requires reflexivity and judgment. Professionalization similarly relies on rationalizing and self-examining deliberative processes. Needless to say, reflexivity and judgment are also at the foundation of practice transformation. Taking practice seriously, however, draws special attention to all those meanings that are woven into practice and that, as such, often remain tacit and inarticulate. With Searle, we call this knowledge, partly tacit, partly reflexive, the "Background,"[64] a notion that is also akin to Bourdieu's "*habitus*."[65]

Background knowledge consists primarily of intersubjective expectations and dispositions, which can be grasped only as embedded in practice. Individuals and groups act, interact, reason, plan and judge, symbolically represent reality, and have expectations of the future within a dominant interpretive backdrop that sets the terms of interaction, defines a horizon of possibility, and provides the background knowledge of the expectations, dispositions, skills, techniques, and rituals that are the basis for the constitution of practices and their boundaries. Background knowledge, however, does "not create uniformity of a group or community, but organize[s] their differences around pervasive understandings of reality."[66] Similarly, *habitus* refers to this embodied stock of unspoken know-how, learned in and through practice, and from which deliberation and intentional action become possible.[67] Contrary to representations, which usually are verbal and intentional, dispositions are often tacit and inarticulate: knowledge that is forgotten as such – unless it is reflexively recovered.

Fourth, practices partake in both *continuity and change* in social and political life. On the one hand, practices are the vehicle of reproduction. Intersubjectivity lives on in and through practice. The performance of practices in socially recognizable ways is the source of ontological stability in social life. At the same time, however, it is also from practices that social change originates. For one thing, practice-qua-performance is a process; change not stability is the ordinary condition of social life. As March aptly put it: "Change takes place because most of the time most people in an organization go about what they are supposed to do; that is, they are intelligently attentive to their environments and their jobs."[68] Stability, in other words, is an illusion created by the recursive nature of practice. For another, new ways of thinking or doing necessarily

---

[62] See Williams, 1991; and Kratochwil, 1989.   [63] Swidler, 2001, 89.

[64] Searle defines the "Background" as "the set of nonintentional or preintentional capacities that enable intentional states to function." Searle, 1995, 129.

[65] Bourdieu defines *habitus* as "systems of durable, transposable dispositions" that constitute people's thought and practices. Bourdieu, 1990, 53. Other theorists use different terms to describe shared knowledge structures: Foucault, 1992 uses the concept of "codes"; Goffman, 1977 refers to "frames"; and Taylor, 1985 suggests "background understanding."

[66] Adler and Bernstein, 2005, 296.   [67] Pouliot, 2008.   [68] March, 1981, 564.

emerge from the contingent "play of practice,"[69] in which meanings are never inherently fixed or stable.

The material/meaningful, structural/agential, reflexive/background, and stability/change attributes of practice acquire concrete and workable theoretical and empirical meaning in the concept of *communities of practice*.[70] Practices develop, diffuse, and become institutionalized in such collectives. A community of practice is a configuration of a domain of knowledge that constitutes like-mindedness, a community of people that "creates the social fabric of learning," and a shared practice that embodies "the knowledge the community develops, shares, and maintains."[71] The knowledge domain endows practitioners with a sense of joint enterprise, which "brings the community together through the collective development of a shared practice" and is constantly being renegotiated by its members. People function as a community through relationships of mutual engagement that bind "members together into a social entity." Shared practices, in turn, are sustained by a repertoire of communal resources, such as routines, sensibilities, and discourse.[72] The community of practice concept encompasses not only the conscious and discursive dimensions and the actual doing of social change, but also the social space where structure and agency overlap and where knowledge, power, and community intersect. Communities of practice are intersubjective social structures that constitute the normative and epistemic ground for action, but they are also agents, made up of real people, who – working via network channels, across national borders, across organizational divides, and in the halls of government – affect political, economic, and social events.

Although an international practices approach suggests a broader ontology for understanding world politics, we do not consider it to be a magic wand with which we can explain all international phenomena. Some of the limits of the approach may lie in its comprehensiveness. At times, one may just need and want to focus mainly on the role of ideas – for example, when looking at IR from a normative perspective. At other times, researchers may be interested in looking at specific decision-making events, which may require holding practices constant. Likewise, explaining the relationship between two variables – for example, terrorism and democracy – may lead researchers to highlight less the practices themselves than the nature of the relationship, on the aggregate, and in particular cases. An international practices approach is also likely to raise methodological challenges – for example, about demonstrating the causal and constitutive effects of practices, while controlling for other variables and processes. As we hope, however, to show in the following section on how practice generates transformation, and as the following chapters demonstrate and

---

[69] Doty, 1997.   [70] Wenger, 1998. In IR, see Adler, 2005, 15–27 and 2008.
[71] Wenger, McDermott, and Snyder, 2002, 28–29.
[72] Wenger, 1998, 72–85, 209.

illustrate, an international practices approach can explain a lot across almost all subfields, such as international security, international political economy, international law and humanitarianism, emotions, and discourse. We take this book, then, as a first and suggestive step for developing the study of international practices, while being well aware of the importance of other approaches, some of the limits of the practice approach, and also the possibilities for future cross-fertilization between a practice framework and other IR approaches.

Framework: how practice generates transformation

Because the aim of this volume is dialogue across paradigmatic divides, this introduction does not encourage contributors to buy into a specific theoretical approach. Rather, it suggests a modular framework that scholars from different traditions can access from their own particular ontological and epistemological perspectives. Paraphrasing Sewell, we ask a simple but crucial question: How does the ordinary unfolding of practice generate transformations?[73] Because practice is suspended between agency and structure, we posit three possible domains of change: in subjectivities (e.g. preferences, dispositions, or intentionality), in practices themselves, or in social orders (e.g. structures, domination patterns, or discourse). We leave it to our contributors to determine on which of these domains they wish to focus. From our simple question above, we posit the following. First, transformation is the ordinary accomplishment of social life; stability is the result of the work of practice – that is, of process and evolution. Second, practice is the accomplishment of agency and more specifically of political contestation, from which transformations necessarily flow. Third, the engine of practice transformation is not only agential but also structural because, locally, practices interact with one another. All in all, change in practice has no other origin than the accomplishment of practice: practice is both *explanans* and *explanandum*.

In order to operationalize this recursivity and make it amenable to empirical research, we encourage our contributors to clarify whether (and for what analytical purposes) they treat practice as *explanans*, *explanandum*, or both. Is practice the driving force of some form of transformation (possibly of practice itself), or is transformed practice the result of some driving forces (possibly including practice itself)? This issue has important consequences for designing the inquiry. In the following paragraphs, we envision two general frameworks that alternatively posit practice as *explanans* or *explanandum*: the lifecycle of practice and the interplay of practices. Note that these frameworks are not mutually exclusive: in combining both, it is possible to grasp the recursivity of practice in producing its own transformation.

[73] Sewell, 1992.

First, one may look at the evolution of a specific practice – that is, its dynamic historicity and contingent processes of transformation over time and space. The focus here is on a practice's lifecycle,[74] which includes, in its ideal-typical form, the generation, diffusion, institutionalization, and fading of a particular competent performance. To be sure, not all practices go through these four phases; it is an empirical matter to determine the ebb and flow of a specific practice in history – whether it ever diffused or institutionalized, for instance. Contemporary practices obviously fall short of meeting the fourth phase, and we can as well imagine "non-practices" that have failed to emerge in the first place despite favorable conditions and supportive agency. The lifecycle of practice, in other words, is not a teleological framework, but a genealogy of the development, however arrested it may be, of a meaningful activity. It is up to the analyst to delineate and explain its space and time horizon. For example, emphasis may be put on generative relationships – that is, instances or episodes of formative interactions which, due to either material or ideational reasons, or both, facilitate the emergence of a new practice. The joint American–Soviet seminars on nuclear arms control of the 1960s; the Helsinki Final Act negotiations in the early 1970s; and the negotiations that preceded Stockholm's first and seminal global environmental conference in 1972, are examples of generative relationships. Alternatively, one may look into the diffusion of a practice – how intersubjective knowledge becomes more widely established in communities of practitioners and thus how the latter expand – or its institutionalization, whereby intersubjective knowledge establishes as social structures. Through iteration, practices may congeal in a variety of social things, such as institutions, objects, taboos, laws, rites, etc. In this sense, international law (i.e. a codified set of norms and prescriptions about international behavior) often serves to inscribe customary practices in "things," that is, in written and agreed-upon principles that will be upheld by given judiciary or political organs. Though ever-evolving, practices tend to have a "core" that is recognized as such by their performers. For example, despite its considerable evolution over the centuries, especially in forms and means, the practice of diplomacy has remained an organized dialogue between more or less independent political communities. Whatever phase(s) the analyst elects to study, in the lifecycle framework practice is the *explanandum*. Depending on one's theoretical leanings, the *explanans* of a practice's lifecycle may be structural or agential, material or symbolic, etc. After all, practice lies at the intersection of these dualisms, as we argued above.

Second, practice may be part of the *explanans* – that is, the determinant of transformation. Again, a plethora of other factors may be summoned in combination with practice – intersubjective structures, material forces, etc. Similarly, a variety of transformations (the *explanandum*) may result from practice-as-*explanans*, including a new distribution of resources, knowledge innovation,

---

[74] See Adler, 1991; and Finnemore and Sikkink, 1998.

new subjectivities, etc. That being said, conceiving of practice-as-*explanans* suggests two main processes of transformation: how practices are performed (agency and contestation) and how practices interact with one another (the interplay of practices). To begin with the latter, we assume that the world is made up of various "constellations of practices,"[75] that is assemblages of communities and their practices that interact, overlap, and evolve. Practices in a constellation, for example, specific and general practices, are interconnected – they share an epoch, a geographical place, a common object, a similar disposition, they react to the same conditions or perform the same functions, etc. It is the permanent state of connectivity and tension inside a constellation of practices that fuels transformation. We envision four main types of relationships among a particular set of practices:

(1) *Parallel existence*: practices are linked in space and/or time but they do not significantly interfere. This may be because these practices belong to different registers of social life, because they perform unalike functions, because they make use of unrelated tools, etc. This type of interaction is the least conducive to transformation because interference is minimal.

(2) *Symbiosis*: practices remain distinct but they form a coherent whole in which the parts (a set of competent performances) are united in a mutually reinforcing relationship (e.g. alliance-making and balancing).

(3) *Hybridization*: interacting practices combine and form a new type of competent performance. Elements of different practices are rearranged into a hybrid new form that replaces past ways of doing. Hybridization fuels on innovative associations, and as such is often equated with creation (e.g. Christian solidarity bred humanitarian intervention).

(4) *Subordination*: practices are variously positioned in a hierarchical relationship. Some practices "anchor" others in making them possible;[76] others are the mere enactment of a deeper practical order (e.g. sovereignty anchors diplomacy). In these hierarchical bundles, one practice may become the dominant form of a set of subordinated practices, which may nonetheless continue to be practiced (e.g. sovereignty/non-intervention may become subordinated to the responsibility to protect).

Of course, none of these scenarios simply "happens" without the intervention of a variety of agents in some form of politics. This is the second process whereby practice may breed transformation. In focusing on different kinds of practical interplays, we do not take a structuralist outlook in which it is the "fit," or lack thereof, among practices that determines their interactions alone. Instead, we want to insist that agency is front and center in the interplay of practice, if only because it is practitioners who, ultimately, are the performers. Put in simple terms, the reason why a given bundle of practices follows a

[75] Wenger, 1998.   [76] Swidler, 2001.

particular scenario and not others has less to do with how it fits altogether – a functional argument – than with how it is *fitted* together as a result of political struggles. The politics of practice concern the ways in which agents struggle to endow certain practices with political validity and legitimacy – or, in Hansen's words, to make a specific practice look like a general one. For instance, new practices emerge out of authoritative definitions of truth and morality as promoted by certain segments of society. Practices transform in order to solve a "real-world" problem; but the problem has to be defined as such in the first place. Politics also plays out in social networks and the possession of valued resources: it is not only the practice *per se* that diffuses, but also its practitioners' ways of engaging with the world. In the ebb and flow of practices, the careers of practices and practitioners interact. As we shall further argue below, practice is eminently political in that it sustains, or undermines, existing patterns of power relations.

Taking stock of this and the previous sections, we believe that a practice-oriented framework can accommodate a variety of theories and paradigms in offering a large menu for choice: (1) whether to concentrate on the material or symbolic dimensions of practice, or both; (2) whether to focus on the structural or agential nature of practice, or both; (3) whether to look into the stabilizing or dynamic aspects of practice, or both; (4) whether to treat practice as *explanandum* or *explanans*, or both; (5) if *explanandum*, what other factors (whatever their ontological status) to conjure in explaining the lifecycle of practice; (6) if *explanans*, what other determinants to add on to practices themselves in explaining transformation; (7) if *explanans*, what type of interplay of practices is generating transformations; and (8) if *explanans*, what transformation the ordinary unfolding of practice produces. Thus, for example, realists can analyze the lifecycle of the balancing practice from a material power perspective, while liberals can emphasize institutions and individuals' choices. Alternatively, English School scholars can emphasize the historical processes via which emerging practices aggregate into international societies (i.e. configurations of practices), while constructivists and poststructuralists may emphasize transformation in collective meanings and discourse as a result of practice. Every author in this book was encouraged to consider those aspects of the practice lifecycle that, so far, they might have neglected, and to look for points of convergence with other approaches. While we expect our contributors to remain faithful to their respective theoretical niche, we anticipate that zooming in on international practices may lead different IR theories to cluster somewhere around the middle of Figure 1.1.

On methodology

This leads us to underline an important point on methodology: we deliberately refrain from imposing any single methodology; rather, we take a pluralistic approach. Accordingly, scholars are expected to use those methods that are

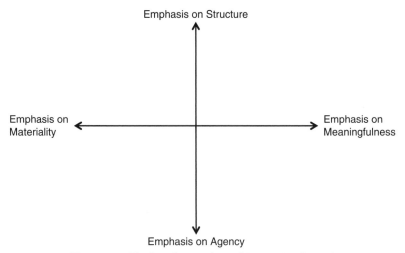

Figure 1.1   The broader ontology of international practices

most adequate from their own unique epistemological and theoretical perspectives. We can contemplate, and actually encourage, a combination of methodologies, and taking some methodologies as complementary. Of course, we are well aware that not all methods are compatible, and that positivism and interpretivism are probably not reconcilable. Our goal is not to minimize well-known differences. Yet we do not want to let epistemological incommensurability become a methodological straitjacket in taking international practices seriously.

Our rationale for taking such a pragmatic stance is two-fold. First, recall that pragmatism rests on the view that what practitioners generally do, as they go on with their lives, is basically "what works" in and through practice. The same goes for social scientists: scholars should select those methodological tools that allow them to "solve" their puzzle. Of course, it is the other members of the community of scientific practice who will assess whether these tools were handled successfully or not. Chances are that certain practitioners will disagree and instead propose other methods that "work better." Such is the nature of the academic enterprise and we encourage scholars to evaluate methods in action rather than through *a priori*, epistemological lenses. Second, we advocate methodological pluralism based on the history of social sciences. In and through practice, interpretivists, positivists, and others have tried a wide variety of tools, through the decades, and with more or less success. Although scholars usually disagree on which methods do a better job than others, we are confident that they would all agree that so far no single method has proven so successful as to completely dislodge the others. Statistical methods capture dimensions of social life that often escape the attention of hermeneutics; and the opposite is also true. As editors, we certainly think that certain methods are better than others, as our own works show. Nevertheless, our own preferences should not distract us from the fact that in the history of social scientific practice, neither discourse analysis nor statistical regression can claim to have explained the whole of social life on its own. So let practice judge how different methods comparatively fare.[77]

An agenda for taking international practices seriously

In this section, we briefly lay out some directions for taking international practices seriously. This exercise is not meant to be exhaustive but suggestive. We identify eight main contributions that a practice-oriented approach to IR could make:

(1) *International practices and practitioners.* Studying diplomacy, the environment, terrorism, deterrence, human rights, balance of power, international law, and a plethora of other international practices raises important research avenues, such as the role of practices in the attainment of preferences or practices' constitutive effects on subjectivity.[78] One important subset agenda here is studying micro-practices and everyday world politics, both of which play a role in bringing about changes in broader security and economic dynamics and rules, thus affecting global governance.

(2) *Anchoring practices.* The power of what Swidler calls "anchoring practices," which symbolically establish the constitutive rules they embody, stems from their encoding of dominant schema, which are never formulated as rules.[79] One of the intriguing aspects of anchoring practices, thus, is their reliance on common knowledge, which implies that they "do not require the time or repetition that habits require, but rather the visible, public enactment of new patterns so that 'everyone can see' that everyone else has seen that things have changed."[80] The reliance of anchoring practices on common knowledge raises interesting research possibilities for rationalists and constructivists alike to research how practices help produce and sustain institutional solutions to international problems.

(3) *Evolution of practices.* When studying international practices from a historical perspective, one has to look back to the generative relationships that made them possible, as well as the socio-political processes that allowed their diffusion.[81] In so doing, a practice lens denaturalizes the taken-for-granted condition of contemporary world politics. International practices are not a-historical patterns of action, but evolving sets of activities that connect with past social and political struggles over the meaning and ruling of the world. Certain practices remain isolated; others triumph over distance, cultural differences, and the passing of time. In addition, historicizing practice

---

[77] Kratochwil, Chapter 2 in this volume.   [78] Bially Mattern, Chapter 3 in this volume.
[79] See Swidler, 2001; and Sending and Neumann, Chapter 9 in this volume.
[80] Swidler, 2001, 87.   [81] Little, Chapter 7 in this volume.

eschews the pitfalls of functionalism and allows for path dependence and other historical effects on current international practice.

(4) *Background knowledge.* Practices' symbiotic relationship with background knowledge suggests a research agenda on ways that tacit and reflexive knowledge combine in the innovation, evolution, and execution of international practices. Equally important is to study the constitutive and causal effects of knowledge on practice, and the effect of competing epistemic interpretations on the reification and institutionalization of practices.[82] Exploring the background knowledge that makes rationality and strategic practice possible may be one of the ultimate payoffs of an IR practice approach. From this perspective, the capacity for rational thought and behavior is above all a background capacity; rationality is "located" not only in people's heads but also in an evolving backdrop of knowledge. When there is no prior experience, communities of practice[83] may play a role in socially constructing traditions around which expectations cluster. Finally, background knowledge plays a role as "focal points" in the construction of practices, strategic or not.

(5) *Communities of practice.* A practice approach in IR begs for a close scrutiny of the role of communities of practice in world politics. Think about our world neither as an assemblage of states nor as divided by borders and lines of national identification, but as transnational communities of practice, based on what people actually *do* rather than on where they happen to live. Then we would see, for example, transnational communities of diplomats sharing a diplomatic culture, common values, and interests that are intrinsic to their practice. We also would see merchants from different countries, even competing countries, who participate in trade practices and share an interest, knowledge, discourse, and identity in learning and applying their practices. We might also see international and transnational lawyers trying to make human rights more legitimate, acceptable, and accessible to people on the global level.[84] We might witness scientists and scholars organizing themselves for worthy causes, such as alleviating world hunger or banning landmines. Explaining social change from a community of practice perspective may both challenge and complement studies of institutional change that focus on social networks, because it relies on a thicker social theory of knowledge diffusion and power relations.

(6) *Power and practice.* As a conceptual tool, the notion of practice helps explain how certain potentialities become tangible and concrete in world politics. It also helps address issues of relative power, interests, order, morality, hierarchy, and legitimacy, and recalls that power is not a capacity but a relation

---

[82] Stein, Chapter 4 in this volume.   [83] See Adler, 2005 and 2008.
[84] Brunnée and Toope, Chapter 5 in this volume.

and that it is both material and symbolic.[85] As Barnes argues: "To engage in a practice is to exercise a power ... what is called the active exercise of a power may equally be called the enactment of a practice."[86] This is because a practice encodes the dominant meanings and doings in a given social and political context.[87]

(7) *Signaling*. Practices are embedded in knowledge and shot through with power, but they also convey information – in other words, political actors use practices and conventions, for example, to signal resolve, make credible commitments, communicate deterrence, rather than aggressive intentions, and signal confidence and stability to prevent economic crises from running out of control. While, for example, an important literature exists on using audience costs to signal resolve in international crises,[88] this literature has yet to focus on the practices political actors use to signal, communicate, and bargain with other actors. This raises the questions why states choose certain practices rather than others, and why some practices may be more successful than others in achieving state objectives.[89] While obviously germane to rationalism, this agenda on practices and signaling also fits with questions of whether and how established practices are used to attain common understandings as part of a communicative action and practical rationality logic.[90]

(8) *Balance of practices*. States may differ not only in their political, social, demographic and economic make-up, material capabilities, and historical cultural contexts that give rise to states, but also in the institutionalized practices of their communities of practice.[91] Alternatively, states may share similar political and economic regimes and values – for example, they may be part of a market-oriented democratic community of states, but still differ in the ways they go about achieving their goals in practice. We envision that differences in the ways states deploy practices in the world scene have structural effects, and that these effects may be as if not more important than material power, interest, and knowledge. We may refer to a practice criterion by which states are stratified in the international arena as "balance of practices,"[92] the balance of institutionalized patterns of competent performances states use to pursue their aims.

Plan of the book

Chapter 2 discusses the semantic and epistemological connotations of practice and the "practice turn" in social theory and explores implications for a practice-

[85] Abrahamsen and Williams, Chapter 12 in this volume.   [86] Barnes, 2001, 20.
[87] Hansen, Chapter 11 in this volume.   [88] Fearon, 1997.
[89] Voeten, Chapter 10 in this volume.   [90] Habermas, 1984.
[91] Ripsman, Chapter 8 in this volume.   [92] Adler and Crawford, 2006.

oriented approach in IR. Analyzing the actual usage of the concept of practice in its varied forms, including its reflexive use by social scientists, Friedrich Kratochwil identifies elements of a generative grammar that American pragmatism articulated in opposition to the Cartesian project and traditional epistemology. Philosophical pragmatism's key implication for a focus on international practices is that truth and validity are practice-relative rather than practice-justifying notions. Kratochwil then explores two episodes, the development of the Chicago School and Stephen Turner's critique of the "practice turn" in social theory, and shows that themes that resurface in the theoretical discussion of practice are part and parcel of an ongoing debate in all social sciences. Kratochwil concludes that a fruitful foregrounding of practices in IR cannot result in a traditional "theory," but ought to disclose distinct elements of human action, including time, contingency, and responsibility.

In Chapter 3, Janice Bially Mattern explores how zooming in on practice, and in particular the ontological move away from traditional dualisms that this move entails, may help conceive of emotions and their role in international politics. Her main claim is that emotions *are* practices. Building on Schatzki, Bially Mattern theorizes emotions as "ways-of-being" in the world. For one thing, as a practical experience emotion is at once a form of agency and a reproduction of structure. For another, as a bodily performance emotion is a doing expressed through human bodies and which engages with objects and the larger social environment. Bially Mattern devises a method of mediated discourse analysis that seeks to capture the "rhythmic integration" of material bodies and linguistic discourses. She concludes with a plea for using human beings, and more specifically their practices, as the central unit of analysis in the study of emotions in world politics.

In Chapter 4, Janice Gross Stein explores how and why, by reflexively shifting the background knowledge on which humanitarian competent performances are based to the foreground, a humanitarian community of practice began a learning process that may be changing not only humanitarian practices but also the community itself. At the core of the discussion and contestation about competencies and standards of practice, says Stein, was the humanitarian community of practice beginning to grapple with power – which was alien to its ethical make-up – and the political roles and responsibilities that grew from their practices. While the conversation among humanitarians led to the development of a few accountability institutions, which promoted continuous feedback and iterative problem-solving, there is not much evidence that learning in and through practice has taken place. This might as well be because the outcomes of this learning process may be less important than its symbolic significance. Through background knowledge and practice contestation, the humanitarian community of practice is continually being socially reconstructed.

Chapter 5 argues that law is created, maintained, or destroyed through day-to-day interactions in multiple and overlapping communities of legal practice.

Drawing together insights from IR constructivist approaches and the legal theory of Lon Fuller, Jutta Brunnée and Stephen J. Toope develop an interactional theory of international legal obligation that suggests that the obligatory effect of international law stems from a "practice of legality." By this they mean that legal norms, which are rooted in particular forms of background knowledge that meet criteria of legality (such as generality, promulgation, and nonretroactivity), are upheld through norm-congruent collective practice. Because agents help develop and uphold norms and their legality through practice across time, this dynamic theory enables scholars to account for the lifecycle of legal norms, their emergence, diffusion, institutionalization, and destruction. Brunnée and Toope argue that a strong community of practice sustains at least the procedural aspects of the global climate regime. Interactional theory suggests that a long-term agreement on emission reductions is unlikely to be attainable unless it is embedded in a vibrant practice of legality.

Patrick Morgan in Chapter 6 traces the lifecycle of Cold War deterrence practices and their transformation after the Cold War. The lifecycle of Cold War deterrence began with a major modification of traditional deterrence in international politics, which was strongly affected by practices handed down by the two world wars. The intensity of the Cold War, combined with nuclear weapons and their delivery systems, provided the impetus for turning deterrence from a standard practice into an elaborate strategy. However, the evolution of deterrence practices that Cold War intellectuals generated slowly nudged the Cold War relationship into behavior and interactions that had the trappings and components of a modest community. Many components of Cold War deterrence practice survived the end of the Cold War and deterrence is now applied to forestall behavior well short of interstate war, including state-sponsored terrorism and nuclear proliferation. In the end, Morgan argues, the Cold War era passed and deterrence looks somewhat superfluous, but security efforts still take place amidst the shadows and echoes of Cold War deterrence practices.

In Chapter 7, Richard Little examines how the idea of practice can be drawn on in a way that helps to reassess the distinction between society and system and thereby, potentially, to resolve the debate that has gone on within the English School between the international system and international society. Criticizing the view that the system is simply the a-social version of society, Little concludes that it is only possible to identify systemic practices in the context of an international society. Little uses the British response to the Spanish Civil War as a case study in which long-standing practices of non-intervention clashed with systemic pressures to intervene. The chapter traces in detail how these conflictual dynamics were resolved in practice. Little concludes that as powerful as systemic imperatives may be, the process of defining the situation in which decision-makers find themselves is, fundamentally, a matter of practice.

In Chapter 8, Norrin Ripsman seeks to integrate the concept of practice into neoclassical realism. The basic insight is that the domestic practices that condition policy-making shape the international practice of balancing. In addition, because domestic practices are themselves partly determined by systemic pressures and balancing responses, there is a recursive interplay between the national and international realms. At the empirical level, Ripsman studies the impact of the practice of bipartisanship on American national security policy from 1945 to 1950. Focusing on a small community of practice located in Washington, DC, the case study helps understand how background knowledge and competent performance mediate structural effects on policy-making. As a result, Ripsman argues, balancing practices differ over time and space as practitioners draw upon an evolved set of institutions, procedures, and practices.

Chapter 9 looks at the issue of international organization (IO) authority and autonomy as resulting from emergent practices rather than from the internal features of IOs and states. Drawing on Swidler's concept of "anchoring practices," Ole Jacob Sending and Iver B. Neumann understand expert knowledge produced and used by IOs in terms of concrete practices that define an infrastructure or reference-point for interaction, rendering strategies for action possible while closing off others. They argue that the World Bank's expertise is embedded in a set of key practices, in particular the Country Policy and Institutional Assessment (CPIA), which annually assesses the performance of client countries according to a set of expertise-based criteria for good policies and institutions. By anchoring more specific practices, such as the Bank's Performance Based Allocation (PBA) system, the CPIA structures the Bank's interaction with donors as well as how donors debate and negotiate. The chapter concludes that practices are productively powerful because they define an infrastructure and a set of tools for actors to use and display in social interaction.

In Chapter 10, Erik Voeten looks into the practice of political manipulation – or, as William Riker called it, "heresthetics." Coming from a rationalist perspective, Voeten seeks to grasp the patterns that skilled political manipulators use in context. He illustrates his analysis with the case of the *Declaration on the Granting of Independence to Colonial Countries and Peoples*, which the United Nations General Assembly (UNGA) adopted in 1960. Voeten explains the creation and application of the resolution through the skills that a number of representatives from former colonies deployed in exploiting external events in ways that conform to typical UNGA practices. The chapter demonstrates that political manipulation, the process of using or shaping the structure of a decision-making environment to one's advantage, satisfies the main elements of practice, including competent performance, background knowledge, and discursivity. In so doing, Voeten reconciles the study of strategy and rationality with a thicker understanding of sociality.

In Chapter 11, Lene Hansen approaches practices from a poststructuralist perspective. Her main claim is that because practice is inherently unstable, there is always political work, in the form of discursive practices, which goes into articulating a specific practice with its shared background knowledge. Closing this politico-epistemic gap is a basic feature of practice, which problematizes its taken-for-granted and routine dimensions. Hansen demonstrates this process with the case of the Muhammad cartoon crisis in Denmark in 2005–2006. Under circumstances of foreign policy crisis, different actors tried to impose a frame of commonality across practices that had no self-evident connection, such as the practice of publishing the cartoons as editorials, or the inscription of the Danish government's actions as part of transatlantic values. Overall, Hansen's chapter shows how poststructuralism and practice-oriented approaches can mutually benefit from one another, particularly in better understanding the political constitution of subjectivities in and through practice.

In Chapter 12, Rita Abrahamsen and Michael Williams build on Bourdieu's sociology to assess contemporary changes in the field of global security. The authors contend that the distinctions between public and private, global and local, are themselves forms of practice and power that agents in the field wield more or less successfully. Empirically, the chapter focuses on the rapid expansion in the activities of global private security companies (PSCs) in civilian, everyday activities in the South African context. Abrahamsen and Williams explain the ongoing reconfiguration of the field through the accumulation of new resources by private military companies, not simply in economic terms but also and primarily the symbolic capital of the public. Among other things, the chapter illustrates how shifts in background knowledge – in this case, the turn to private security strategies – can empower certain agents as competent and reasonable players in a field.

Finally, in Chapter 13, Raymond D. Duvall and Arjun Chowdhury provide a concluding statement in the form of a sympathetic critique of the centering of practices, as proposed and exemplified in this volume. While endorsing the focus on practices they pose three challenges that they intend as problems which, if confronted, would strengthen scholars' ability to take a practice approach more productively. Those challenges concern three questions; respectively, how in the practice of scholarship the subject of practices, the relationship of practices to meaning, and processes of change are theorized. They address these questions primarily through a critique of the conceptualization of practices as competent performances, arguing that that conceptualization limits the theoretic and analytic promise of the centering of practices. They conclude with some methodological suggestions for the study of practices understood as both competent and "incompetent."

References

Adler, Emanuel, 1991. Cognitive Evolution: A Dynamic Approach for the Study of International Relations and Their Progress. In *Progress in Postwar International Relations*, edited by Emanuel Adler, and Beverly Crawford, 43–88. New York: Columbia University Press.

2002. Constructivism in International Relations. In *Handbook of International Relations*, edited by Walter Carlsnaes, Thomas Risse, and Beth A. Simmons, 95–110. Thousand Oaks: Sage.

2005. *Communitarian International Relations: The Epistemic Foundations of International Relations*. New York: Routledge.

2008. The Spread of Security Communities: Communities of Practice, Self-Restraint, and NATO's Post-Cold War Evolution. *European Journal of International Relations* 14 (2): 195–230.

Adler, Emanuel and Steven Bernstein, 2005. Knowledge in Power: The Epistemic Construction of Global Governance. In *Power in Global Governance*, edited by Michael Barnett and Raymond D. Duvall, 294–318. Cambridge: Cambridge University Press.

Adler, Emanuel and Beverly Crawford, 2006. Normative Power: The European Practice of Region-Building and the Case of the Euro-Mediterranean Partnership. In *The Convergence of Civilizations: Constructing a Mediterranean Region*, edited by Emanuel Adler, Federica Bicchi, Beverly Crawford, and Raffaella A. Del Sarto, 3–47. Toronto: University of Toronto Press.

Adler, Emanuel and Vincent Pouliot, 2011. International Practices. *International Theory* 3 (1): 1–36.

Adler-Nissen, Rebecca, 2008. The Diplomacy of Opting Out: A Bourdieudian Approach to National Integration Strategies. *Journal of Common Market Studies* 46 (3): 663–684.

Ashley, Richard, 1987. The Geopolitics of Geopolitical Space: Toward a Critical Social Theory of International Politics. *Alternatives* 12 (4): 403–434.

Barnes, Barry, 2001. Practice as Collective Action. In *The Practice Turn in Contemporary Theory*, edited by Theodore R. Schatzki, Karin Knorr Cetina, and Eike von Savigny, 17–28. New York: Routledge.

Bernstein, Richard J., 1971. *Praxis and Action*. Philadelphia: University of Pennsylvania Press.

Bigo, Didier, 1996. *Polices en réseaux. L'éxpérience européenne*. Paris: Presses de Sciences Po.

Bourdieu, Pierre, 1977. *Outline of a Theory of Practice*. New York: Cambridge University Press.

1990. *The Logic of Practice*. Stanford: Stanford University Press.

Brunnée, Jutta and Stephen J. Toope, 2010. *Legitimacy and Legality in International Law: An Interactional Account*. New York: Cambridge University Press.

Büger, Christian and Frank Gadinger, 2007. Reassembling and Dissecting: International Relations Practice from a Science Studies Perspective. *International Studies Perspectives* 8 (1): 90–110.

Bull, Hedley, 1995 [1977]. *The Anarchical Society: A Study of Order in World Politics*. 2nd edn. New York: Columbia University Press.

Butler, Judith, 1990. *Gender Trouble: Feminism and the Subversion of Identity*. New York: Routledge.

Buzan, Barry and Richard Little, 2001. Why International Relations Has Failed as an Intellectual Project and What to Do About It. *Millennium* 30 (1): 19–39.

Cook, Scott D. N. and John Seely Brown, 1999. Bridging Epistemologies: The Generative Dance Between Organizational Knowledge and Organizational Knowing. *Organization Science* 10 (4): 381–400.

Corradi, Gessica, Silvia Gherardi, and Luca Verzelloni, 2010. Through the Practice Lens: Where is the Bandwagon of Practice-based Studies Heading? *Management Learning* 41 (3): 265–283.

De Certeau, Michel, 1990. *L'Invention du Quotidien 1. Arts de faire.* Paris: Gallimard.

Der Derian, James, 1987. *On Diplomacy: A Genealogy of Western Estrangement.* Oxford: Blackwell.

Der Derian, James and Michael J. Shapiro, eds., 1989. *International/Intertextual Relations: Postmodern Readings of World Politics.* Lexington: Lexington Books.

Doty, Roxanne Lynn, 1996. *Imperial Encounters: The Politics of Representation in North–South Relations.* Minneapolis: University of Minnesota Press.

  1997. Aporia: A Critical Exploration of the Agent–Structure Problematique in International Relations Theory. *European Journal of International Relations* 3 (3): 365–392.

Fearon, James D., 1996. Rationalist Explanations for War. *International Organization* 49 (3): 379–414.

  1997. Signaling Foreign Policy Interests: Tying Hands Versus Sinking Costs. *The Journal of Conflict Resolution* 41 (1): 68–90.

Finnemore, Martha and Kathryn Sikkink, 1998. International Norm Dynamics and Political Change. *International Organization* 52 (4): 887–917.

Foucault, Michel, 1980. *Power/Knowledge: Selected Interviews and Other Writings 1972-1977.* Edited by Colin Gordon. New York: Pantheon.

  1992. *The History of Sexuality: The Use of Pleasure.* London: Penguin.

Friedrichs, Jörg and Friedrich Kratochwil, 2009. On Acting and Knowing: How Pragmatism Can Advance International Relations Research and Methodology. *International Organization* 63 (4): 701–731.

Garfinkel, Harold, 1967. *Studies in Ethnomethodology.* Englewood Cliffs: Prentice Hall.

Gheciu, Alexandra, 2005. *NATO in the "New Europe": The Politics of International Socialization after the Cold War.* Stanford: Stanford University Press.

Giddens, Anthony, 1984. *The Constitution of Society: Outline of the Theory of Structuration.* Berkeley: University of California Press.

Goffman, Erving, 1959. *The Presentation of Self in Everyday Life.* New York: Doubleday.

  1977. *Frame Analysis: An Essay on the Organization of Experience.* Cambridge, MA: Harvard University Press.

Goldstein, Judith and Robert Keohane, eds., 1993. *Ideas and Foreign Policy: Beliefs, Institutions, and Political Change.* Ithaca: Cornell University Press.

Guzzini, Stefano, 2000. A Reconstruction of Constructivism in International Relations. *European Journal of International Relations* 6 (2): 147–182.

Haas, Peter M and Ernst B. Haas, 2002. Pragmatic Constructivism and the Study of International Institutions. *Millennium* 31 (3): 573–601.

Habermas, Jürgen, 1984. *The Theory of Communicative Action.* Vol. 1. Translated by Thomas McCarthy. Boston: Beacon Press.

Hellmann, Gunter, ed., 2003. Are Dialogue and Synthesis Possible in International Relations? *International Studies Review* 5 (1): 123–153.

2009. Pragmatism and International Relations. *International Studies Review* 11 (3): 638–662.

Hopf, Ted, 2002. *Social Construction of International Politics: Identities and Foreign Policies, Moscow, 1955 and 1999.* Ithaca: Cornell University Press.

2010. The Logic of Habit in International Relations. *European Journal of International Relations* 16 (4): 539–561.

Huysmans, Jef, 2002. Shape-shifting NATO: Humanitarian Action and the Kosovo Refugee Crisis. *Review of International Studies* 28 (3): 599–618.

Jackson, Patrick Thaddeus and Daniel H. Nexon, 1999. Relations before States: Substance, Process and the Study of World Politics. *European Journal of International Relations* 5 (3): 291–332.

Jervis, Robert, 1976. *Perception and Misperception in International Politics,* Princeton: Princeton University Press.

Katzenstein, Peter J., 2010. A World of Plural and Pluralist Civilizations: Multiple Actors, Traditions, and Practices. In *Civilizations in World Politics: Plural and Pluralist Perspectives,* edited by Peter J. Katzenstein, 1–40. New York: Routledge.

Katzenstein, Peter J. and Rudra Sil, 2008. Eclectic Theorizing in the Study and Practice of International Relations. In *The Oxford Handbook of International Relations,* edited by Christian Reus-Smit and Duncan Snidal, 109–130. Oxford: Oxford University Press.

Keck, Margaret E. and Kathryn Sikkink, 1998. *Activists Beyond Borders: Advocacy Networks in International Politics.* Ithaca: Cornell University Press.

Keohane, Robert O. and Joseph S. Nye, 2001 [1977]. *Power and Interdependence,* 3rd edn. New York: Longman.

Kissinger, Henry A., 1973 [1957]. *A World Restored: Metternich, Castlereagh and the Problem of Peace, 1812–1822.* Gloucester, MA: Peter Smith.

Koivisto, Marjo and Tim Dunne, 2010. Crisis, What Crisis? Liberal Order Building and World Order Conventions. *Millennium* 38 (3): 615–640.

Kratochwil, Friedrich V., 1989. *Rules, Norms, and Decisions: On the Conditions of Practical and Legal Reasoning in International Relations and Domestic Affairs.* New York: Cambridge University Press.

2007. Of False Promises and Good Bets: A Plea for a Pragmatic Approach to Theory Building. *Journal of International Relations and Development* 10 (1): 1–15.

Krebs, Ronald R. and Patrick Thaddeus Jackson, 2007. Twisting Tongues and Twisting Arms: The Power of Political Rhetoric. *European Journal of International Relations* 13 (1): 35–66.

Krotz, Ulrich, 2007. Parapublic Underpinnings of International Relations: The Franco-German Construction of Europeanization of a Particular Kind. *European Journal of International Relations* 13 (3): 385–417.

Latour, Bruno, 2005. *Reassembling the Social: An Introduction to Actor–Network Theory*. New York: Oxford University Press.

Leander, Anna, 2005. The Power to Construct International Security: On the Significance of Private Military Companies. *Millennium* 33 (3): 803–826.

Legro, Jeffrey W., 1996. Culture and Preferences in the International Cooperation Two-Step. *American Political Science Review* 90 (1): 118–137.

March, James G., 1981. Footnotes to Organizational Change. *Administrative Science Quarterly* 26 (4): 563–577.

Mead, George Herbert, 1934. *Mind, Self, and Society*. Chicago: University of Chicago Press.

Mérand, Frédéric, 2008. *European Defence Policy: Beyond the Nation State*. New York: Oxford University Press.

Mitzen, Jennifer, 2006. Anchoring Europe's Civilizing Identity: Habits, Capabilities, and Ontological Security. *Journal of European Public Policy* 13 (2): 270–285.

Moravcsik, Andrew, 2003. Theory Synthesis in International Relations: Real not Metaphysical. *International Studies Review* 5 (1): 131–136.

Neumann, Iver B., 2002. Returning Practice to the Linguistic Turn: The Case of Diplomacy. *Millennium* 31 (3): 627–651.

2003. International Relations as Emergent Bakhtinian Dialogue. *International Studies Review* 5 (1): 137–140.

Onuf, Nicholas Greenwood, 1989. *World of Our Making: Rules and Rule in Social Theory and International Relations*. Columbia: University of South Carolina Press.

Polanyi, Michael, 1983. *The Tacit Dimension*. Gloucester, MA: Peter Smith.

Pouliot, Vincent, 2008. The Logic of Practicality: A Theory of Practice of Security Communities. *International Organization* 62 (2): 257–288.

2010a. *International Security in Practice: The Politics of NATO–Russia Diplomacy*. Cambridge: Cambridge University Press.

2010b. The Materials of Practice: Nuclear Warheads, Rhetorical Commonplaces and Committee Meetings in Russian–Atlantic Relations. *Cooperation and Conflict* 45 (3): 294–311.

Rasche, Andreas and Robert Chia, 2009. Researching Strategy Practices: A Genealogical Social Theory Perspective. *Organization Studies* 30 (7): 713–734.

Reckwitz, Andreas, 2002. Toward a Theory of Social Practices: A Development in Culturalist Theorizing. *European Journal of Social Theory* 5 (2): 243–263.

Reus-Smit, Christian, 1999. *The Moral Purpose of the State: Culture, Social Identity, and Institutional Rationality in International Relations*. Princeton: Princeton University Press.

Rorty, Richard, 1982. *Consequences of Pragmatism*. Minneapolis: University of Minnesota Press.

Ryle, Gilbert, 1984. *The Concept of Mind*. Chicago: University of Chicago Press.

Schatzki, Theodore R., 1996. *Social Practices: A Wittgensteinian Approach to Human Activity and the Social*. New York: Cambridge University Press.

Schatzki, Theodore R., Karin Knorr Cetina, and Eike von Savigny, eds., 2001. *The Practice Turn in Contemporary Theory*. New York: Routledge.

Schelling, Thomas C., 1980 [1960]. *The Strategy of Conflict*. Cambridge, MA: Harvard University Press.

Seabrooke, Leonard and Eleni Tsingou, 2009. Power Elites and Everyday Politics in International Financial Reform. *International Political Sociology* 3 (4): 457–461.

Searle, John R., 1969. *Speech Acts*. New York: Cambridge University Press.

1995. *The Construction of Social Reality*. New York: Free Press.

Sewell, William H., 1992. A Theory of Structure: Duality, Agency, and Transformation. *American Journal of Sociology* 98 (1): 1–29.

Swidler, Ann, 1986. Culture in Action: Symbols and Strategies. *American Sociological Review* 51 (2): 273–286.

2001. What Anchors Cultural Practices. In *The Practice Turn in Contemporary Theory*, edited by Theodore R. Schatzki, Karin Knorr Cetina, and Eike von Savigny, 83–101. New York: Routledge.

Taylor, Charles, 1985. *Human Agency and Language: Philosophical Papers 1*. New York: Cambridge University Press.

1993. To Follow a Rule ... In *Bourdieu: Critical Perspectives*, edited by Craig Calhoun, Edward LiPuma, and Moishe Postone, 45–60. Chicago: University of Chicago Press.

Tilly, Charles, 2006. *Why? What Happens When People Give Reasons ... and Why*. Princeton: Princeton University Press.

Toulmin, Stephen, 2001. *Return to Reason*. Cambridge, MA: Harvard University Press.

Turner, Stephen P., 1994. *The Social Theory of Practices: Tradition, Tacit Knowledge, and Presuppositions*. Chicago: University of Chicago Press.

Villumsen, Trine, Forthcoming. *The International Political Sociology of Security: Rethinking Theory and Practice*. New York: Routledge.

Waltz, Kenneth N., 1979. *Theory of International Politics*. Reading, MA: Addison-Wesley.

Wendt, Alexander, 1999. *Social Theory of International Politics*. New York: Cambridge University Press.

Wenger, Etienne, 1998. *Communities of Practice: Learning, Meaning and Identity*. New York: Cambridge University Press.

Wenger, Etienne, Richard McDermott, and William M. Snyder, 2002. *A Guide to Making Knowledge: Cultivating Communities of Practice*. Boston: Harvard Business School Press.

Wiener, Antje, 2008. *The Invisible Constitution of Politics: Contested Norms and International Encounters*. New York: Cambridge University Press.

Williams, Michael C., 1991. The Future of Strategy. Working Paper 3. Toronto: Centre for Strategic and International Studies, York University.

2007. *Culture and Security: Symbolic Power and the Politics of International Security.* New York: Routledge.

Wittgenstein, Ludwig, 1958. *Philosophical Investigations.* Oxford: Blackwell.

Zürn, Michael and Jeffrey T. Checkel, 2005. Getting Socialized to Build Bridges: Constructivism and Rationalism, Europe and the Nation-State. *International Organization* 59 (4): 1045–1079.

2 | Making sense of "international practices"

FRIEDRICH KRATOCHWIL

Introduction

Now that the "practice turn" in social theory has reached International Relations (IR), a new great debate seems to be in the offing. Observers of previous "turns" might be skeptical of the promissory notes, not only because of experience, but also because this new focus on "practices" seems even less well defined. The spectrum ranges from adherents of "implicit knowledge" and habits à la Polanyi[1] to Giddean grand theory focusing on the dialectics of agency and structure.[2] It encompasses "social" epistemology stressing the communal aspects of knowledge production,[3] Bourdieu's emphasis on "*habitus*" and *doxa*,[4] and Oakeshott's "habits" and "knowing how" rather than "knowing why."[5] Thus, the call to foreground practices might make for heated debates but illumination by low wattage, given the heterogeneity of the different vocabularies.

Such problems are usually "solved" by a "working definition" imposing some order. Yet, frequently "working definitions" hide deep conceptual disagreements and emerge from intense negotiations among the participants in a research project. While such a preliminary agreement might be the price for getting along, nothing in this procedure guarantees that this "consensus" is "fruitful," as it depends on who participates and on who is setting the terms of the debate. Two of the more recent "collective" research programs – one on "ideas,"[6] the other on "judicialization"[7] – illustrate these problems: By nobly forgoing any engagement with the common uses of the crucial terms and their theoretical reflections, and by settling conceptual issues largely by fiat, we were treated to an amicable but rather shallow conversation among friends.

Thus proceeding according to standard taxonomic principles and taking the precision of a clear "reference" as a yardstick might make for bad heuristics. Not only do we face difficulties in levels of abstraction, i.e. the inverse relationship between denotational and connotational scope,[8] we also have the problem

---

[1] Polanyi, 1958. [2] Giddens, 1979. [3] Fuller, 1991. [4] Bourdieu, 1977.
[5] Oakeshott, 1975. [6] Goldstein and Keohane, 1993. [7] Abbott *et al.*, 2000.
[8] Sartori, 1970.

that the concepts of the social world do not simply correspond to some external "givens." Meaning is constituted by links to other concepts rather than by a match between a concept and its object. Hence, if we are interested in how a society "works," we must know how people communicate, *use* the concepts, and connect them with actions. In addition, we better realize that our concepts have their "history," and that changes cannot be construed as an ever-more accurate approximation to a fixed reality. For example, to see politics as a "contract" rather than as a "body" represents a conceptual revolution, as the seventeenth century showed. Yet, the new understanding does not mean that a previous "error" was corrected and we are now closer to the "truth."

These are powerful reasons for not solving conceptual problems by fiat or consensus among researchers, but for analyzing first the semantic field within which a concept functions, and then examining the linkages of this semantics to actions and changing practices. Thus we have to take two steps, one involving the analysis of actual usage of the concepts – instead of construing some idealized version and imposing it on ordinary language – and the second addressing the "archeology" of the concepts and their "reflexive" use by social scientists.

To analyze "practice" in these terms is the task of this chapter. Given that our concepts are formed by the extension of paradigmatic cases and by analogies,[9] I argue that the search for a common core representing the "essence" of a phenomenon in a concept is futile. Instead, as Wittgenstein argued, concepts are clusters, which are like a rope in which string is linked to string without one necessarily going through the whole length. Staying within the imagery of weaving but adding more complexity, we have to examine not only how the strings are interwoven, but must also realize that their intertwining shows significant variation. Thus, a "section" might not be a representative sample and "historicity" discloses itself only through time.

Our point of departure, calling "practices ... competent performances,"[10] appears to avoid those pitfalls, even if one can remain (with Duvall and Chowdhury[11]) skeptical about the claim that practices could serve the function of a "gluon" in the field. Here the metaphor of a "force" that makes things to hang together also points in a different direction as the argument of a "conversation" among people coming from different theoretical orientations. But precisely since no "conversion," knock-out "testing" of different approaches – the favorite pastime of dissertations where usually three different approaches are subjected to scrutiny – or grand theoretical "synthesis" is proposed here, we actually might address real political and social problems instead of losing ourselves in methodological quibbles or meta-theoretical abstractions. The conceptualization of practice here is sufficiently broad to allow for an investigation of the *ordinary language*

---

[9] See Davis, 2005; and Lakoff and Johnson, 1999.
[10] Adler and Pouliot, Chapter 1 in this volume.
[11] Duvall and Chowdhury, Chapter 13 in this volume.

uses, while also providing clues to the more "reflexive" *uses* of the term in the social sciences, as I shall try to show below.

Based on this examination, it seems that the various contributions subsumed here under the shorthand of "international practices" represent more than an agglomeration of fads. Instead, they share some elements of a generative grammar for approaching action and meaning that American "pragmatists" had articulated. Their opposition to the Cartesian project and traditional epistemology was based on the recognition that the conception of an "absolute standpoint" and of "nature" as ontologically given had been thoroughly undermined by modern logic and modern science alike. Revisiting these debates is therefore not simply an excursion into the "history of ideas" that can be left to some historians or arm-chair philosophers; as such a "detour" might add some luster to the enterprise but is otherwise unrelated to our research. Instead, I claim that understanding these debates is *central* to our work, as here the links between agency and ideas, social structures and meanings, stability and change are vetted.

In short, if the foregrounding of practice in IR is to succeed, it should take this pragmatic criticism seriously and develop a better conceptualization of social action. This requires a new answer to the problem of order, traditionally dealt with either in Hobbesian terms (imposition), or through the "internalization" of norms whereby "society" results simply from the coincidence of "ideas" held by individuals. I argue that thereby entirely implausible conceptual moves have to be made, ranging from the incoherence of the "desire plus belief" model of action to "causal pathways" shepherding ideas into individual minds.

But a focus on practice also requires embedding the practice of knowledge-production in wider social processes. After all, communities of scientists are not entirely autonomous but frequently have to "answer" to other authorities. This becomes especially obvious in medical research and experiments involving persons but it also leads to debates and formal proceedings in all areas, when, e.g., granting agencies have to decide on funding one type of research rather than another. Here resort to scientific standards is – contrary to the epistemological ideal – not the only yardstick. For one, all, or several of the proposals might satisfy the criteria applied by the practitioners in question. Two, new departures might also require changes in traditional methodologies – as, e.g., biology cannot satisfy the ideal of the coincidence of explanation and prediction. Three, different "schools" in a field might proffer different "proofs" and "consultants" and peer-reviewers are then supposed to mediate the controversies. Procedural fairness becomes now increasingly important. The assessment of costs, risks, and the "promises" of particular research proposals have inevitably elements of genuine uncertainty. All of this is far removed from the naïve notion of "conjectures and refutations" as near-automatic truth-finders and of "science" as a self-encapsulated enterprise, since pragmatic and utility criteria also inform the final assessment. Finally, investigating how different practices are nested, bundled, or subordinated we cannot simply assume that here a functional logic prevails or that the cunning of reason is working itself out, as so many narratives of progress and the end of history suggest. Instead we are directed, as Adler and Pouliot correctly suggest, to the sites of *political struggles* where these assemblies occur, notwithstanding the rhetoric of "best practices," or of the universality of norms or values embedded in them.

On the other hand, the focus on practices outlined by Adler and Pouliot demonstrates its fruitfulness even in the case of extreme conflict. Patrick Morgan's study of the transformation of deterrence[12] shows that the Cold War – far from instantiating the "nature" of politics as realist "theory" about hegemonic conflicts seemed to suggest – was in its practices decisively shaped by antecedent historical experiences, cultural factors (such as the fear of totalitarian-ism), and military routines (such as targeting practices) that pushed deterrence more towards the pole of total war as opposed to a possible minimum deterrence stance. But even out of seemingly unbridgeable conflicts the search for "peace without community" continued in a complex interplay of technological change, changes in the epistemes and in the accretion of new practices that were reluc-tantly adopted by US and Soviet decision-makers and their military. The inter-action of these changes fundamentally altered the old repertoires of seeking security through unilateral measures, aimed at victory and/or survival, and allowed for better crisis management, and later paved the way for the system-transforming change that ended the Cold War.

Having outlined the scope of the chapter, my argument takes the following steps: the next section examines the ordinary use of "practice" and "practices." The goal is to map rather than to develop an ideal-type. The third section deals with pragmatism in general and the fourth section examines two episodes of a "practice turn" in sociology, because the battle-lines were originally drawn there between the old epistemological project and the new ways of knowledge-production. The first episode resulted from the encounter of reform-minded sociologists at Chicago with pragmatism and its emphasis on problem-solving rather than "theory." The second more recent episode was more methodolog-ically oriented. Here Turner's *Social Theory of Practices* serves as my foil.[13] A brief summary (section five) concludes the chapter.

The uses of "practice"

The term "practice" has quite different meanings depending on whether it is in the singular or in the plural. "Practice" (*praxis*) is thus a collective singular encompassing various more specific "practices," but it also attains its meaning from its opposition to "technique" or "production" (*techne* or *poiesis* in Aristotle's taxonomy). Underlying the Aristotelian project, reverberating in our vocabula-ries, is the issue of which type of knowledge is necessary for different activities. For

---

[12] Morgan, Chapter 6 in this volume. [13] Turner, 1994.

the "making" of things *techne* serves as the template, while *poiesis* covers also the case of creative endeavors. "Theory," on the other hand, concerns the "view" of things as they are. Thus *praxis* is neither theoretical nor productive. Rather *praxis* provides yardsticks for *action* and for availing oneself of more specific practices. As the latter could easily shade off into a "technique," i.e. selecting a practice that "works" – particularly when questions of ends remain unaddressed – another criterion becomes important, if one wants to "*act well*," as Aristotle puts it. Since we usually act in social contexts, others' interests and possible interferences have to be addressed. This adds a moral dimension to action distinguishing the latter from events, from the production of things, and from theoretical speculation.

Often, this moral dimension of action and *praxis* is overlooked and treated only elsewhere – for example, when we discuss the shifting of blame, the pathologies of working bureaucratically "by the rule-book," or the shirking of responsibility in organizations. After all, following rules can be one of the most effective ways of sabotage, as the "job actions" of air-controllers (who are not allowed to strike) shows. Similarly, following "best practices" is an effective way of avoiding criticism even if the intended goal remains unachieved, or the strategies are actually counterproductive. In this context, Chapter 9 by Sending and Neumann in this volume provides much food for thought on how the assumption of "one size fits all" exacerbates problems rather than solves them.[14] Moreover, Janice Gross Stein's Chapter 4 in this volume shows how "doing the right thing," as specified by the deontologically framed rules of humanitarianism, often prevents a critical examination of the problems while safeguarding the "moral" standing of dangerous and harmful actions.

Furthermore, when we turn to *practicing* something, we face several ambiguities. First, we use the term for disciplining efforts, as when we are trying to get something right through repetition until it is done nearly automatically. If I want to perform Beethoven's violin concerto, I'd better practice the difficult octaves until I play them effortlessly and without conscious control. But second, we also use "practice" when we want to distinguish the seriousness of a performance from mere exercises, where we go only through the motions.

The first meaning is well in line with Foucault's studies about self-fashioning, with some aspects of Bourdieu's arguments about *habitus*, or even with Polanyi's notion of "tacit knowledge." Of course, the contradiction remains that both a simple form of habituation and one of knowledge-production are lumped together. Yet, Skinnerian conditioning is something entirely different from the "givens" in a field that are "self-understood" and that determine the bounds of sense. Thus, the focus on "routine" in which both modes of training converge – one stressing conditioning, the other cognitive factors – hides important differences.

[14] Sending and Neumann, Chapter 9 in this volume.

The second meaning of practice (as "performance") comes close to transcending our conventional understanding. In this context, one could mention Flyvbjerg's[15] virtuous performances of masters in the field or Bourdieu's Kabyle clansman.[16] For instance, the latter teaches his fellows a lesson by not using the usual strategies of redressing a wrong. In his refusal he provides a new example for honor and its defense. But here we encounter perhaps a charismatic breakthrough rather than an established practice. After all, the charismatic leader is – contrary to what Weber suggests – not a simple non-conformist but appeals to his group on the basis of widely shared practices which are now transcended or given new meaning. Only by keeping the social bond with his followers can the non-conformist leader remain charismatic,[17] instead of becoming a law-breaker.

Certain performances, though, are again closer to normal practices, because frequently they have to follow painstakingly the underlying rules. Ceremonies and rituals come to mind. As they often have their roots in magic, all prescriptions must be observed scrupulously, even though these rituals might eventually result in the seemingly chaotic "collective effervescence" that Durkheim mentions when describing communal rituals in primitive religions.[18]

The use of the *adverbial form* of practice – calling something "practical" – stresses again the more normal recurrent dimension of situations which are, however, not reducible to routines or habits. Instead, it comes attached to a stronger evaluative dimension, emphasizing the creative character of the solutions. After all, the "practical" might not be the habitual.

The last remark draws attention to another dimension of practices that emphasize skill and judgment, or the "craft" dimension of practice. Acting in this way entails making use of knowledge and skills but on the basis of the particular circumstances of a case. This involves "judgment," which is specifiable neither by rules nor by the traditional inference patterns. In this sense, we practice law, medicine, or "statecraft" (albeit in a looser sense). At issue is a quick and comprehensive diagnosis of the situation rather than its subsumption under a law or an inductive inference. "Completeness" and timeliness become now important criteria. Aristotle's emphasis on recognizing the right moment, the *kairos*, stands in stark contrast to formal rigor and a-historical validity of nomic assertions. Experience and the ability *to reason from case to case* are necessary instead of applying universal laws. "Prudence" rather than "theory" guides the analysis.

This last point corrects the impression that the relevant distinctions can be subsumed under the rubric of "professional" activities. While certainly some professionals are engaged in practical activities, not all are. It would be odd to say that someone practices engineering, even if she has an office, like a doctor or a lawyer, and acquired her status through certifications. Similarly, some

---

[15] Flyvbjerg, 2001.   [16] Bourdieu, 1974.   [17] Alberoni, 1984.   [18] Durkheim, 1965.

simple as well as complicated activities – even those with a practical import such as cooking or building a car – are not "practiced." The former uses rules (recipes), while the latter involves stringent models and optimization criteria based on physical laws. These examples suggest that we make distinctions between instrumental actions, and productive and practical activities, despite considerable overlaps.

Another sense of "practice" is involved when we speak of assemblies of interrelated actions by several persons, as in Bratman's collective intentions.[19] Examples are playing a duet or hunting together. These actions must "mesh" – provided by the score or the strategy – and they involve continuous collaboration. The participants monitor each other's actions and make necessary adjustments in order to reach the goal. Simply working by the rules, or following the score irrespective of what the other(s) is (are) doing, is likely to derail the project. That a pack of wolves, hunting together, forms such collective intentions should caution us in deriving such endeavors from the cognitive "application" of rules. Furthermore, the necessarily continuous coordination is badly conceived as executing a script that is the efficient cause, precisely because the "finality" of action makes constant adjustments necessary, something that contradicts the notion of efficient cause that results in identical effects.

The example of collective intentions leads to the general problem of "institutions," which provide the cognitive enabling conditions for collective intentions, even though the latter might rest on, or work in tandem with, some pre-cognitive mimetic and motoric abilities. Institutions have often been defined as "settled practices." Searle has elaborated on the peculiarities of institutional practices and on two aspects in particular. They concern the "artificial character" of institutions and their roots in language via "status ascriptions,"[20] a point made already by Aristotle in *Politics*. Animals might form some collective intentions, but not even the slyest dog "purchases" his can of dog-food when he drops a dollar in front of his master's feet and gets rewarded for this act. The conditioned "habit" and the ensuing interplay do not entail an understanding of the institution of money, since this would require familiarity with such practices as "saving," "investing," even "paying debts."

Finally, there is the famous distinction between theory and practice. Practice means the actual conduct, while theory denotes an idealized form or hypothetical construct. Examples are game theory or Rawls' defense of "ideal theory" even for practical matters, exemplified by his "veil of ignorance."[21] Such a distinction has two conflicting corollaries. On the one hand, in privileging "theory" as a mode of knowledge, the deficiencies of actual practice appear to result from the inherent limitations of prudential reasoning rather than from

[19] Bratman, 1992.   [20] Searle, 1995.   [21] Rawls, 1971.

the complexities of situations or the difficulty of "applying" abstract principles. On the other hand, by using the distinction *against* this privileging move we arrive at an indictment of "theory." After all, even in natural science the actual practice of knowledge generation diverges significantly from its rational "reconstruction" in textbooks.

The last problem allows again for a "stronger" and a "weaker" interpretation. The weaker version focuses on considerable differences *within science* itself, such as between theoretical and experimental physics. In the stronger version, the issue is rather the identification of the "actual" with science *tout court*. As Michael Lynch put it:

> The accent is realistic but this genre of realism is more akin to *cinéma vérité* than to the philosophy of scientific realism. Far from invoking the real nature of an asocial universe to account for scientific developments, this brand of social and historical realism implies an unblinking attempt to produce down to earth and perhaps unflattering documentary portrayals. The practical reality is not invisible and abstract, it is commonplace and on the surface.[22]

This interpretation gives the "practice turn" in social theory its bite. Before we decide which version to embrace, and which lessons we might have to learn for IR analysis, it is useful to examine first some of the central tenets of pragmatism, the *spiritus rector* of the "practice turn" in social theory.

Pragmatism

Rather than sketching the common core all pragmatist thinkers share, I treat it as an open question. Peirce, who is perhaps closest to the traditional epistemological concerns, focused increasingly on the community of scientists rather than on reason and its categories. He insisted that his approach was "pragmaticist" rather than pragmatic, precisely because he did not want to be identified with James and Dewey.[23] Similarly, Dewey was critical of James' individualism that allowed too little space for the "social," by focusing on the justification of individual beliefs. Thus, the diversity among pragmatism's protagonists made for lively debates but not for a grand "synthesis."

If there is a *common theme* (rather than a common core) running through those expositions and conversations, it is the coming to terms with the end of speculative philosophy (after Hegel and Nietzsche's "death of God") and with the advances of science, particularly biology. Both developments inverted the traditional hierarchy between metaphysics (theory) and practical knowledge.

---

[22] Lynch, 1997, 338.
[23] Peirce thought that this neologism was so "ugly enough to be safe even from kidnappers." Peirce, 1952, 276–277.

Of course, for a while it seemed that "nature," speaking to us directly through "science," could provide the ultimate foundation. But with the disenchantment of nature, the big questions of philosophy could no longer be answered in the traditional fashion; rather, one had to "get over them," as Dewey suggested.[24]

Dewey saw clearly that the substitution of God by nature was to exchange the placeholders while preserving the old metaphysical framework, where the "true" was permanent and fixed, and the fleeting and contingent was "defective." Yet, since our conceptual frameworks developed out of particular choices in philosophy, one has to examine such a fundamental presupposition since they establish the "hierarchy" in the modes of knowing. Practical knowledge is devalued because of its "contingent" character, while "theory," dealing with the universal and unchanging, is extolled. Thus, despite the fierce debates in philosophy, most quarrels barely scratched the surface, as Dewey suggested:

> Special theories of knowledge differ enormously from one another. Their quarrels with one another fill the air ... Some theories ascribe the ultimate test of knowledge to impressions passively received, forced upon us ... Others ascribe the guarantee of knowledge to synthetic activity of the intellect. Idealistic theories hold that the mind and the object known are ultimately one; realistic doctrines reduce knowledge to an awareness that exists independently ... they all make one common assumption. They all hold that the operation of inquiry excludes any element of practical activity that enters into the construction of the object known ... For according to them the "mind" constructs the known object not in any observable way, or by means of practical overt acts having a temporal quality, but by some occult internal operations ...
>
> The theory of knowing is modeled after what was supposed to take place in the act of vision. The object refracts light to the eye and is seen; ... A spectator theory of knowledge is the inevitable outcome.[25]

Yet, after Darwin, it became difficult to argue that "reality" was complete, "out there," only to be discovered. It implied that the identification of truth with an unchanging nature was mistaken. Such a stance could not deal with the always preliminary character of any established "truth," and with nature's changes itself. It forced upon a critical observer the radical conclusion that the old hierarchy of theory and practical knowledge had to be inverted, and that the notion of truth as "certainty" or indubitability, exemplified by Descartes, was essentially misleading. A brief discussion of both points seems necessary.

As to the always preliminary character of what counts as "truth," the example of the "positivist" Popper is instructive. On the one hand, he is aware that most of our theories are probably wrong and that they will have to be revised. On the other hand, he clings to a notion of "the truth" which is derived from metaphysics. Revisions can then be interpreted as "progress," as coming nearer

[24] Dewey, 1981, 41.   [25] Dewey, 1984, 18–19.

to the truth, while simultaneously never actually getting there (because otherwise revisions could not occur). In squaring the circle, Popper introduces the notion of *verisimilitude*.[26]Aside from the question whether such a "reconstruction" is a fitting description of what goes on in science – here Kuhn's criticisms and the detailed accounts of the history of science are critical – this move involves him in a logical contradiction.

If nature is not simply "there" speaking to us directly, and if we have access to it only through our (fallible) theories, we have no independent way of assessing whether we are "closer." All we can say is that we are somewhere else, but not that we are nearer, because this would presuppose some direct knowledge. Only by knowing *a priori* a goalpost could we judge whether we have come nearer to it. In addition, the spatial metaphor is inappropriate. "Progress" in science consists largely in asking *entirely new* questions, which were inconceivable before, rather than in exhausting step by step a *given* area.

This means that both in science and in assertions about "The Truth" something else is going on. The "belief in truth" and its indictment of "relativism" serve as quasi-religious grounds. As Rorty suggests, "[t]he premise of philosophy is that there is a way things really are – what humanity and all the rest of the universe are and always will be, independent of any merely contingent human needs and interests. Knowledge of this is redemptive . . . The striving for Truth can take the place of the search for God."[27]

The issue raised by looking at science and knowledge generation as a social practice brings into focus the productive roles of the investigator and the community. It foregrounds the actual activity of the investigator and the critical reflection on its own presuppositions rather than assuming an Archimedean point. Consequently, both Peirce and James adamantly opposed the epistemological project, based on Descartes. In his "Some Consequences of Four Incapacities," Peirce rejects both Cartesian principles as foundational for knowledge: radical doubt (or the empty self-reflection of an abstract self) and "clear and distinct ideas" which are based on question-begging presuppositions:

> We cannot begin with complete doubt. We must begin with all the prejudices which we actually have when we enter upon the study of philosophy. These prejudices are not dispelled by a maxim, for they are things which do not occur to us can be questioned. Hence this initial skepticism will be a mere self-deception and not a real doubt . . .
>
> In science in which men come to agreement, when a theory has been broached, it is considered to be on probation until this agreement is reached. After it is reached, the question of certainty becomes an idle one, because there is no one left who doubts . . .
>
> Philosophy ought to imitate the successful sciences in its methods, so far as to proceed only from tangible premises which can be subjected to careful

[26] Popper, 1965, Chapter 10.   [27] Rorty, 2004, 11.

scrutiny, and to trust rather *the multitude and variety of its arguments than to the conclusiveness of any one.*[28]

In short, the experience of the world is not like receiving passively some inputs from reality which leave their marks on our sense organs; the mind is also not a simple container but rather a stream of continuous adjustments in which impressions are sorted, selected, combined, and formed into images. Far from being adequately conceived as a passive *tabula rasa*, apprehending the world involves a selective and purposeful *activity*. This stress on action underlying perceptions distinguishes pragmatists from empiricists like Locke or Hume, despite their constant emphasis on "experience."

Consequently "truth" cannot be some "stagnant, ontological wonder-sickness" of philosophers such as Schopenhauer.[29] In an ever-changing world "truth" is not a property of a fixed "world out there," but it is better thought of as a process by which we "verify" some assertions while rejecting others.[30] In "The Sentiment of Rationality," James suggests – much like Rorty after him – that such a conception of truth had its own justification, and that it neither needed an unchanging world, as the old ontology maintained, nor universal and a-historical categories of reason, as Kantians or transcendentalists suggested. To this, Peirce would add that this experience is not one of individuals or their "minds" but a *communal* affair, by which ideas and hypotheses are vetted. Their acceptance is based on intersubjective understandings, which also provide the criteria – i.e. the "external permanency"[31] as he calls it – and allocate the burdens of proof.

This orientation implies turning away from abstractions and ideal conceptions, from *a priori*s, axioms, and the ideal of compelling demonstrations, to arguments and justifications. Irrespective of which version we prefer, James, Dewey, or Peirce, the result is an exact reversal of the assumptions underlying classical thought. "Truth" is not simply given, revealed, or intuited by theoretical reason; rather, it results from *practical activity*, from learning and contestation. But this means that both conceptions of "Truth" – i.e. as coherence (as in logic) and as correspondence (to the "world out there") – turn out to be poor philosopher's stones. Not certainty but *the concrete problem situation* and the way of *coping* with it now become central.

The move away from theoretical preoccupations to practical problem-solving is not limited to some simple deliberation about the most adequate means for a chosen end. Dewey rejected psychological models based on the stimulus/response scheme of efficient causality and he criticized instrumental rationality in explaining problem-solving in situations requiring actions (i.e. those that could not be handled by habits or unquestioned routines). Both

---

[28] Peirce, 1997, 4–5. Emphasis added.   [29] James, 1977b, 22.
[30] See James, 1977a and 1977c.   [31] See Peirce, 1955a, 18 and 1955b, 26–31.

approaches, he contended, provide a misleading and truncated version of actual choice-process. The first assumes that the stimuli of environment call forth the responses causally. It hides the problem that the actor must *decide* which stimuli bombarding him have to be selected according to their relevance to a problem at hand. Action and choice are necessary only when something disruptive occurs. Second, models of "rational action," i.e. the realization of pre-set ends through maximizing action, are also conceptually not rich enough to deal with the complexities of choice. We never stand outside the situation having a complete, ordered set of alternatives, and human action is also teleological only in a quite diffuse fashion. Thus, in concrete choice situations, ends and means are being continuously adjusted until a dominant motive – all things considered – emerges.

Certain themes addressed by pragmatism suggest that there exists indeed a family resemblance among the different uses of "practice" mentioned above. This has important consequences for social analysis. *First*, the subversion of the theoretical ideal shows that the template of acting provides a better under-standing for what goes on in science than a model based on demonstration or "indubitability." In addition, the Darwinian revolution – later reinforced by modern physics and "Schroedinger's cat" problem – demonstrated that nature is not fixed, and that knowing it is not like "lifting a veil" from an eternal, pre-existing reality.[32]

Second, the activity of the researcher and the community with its routines in knowledge-production replaced the old notion of a single (universal) "observer." A more constitutive understanding of the investigator and the community of practitioners emerged. These points were adopted only reluc-tantly by "mainstream" social science and at different speeds in different disciplines. The observer's constitutive role remained for the longest time controversial. When it was broached by some constructivists, the epistemolog-ical "consensus" in IR treated such attempts as pernicious pleas for "relativism." Most disciplines were, however, willing to accept the role of the "scientific community," leading to several conceptualizations. It ranged from IR's focus on epistemic communities – stressing cognitive factors and even cognitive evolution[33] – to more "habit-"driven models in sociology like Bourdieu's *habitus* and the role of "doxological" conflict among scientists.[34]

A *third* theme emerges from the distinction between "practice" as unreflec-tive habit and as something requiring judgment in the application of rules. Here pragmatism has contributed largely to the second theme by insisting on the "performative" aspects of action, while "science studies" focused on the first. For example Latour[35] and his followers stressed the unintentional part of action and social organization and named as the crucial element the interface

---

[32] Zeilinger, 2003.   [33] Adler, 1991.   [34] Villumsen, 2008.
[35] Latour and Woolgar, 1979.

of researchers and their artifacts. This goes from the simple design of questionnaires, determining the "importance" of information, to sophisticated laboratory machines and the "reverse adaptation" they can engender. In this sense, machines and programs set the limits of what can be asked and what makes sense, thereby calling into question the classical goal/means distinction in our conception of instrumental rationality. While pragmatists questioned the adequacy of this model from the perspective of intentional action, Latour and his followers raised doubts from the perspective of means.

Lastly, there is a *fourth* theme that shows some resemblance to the "performance/habit" tension but seems to transcend it. It is the argument about "virtuoso" performances transcending all habit but also all conscious rule-following. Nevertheless, it cannot be something so radically different that it is unrecognizable as being part of a particular practice. Thus, when the Kabyle clansman does not ask for redress from the perpetrator – as prescribed by traditional norms – but engages in some new form of "shaming" by complaining to his brother, there has still to be some shared understanding that this response "belongs" to a process of "righting wrongs." It cannot be a purely idiosyncratic act, such as making a somersault or pulling a donkey's tail. In the specific case the clansman could use the norm that only "worthy" people can give satisfaction while the perpetrator had no "honor." As indicated above in the discussion of the "charismatic leader," it seems that only a re-conceptualization of social action can address this problem, since the conventional distinction between "routine" and "exceptional" action hardly provides the necessary tools. The next section on pragmatism's impact on American sociology should be read in this light, i.e. not as a disciplinary history but as a clarification of action analysis.

The impact of pragmatism on American sociology

In this section I focus on two episodes in which pragmatism informed most visibly the discussion in sociology: one, the period of the "Chicago School" which found its most noticeable expression later in the "symbolic interactionism" of Mead, Blumer, and Goffman; the other, more recent, episode was occasioned by Turner's book on practices and their puzzles. Both debates illustrate the main controversial issues and are therefore important also for the IR community.

The old Chicago School of sociology with its emphasis on social reform, on experiential knowledge, and on painstakingly conducted empirical research for solving concrete social problems provided a fertile ground for pragmatic thought.[36] William Isaac Thomas, a Chicago graduate and later a faculty member of the sociology department, was one of the first to link pragmatism

---

[36] For a general discussion see Joas, 1993, particularly Chapter 1.

and sociological research. In his *Source Book for Social Origins*,[37] Thomas criticized the dominant modes of causal explanations of behavior in terms of biological determinants, whether racial or psychological, and shifted attention to cultural factors. But neither were individuals for him simply the "executors" of scripts provided by "society" which was crucial for the analysis of change. A loss of traditional orientation did not have to lead to anomie and disorientation. Rather, new cultural forms engendered new institutions, thereby establishing a new equilibrium between disintegration and reorganization. In his famous study on Polish immigrants (together with Znaniecki),[38] he showed that social change did not consist in substituting "modernity" for tradition, eliminating, e.g., ethnic or family ties, but in constructing a new configuration of these elements.

In this environment George Herbert Mead developed his "social psychology" and in particular the famous distinction between the "I" and the "me," a distinction dating back to William James. Convinced that "self-reflectivity" – neither in the empty Cartesian form nor in the transcendental subject *à la* Kant – provided the key to human sociality, he showed how human sociality differed from that of other species. Although Aristotle had already pointed to the constitutive nature of language in his *Politics*,[39] at Mead's time the recovery of language as an intersubjective phenomenon had to cope with deeply ingrained notions of (methodological) individualism, the "causal" nature of explanations, and a naturalistic concept of social "science."

For that reason, pragmatism became a liberating influence, as it allowed one to question these assumptions. In the end, Mead conceived a new theory of communication. Taking issue with Royce's theory of imitation Mead argued that this was like putting the cart before the horse.[40] For him, actions were not simple responses to stimuli, since it is precisely the inhibition of an automatic response and the orientation towards the other that constitutes social action. The first function of even a "gesture" is "the mutual adjustment of changing response to changing social stimulation."[41] Thus, the "social" cannot be discovered by adding up individual responses to internal or external stimuli, but has to be found in a specific form of cooperation that requires monitoring and mutual adjustment instead of simple repetition and imitation:

> The likeness of the actions is of minimal importance compared with the fact that the actions of one form have the implicit meaning of a certain response to another form. The probable beginning of human communication was in cooperation, not in imitation. Where conduct differed and yet the act of the one answered and called out the act of the other.[42]

---

[37] Thomas, 1909.   [38] Thomas and Znaniecki, 1996.   [39] Aristotle, 1981, 60 (1253a7).
[40] Joas, 1985, Chapter 5.   [41] Mead, 1910, 398.
[42] As quoted in Joas, 1985, 99–100. Originally in Mead, 1909.

In addition, human communication is superior to mere signs or gestures as it operates via significant symbols, in other words through an anticipation of "others' responses" (the "me"), while action results from the tension between the "me" and the "I." This tension allows for creative innovation and not only for the re-enactment of fixed roles.

Actors are, therefore, not normative "dopes" implementing the expectations of others, but in each interaction the decisive criterion is whether the parties can "go on." Two reasons support this: *First*, the "me" represents the expectation of significant others but precisely because we have usually more than one "other," we have to manage conflicts between these expectations. Thus, different from the "I" or self, which has to give coherence to all of my actions, one way of managing role-conflicts is to allow different "mes" to appear in different situations (at school I am a teacher, at home a husband). Only in well-specified games, the "rules of the game" become the "generalized other," thus allowing for less leeway. By developing the ability of taking the role of the other, an actor develops reflexivity and avoids the solipsism of Cartesian pure reflection. She also induces the other through "alter-casting" to become part of a common understanding of what is going on.[43]

Second, actors are not normative dopes, because situations are usually ambiguous and allow for "bending" the rules. This introduces new meanings and allows for innovation in coping with social problems. Sometimes these "interstitial changes" result through time in fundamental reconceptualization. For instance, Chapter 12 by Abrahamsen and Williams in this volume shows quite nicely how "security" became a "commodity" after having mutated from a "task" to a "[public] good," and finally to a tradable good. Sometimes fundamental environmental changes make playing the international game according to a traditional practice such as "non-intervention" difficult or impossible, as Little points out in Chapter 7 in this volume. Thus the crude dichotomy between "interests" and "rule-following" that has dominated the debate hardly captures these complexities. Sometimes the change is more explicit, involving deliberate new rule-making, as in cases of regimes or constitutional arrangements.

This view on rules is predicated on the constitutive surplus of rules instead of simply engaging in repetition. Freud correctly diagnosed mindless repetition as a "compulsion" depriving the individual of his agency and making him appear as a victim of circumstances. Instead, rule-following allows us to experience

---

[43] As a matter of fact one of Mead's surprising implications is that the creation of "inanimate" objects in the cognitive development of individuals crucially depends on the capacity of role-taking which has been acquired in social contexts. As Joas suggests, only in this way does the hand–eye coordination "create" permanent objects rather than leaving the individual with a series of unconnected polysensory experiences. Only in this way do we connect the different experiences and attribute them to an "object" that offers a kind of "active" resistance that emanates from the "inside" of objects rather than being just a property of their surface. Joas, 1985, 153 ff.

change in a meaningful fashion. This has important implications for both "society" and the "self." The self, reflecting upon itself, is not gazing at a frozen image as when looking in a mirror. Rather, the individual understands her present predicament in the light of past experiences, opening up the horizon for future action by "playing through" different options for realizing her "projects." Identity is not ascertained by an act of pure self-reflection but by a person's active involvement in interactions and projects. Somebody who does not remember can make little sense out of the present, which then appears as a meaningless stream of impressions. Equally, someone who sees no future is prevented from acting. Thus, *the "self" is accessible to us through our actions and the reactions we experience.* This is the upshot of Mead's distinction between "I" and "me," and of the link between "historical" reflection and projects.[44]

Compared with these rather far-reaching implications for a theory of action, the second debate seems rather shallow. As it is largely methodology-driven it consists of some well-known arguments against the fuzziness of the concept of practice and rule-following. Here Turner's book has been decisive for setting the terms of the debate.[45] His attack on "practice mongers" takes the familiar route of showing the imprecision of the term by comprising a cognitive and performative version of practice (the latter stressing competences or skills).

Turner criticizes the notion that the acquisition of competences must be explained in terms of people "sharing" some common understandings or rules. Rather, he suggests, the "uniformity" of such performances can be explained in terms of individually acquired habits or bodily routines. Allegedly, if practices are to have any explanatory standing, they must refer to objectively ascertainable regularities, i.e. must have some "psychological reality and causal effectiveness." On the other hand, if individual habits are "personal" (thus conforming to a strict methodological individualism), one must explain their uniformity, as well as their generational transfer. Therefore, much of the book is an attack on those sociological theories that use a common social substratum as an *explanans*, such as Durkheim's "collective mind" where "social facts" are allegedly located. But such constructions, Turner objects, "required one to believe in a process of transmission, of the insertion of the collective objects into the individual mind or body, that simply defies credulity when fully understood."[46]

Two problems emerge. As to the first: The easiest solution would be to deny any "cultural" element and see the problem of action and social reproduction (Turner's problem of transmission) simply as a process of physical conditioning, in line with strict behaviorism. Turner avoids that route, because he thinks that such action explanations are deficient. Yet, as any culturalist, he has to explain the processes of "learning," "socialization," and "internalization." This

---

[44] For a similar argument on the need of historical reflection not based on Mead, but rather on Bull's argument for a "classical" approach to politics, see Kratochwil, 2006.

[45] Turner, 1994. [46] Turner, 1997, 345.

leads to the second problem. Studying this inculcation involves unobervables, like "minds" and "intentions." Turner wants to resort to such theoretical props only if they have causal significance. But since we have no direct access to internalization processes, we remain uncertain whether people share the "same thing," i.e. that their overt behavior is the effect of the same value or norm "causing" the action. After all, people could come to the same act by a different route, or they could have learned different things from the same norm.

This criticism is valid since the reversal of the causal inference from the effect to an alleged cause is logically faulty – Hume's famous problem of induction comes to the fore – save in inferences via the *modus tollens*.[47] Turner's conclusions are, however, plausible only if we (rather dogmatically) have already decided that only causally efficient explanations are "proper" explanations. Holding on to a strict efficient causality, Turner maintains that no "sharing" is necessary. Consequently, "social facts" have no standing and they can best be understood as the coincidence and aggregation of individual acts, fully explainable in terms of the acquisition of individual habits.

These heady claims result more from conceptual confusions than from well-founded objections. Let us begin with the notion that explaining something is tantamount to establishing a "causal link." While efficient causality certainly is an "explanation" not all explanation shares this form, as the discussion of "constitutive explanation" shows,[48] not to speak of the fact that what *serves* as an explanation is not free-standing but highly context-dependent.

When an interstate highway bridge collapses, for example, next day's newspapers will attribute it to the earthquake that occurred. However, when an investigation examines the case the causal attribution might quickly lose its explanatory value when such things as shoddy workmanship or the crass violations of building codes are cited. Here the conjunction of several independent, necessary, but insufficient "causes" does the explaining. And things get even more complicated when we find out that the decision of the zoning board and planning commission to build the bridge in this particular location (despite its unstable foundations) instead of choosing a safer alternative 20 miles north, was due to the corruption of several board members. In that case, the earthquake – while not irrelevant – loses its status of an "explanation," as questions of responsibility now attain prominence. In short, we ask for explanations in a variety of contexts that cannot all be forced into the Procrustean bed of causal efficiency.

Similar difficulties arise with Turner's assertion that all social phenomena must be explained in individual terms. Despite this being a basic tenet of methodological individualism, it is untenable, even logically, since it involves

---

[47] This is the reason why Popper makes "refutability" rather than degrees of "confidence" his demarcation criterion for "science." Popper, 1968.

[48] Wendt, 1999, particularly Chapter 2.

two fallacies working in tandem. The first is the fallacy of composition: what is true of the parts need not be true of composites and vice versa. For example, both pickles and chocolate pudding might be "good," but it does not follow that the composite is also "good." Similarly, corporations are "owned" by the shareholders, yet the latter do not own the assets of the corporation. These examples should make us suspicious of the ideal of methodological individualism, despite its popularity, as its plausibility results from the "fallacy of misplaced concreteness."

Similarly, Turner's criticism of the murky concept of "tacit knowledge" or of unreflective habit are well taken and to the point, but two problems remain if we dismiss the "tacit knowledge" argument entirely. One is that many practices seem to involve some skills whose exercise can be described in rule-form without really capturing what is going on. For instance, a student who learns from his master how to paint an ear will not only see how the master does it, but the master's criticism will contain some "tips" ranging from holding the paint-brush differently to encouraging bolder strokes and paying attention to certain curves. Saying that the student learns by "following the rules" is somewhat odd, particularly since the instructions are not in rule-form, but are situation-specific "commands."[49] The student either gets the hang of it or not. He has "learned" when he can "go on" and for example paint an ear from a different perspective. Similarly, the girl who has learned to ride a bicycle no longer needs stabilizing props.

In both cases, the rules were not really "applied," as in applying a paragraph of the penal code to a criminal act. Even if one argued that in riding a bike the girl actually follows rules based on mathematical equations, showing her such calculations or subjecting her to calculus classes would hardly improve her bike-riding. Thus, it is somewhat beside the point to focus on whether the student or the girl "shared" the respective rules. Besides, in both cases the issue is not an exact reproduction brought about by an efficient cause but rather the ability to "go on" and do things somewhat differently.

Rule-following seems to encompass a variety of ways in which we become competent performers. Some things we "pick up" through pure imitation, like when learning to speak by forming words out of sounds. But when we construct sentences, the underlying grammatical structures remain largely unknown until we learn another language. Yet, we should not forget that the corrections we receive from parents, friends, and teachers on how "one speaks properly" form a crucial part of this process. Thus, we learn through imitations, corrections, and "tips" as in the case of the painter, even though here, as in the case of articulating words, the learning is less cognitive than involving the acquisition of "how to" capacities. Finally, in certain circumstances we actually *need* to follow explicit rules not only to be competent actors, as in the case of a judge. None of

---

[49] On this distinction and its implication for law (and social theory) see Hart, 1961.

her decisions would have any validity without an explicit invocation of rules and norms as "reasons."

To that extent, the reduction of all these different actions to "habit" seems sterile, not to mention the ambiguity of "habit" itself. Is the habit of putting my house-keys in a bowl the same as the "disciplinary" decision to rise at 7 every morning, even if I do not wake up without an alarm clock? Both cases can be described as "habits," but they involve rather different things. Finally, is it sensible to call complicated interactions involving continued cooperation, such as playing soccer, "habits"? The participants are required precisely not to do the "same" thing – Turner's acid test for whether people act on the basis of having something in common – but to engage in continued mutual adjustment.

Thus, by using "rule" as a *descriptive* term for observable regularities based on efficient causes Turner misses the function of rules as providing reasons for actions, "all things considered." They do not work like causes precisely because they are not designed for creating identical responses or reproductions of imaginary, abstract situations. Rather, they enable people "to go on," and thereby also change the processes of social reproduction. "Same" is not simply the exact copy but specified by a *tertium comparationis* or a (contestable) analogy. For instance, apples and oranges are the "same" (fruit) for some purposes – if compared to machines or birds – but not for all purposes. Without further specification, the meaning of the term "same" cannot be determined.

In Chapter 11 in this volume, Hansen shows how the "same" incident (caricatures of the prophet Muhammad) had different consequences depending on whether it was treated within the set of diplomatic practices or constitutional politics. That a different framing of the issue results in different outcomes does not entitle us to deny the existence of various practices, even though observing the "case" through time and tracing the various stages of contestation does not let us predict the outcome from the panoply of rules.

Thus, the naïve objection to a practice approach that attempts to "test" it by proving the "non-existence" or epiphenomenal character of rules is unconvincing. For one, actions are nearly always overdetermined allowing for different interpretations. More importantly, the complexities arise not from the non-existence of rules but from the complex interdependence of various simultaneous games. Here opportunities of deception and manipulation abound, as do the opportunities for calling into question the "background knowledge" used for assessing "competence" of an actor's performance, a problem Voeten addresses.[50] In other words, not the "non-existence" but the *existence* of several practices and their combination create the puzzle. Solving it far exceeds the binary logic underlying the usual "tests" according to which something is or is not so (*tertium non datur*). Finally, since norms are counterfactually valid, their

---

[50] Voeten, Chapter 10 in this volume.

influence on decision-making cannot be reduced to a question of observable "existence" but requires a different "test."

Turner is aware of these complications, yet he seems to adhere to a conception of language in which words function as exact matches of outward phenomena. This "descriptivist" fallacy, however, is nonsensical even for a positivist research agenda where concepts are "precise" when they match objects of the world "out there." Such arguments break down quickly when we consider certain "factual" properties such as "big" or "small." What is big or small cannot be decided by the "facts," because there is no fact of the matter. A deviation of 1 mm is enormous for a computer-chip producer but irrelevant to a builder of a 50-storey office tower. Therefore, such terms are not free-standing and do not assign meaning in simple referential operations; their meaning depends on the *use of the terms* instantiating the relevant practices of a field.

This raises a second point. One can describe bicycle-riding in various ways. For example, one can observe and employ propositions in order to describe and explain, while another description might focus on the actor and her abilities of "how to do it." Privileging the first account prevents, however, an understanding of the "how to" element in practical activities because it assumes that practice can be illuminated only by subjecting it to a "theoretical" treatment. Thus as Brunnée and Toope show,[51] learning a language or legal reasoning is not like putting external things into one's mind but involves rule-governed interactions by which we generate and maintain collective understandings. Here neither spatial analogies nor attention to free-standing fixed rules of a "pure theory" of law are helpful.

Most of Turner's puzzles are due to his use of problematic spatial metaphors: How do the rules get in the actor's (private) mind? Turner's vocabulary, coming close to a Freudian slip, is telling. He is worried about the "*location*" of rules and about how they get into the minds of individuals, how they are "possessed" or "not possessed."[52] In other words, rules are like parcels in transition. One "owns" them after having received them and put them into the "mind," which is apparently a container. This is as fruitful as asking where "numbers" are located, or whether and how we possess them, particularly if we are bad at arithmetic. Similarly, Bially Mattern argues that students of emotions – who seem all aware that their subject matter does not fit the traditional ontological and epistemological categories – usually end up belying their own arguments by squishing "emotions" in an either/or framework of causal inference instead of seeing them as "enactments" that emerge from the interaction between cognition and physiology, nature and culture, agency and structure.[53]

The main problem here is to treat practices like "things" and subject them to physical (spatial) criteria instead of seeing them as *significations*, accessible to us

---

[51] Brunnée and Toope, Chapter 5 in this volume.
[52] Turner, 1994, particularly Chapter 4, 60 ff.   [53] Bially Mattern, Chapter 3 in this volume.

through the analysis of semantic fields and the actions which are thereby authorized, demanded, or enjoined. As Doty maintains:

> Practices are generally embedded in discourses which enable particular meanings to be signified. However discourses do not mechanically or instrumentally produce practices, nor do practices mechanically . . . reproduce a particular discourse. Rather there is a dimension of indeterminacy or "play" to practices . . . Practices, because of their inextricable link with meaning, have an autonomy which cannot be reduced to either intentions, will, motivations or interpretations of choice making subjects or top the constraining and enabling mechanisms of objective but socially constructed structures. Practices overflow that which can be accounted for in purely structural or agentic terms.[54]

From this a new research program emerges that is no longer stymied by the conceptual morass of classical metaphysics from which pragmatism tried to liberate us. A focus on practice in IR can hopefully transcend these traditional conceptual confusions, turn us away from those blind alleys, and open up new vistas and avenues for fruitful research.

Conclusion

This chapter has sought to make sense of the turn to "practices" in social theory and discuss its implications for IR. I addressed first the different uses of the term "practice" and then showed how these uses are reflected in the present discussions. This involved me in a conceptual analysis that owes more to ordinary language philosophy, and pragmatism than to the classical taxonomic method of mainstream social science. This choice was justified not only by the problematic nature of traditional epistemology but also by the heuristic fruitfulness of such an approach. This claim obliged me to show that the divergent uses of the term, which I examined in the second section, are related or represent direct responses to the "pragmatist" challenge that tried to deal with the failure of the epistemological project and the Hegelian interpretation of "history" (treated in the third section).

On the continent Nietzsche, and later Heidegger and Gadamer, took up this challenge; the American response was characterized by a distinct orientation to social reform and by a reconceptualization of action, rejecting both the stimulus/response and the "desire plus belief" models. Having shown that the hierarchization of the different modes of knowledge (putting theoretical knowledge first) was the result of conceptual choices in antiquity, which survived the demolition of ontology by Hume and Kant, Dewey and some fellow pragmatists attempted to formulate new criteria by which knowledge could be assessed. The

---

[54] Doty, 1997, 377.

revolutionary result of their – otherwise rather diverse – speculation was that truth and validity were *practice-relative* rather than *practice-justifying* notions.

To address some of the implications for the social sciences, I revisited two episodes of a "practice turn" in sociology: the older represented by the Chicago School of sociology, and the newer, championed by Turner, which was more methodology-driven, but more limited in depth and scope (the fourth section). I wanted to show how certain themes resurface again and again and are of interest to all social sciences, how the present research program on practices can be placed within the larger disciplinary history, and how its potential for developing better heuristics can be assessed. Those who may have hoped to see a new "theory" emerge may be disappointed.

But my point is that a focus on practice cannot end up in a traditional "theory," but foregrounds distinct elements of human action that are neglected or misleadingly treated when they are subjected to criteria of "theory." Doing justice to the problems of action means that time (not a-historicity), contingency (and not universality), responsibility (and not efficient causality), purpose (not "eternal verities"), and context (not the "view from nowhere") are defining characteristics that cannot be neglected by applying "theoretical" standards. The discussion of "meaning" of concepts, i.e. of their *use in context* (rather than their reference to "objects") and of what *serves* as an explanation elaborated on this problem. Thus the meaning of the sentence "Castro is a communist" cannot be ascertained by some deictic procedure but by becoming aware of the pragmatic context and the underlying practices, i.e. whether this utterance is used in a discussion of the Politburo of the former CPSU, or in a briefing of the US president by the CIA director.

This realization defeats, then, all attempts to get at the "real" meaning of our concepts via generalizations and some of the other criteria of theory-building, such as matching the concept with the "world out there." Instead of starting with abstracting from contexts and situations, we have to *begin* with them, as pragmatism suggests, but must then interrogate the silent presuppositions of our actions and understandings, precisely because no absolute "view from nowhere"[55] is possible. This does not mean that all our views are incommensurable and the actions based on them are then simply self-justifying, but it *does* mean that we have to face the dilemmas entailed by "naming" (as Hobbes was so keenly aware), and by our judgments whether or not something shall count as an (in-)competent performance, or as a transgression, as Duvall and Chowdhury point out.[56] That the "bounds of sense" are contested and also provide the fissures where conflicts emerge and the social fabric rends is hardly news. Thus, no status quo bias or Parsonian predilection for an "integrated" social system is implied by the focus on practices, although it should be obvious that the unintended can be assessed only in relation to the intended, the incompetent

---

[55] Nagel, 1986.   [56] Duvall and Chowdhury, Chapter 13 in this volume.

only in relation to the competent, the transgression only in regard to the "normal." The point here is that this is an observation of a semantic relationship, not an endorsement of any particular, a-historical instantiation of the terms.

Foregrounding practices and their enactment offers thus a new perspective on social action rather than a new "theory." Very much like constructivism which had undermined the idea of a "fixed reality" and which was – contrary to attempts to define a *via media* between liberalism and realism[57] – not a "theory" of international relations,[58] a focus on practices is not a new "paradigm" that ends all debates in the field. Just as I thought *then* that no new "orthodoxy" was needed,[59] so I think *now* that people can engage meaningfully in a spirited conversation across methodological lines (and above all, *do* exciting research) if they address problems of *praxis*, which the "quest for certainty," as criticized by Dewey, has prevented for so long.

References

Abbott, Kenneth W., Robert Keohane, Andrew Moravcsik, Anne-Marie Slaughter, and Duncan Snidal, 2000. The Concept of Legalization. *International Organization* 54 (3): 401–419.

Adler, Emanuel, 1991. Cognitive Evolution: A Dynamic Approach for the Study of International Relations and Their Progress. In *Progress in Postwar International Relations*, edited by Emanuel Adler and Beverly Crawford, 43–88. New York: Columbia University Press.

Alberoni, Francesco, 1984. *Movement and Institution*. New York: Columbia University Press.

Aristotle, 1981. *Politics*. Translated by T. A. Sinclair. Harmondsworth: Penguin.

Bourdieu, Pierre, 1974. The Sentiment of Honor in Kabyle Society. In *Honor and Shame: The Values of Mediterranean Society*, edited by Jean G. Péristiany, 191–242. Chicago: University of Chicago Press.

   1977. *Outline of a Theory of Practice*. New York: Cambridge University Press.

Bratman, Michael, 1992. Shared Cooperative Activity. *The Philosophical Review* 101 (2): 327–341.

Davis, James W., 2005. *Terms of Inquiry: On the Theory and Practice of Political Science*. Baltimore: Johns Hopkins University Press.

Dewey, John, 1981. The Influence of Darwinism on Philosophy. In *The Philosophy of John Dewey*, edited by John J. McDermott. Chicago: University of Chicago Press.

   1984. The Quest for Certainty. In *Later Works, 1925–1953*. Vol. 4, 1929, edited by Jo Ann Boydston. Carbondale: Southern Illinois Press.

Doty, Roxanne Lynn, 1997. Aporia: A Critical Exploration of the Agent–Structure Problematique in International Relations Theory. *European Journal of International Relations* 3 (3): 365–392.

[57] Wendt, 1999, Chapter 1.   [58] Kratochwil, 2008.   [59] Kratochwil, 2000.

Durkheim, Émile, 1965. *The Elementary Forms of the Religious Life*. New York: Free Press.

Flyvbjerg, Bent, 2001. *Making Social Science Matter: Why Social Inquiry Fails and How it Can Succeed Again*. Translated by Steven Sampson. Cambridge: Cambridge University Press.

Fuller, Steve, 1991. *Social Epistemology*. Bloomington: Indiana University Press.

Giddens, Anthony, 1979. *Central Problems in Social Theory: Action, Structure, and Contradiction in Social Analysis*. Berkeley: University of California Press.

Goldstein, Judith and Robert Keohane, eds., 1993. *Ideas and Foreign Policy: Beliefs, Institutions, and Political Change*. Ithaca: Cornell University Press.

Hart, H. L. A., 1961. *The Concept of Law*. Oxford: Clarendon.

James, William, 1977a. Pragmatism and Radical Empiricism. In *The Writings of William James*, edited by John J. McDermott, 311–317. Chicago: Chicago University Press.

1977b. The Sentiment of Rationality. In *The Writings of William James*, edited by John J. McDermott, 318–344. Chicago: Chicago University Press.

1977c. Pragmatism's Conception of Truth. In *The Writings of William James*, edited by John J. McDermott, 429–443. Chicago: Chicago University Press.

Joas, Hans, 1985. *G.H. Mead: A Contemporary Re-Examination of His Thought*. Translated by Raymond Meyer. Cambridge: Polity Press.

1993. *Pragmatism and Social Theory*. Chicago: University of Chicago Press.

Kratochwil, Friedrich, 2000. Constructing a New Orthodoxy? Wendt's "Social Theory of International Politics" and the Constructivist Challenge. *Millennium* 29 (1): 73–101.

2006. History, Action and Identity: Revisiting the "Second" Great Debate and Assessing its Importance for Social Theory. *European Journal of International Relations* 12 (1): 5–29.

2008. Constructivism: What it is (Not) and How it Matters. In *Approaches and Methodologies in the Social Sciences: A Pluralist Perspective*, edited by Donatella della Porta and Michael Keating, 80–99. Cambridge: Cambridge University Press.

Lakoff, George and Mark Johnson, 1999. *Philosophy in the Flesh*. New York: Basic Books.

Latour, Bruno and Steve Woolgar, 1979. *Laboratory Life: The Social Construction of Scientific Facts*. London: Sage.

Lynch, Michael, 1997. Theorizing Practice. *Human Studies* 20 (3): 335–344.

Mead, George Herbert, 1909. Social Psychology as Counterpart to Physiological Psychology. *Psychological Bulletin* 6 (12): 401–408.

1910. Social Consciousness and the Consciousness of Meaning. *Psychological Bulletin* 7 (12): 397–405.

Nagel, Ernst, 1986. *The View from Nowhere*. Oxford: Oxford University Press.

Oakeshott, Michael Joseph, 1975. *On Human Conduct*. Oxford: Clarendon Press.

Peirce, Charles S., 1952. *Collected Papers*. Vol. 5, *Pragmatism and Pragmaticism*, edited by Charles Hartshorne and Paul Weiss. Cambridge, MA: Harvard University Press.

    1955a. The Fixation of Belief. In *Philosophical Writings of Peirce*, edited by Justus Buchler, 5–22. New York: Dover.

    1955b. How to Make Our Ideas Clear. In *Philosophical Writings of Peirce*, edited by Justus Buchler, 23–41. New York: Dover.

    1997 [1868]. Some Consequences of Four Incapacities. In *Pragmatism: A Reader*, edited by Louis Menand, 4–7. New York: Vintage Books.

Polanyi, Michael, 1958. *Personal Knowledge*. Chicago: University of Chicago Press.

Popper, Karl R., 1965. *Conjectures and Refutations: The Growth of Scientific Knowledge*. New York: Harper & Row.

    1968. *The Logic of Scientific Discovery*. New York: Harper & Row.

Rawls, John, 1971. *A Theory of Justice*. Cambridge, MA: Harvard University Press.

Rorty, Richard, 2004. Philosophy as a Transitional Genre. In *Pragmatism, Critique, Judgment: Essays for Richard J. Bernstein*, edited by Seyla Benhabib and Nancy Fraser, 3–28. Cambridge, MA: MIT Press.

Sartori, Giovanni, 1970. Concept Misformation in Comparative Politics. *American Political Science Review* 64 (4): 1033–1053.

Searle, John, 1995. *The Construction of Social Reality*. Harmondsworth: Penguin.

Thomas, William I., 1909. *Source Book for Social Origins: Ethnological Materials, Psychological Standpoint, Classified and Annotated Bibliographies for the Interpretation of Savage Society*. Chicago: Chicago University Press.

Thomas, William I. and Florian Znaniecki, 1996. *The Polish Peasant in Europe and America: A Classic Work in Immigration History*, edited by Eli Zaretzky. Urbana: University of Illinois Press.

Turner, Stephen P., 1994. *The Social Theory of Practices: Tradition, Tacit Knowledge, and Presuppositions*. Chicago: University of Chicago Press.

    1997. Bad Practices: A Reply. *Human Studies* 20 (3): 345–356.

Villumsen, Trine, 2008. *Theory as Practice and Capital: NATO in a Bourdieusian Field of Security in Europe: Towards a Sociological Approach to IR*. Copenhagen: Copenhagen University Press.

Wendt, Alexander, 1999. *Social Theory of International Politics*. New York: Cambridge University Press.

Zeilinger, Anton, 2003. *Einsteins Schleier*. Munich: Beck.

PART II

Practices and their background

3 A practice theory of emotion for International Relations

JANICE BIALLY MATTERN[*]

There is growing appreciation among International Relations (IR) scholars that emotion matters fundamentally to the dynamics of world politics. But discerning and establishing just *how* has proven rather difficult. At the heart of the problem is that the phenomenon of emotion does not "fit" conveniently into any of the usual orienting categories used in IR. Emotions are the embodied experiences of concrete persons but they are not actually the "properties" of those persons. Rather than things people have, emotions are contingent ways-of-being human – that is, experiences of human *being* – that emerge from interactions between agencies and structures of both material and social sorts. They are neither substance nor process, neither natural nor cultural, neither cognitive nor physiological. In the context of IR, this means that it makes little sense to try to apprehend emotions through the levels-of-analysis framework that organizes the field. For those interested in understanding the role of emotion in world politics, the daunting questions begin with how one begins.

I found myself facing these questions during the course of an ongoing research project when I came to suspect that emotion was a key force in producing the outcome that interested me. Since this was not what I had expected, pursuing my suspicion meant taking a considerable detour to figure out how other scholars had managed to study emotion. What I found, both in and outside of IR, is that most scholars have met the challenge by dodging it. In IR, in particular, the existing literature on emotion succeeds in examining its role in world politics only to the extent that it wittingly or unwittingly assumes away the ontological complexity of emotion. It was in this context – that is, in search of a way to conceptualize, theorize, and perform empirical research on emotion in world politics – that I stumbled into practice theory.

In this chapter, I argue that practice theory offers a framework that embraces, rather than assumes away, the ontological complexity of emotion. It offers a way to fathom emotion that does not reduce that phenomenon to one or the other of the categories it exceeds. Because of this, practice theory lays the

[*] The author is grateful for written feedback on earlier versions of this chapter from Emanuel Adler, Bentley Allan, Jonathan Mercer, Jennifer Mitzen, Vincent Pouliot, Janice Gross Stein, and Alexander Wendt.

foundation from which it is possible to develop a theory of the impact of emotions on world politics that is logically consistent with the phenomenon itself; and an empirical research method that is capable of capturing emotion (as opposed to some inadequate proxy of itself) literally *in action*. In short, in offering the emotion researcher a conceptually solid point from which to begin, the practice perspective on emotion clears the way for more compelling research into how emotions matter in world politics.

As a matter of positioning this chapter relative to the rest of this volume, a few points bear emphasis. First, this chapter is less about practice as *explanans* or *explanandum* than it is about the value of *practice theory* as a *heuristic* through which we might better evaluate emotions as *explanans* of various outcomes in world politics. Of course, were it that emotions really *are* practices (as opposed to being usefully modeled as such) it would be accurate to say that I am interested in (emotional) practices as *explanans*. Tempted though I am by the notion that emotions actually are practices, I do not venture to argue that here. Second, the whole of my argument – from my conceptualization of emotions as practices, to the theoretical and methodological directions that I argue this implies for emotion research in IR – is rooted in and derived from the very specific practice theory of Theodore Schatzki.[1] This means that aspects of my chapter imply considerable departures from the terms of Adler and Pouliot's necessarily more general framework.[2]

Key among them is that I take practice as offering IR not a *broader* ontology but one that is *at least* as restrictive – albeit more complex – than the various ontologies that currently pepper the field. The source of this difference is that, with Schatzki, I take practices as unique from other forms of action only in that practical action is conceptually and analytically irreducible to more elementary, constitutive forces (as I suggest below, Adler and Pouliot adopt a rather more flexible position on this). This strong claim indicates that practices cannot *cluster around* the intersection of the axes as in Adler and Pouliot's Figure 1.1 (p. 22), but rather can unfold only *at* the intersection itself; only where it is impossible to disentangle agency from structure, social meaning from material fact.

From this difference follows another, which is that whereas Adler and Pouliot interpret practice as an ontological and epistemological "gluon" that cuts across IR "isms,"[3] I understand practice theory as outlining an "ism" in its own right. Just as rationalism, for instance, builds its particular account of social order on the back of a specific individualist ontology of human beings, "practice-ism" (or anyway, my Schatzki-inspired version) builds its account of social order on the back of a post-Cartesian, post-individualist ontology of human being. As I turn now to arguing, adopting this practice ontology makes a

---

[1] All references to Schatzki's practice theory are specifically to Schatzki, 1996.
[2] Adler and Pouliot, Chapter 1 in this volume.   [3] *Ibid.*

considerable difference in how one can theorize and research the role that emotion plays in world politics.

The emotion problem

In this section, I lay out the emotion problem in IR. I argue that when faced with the challenge of developing theoretically tractable and empirically researchable propositions about the role of emotion in world politics, emotion scholars in IR have done what emotion researchers in so many other fields have done: they have responded to the elusive complexity of emotion by seeking to simplify the phenomenon. The result is that they (wittingly and unwittingly) "squish" emotion into one or another side of the categories it exceeds. This solution has come with a cost for, in approaching emotion as a product of either/or types of causal forces, emotion researchers in IR end up belying their own arguments about how emotion matters in world politics. In fact they end up ironically indicating that emotion *per se* does not have a *distinctive* impact on world politics. Its effects are more fundamentally reducible to the work of willing agents, or determinative material or social structures.

Few IR scholars would deny the importance of emotion to world politics but, until recently, only a few have endeavored to understand the ways in which this is so. In the last decade this has begun to change. In her seminal article, Neta Crawford reminded IR of the "passions" upon which theories of international politics and security depend, paving the way for scholars to explore emotions not just as properties of decision-makers but as forces within the broader dynamics of world politics among collective actors.[4] Crawford's entreaty, combined with growth in constructivist theorizing and the events of 9/11, has prompted IR scholars to turn their attention to this previously marginalized area of study. A burgeoning body of research now exists that inquires into the role of emotion in a wide range of global political dynamics, including state rationality and the logic of deterrence,[5] the war on terror,[6] patterns of ethnic and civil conflict,[7] the explosion of violence between states and transnational actors,[8] national reconciliation,[9] and political identity formation.[10]

As in any emerging literature, however, foundational questions remain – not least how to cope analytically with the complex nature of emotion. Although common parlance suggests that emotions are "things" that individuals "have," experts have increasingly come to appreciate a more subtle ontology and epistemology of emotion. At its clearest, "emotion is one of a large set of differentiated biologically based complex conditions" that is constituted, at

---

[4] Crawford, 2000.   [5] See Mercer, 2005 and 2010.
[6] See Bennett, 2002; and Saurette, 2006.   [7] See Kaufman, 2001; and Petersen, 2002.
[8] Appadurai, 2006.   [9] Edkins, 2003.
[10] See Campbell, 1998; Hutchison, 2008; and Hutchison and Bleiker, 2008.

the very least, by *mutually transformative interactions* among biological systems (e.g. cognition, physiology, psychology) and physical and socio-cultural ones.[11] Emotions, that is, are energies or capabilities, which are acquired by individuals through complex engagements with objects and others in the world.[12] Key here is the fact that the human body is an open system, which responds to its environment by developing its capacities.[13] While emotion, in general, is one such type of capacity, the particular emotional experiences of which one becomes capable are socially, historically, and personally contingent. Far from universal, then, emotions are emergent from and irreducible to agency or structure, substance or process, nature or culture.

Given the complex, emergent character of emotion the challenge for researchers has been how to develop a conceptual system that appropriately "acknowledges the complexity of emotional functions" while still effectively capturing their discreteness as phenomena.[14] While conceptual integrity is a prerequisite for achieving "substantive conclusions . . . with scientific merit" it remains unclear how to conceptually disentangle the phenomenon of emotion from its constitutive forces and effects.[15] For instance, recent research in neuroscience indicates that even though the intellectual dimension of emotional awareness (cognition) and the unconscious dimension of bodily affect (physiology) interact in the production of emotional experience they can also be independent processes, with the affective arising before the cognitive, or the cognitive occurring without the affective.[16] In other words, it is not just that emotional experiences are complex emergent phenomena but that the combination of forces from which they are emergent varies from context to context. The result is that the field of emotion research is "rife with basic disagreements about crucial conceptual definitions."[17]

The "wise" solution, as Ronald De Sousa puts it, is "to rephrase the question."[18] Rather than asking, "How can I conceive of emotion in a way that reflects its complex and variable dichotomy-eluding ontology?" scholars have pursued their research on emotion by asking "What conception of emotion can offer the most explanatory purchase?" In other words, the field has solved the "problem" of the elusive ontology of emotion by focusing instead on epistemology; on *the site* or *force through which* the emotional experience becomes known to those in its throes, and to researchers. The result is a literature organized around three broad analytics: those that emphasize the cognitive or intellectual dimensions of emotion;[19] those that emphasize its physiological or

---

[11] Clore and Ortony cited in McDermott, 2004, 692.   [12] De Sousa, 2008.
[13] See Park, 2006; Dunbar, 2003; and Wolfe, 1997–1999.   [14] De Sousa, 2008, 12.
[15] Marcus, 2000, 225.   [16] See *ibid.*, 224; and Fisher and Chon, 1989.
[17] Marcus, 2000, 224.   [18] De Sousa, 2008, 12.
[19] See Nussbaum, 2001; and De Sousa, 1987.

affective dimensions;[20] and those that emphasize the forces of the socio-cultural environment in which the emotional body is situated.[21]

The emerging body of emotion research in IR largely reflects this analytic trend: attuned though scholars are to the complex emergent ontology of emotions, they tend, even if unwittingly, to focus for analytic purposes on one or another of its constitutive forces. For instance, Stephen Rosen accepts the significance of social environment and cognition in constituting emotional functions but, to make emotion tractable, adopts an evolutionary view in which those forces are reduced to biological imperatives of survival.[22] Jonathan Mercer, who is also concerned about "getting lost" in the ontological complexity of emotion, resolves the problem by instead emphasizing the cognitive. On his account, emotion is analyzed as the "substrate" of such thought-based constructs as rationality and belief.[23] Even Roland Bleiker and Emma Hutchison, who are bothered by such reductive tendencies, end up reducing emotion to one of its constitutive components.[24] In focusing their attention on visual media (e.g. art, film) as a site of collective emotional expression and stimulation, they marginalize the cognitive and embodied aspects of emotional experience in favor of a focus on its social ones.

Intentional or not, the "streamlining" of emotion into biological, cognitive, and social analytics has been fruitful from the perspective of getting on with the business of studying emotion in world politics. Whereas Rosen's biological determinism enables him to explain the curious obsession of military leaders with social status, Mercer's cognitive bias supports the ground-breaking argument that credibility, and so the logic of deterrence, is constituted by emotional beliefs. Bleiker and Hutchison's unintended reduction of emotional functionality to social representations also pays dividends. Their focus on visual media makes possible the argument that emotion played a much larger role in shaping the political impact of 9/11 than "had the news of the attack been communicated by texts alone."[25] Given that such innovative propositions about the role of emotion in the dynamics of world politics was made possible by the framing of emotion research in epistemological terms, De Sousa's suggestion appears wise indeed.

And yet, upon deeper reflection the benefits of the epistemology-first focus appear less certain. The heart of the problem is that it is impossible to adopt any epistemological analytic that does not also imply specific ontological foundations, which then tend to become reified in the theorizations and insights that follow. Hence, from biological analytics of emotion tend to arise accounts of

---

[20] See Panskepp, 1998; and LeDoux, 1996.
[21] See Kövecses, 2000; Barrett, 2006; and Fisher and Chon, 1989. This taxonomy is from De Sousa, 2008.
[22] Rosen, 2005.   [23] Mercer, 2010, 25 and 11.   [24] Bleiker and Hutchison, 2008.
[25] *Ibid.*, 130.

world politics in which emotions appear as materially determined, naturally given forces; from cognitive analytics tend to arise accounts in which emotions appear as instrumental tools in the repertoire of reasoning agents; and from social analytics tend to arise stories in which emotions are simply one among many social structures or discourses that constitute subjects. In other words, the pursuit of analytic clarity about the distinctive effects of emotion ironically ends up rendering emotion indistinguishable from other forces.

Consider, for instance, Jacques Hymans' acclaimed research on nuclear politics.[26] Although he begins with a sophisticated account that recognizes the socio-cultural, cognitive, and physiological dimensions of emotions, Hymans, like Mercer, makes cognition the cornerstone of his analytic framework. Arguing that beliefs about national identity constitute different emotional dynamics that in turn inspire decision-makers to make a variety of different nuclear choices, Hymans tells a story in which emotions appear all but indistinct from the rational calculations about beliefs from which they emerge. The result is a story about nuclear politics that is virtually impossible to differentiate from the traditional strategic security stories about nuclear proliferation that have long dominated the field. Even Mercer, who puts emotion *before* cognition, ends up telling a story in which emotional functionality appears as an empty set or a conceptual placeholder rather than a substantive experience with particular cognition-shaping features. Instead of the story he wants to tell – about the process by which emotional experience constitutes rationality and credibility – Mercer ends up with a story about how cognition assimilates emotional information. In both cases, one learns little about the role of emotion *per se* in world politics and quite a lot about that of reasoning agents.

The "emptying" of emotion from emotion research occurs in a different way in Andrew Ross' otherwise theoretically exquisite account of the role of emotion in political violence.[27] Like Bleiker and Hutchison, Ross is uncomfortable with the denuded notion of emotion that follows from an analytic emphasis on its constitutive components. However, whereas Bleiker and Hutchison seek a remedy in an explicit turn to the social framework, Ross seeks a remedy in stepping away from the epistemology-first approach to studying emotion. Directly deriving his theory of emotion in world politics from the complex, emergent ontology of the phenomenon, he argues that emotion can be understood holistically as a form of human energy or "capability." Key here is that emotion is a *unique* form of human experience that not only shapes cognition but also produces cognitively unmediated affect.[28] Acknowledging that *some* emotional experiences are consciously felt and rationally manipulated, Ross points out that *all* emotions entail an affective experience. In this way, even conscious emotions entail some unreflective affective "excess" and it is, in Ross'

---

[26] Hymans, 2006.   [27] Ross, 2006.   [28] *Ibid.*, 202–204, 212.

view, this excess that makes emotion a unique force in the dynamics of political violence.[29]

Ross' account is remarkable in that it effectively theorizes a "something" – elusive to other IR researchers – that makes emotion more than the sum of its parts.[30] In this way it promises to move emotion research past the simplifying frameworks that evacuate the phenomenon of its very distinction. Yet when it comes to "finding" the affective excess, or the unique qualities, that he argues distinguishes emotion from other forms of human experience – that is, when it comes to epistemology – Ross falls back into reductionism. Recognizing that we cannot get into heads or bodies to distinguish the character and effects of the inarticulable experiences being lived by those in the throes of emotion, Ross suggests that we can interpret such experiences by tracing "circulations" of affect through publics. Hence, Ross argues that the militarist US response to the 9/11 attacks was made possible by an affective energy or mood among Americans; a mood that was both cognitively and unreflectively activated through the circulation of particular images and representations that had become historically entrained among Americans to evoke emotions "conducive to militarist response."[31] Yet Ross merely asserts, rather than empirically illustrates, the embodied experience of emotional militarism that he posits was activated among Americans by the circulation of such images. Rather than capturing the character and effects of the affective energy allegedly contained within those social circulations, Ross ends up with a story more plausible as an account of strategically manipulated public discourses.[32]

From the perspective of advancing knowledge on the role of emotion in world politics, it is discouraging that research designed so self-consciously to avoid reducing emotion to its constitutive phenomena would fail to do so. And yet, contained within Ross' work is an important opening from which to remedy this shortcoming. In approaching emotions as experiences that become available to a human being through complex interactions among biological (physiological and cognitive) and social forces, Ross implicitly fathoms emotions as practices. By explicitly recognizing and systematizing this ontology, we can uncover better ways to study emotion in world politics.

---

[29] See also Edkins, 2003.

[30] Others attuned to the need to theorize emotion as more than the sum of parts have merely concluded that there is something mystical or magical about emotion that exceeds our grasp. They make no effort to account for that excessive dimension, though. Ross, 2006, 211.

[31] Ross, 2006, 213.

[32] For such an account, see Krebs and Lobasz, 2007. Saurette's Deleuze-inspired model of emotion (2006) confronts similar methodological problems as those faced by Ross. In other work, Ross argues that discourse is an embodied practice as well as an intellectual one consisting of cognitive content and social meaning (Ross, Forthcoming). Yet since he offers no way to distinguish those aspects of discursive action that issue from embodied affective experiences from those aspects of discursive action that issue from intellectual choice, it is empirically impossible to parse his claim that the former does distinctive work.

The ontology of practice

Emotion scholars across disciplines often imply that emotions have something to do with practices. Hate, for instance, is commonly used not as a noun (i.e. hatred) but as an adjective that modifies the word "practices" (i.e. hateful).[33] Alternatively, the existence or presence of particular emotions (e.g. fear) in a given context is depicted in connection to specific social practices (e.g. aggressive posturing). And yet, the connection between emotion and practice has been made mostly in casual ways, proffered without sustained analytic reflection on the character of the relationship between emotion and practice.[34] In this section, I develop the theoretical basis upon which I seek to remedy this with a practice theory of emotions. My core burden in this section thus echoes that of Adler and Pouliot in Chapter 1 in this volume: to characterize practice and clarify the nature of a practice perspective as an analytic framework from which to approach the social world.

As a starting point, recall that practices are competent performances; they are "doings" or routines of action – e.g. teaching, buying a cup of coffee, conducting international diplomacy – that carry specific meanings within particular cultural, historical, and material space. Practice theory, however, gives us leverage on more than just "how things are done around here." As Theodore Schatzki argues, practice theory is a theory of how humans "do" their very being-in-the-world. Practices, he argues, are the foundations, or the smallest units, of social life. From local neighborhood to world politics, practices organize human life, establish social order, and transform the orders they create.

The logic of Schatzki's bold propositions can be traced back to his account of practical ontology. Along with most of other theorists of practice, including Adler and Pouliot, Schatzki posits that practice rests on a unique ontology. The question is precisely how. Echoing other practice theorists, Adler and Pouliot argue that what makes the ontology of practice unique is that practice is "suspended" between structure and agency, materiality and sociality.[35] Hence, while other forms of action may also entail and combine these basic components of social life,[36] only practice actually exists or "unfolds" in the distinct ontological space where all four components converge. Practices, after all, are *competent performances* while other forms of action are not; and competence necessarily involves sociality and structure while performance necessarily

---

[33] Natter, 2001.

[34] Partial exceptions exist. Durkheim described emotions as cognitive fictions produced "outside in" through the embodied conduct of social rituals (Fisher and Chon, 1989). Others focus on the ways that such embodied rituals (especially "emotive" speech) induce emotions in the form of lived affective experiences. See Massumi, 2002; and Reddy, 1997.

[35] Adler and Pouliot, Chapter 1 in this volume.

[36] Biological reflexes, for instance, entail both materiality and structure.

involves materiality and agency. In this way, practice is not possible without all four components of social life.[37]

There is a problem, however, for to say that practice is not possible without all four components of social life is not necessarily to defend the claim that practical action rests on unique ontological ground. Quite the contrary, this formulation risks conflating two very different views of practical ontology: one in which practice is ontologically *suspended* between sociality, materiality, agency, and structure; and one in which practice is an ontological *amalgamation* of these components of social life. While Adler and Pouliot use these concepts as if they are continuous and compatible with each other, one ought not do so. After all, something that is suspended between other components is distinct from them. In contrast, an amalgamation is a composite phenomenon that can still be reduced to its original components. Insofar as practice rests on an amalgamated ontology, practical action might just as well be analyzed in terms of the contributions of each of its ontological components. Doing so disaggregates practices into the very ontological dichotomies that, according to practice theory, practice exceeds. In fact, if one accepts that practice has an amalgamated ontology, practice hardly seems like a distinct form of social action. At best, it appears as a complex form of other forms of action; and, at worst, it becomes analytically indistinguishable from them.

For an example of this one need look no further than the debate between Bourdieu and his critics. Because Bourdieu (unwittingly) adopts an amalgamated practical ontology, his critics are able to disaggregate it into its component parts, upon which they find that Bourdieu has not sufficiently considered agency. The result, they argue, is that practical action in Bourdieu's model becomes analytically indistinct from structurally driven forms and equally as a-historical.[38] Etienne Wenger's "communities of practice" framework has been charged with the same problem in reverse. The rather minimal contribution of structure to his amalgamated practical ontology fashions practical action so that it is analytically indistinguishable from agent-driven action.[39] In either case, practical action collapses into some other form of action because practice theorists have failed to capture the unique ontology of practice. It is into this breach that Schatzki steps, endeavoring to clarify the precise way in which practice is ontologically distinct from other forms of action.

Using the apparent failure of Bourdieu's practice theory as his jumping off point, Schatzki argues that the problem lies with the way both Bourdieu and his

---

[37] In the case of competence, a "doer" only acquires the technical knowledge and social understanding to properly perform a practice in light of her access to and recognized position within the relevant symbolic and social orders. In the case of performance, the very possibility of action depends upon an animate physical presence, a being, with the capacity to take action. Adler and Pouliot, Chapter 1 in this volume.

[38] Farnell, 2000.   [39] Cf. Mutch, 2003.

critics imagine the "nexus" or "fulcrum" in which practice unfolds. They do not imagine it as producing a distinctive phenomenon: one that is *emergent* from the complex interplay between agency, structure, materiality, and sociality; one within which these original components dissolve and become indistinct from each other. Instead they see the fulcrum as a meeting point or intersection at which each component retains its elemental form. The result is that both Bourdieu and his critics remain "trapped" within the very dichotomies that practice is thought to elude. To illustrate, Schatzki notes that while Bourdieu and his critics disagree over whether he really "locks out" agency, *both sides* implicitly agree that practical knowledge itself is devoid of agency. After all, practical action rests on tacit and unreflective knowledge, or what Adler and Pouliot call the "Background."[40] It follows that Bourdieu and his critics assume that agency comes from "the mind," in the Cartesian sense of reflective, cognitive, processes.[41] They abide, that is, by the Cartesian mind/body dichotomy. Schatzki, in contrast, proposes that there is no reason to expect that cognitive, reflective actions are the only kind of actions that exude agency. In fact, the key to appreciating the suspended ontology of practice lies in recognizing other forms of agency – especially those entailed in "the body."[42]

Toward this end, Schatzki offers a post-Cartesian account of agency. Approaching agency as a force of creativity, or the ability to do things differently, Schatzki argues that agency is a *result* of practice rather than its source.[43] Just as the score from a football game is an accomplishment of the practice of playing football so is agency an accomplishment of a practice: specifically, the practice of *being human*. Whereas the practice of football involves the

---

[40] The problem, argue critics, is that tacit and unreflective as practical knowledge is, its practitioners appear as mechanistic carriers and executors of competencies they "inherit" from the *habitus*; and practical action devolves into a self-reinforcing "locked-in" structure that is impervious to change (Reckwitz, 2002). Bourdieu, interestingly, does not dispute that practical knowledge translates to action in a mechanistic way but instead argues, as do Adler and Pouliot, that agency still creeps in. Bourdieu tries to avoid structural determinism by suggesting that the *habitus* only *disposes* bodies to do certain things; that it is *generative*, providing resources that agents can use to improvise practice. Yet, Bourdieu "offers no account of how agents draw on their habitus as a resource of some kind" – that is, of where they get their improvisational creativity (Farnell, 2000, 402–403). This problem persists in the Bourdieusian practice literature in IR. See Pouliot, 2008; and Jackson, 2008. Adler and Pouliot assert that background knowledge "does not create uniformity of a group" and they argue that there is always "wiggle room for agency even in repetition" but they do not offer a theoretical account of how this is possible. Adler and Pouliot, Chapter 1 in this volume.

[41] Farnell, 2000.

[42] I place this in scare quotes because part of Schatzki's agenda is to problematize the very idea of the body as distinct from the mind.

[43] Compare to Adler and Pouliot, Chapter 1 in this volume. Though often conflated with individuality and individualism, Schatzki sees agency as a broader phenomenon of which individualism/ity is one effect.

competent performance of specific techniques for playing ball (throwing, catching) the practice of being human involves the competent performance of specific techniques for expressing one's *way-of-being human* to other humans. As Schatzki argues there are four dimensions to way-of-being human: states of conscious awareness, like feeling itchy or hearing a sound; intellectual conditions, like attitudes, beliefs, and interpretations; behaviors, or what one is doing, like buying coffee; and emotion, or how one is experiencing their own existence in the world at a given moment. While I return to these below (especially emotion), for now the point is that one becomes human only to the extent that one makes present to other humans one's way-of-being.[44] In this way, agency emerges from being human, where being human, rather than an innate condition, is itself a practical activity.

What, then, is it about the practice of being human that creates agency? In certain respects, the practice of being human is like all practices. For one, a being acquires the knowledge and competency for its performance in and through concrete social relations in specific social contexts.[45] That is, one learns how to express one's being – how to "do" one's human being – by acquiring the social understandings and technical skills appropriate for making a given way-of-being intelligible to other humans within a given social and symbolic order. Also like with all practices, the performance of human being (i.e. self-expression) reproduces the social structures from which it emerges by positioning those who perform it according to the degree of competency of their performance; that is, in terms of how recognizable and intelligible their human way-of-being is to those at the "core" of the practice.[46] In this sense, the practice of being human generates a human social order within which it positions its practitioners.

Unlike other practices, though, the practice of being human is both a practice in its own right and a necessary and inevitable component of other practices. Put differently, *all* practices also enact or do human being because being human is done by making present one's way-of-being in the world to others. All practices do this at some level. From those that emerge overtly to serve the purpose of self-expression, like talk therapy, to those that at first blush seem irrelevant to self-expression, like football, all practices necessarily express some dimension of their practitioners' way-of-being to other humans. Consider football. Not only does its enactment "do" the playing of football but for others to whom the practice of football is intelligible it also expresses the practitioner's behavioral way-of-being in the world; that is, *what he is doing*. Indeed, depending on a variety of factors the doing of football might express its practitioners' way-of-being along other dimensions as well – from the conscious to the intellectual to the emotional. In this way, no matter what else a practice does,

---

[44] See also Varela, 1995.   [45] Adler and Pouliot, Chapter 1 in this volume.   [46] *Ibid.*

all practices organize their doers within the social structures from whence the practice emerged in a process that generates and stabilizes human social order.

Second, practices of being human (and therefore all practices) create agency because, as Schatzki argues, bodies simply exceed the self-expressive routines of practical action that they perform. Insofar as each body is biologically unique, its being-in-the world is also distinctive in ways that simply cannot be rendered intelligible (often even to the being herself) through self-expressive practices.[47] However, precisely because these ineffable ways-of-being are biologically grounded, they cannot help but inflect the way that a given practitioner performs the competent techniques of a given self-expressive practice in a given moment. Hence, no matter how local and cohesive the practice, and no matter how competent its performers, different practitioners will always perform it in somewhat different ways. Through movement and comportment, tone and pitch, position, appearance, and orientation, human bodies, unlike machines, *exceed* the techniques they perform. They make present, even if unintelligibly so, those aspects of a performer's being that are lost, evacuated, or otherwise rendered inexpressible with available practical techniques.

This bodily excess, argues Schatzki, is agency. Unintelligible as bodily excess is to others, even in the midst of other socially meaningful performances, it materializes as a surprise within the social space of its performance. Because it is other than what is expected, bodily excess amounts to creativity that can contribute to a transformation, not only in the particular practices into which it "leaked" but also potentially into the order of human social life generated by those practices.[48] Of course, understood this way, agency is not a property of the human being (i.e. of either mind or body) but a momentary effect created by the competent performance of practical techniques of self-expression that "do" being human. But since all practices "do" human being and since each human being is competent in any number of practices, the potential sources of agency are infinite, as are the potentially transformative effects of each "leak."[49] As Schatzki explains, humans do their being at the nexus of a unique, contingent constellation of practices such that a practitioner's competencies in one domain become his bodily excess in the next.

Against the backdrop of Schatzki's post-Cartesian account of agency, it becomes possible to appreciate the unique ontological status of practice. First,

---

[47] Schatzki, 1996, 54.

[48] It bears emphasis that were it not a stable routinized practical setting there would be no stable expectations in the first place, and hence, there could be no discerning difference or creativity. In this way, agency is impossible outside of practice.

[49] The physiological and/or cognitive excess that extrudes into a being's competent performance of self-expression distinguishes her from other performers. In this way, the practice of self-expression not only constitutes a being as human in the human world but also makes socially possible the distinction between human beings. Because the practice of being human produces agency it makes possible the individual.

practice depends upon and reproduces social structure but it also produces the material agency that transforms itself. Second, however, more than just simultaneously entailing all these components, practice renders them so mutually imbricated that they become indistinguishable from each other and practice becomes reducible to none. While structure is necessary for the emergence of practice, practice does what structure cannot: it generates human being. In turn, while practice creates agency, agency does what practice cannot: it transforms practice. In fact, it is only because practice creates agency that practice is distinguishable from structure. In transforming the practices from which it evolves, agency keeps practice from ossifying into a static structure. Against this backdrop, practice appears as far more than an agglomeration of other components of social life. It is a moment of "doing" (a moment in the doing of human being) when structure becomes agency, when sociality becomes materiality, and when continuity becomes change. Practice is a component of social life in its own right.

This last point bears emphasis. On Schatzki's rendering, practice is the fundamental component of social life for it appears that there is no form of social action that is not also a component of some practical action. For one, purely agent-driven action is simply impossible. Not only is there is no such thing as an agent *per se* but agency, as a force of difference-making creativity, presupposes an intelligible status quo against which cognitive and/or physiological excess stands out. In this way, agency is always bound up with practical action. And while structurally driven action is theoretically possible, it can only exist when forces are brought to bear on inanimate bodies or machines outside of social relations. In this way, structurally driven action is, by definition, socially uninteresting. It only becomes socially interesting when structure becomes encoded in the doings of human being – that is, when it becomes an agency-producing practice.

Given practice as the fundamental unit of social life, the potential contribution of practice theory to IR is nothing less than a full transformation of how scholars approach the field. To take a practice perspective on world politics is to do more than just "add practice to world politics and stir." It is to ask how practice *is* world politics; it is to ask how practice organizes and transforms the human social order that IR scholars call world politics. In this way, the practice perspective on IR constitutes an "ism" in its own right.[50]

Emotional practices

I have argued that research on emotion in IR succeeds only by analytically reducing the dichotomy-eluding, emergent phenomenon of emotion to the constitutive components to which it cannot be analytically reduced. I have

---

[50] Adler and Pouliot also see practices as a foundation for the order of human life, but given this discussion this view sits uneasily with their broad view of practices as a "gluon" and not an "ism."

further argued that Schatzki has modeled practice, a similarly dichotomy-eluding, emergent phenomenon, in a way that overcomes these problems. In this section, I bring practice theory into contact with emotion theory in order to examine whether and how the practice heuristic might offer some more compelling leverage on emotion. I argue not only that it is conceptually appropriate to model emotions as competent performances but also that in doing so we gain new ways to think about how emotions might matter in the social world – and, by extension, world politics.

When it comes to approaching emotions as practices Schatzki is, unfortunately, of little help. Certainly, Schatzki recognizes the centrality of emotion to human being and social order. Indeed, as noted above, Schatzki takes emotion as one of the four dimensions of human ways-of-being that one might express through practice. And yet, Schatzki treats emotion, itself, as a given; as an internal experience of existence, the externalization of which through expressive practices constitutes one's human being. While I share Schatzki's view of emotion as a way-of-being, and of practice as expressing emotion, the developments of emotion theory, as laid out above, suggest that we might also think of emotions – that is, the very experience of "having" a particular affect – as themselves as practices. After all, if emotions are capacities that beings acquire in and through the complex interplay among biological (physiological and cognitive) and social forces, a practice perspective is as well suited to analyzing emotions as it is to football. Doing so involves considering not, as Schatzki does, how beings express emotions *through* practices but rather how beings acquire the competency to "do" a given emotion; and how the "doing" of that emotion affects (literally) the social orders from which the emotional practice emerged in the first place.

Understood this way the challenge is whether it makes sense to approach emotions as competent, socially meaningful, bodily performances. Some aspects of this idea ought to be uncontroversial, not least that emotions are bodily phenomena. Whether cognitively processed or entirely unmediated by cognition, emotions are biologically grounded, subjectively experienced phenomena that cannot be apprehended without analytic attention to the human body. It ought also to be relatively uncontroversial to propose that emotions are socially meaningful. While the meanings of different emotions vary from context to context, emotions are nothing if not socio-linguistic categories through which humans tacitly or reflectively convey information to others about how one is doing.[51] In this way, Schatzki is right to propose that the expression of emotion makes a being present to other humans. However, to approach an emotion as a practice is to treat emotions not as strictly internal phenomena that can only be externalized through expressive practices.[52] It is to

---

[51] Lutz, 1988.
[52] I agree with Schatzki, though, that emotion can also be expressed through various other practices beyond that of its own doing.

take emotion, itself, as an expressive social practice. It is to say that emotional ways-of-being become socially intelligible as bodies competently perform the techniques that bring them into being.

The idea that emotions are competent performances or actions (no less ones that are intelligible to others) calls for a more sustained defense. After all, competent performances are things that people (intentionally or not) *do*; and, in fact, that they learn how to do through social engagements. In contrast, emotion, in the lay imagination, is something that naturally happens to people without effort. And yet, as argued above, current research on emotion suggests that there is a lot less difference between practical action and the process by which a given emotional experience is created. Just as practical action (even that which is cognitively mediated) is ultimately rooted in the unreflective "Background," so are emotions. Emotions, of both the cognitive and cognitively unmediated sort, "happen" only as a result of a series of physiological bodily doings. For instance, the experience of excitement is the result of all kinds of biological actions that literally move and change the way a being exists in the world in a given moment. These may include physiological actions that create, say, increased heart rate, sweaty palms, and a burst of adrenaline; psychological actions that ameliorate one's mood; and cognitive actions that generate a heightened sense of expectation. In any case, emotions do not happen; they are done. Like football games, and all other practices, emotions happen through the labor of the human biology.[53]

Second, the ability, or labor-capacity, to "do" a given emotion is not given to bodies by nature. Rather, as noted above, the biological capacity to create a particular emotional experience is something that humans develop as the open biological system traditionally called "the body" interacts with the environments within which the being is positioned. Consider fear. Like any emotional way-of-being in the world, fear exists as a specific flow of sensations and feelings, which are produced in the body by the stimulation of a particular complex of biological processes. And yet at every level the activities involved in constituting fear are contingent. At the cultural level, the contingency concerns which sensations and feelings "count" as fear; at the biological level, the contingency concerns the particular complex of physiological and/or cognitive processes entailed in constituting and expressing fear-associated sensations and feelings; and at the level of the environment, the contingency concerns the kind of stimuli that will activate those biological processes. In short, a being *learns* how to experience, understand, and recognize fear. In other words, emotions are not *just* doings; they are competent ones.

---

[53] Haraway, 1990. While the physiological actions that "do" emotion are clearly different from those that "do" a football game (e.g. less complex, involving the integration of competencies from fewer biological and social sites) the analytic category is identical. Both involve mobilizing or animating bodily forces in ways that re-orient the body's way-of-being in the world.

Of course, as the practice perspective notes, practical competency is learned in and through social engagements within a particular social structure (e.g. *habitus*). This is true, emotion research confirms, even when it comes to the unreflective physiological competencies necessary to "do" a given emotion.[54] Specifically, both the physiological dynamics underlying the lived bodily experience of a given emotion (e.g. fear) and the neuro-cognitive processes that allow one to recognize it as such, develop through engagement in the social world that touch off an ultra micro-dynamic called entrainment or enactment.[55] In this organic process, physiological systems become integrated with, or entrained to, the rhythm of social interactions such that those interactions automatically (i.e. without cognitive reflection) provoke the activation of a particular complex or flow of sensations and feelings. Bodies in war zones, for instance, may become entrained to activate adrenaline, increased heart rate, and a sense of doom in response to a loud explosion. For suburban partygoers, a similar sound (fireworks or a popping cork) might also be entrained to the activation of adrenaline and increased heart rate but along with spontaneous laughter and a sensation of well-being. In this sense, the physiological competence to produce certain types of lived experiences (e.g. doom vs. well-being) emerges through sociality. So does the neuro-cognitive competence to make sense of a particular bodily experience as an instance of a particular emotion. Heart-racing doom only becomes conscious as an experience of fear – rather than, say, anxiety or depression – through the socially constituted emotion-concepts that make possible the cognitive process of categorization.[56]

As with all competent performances, the practical actions that "do" emotion carry social meanings and have social effects. For one, emotional practices reproduce the social structures from whence they emerged. When a being enacts the physiological routines of fear (e.g. heart-racing doom) in response to an appropriate stimulus (e.g. an explosion) in an appropriate social context (e.g. a war zone) she reinforces the social, physiological, and cognitive knowledge that binds war-zone explosions to heart-racing doom and the concept of "fear." Interestingly, the mutually reinforcing dynamic between emotional practices and the structures from which they emerge may offer some insight into one of the fundamental puzzles about emotion: how it is that we can speak of specific emotions (fear, joy) as if they are durable, universally recognizable substances even though their social and subjective content varies considerably across time and internal experience.

It may also offer some insight to how it is possible for others to know or apprehend the emotional experience of another. Key here is that because emotional practices emerge from specific meaning-laden social structures, the practical actions that "do" emotion also unreflectively express the way-of-being that they create. Hence, among humans that do their being in a war zone, a

---

[54] Colombetti and Thompson, 2008.   [55] Collins, 2004.   [56] Lakoff and Johnson, 1999.

body in the throes of doing sweaty-palmed doom is recognized as a fearful human being. The implication is that whether or not an emotional practitioner attempts to make her emotional way-of-being present to others through an explicitly expressive practice (like conversation), emotions, as practices, cannot help but express themselves. The competent bodily performances of the emotional practitioner always unreflectively make present to those similarly socially and physiologically entrained the emotional experiences of being that they enact. It logically follows that emotion is actually no more an internal, subjective experience than it is an external, intersubjective one. As practices, emotions are as much a public event as a private way-of-being. They happen, as it were, across levels of analysis.

Since emotional practices, like all practices, express one's way-of-being human they are part of what constitutes human social order. More precisely, practices "sort" human beings into appropriate social positions, assigning identities and drawing boundaries in a manner consistent with the degree of a practitioner's competency. In the context of emotional practices, enacting and expressing an appropriate emotion in an appropriate context not only makes one's individual way-of-being present but, to the extent that one's performance is intelligible, emotional practices "surface" their practitioners as belonging to, or foreign to, a given social space.[57] For instance, the suburban partygoer that responds to the sound of a popping cork by (consciously or unconsciously) running for cover expresses a lack of emotional competence.[58] His body-in-action expresses an emotion that reveals him as socially "unlike" the others. Through this process emotional practices clarify social boundaries and lay the foundations upon which identities and interests develop and are reproduced.

Finally, and also as with all practices of being human, emotional practices create agency. They "leak" potentially transformative forces of creativity into both the emotional practice and the social order it generates. Indeed, neuroscientific research on emotion empirically establishes what practice theory theorizes: that each human body is physiologically unique and uniquely situated at a contingent nexus of structures. As it acquires practical (physiological) competencies within one context, it carries them into the next.[59] Emotional practices, as such, are never uniformly performed by their practitioners but, instead, shot through with "complexities, differences and particularities."[60] For instance, bodily experiences of fear in a war zone may be constituted and expressed with varying degrees of arousal, types of facial expression, and behavioral reactions. Even the most deeply entrained bodies exceed the practical techniques that "do" any given emotion.

---

[57] Ahmed, 2004.

[58] Note that entrainment carries across context until the body "catches up" to a new social environment.

[59] Damasio, 2005.   [60] Schatzki, 1996, 12.

Whether cognitively processed or not, such variations introduce creativity into practical actions which, when passed along "interaction chains" or "circulated" through a social space, contribute to altering, and even transforming, the practice and the social order it establishes.[61] To concretize this consider "the wave" – a sporting event ritual in which successive groups of spectators briefly stand and raise their arms. Understood as a practical technique for performing and expressing the emotional practice of solidarity, the wave emerged as creative variation on such traditional solidarity-enacting techniques as clapping and cheering.[62] In this way, the emotional practice of solidarity evolved as a result of the "leaking" unintelligible excess of its own performance.

In fact, the wave did more than merely expand the repertoire of ways to enact and experience solidarity. In many cases, it actually transformed the boundaries, identities, and behaviors among sports fans. For instance, fans at the University of Michigan became internally divided as this emotional practice of solidarity encroached on the competent performance of other practices – for instance, intellectual ones like concentrating, and practices of conscious awareness ones like seeing the game. Indeed, for many Wolverine fans, the wave became an entrained trigger for the emotional experience and expression of frustration.[63] Key here is that emotional practices are not discrete but connected to each other and to other types of practices through the very human beings they produce. Emotional practices and their transformation ripple outward, literally affecting stability and change in other spheres of human life and social orders. The question is how they might do so in the spheres of human social order that we call world politics.

Human being as unit of analysis

I have argued that to approach emotions as practices is to understand them as socially meaningful, competent bodily performances that simultaneously constitute and express one's experience of being, generate human social order, and create the agency that transforms it. It is, that is, to conceptualize emotions as having a "suspended" ontology that is irreducible to its constitutive parts. So what gains are to be had by such conceptual labor? In this section I indicate a number of basic theoretical and methodological directions for IR that follow from taking a practice perspective on emotion. Although it is not possible to fully develop these suggestions here, my wager – to be settled, I hope, in the context of the ongoing research project that precipitated this inquiry in the first place – is that these trajectories will ultimately enable better traction on the question of how emotions matter in world politics. The reason, as I now

---

[61] Collins, 2004.
[62] Jennifer Lee, "Lost in Translation: A Chinese Cheer," *New York Times*, August 13, 2008.
[63] Myra A. Oltsik, "Don't Take My Wave Away," *New York Times*, July 8, 1984.

suggest, is that a (Schatzki-inspired) practice perspective encourages theories and methods for IR research that embrace, rather than assume away, the complexity of emotion.

First, and above all, the practice theory outlined here takes emotions outside the levels-of-analysis framework within which studies of emotion in IR have tended to become ensnared. As noted above, because many extant approaches have tended to "fall back" into treating emotion as an internal, subjective experience of individuals, much emotion research has been dogged by the question of how an individual's emotional experience can become woven into the life of collective actors in world politics. While those interested in particular foreign policy decisions have been able to sidestep the question, such is not an option for those interested in placing emotion within the world political system. The practice perspective can do so for it offers the conceptual tools by which to connect the internal, subjective experience of emotion with the social, inter-subjective world from which a being's capacity for that experience emerges. Armed with a practice perspective the key theoretical question is not how emotion "scales up" to international life but, rather, the ways in which emotional practices structure and organize the various domains of international life. How, as Adler and Pouliot ask, do emotional practices emerge, diffuse, become institutionalized, and fade in different domains of world politics? And how, in that process, do they shape, alter, and even transform the logic of those domains?

Second, given the "suspension" of emotional practices around or beyond the levels of analysis, a practice perspective would pursue such questions through an analytic focus on human being (that is, on the doing of being human). After all, as context-contingent bodily routines that express and constitute a human's experience of being in a given moment, emotions exist in their unfolding; they are accomplished in and through human bodies as they perform such constitutive and expressive routines. It bears emphasis that to focus on human being is not the same thing as to focus on the individual, or first level of analysis, nor therefore does this focus imply sacrificing analytic purchase on the role of emotion in the international system. After all, given that being human is a context-contingent social accomplishment that one achieves only to the extent that one competently expresses oneself within that social order, the social organization of a given domain of world politics (e.g. international security) is encoded within the emotional performances of its embodied human practitioners. In this way, an analytic focus on the emotional practices that do human being in the domain of, say, international security allows one to expose the social contours of the international security system, including its associated configuration of identities and interests. A practice theory of emotion, as such, makes possible an emotion-based theory of international stability.

Third, and by the same logic, a practice theory of emotion also makes possible an emotion-based theory of international change. Recall that

emotional practices, like all practices, entail the forces of their own transformation and, by extension, the transformation of the various social orders
that they constitute. Hence, one might theorize the process by which the
creative excess, or agency, produced in the performance of an emotional
practice alters both the emotional practice itself and the human social order,
identity, and interests that characterize the international domain (e.g. international security system) within which it is practiced. Alternatively, one might
theorize change by beginning with an appreciation for the fact that all humans
are positioned at the nexus of multiple structures, practices, and social orders.
In this case the theoretical suggestion is that emotional practitioners within the
international security system might "leak out" or "carry in" potentially transformative emotional practices from the other domains to which they are
connected. A practice theory of emotion, in other words, guides IR scholars
to model emotion as a system-level force, the transformative effects of which
ripple outward from the bodily excess of practitioners in the throes of enacting
an emotional practice.

Of course since agency is, by definition, unintelligible (unexpected, surprising) within the symbolic system of the order into which it ripples or leaks, a
practice theory of emotion also encourages IR scholars to theorize about which
leaks of agency come to matter?; through which kind of emotional practices?;
expressed through which human beings?; occupying which kinds of social
positions within the human social order of which kinds of international
domains? Precisely because not all ripples or leaks of agency matter, a practice
theory of emotion guides us to an emotional theory of international change in
which the analytic gaze remains firmly fixed on concrete human beings in the
act of doing their beings as human in concrete settings.

Fourth, precisely because of the importance of remaining attuned to the
concrete, contingent circumstances in which emotional practices are enacted, a
practice theory of emotion demands an anthropological empirical research
method. It demands a method that reads the social world through real
human beings, interpreting their "doings" not in reference to abstract criteria
but in reference to the local criteria of the social environment within which they
are positioned.[64] In the context of IR this means that an analyst must become
deeply enough immersed in a domain of international political life to be able to
make sense of the specific combinations of conscious and unconscious bodily
routines enacted by people in that domain; and to connect those routines to the
constitution and expression of particular different emotions, or experiences of
being. In other words, it requires the analyst to decode the international social
meanings expressed by human bodies-in-action in particular international
social settings.

[64] Jackson, 2009.

But if an analyst is to successfully draw out or rule out connections between particular emotional practices and specific international political outcomes, a far more structured methodology is also needed; one that prevents the researcher from unwittingly parsing emotional practices and their observed effects into the ontological and epistemological categories between which practical action must remain suspended. After all, insofar as the researcher reduces emotional practices to their constituent components she has done no better than other approaches to emotion at capturing the effects of emotion *per se* in world politics. One promising method in this regard is *mediated discourse analysis*, a technique that emphasizes the body-in-action within a given discursive (i.e. social) order.[65] What makes mediated discourse analysis unique is that it uses socio-linguistic techniques to guide the analyst's focus toward the degree of a practitioner's physiological entrainment with established discursive triggers across a variety of domains. Since degree of entrainment encompasses the variations in the way a practitioner enacts emotional competencies, a mediated discourse analysis ensures not only that the analyst never extracts the social from its material basis but also that she never locates agency apart from the reproduction of structure. In this way, mediated discourse analysis promises a technique for "finding" emotion in real bodies in real-world politics while guiding the analyst without "squishing" emotion into one or another side of the ontological categories that it exceeds.

Finally, it is worth noting the potential applicability of these practice-inspired theoretical and methodological directions to the study of any kind of international practice – from deterrence to balancing to humanitarianism. If this underscores why I take practice theory as establishing an "ism," it also raises a cautionary warning about practice theory in general and its application to emotions in particular. If all actions can be viewed as component parts of some practice, and if practice is the fundamental unit of social life, then practice becomes everything and nothing at all. Accordingly, if the practice heuristic is to be any more effective than extant theories at capturing *emotion* in world politics (as opposed to practice itself) it is crucial to be analytically and empirically vigilant about teasing emotional practices out from the various other emotional and non-emotional practices with which they are inevitably imbricated, interconnected, and otherwise "aggregated."[66]

The challenge in the case of emotion is that emotion is both a practice in its own right and an experience of being that can be expressed through other practices. Recall here that all practices, no matter their primary accomplishment, are also practices that do human beings. All practices position their doers in a social order because they make present the doer's way-of-being along some dimension. Hence, we might find the practice of say, joy, enacted directly; we might find it nested within another practice (say, football) in the sense that the

---

[65] See Scollon, 2001 and 2005.   [66] Adler and Pouliot, Chapter 1 in this volume.

two are being performed simultaneously; or we might find that there are particular ways of practicing football that *themselves* constitute and express joy. What is more, since a practice can express a doer's way-of-being along more than one dimension, we might find ways of practicing football that simultaneously "do" joy and, say, an intellectual attitude such as optimism.

While ultimately the bounds of practice and its relationship to other practices must be sorted out empirically, the only way to prevent practical analysis from devolving into a useless catch-all is by remaining firmly anchored in the analytic distinction among different practical domains: in this case, among emotion and other ways-of-being in the world. As Schatzki indicates, we can distinguish practices that express sensory, intellectual, and behavioral ways-of-being from those that express emotional ways-of-being according to what they tell us about a being's existence in the world in the moment of their performance. Whereas the former three address "why" and/or "what" aspects of being, emotional practices – whether discrete, nested, or channeled through another practice – address the "how" aspects. The key to analyzing emotional practices in world politics is to focus on the competent performances that, in the moment of their enactment, express how the "doer" is experiencing her own existence as a being in the human world.

References

Ahmed, Sara, 2004. Affective Economics. *Social Text* 22 (2): 117–139.

Appadurai, A., 2006. *Fear of Small Numbers*. Durham, NC: Duke University Press.

Barrett, Lisa F., 2006. Solving the Emotion Paradox: Categorization and the Experience of Emotion. *Personality and Social Psychology Review* 10 (1): 20–46.

Bennett, William J., 2002. *Why We Fight: Moral Clarity and the War on Terrorism*. New York: Doubleday.

Bleiker, Roland and Emma Hutchison, 2008. Fear No More: Emotions and World Politics. *Review of International Studies* 34 (1): 115–135.

Campbell, David, 1998. Why Fight: Humanitarianism, Principles, and Post-Structuralism. *Millennium* 27 (3): 497–521.

Collins, Randall, 2004. *Interaction Ritual Chains*. Princeton: Princeton University Press.

Colombetti, Giovanna and Evan Thompson, 2008. The Feeling Body: Toward an Enactive Approach to Emotion. In *Developmental Perspectives on Embodiment and Conciousness*, edited by Willis F. Overton, Ulrich Müller, and Judith Newman, 45–68. New York: Lawrence Erlbaum.

Crawford, Neta C., 2000. The Passion of World Politics: Propositions on Emotions and Emotional Relationships. *International Security* 24 (4): 116–156.

Damasio, Antonio R., 2005 [1994]. *Descartes' Error: Emotion, Reason, and the Human Brain*. Rev. edn. New York: Penguin.

De Sousa, Ronald, 1987. *The Rationality of Emotion*. Cambridge, MA: MIT.
    2008. Emotion. In *The Stanford Encyclopedia of Philosophy* (Fall 2008 edn.), edited by Edward N. Zalta. Available at http://plato.stanford.edu/archives/fall2008/entries/emotion. Accessed October 29, 2010.

Dunbar, R. I. M., 2003. The Social Brain: Mind, Language, and Society in Evolutionary Perspective. *Annual Review of Anthropology* 32: 163–181.

Edkins, Jenny, 2003. *Trauma and the Memory of Politics*. Cambridge: Cambridge University Press.

Farnell, Brenda, 2000. Getting Out of the Habitus: An Alternative Model of Dynamically Embodied Social Action. *Journal of the Royal Anthropological Institute* 6 (3): 397–418.

Fisher, Gene A. and Kyum Koo Chon, 1989. Durkheim and the Social Construction of Emotions. *Social Psychology Quarterly* 52 (1): 1–9.

Haraway, Donna J., 1990. *Simians, Cyborgs, and Women: The Reinvention of Nature*. New York: Routledge.

Hutchison, Emma, 2008. The Politics of Post-Trauma Emotions: Securing Community after the Bali Bombing. Working Paper 2008/4. Canberra: Department of International Relations, Australian National University. Available at http://ips.cap.anu.edu.au/ir/pubs/work_papers/08-4.pdf. Accessed November 9, 2010.

Hutchison, Emma and Roland Bleiker, 2008. Emotional Reconciliation: Reconstituting Identity and Community after Trauma. *European Journal of Social Theory* 11 (3): 385–403.

Hymans, Jacques E. C., 2006. *The Psychology of Nuclear Proliferation: Identity, Emotions, and Foreign Policy*. Cambridge: Cambridge University Press.

Jackson, Patrick Thaddeus, 2009. Situated Creativity, or, the Cash Value of a Pragmatist Wager for IR. *International Studies Review* 11 (3): 656–662.

Jackson, Peter, 2008. Pierre Bourdieu, the "Cultural Turn" and the Practice of International History. *Review of International Studies* 34 (1): 155–181.

Kaufman, Stuart J., 2001. *Modern Hatreds: The Symbolic Politics of Ethnic War*. Ithaca: Cornell University Press.

Kövecses, Zoltán, 2000. *Metaphor and Emotion*. Cambridge: Cambridge University Press.

Krebs, Ronald R. and Jennifer K. Lobasz, 2007. Fixing the Meaning of 9/11: Hegemony, Coercion, and the Road to War in Iraq. *Security Studies* 16 (3): 409–451.

Lakoff, George and Mark Johnson, 1999. *Philosophy in the Flesh: The Embodied Mind and its Challenge to Western Thought*. New York: Basic Books.

LeDoux, Joseph, 1996. *The Emotional Brain*. New York: Simon & Schuster.

Lutz, Catherine, 1988. *Unnatural Emotions: Everyday Sentiments on a Micronesian Atoll and their Challenge to Western Theory*. Chicago: University of Chicago Press.

Marcus, George E., 2000. Emotions in Politics. *Annual Review of Political Science* 3 (1): 221–250.

Massumi, Brian, 2002. *Parables for the Virtual: Movement, Affect, Sensation*. Durham, NC: Duke University Press.

McDermott, Rose, 2004. The Feeling of Rationality: The Meaning of Neuroscientific Advances for Political Science. *Perspectives on Politics* 2 (4): 691–706.

Mercer, Jonathan, 2005. Rationality and Psychology in International Politics. *International Organization* 59 (1): 77–106.

——— 2010. Emotional Beliefs. *International Organization* 64 (1): 1–31.

Mutch, Alistair, 2003. Communities of Practice and Habitus: A Critique. *Organization Studies* 24 (3): 383–401.

Natter, Wolfgang, 2001. From Hate to Antagonism: Toward an Ethics of Emotion, Discussion, and the Political. *Political Geography* 20 (1): 25–34.

Nussbaum, Martha C., 2001. *Upheavals of Thought: The Intelligence of Emotions.* Cambridge: Cambridge University Press.

Panskepp, Jaak, 1998. *Affective Neuroscience: The Foundations of Human and Animal Emotions.* New York: Oxford University Press.

Park, Hyung Wook, 2006. Germs, Hosts, and the Origin of Frank Macfarlane Burnet's Concept of "Self" and "Tolerance." *Journal of the History of Medicine and Allied Sciences* 61 (4): 492–534.

Petersen, Roger D., 2002. *Understanding Ethnic Violence: Fear, Hatred, and Resentment in Twentieth Century Eastern Europe.* Cambridge: Cambridge University Press.

Pouliot, Vincent, 2008. The Logic of Practicality: A Theory of Practice of Security Communities. *International Organization* 62 (2): 257–288.

Reckwitz, Andreas, 2002. Toward a Theory of Social Practices: A Development in Culturalist Theorizing. *European Journal of Social Theory* 5 (2): 243–263.

Reddy, William M., 1997. Against Constructionism: The Historical Ethnography of Emotions. *Current Anthropology* 38 (3): 327–351.

Rosen, Stephen P., 2005. *War and Human Nature.* Princeton: Princeton University Press.

Ross, Andrew A. G., 2006. Coming in from the Cold: Constructivism and Emotions. *European Journal of International Relations* 12 (2): 197–222.

——— Forthcoming. *Beyond Hatred: Violence, Identity, and Justice in an Age of Terror.* Chicago: University of Chicago Press.

Saurette, Paul, 2006. You Dissin' Me? Humiliation and Post-9/11 Global Politics. *Review of International Studies* 32 (2): 495–522.

Schatzki, Theodore R., 1996. *Social Practices: A Wittgensteinian Approach to Human Activity and the Social.* New York: Cambridge University Press.

Scollon, Ronald, 2001. *Mediated Discourse: The Nexus of Practice.* London: Routledge.

——— 2005. The Rhythmic Integration of Action and Discourse: Work, the Body and the Earth. In *Discourse in Action: Introducing Mediated Discourse Analysis,* edited by Sigrid Norris and Rodney H. Jones, 20–31. London: Routledge.

Varela, Charles R., 1995. Ethogenic Theory and Psychoanalysis: The Unconcious as a Social Construction and a Failed Explanatory Concept. *Journal for the Theory of Social Behavior* 25 (4): 363–385.

Wolfe, Charles T., 1997–1999. Proprioception. *Artbrain – Journal of Neuro-Aesthetic Theory* 1. Available at www.artbrain.org/proprioception. Accessed October 29, 2010.

4 | Background knowledge in the foreground: conversations about competent practice in "sacred space"

JANICE GROSS STEIN

Introduction: communities of practice

The modern humanitarian community, given voice by Henri Dunant, the founder of the Red Cross in 1863, constituted itself from its earliest days as a "community of practice." This chapter examines the contemporary transformation of this community through practice, the unfolding of its life with the competency of practice at the epicenter of the change.

I treat practices, following Adler and Pouliot, as "competent performances" and "socially meaningful patterns of action."[1] A "community of practice is a configuration of a *domain of knowledge* that constitutes like-mindedness, a *community of people* that 'creates the social fabric of learning,' and a *shared practice* that embodies 'the knowledge the community develops, shares, and maintains.'"[2] In a strong statement of the understanding of practice, practice can be performed "correctly" or "incorrectly," well or badly.[3] Practice is competency.

Competency has been taken for granted since the end of the Second World War among the small group of large non-governmental organizations (NGOs) that delivered emergency humanitarian assistance. Two decades ago, for reasons I shall examine, that background knowledge began to seem inadequate to some within the community, to some policy analysts who watched this community closely, and to states that funded the community's work. This is a story,

---

[1] Adler and Pouliot, Chapter 1 in this volume.

[2] *Ibid.* Emphasis added. Adler and Pouliot continue: "The community of practice concept encompasses not only the conscious and discursive dimensions and the actual doing of social change, but also the social space where structure and agency overlap and where knowledge, power, and community intersect. Communities of practice are intersubjective social structures that constitute the normative and epistemic ground for action, but they are also agents, made up of real people, who – working via network channels, across national borders, across organizational divides, and in the halls of government – affect political, economic, and social events."

[3] Barnes, 2001. For a critique of competency as the core of practice, see Duvall and Chowdhury, Chapter 13 in this volume.

then, of background knowledge pushed to the foreground and of the demand for change that is centrally focused on the practices of the humanitarian community. It is a contest over doing, where leaders of these large organizations – CARE, Médecins sans Frontières (Doctors without Borders, MSF), Oxfam, CARITAS – struggled over the legitimacy of their practices. This story fits nicely within one phase of the lifecycle of a community of practice, an attempt at transformation that grows out of important changes in the international political and social order.

The chapter begins by exploring the changing structures that contributed to the foregrounding of background knowledge. Deepening globalization, retreating but regulating states, and a changing strategic environment all enabled a discussion that began among policy analysts and leaders of some humanitarian organizations who began to worry actively that they were "doing harm." Agency and structure overlapped as the leaders of humanitarian organizations began a fierce debate, where the ethical foundations of humanitarian practices were challenged by consequentialist logics and arguments. These were bitterly contested conversations, wrapped in a language of "doing": doing good and doing harm. From these conversations about practices – their standards, their competencies, their accountabilities – came a difficult discussion about power and responsibility. These conversations reshaped practice and the community as leaders talked about practices in new and often uncomfortable ways.

This is not, however, a straightforward story of change. It is also a story of resistance, of the embedding of practice, and of attachment to practice. The contested conversation about practice, laced in the normative language of "doing the right thing," paradoxically often worked to forestall changes in practice. The conversation about competing normative logics at times masked the fierce controversy about practices and gave legitimacy to those who said: "This is the way we do things." The conversation anchored in practice, about "doing good," at times blocked a more deeply critical examination while it safeguarded the moral standing of embedded practices.

Communities of practice and learning

How is competency or correctness established within a community? These terms imply some standard against which practice can be judged.[4] In the first instance, one can understand these standards as implicit or "inarticulate." They are implicit because practice rests on a stock of background knowledge that is shared. This background knowledge, as Adler and Pouliot argue, is itself practical, oriented towards competency in skill. It is about "doing" in the world. This formulation of practice as competency, transmitted, shared, and

---

[4] Kratochwil, Chapter 2 in this volume, explores the complexity of rules and rule-following.

constructed through performance, constituted as background knowledge is, however, more complicated than it first appears.

Practice is constructed collectively, by a community. Although practice is performed by an individual, it acquires meaning only through collectively shared understandings of competency, of what is well done or poorly done. Without that broader understanding, it would be difficult to construe individual "doing" as practice; that kind of doing would be devoid of any kind of standard. It is in this sense that, as Adler and Pouliot argue, practices join together people or organizations that share an interest in doing and that share standards of competence that have been internalized over time. Practitioners who deliver emergency assistance to distant strangers in need constitute a community of practice. The humanitarian community relies on background knowledge that has developed over time, a form of "inarticulate know-how" or "tacit, taken-for-granted knowledge," which anchors reasoning, expectations, and judgment among practitioners delivering tents, providing emergency medical aid, and supplying clean water. Staff of the large organizations – CARE, MSF – will say simply: It is "the way we do things."[5] That phrase is often a coded reference to their expertise and to the inexperience of the large numbers of smaller, less-seasoned organizations that arrive quickly at the scene of an emergency.

The fundamental questions this chapter asks are two: How do practices within a *community transform and change?* And *how do changing practices reconstitute communities of practice?* I argue that, within the humanitarian community, *change in practices occurs when new problems arise that challenge existing knowledge and/or when some of the influential members of the community want to "do good" better.* It is when they wanted to "'do good' better" – improve the delivery of emergency assistance after a natural disaster, improve the management of refugee camps, avoid the distorting effects of food aid – that some members of the community began, two decades ago, to push background knowledge into the foreground in a conscious attempt to examine what they were doing and whether they could do what they were doing better.

This examination is necessarily conscious rather than unconscious, explicit rather than tacit, and reflective rather than reflexive.[6] I call this process

---

[5] For this discussion, see Bourdieu, 1990; and Searle, 1995.

[6] Inferring from the individual to the collective is an anthropomorphic sin, but there are intriguing parallels. New research in neuroscience establishes that the overwhelming majority of decisions that people make are unconscious, that we are unaware of the processes and the decision. We just "do." Moreover, these unconscious processes are shaped predominantly by the amygdaline and limbic systems in our brains, the circuitry that processes emotions. We become "aware" or conscious when emotion and cognition conflict at manageable levels of intensity or when existing repertoires do not have programs to process the stimulus that we are receiving. I argue that some of the same triggers operate at the collective level. See Stein, 2010; and Rouse, 2007.

"learning," a process where structure and agency overlap to provoke reflection. The humanitarian community, like other communities of practice, knows "the way we do things" but, in response to criticism, or failure, or new knowledge, or discovery from doing – is open to new experiences, to new practical knowledge of what works better, to contingency – what works better here and what works better there – and to the social importance of sharing that knowledge broadly through the community. In the process of learning and sharing, knowledge becomes ever-more explicit, discursive and, at times, representational until, well established, it recedes again into the background.

That knowledge can hardly be expressed apart from practice does not imply that it is not expressed. Indeed, "learning" within a community of practice is closely connected to practice and is expressed through practice. "Teaching" is often done by example, through demonstration, without words but, even under these conditions, learning is reflective and in the foreground. At times, learning that is articulated and verbalized as standards is renegotiated by members who simultaneously "learn by doing" and share knowledge among themselves. These negotiations are not neutral but rather are shaped by the power and politics of the environment in which the community of practice exists and by the power and politics within. Over time, in the lifecycle of a community of practice, the "new" knowledge is assimilated into and modifies existing knowledge and, only then, when it is accepted, does it gradually recede into the background.

In this chapter, I examine a debate about competent practice as an occasion for learning within the humanitarian community. Practice is a central component within the community which is committed to alleviating suffering and to helping distant strangers. What it does, in other words, is central to who this community is; it is defined by its practices. It is this enmeshment of identity and practice within the humanitarian community, along with deep controversy about competing logics, which made the debate about competent practice so difficult and painful.

A conversation about standards of practice – a debate that occurs frequently within communities of practice – is never easy. What is considered "competent" at any moment in time and space is a normative judgment. It reflects not only "what we do," but "what we think we should do," and "how we think about what we should do." A debate about the competency of practice is always difficult and often threatening, because it speaks not only to "what is in" and "what is out" but also to "who is in" and "who is out." In this sense, it is constitutive of a community. Those who do not share the standards of competence cannot for long be part of a community that is defined by its commitment to practice. Practice created the community, but in an ongoing process of learning about "best practices," the community reshapes practice over time and, in so doing, reshapes itself.

"Doing good" has been the animating principle of the humanitarian community since the modern beginnings of humanitarianism in the mid-nineteenth century. Drawn together by a shared commitment to kindness to strangers and a sense of joined enterprise, the humanitarian community has focused on practice. Yet the humanitarian community has divided time and again in debates about standards of practice.[7] It is through deeply political debates about standards of practice that humanitarians have defined and redefined themselves over time. It is in this sense that conversations about practice, about "doing good better," or about "do no harm" – these two are not the same debates – have shaped and transformed the modern history of humanitarianism.

I look at the debate about standards of practice in the humanitarian community since 1990 to address several questions. I ask first what enabled this latest debate about standards of practice within the humanitarian community. Communities of practice, as Adler and Pouliot argue, are suspended between structure and agency.

I begin with the role structure played in moving knowledge from the background to the foreground. How did structure help to call into question what had been previously taken for granted? Structure alone cannot explain the reopening of what had been taken for granted. It can be a trigger to learning, but agents are essential to a process of foregrounding knowledge. I move back and forth in this chapter between agents and structure.

Who is the "practitioner" in this story? It is the engineer connecting water pipes after an emergency. It is the staff at "head office," increasingly professionalized and bureaucratized, that is appealing to governments and donors for funds to sustain the engineer "in the field." And it is leaders of humanitarian organizations who come together in forums to consider their practices, the consequences of these practices, and the critiques leveled at a community that allegedly did not reflect enough on what it did. This is a story about a *community* of practice, a collective that is very loosely institutionalized in a formal way but, in the last two decades, met often to talk about what it was doing. This community works at the interface of large states and powerful international agencies and with those who have fallen victim to history and desperately need, at least for the moment, the kindness of strangers.

This story aggregates across levels as the narrative unfolds. The story opens with individual members of the humanitarian community – Mary Anderson, Alex de Waal, David Rieff – who write critically about what the humanitarian community is doing and the dangerous consequences in the field. Their criticisms ignite a firestorm of controversy, an admixture of acknowledgment and resistance. Large and influential members within the humanitarian community – MSF, Oxfam, CARE, World Vision – then begin processes of critical self-examination about standards of practice. These processes gradually diffuse throughout the humanitarian community and lead to community-wide responses. When the community responds through new institutions and new

---

[7] Barnett, 2011.

standards of competent practice, the community of practice begins to reconstitute itself. Agents change, in other words, during the lifecycle of learning where background knowledge is foregrounded, interrogated, transformed, codified, and then gradually recedes into the background.

The debate about humanitarian practice

The ethic of humanitarian action, as its president noted in 1999 when accepting the Nobel Peace Prize for MSF, is constructed as an "ethic framed in a morality" that is not reducible to "rules of right conduct and technical performance."[8] It was not coincidental that James Orbinski utterly rejected a conception of humanitarianism rooted in competent practice and returned to the universal ethical principles which the founders of modern humanitarianism articulated. Formalized by the International Red Cross, the humanitarian community espouses seven fundamental principles: humanity, impartiality, neutrality, independence, voluntary service, unity, and universality.[9] Orbinski returned to these principles at a time when the humanitarian community faced unprecedented criticism, from both without and within, of what it was doing, of its practices.

The humanitarian community today consists of tens of thousands of NGOs and individuals that accept these principles and work to alleviate the suffering of others. In this chapter, I look only at those who deliver emergency assistance in the context of violent conflict or natural disasters. Despite the large numbers of organizations that deliver help, there are perhaps a dozen, large humanitarian organizations that have deep experience in the delivery of emergency assistance. Large organizations like the International Committee of the Red Cross and Red Crescent, CARE International, World Vision, CARITAS International, Save the Children, Oxfam, Catholic Relief Services, Christian Aid, People in Aid, MSF, and more recently, Africa Humanitarian Action and Islamic Relief, are the leaders in the delivery of humanitarian assistance in emergencies, and many have expanded their mission from relief to development after a crisis eases. It is they who have led the latest conversation about competent practice within the humanitarian community.

It would have seemed inconceivable two decades ago that these humanitarian organizations delivering emergency assistance in war zones would spend any time debating standards of competent practices. Their virtue was unassailable and unassailed. Good intentions were enough to confer legitimacy and, consequently, the competence of practice was taken for granted, in the background, unproblematic. This is no longer the case.

---

[8] Orbinski, 1999.   [9] International Red Cross and Red Crescent Movement, 1965.

Today leaders within the humanitarian community are intimately familiar with voluntary codes of conduct, humanitarian charters, and other standards for the delivery of relief. They have built an active learning network to gather and share the lessons learned from humanitarian practice.[10] In the United Kingdom, the five biggest NGOs have agreed to build "quality assurance" into their practices. Oxfam International has agreed on common program standards across its eleven member organizations. The most influential code was developed by the International Red Cross and Red Crescent Movement. Today, the Disasters Emergencies Committee (DEC), the committee representing the largest humanitarian organizations in the United Kingdom, which organizes joint appeals in times of emergencies, uses the Red Cross principles and code, as well as the codes of good practice developed by the SPHERE Project, NGOs in Disaster Relief, and the People in Aid Code. Humanitarian agencies often prominently display these codes on their websites, a display which is probably more likely to be noticed by potential funders than by potential beneficiaries.[11]

The debate about practice exploded in the 1990s and gripped these large organizations within the humanitarian community. A normative question – whether and how practices should change to become more accountable, what standards of competency are appropriate, how humanitarians could "do good better" – was and is deeply disputed among humanitarians who work in war zones. In this debate that erupted among humanitarians, background knowledge became the subject of contestation. For the first time, the possibility of "doing harm" was foregrounded within this community of practice.

Practice pushed to the foreground: structure and agency

Why did practice become the subject of deep controversy? Structure tells an important part of the story. The debate about standards of competency was pushed from outside the community. At a time of neo-liberal orthodoxy, states withdrew from the direct delivery of emergency assistance and increasingly contracted, directly or indirectly, the large humanitarian organizations to provide a broad range of services in emergencies.

Between 1990 and 2000, aid levels rose from $2.1 billion to $5.9 billion, a nearly three-fold increase. Moreover, as a percentage of official development assistance, humanitarian aid rose from an average of 5.83 percent between 1989 and 1993 to 10.5 percent in 2000.[12] A few donors were responsible for

---

[10] See SPHERE Project, 2004; and HAP Project, 2001.
[11] As Barnett (2008b, 254) notes: "Because organizations are rewarded for conforming to rules and legitimating principles, and punished if they do not, they will tend to model themselves after those organizational forms that have legitimacy." See also Barnett, 2008a.
[12] See Macrae, 2002, 15; and Randel and German, 2002.

much of this increase, and they now constituted an oligopoly. The United States was the lead donor by a factor of three; in 1999, for instance, its outlays exceeded the total assistance of twelve large Western donors. The second largest donor is the European Community Humanitarian Organization (ECHO), followed by the United Kingdom, several European countries, Canada, and Japan.

In return for this increase in giving, many donor states wanted evidence that their money was being well spent. They did not consider good intentions as a guarantee of competency and increased their monitoring and regulation of large, nationally headquartered, humanitarian NGOs. Even as they became physically absent, states became increasingly present as regulators, interested in "outcomes" and "accountability." States began introducing mechanisms that were intended to control the way their "implementing partners" spent the money. As states retreated from program and service delivery, they instrumentalized humanitarian organizations and increasingly thought of them as their agents.

In this new ecology, states are one step removed, no longer practitioners, but regulators and monitors of practice. The disbursement of large amounts of public money to humanitarian organizations increased the tendency for states to steer those who were rowing a boat of significant size. Paradoxically, when the state was present, the degrees of separation between state and humanitarian organization in "the field" were greater. Humanitarians could talk of "sacred space" and moral obligation, with practice in the background. No longer.

Deepening processes of globalization also helped to push background knowledge into the foreground. With the growth in the size and complexity of a small number of the largest humanitarian organizations came professionalization and institutionalization. Openness to the "professional" language of evaluation, outcome mapping, and "results" grew out of the rationalization and institutionalization of humanitarian organizations that were now embedded within wider processes of globalization.[13] Along with organizations in the private and public sectors, organizations operating in humanitarian space increasingly needed specialized training and skills, specialists in human resources, business and finance officers, and all the other attributes of large and complex organizations that deliver services through global networks.

The People in Aid Code, to which DEC members are signatories, outlines guidelines for proper staff management, and human resources policies and a set of indicators that establish benchmarks for evaluating compliance with these standards. It notes in its discussion of its human resources strategy that humanitarian agencies must develop and monitor "operational plans and budgets" in order to "reflect fully our responsibilities for staff management, support, and development and well-being."[14] The demonstration of effectiveness in these areas is not simply for internal consumption but rather, as the report by People in Aid demonstrates, central to their activities:

[13] Hopgood, 2008.   [14] People in Aid, 2003, 8.

The Code is more than merely making staff better at their jobs or happier in their role; it is about organizational effectiveness ... Sometimes external factors prompt action towards effectiveness; host governments, partners and the wider community all need the reassurance that the agencies with which they work will demonstrate professionalism in all their activities. Donors require that their funds be committed to agencies that can demonstrate effective human resource management. For example, the Disasters Emergency Committee (DEC), which raises substantial funds from the British public in times of crisis internationally, states that members need to have "a demonstrable commitment to achieving People in Aid standards and a willingness to be evaluated against them."[15]

The professionalization and rationalization of deepening processes of globalization was internalized by the largest organizations within the humanitarian community. It was given voice by codes of conduct that, for the first time, formalized and articulated standards of competent performance.

Not all the big humanitarian organizations agreed. MSF, for example, refused to participate formally in the development of the SPHERE code, a shared project by many of the largest agencies. MSF considered the demands of donors to codify practice as insulting, as a challenge to both its virtue and its competence.[16] It viewed the demand to demonstrate the competency of its practice through codified rules of conduct as simplistic, and as an affront to an organization that responded to a higher calling. Understandably, the fact that it raised the overwhelming amount of its funds from individual donors and accepted very little from national or international agencies made it much easier for its president to resist a conversation about accountability, and competency, and to insist, as he did, on an "ethic framed in a morality" that is not reducible to "rules of right conduct and technical performance."[17]

In contrast, Islamic Relief, a large Muslim humanitarian organization, quickly agreed to the importance of codes of conduct for competent practice, but did so for quite different reasons. Established in 1984 in response to the humanitarian crises in Ethiopia and the Sudan, Islamic Relief is a religious agency headquartered in Birmingham, UK, with an annual budget in 2007 of approximately $75.9 million, operations in twenty-four countries, and with liaison offices in twelve countries.[18] Like many other humanitarian agencies, Islamic Relief's mission evolved in the 1990s to include a long-term development focus, and then it expanded further after the Tsunami of 2004 and the earthquake in Pakistan in 2005.[19]

---

[15] *Ibid.*   [16] Interview by the author with senior MSF official, February 18, 2008. Geneva.
[17] Interview by the author with James Orbinski, May 5, 2009. Toronto.
[18] UK Charity Commission, n.d., Charity No. 328158 (Islamic Relief).
[19] Regarding the origin of Islamic Relief, see Islamic Relief, n.d.; and Kirmani and Khan, 2008.

After September 11, the virtue and legitimacy of Islamic Relief was called into question. As an Islamic agency headquartered in a Western country, Islamic Relief found itself subject to scrutiny. Although Islamic Relief raises 90 percent of its funds from individual donors, as does MSF, like all Islamic charities it found itself the object of suspicion that it could be used to channel funds from "terrorist" organizations. Islamic Relief is, organizationally speaking, a relatively "young" agency, as are many Islamic humanitarian agencies. Islamic agencies began as humanitarians in the 1980s in places like Algiers, Beirut, Cairo, Gaza, and Tehran, and it was another decade before they developed significant international relief programs.[20] Once these relatively young agencies went global, though, they began to feel pressure from within and outside the sector to comply with its evolving standards of competent practice. In a climate of suspicion, obvious compliance brought significant benefits. In response to these challenges, Islamic Relief initiated several reforms. As one senior staff member observed:

> Islamic Relief has to be good at what it does. Effective and efficient. Focused and knowledgeable. We should not have to struggle to meet minimum standards; instead, we should help to develop those standards ... We need that to survive in a world that often looks at Muslim charities with suspicion. To get to that leadership position, we need to perform better than we do now. Performing better has to do with structure, process, job satisfaction, cordial relations, a positive work environment, technical expertise, and priority-setting.[21]

What did Islamic Relief do? First, it established its own mechanisms to demonstrate its accountability to both donors and beneficiaries. Islamic Relief's Quality Management System (IRQMS) sets the standards by which staff in Islamic Relief field offices can both self-assess their work and be evaluated from headquarters in three key areas – policy and governance, program management, and office management – across seventeen indicators. By training and working closely with staff to meet at least the first of three levels of quality management and by holding periodic reviews, country directors try to improve performance.

Islamic Relief also paid attention to transparency. It tried to provide more and better information about its projects to beneficiaries or stakeholders. It also encouraged participation by partner agencies, institutional donors, and beneficiaries through the lifecycle of a project. By engaging stakeholders in identifying needs, developing the project, and implementing and monitoring its

[20] For data on the increase in the number of Islamic aid agencies in Africa from 1980 to 2000, see Salih, 2004.
[21] Interview by Laura Thaut, July 30, 2008. Birmingham, UK. Cited in Thaut, Barnett, and Stein, 2011.

progress, Islamic Relief believes its projects have a better chance of meeting evaluation standards.

Islamic Relief also improved its monitoring of performance management. It considers self-monitoring and auditing to be central in establishing accountability and demonstrating competence to its stakeholders. Progress assessments are conducted at several levels, both internally, within field offices and by external staff depending on the size of the project. Different evaluation techniques are used at the project, program, country, regional, sectoral, and global levels. For example, at the program level, similar water-related programs must be reviewed annually by the field office with country director oversight, as well as undergo a "Full Field Office Appraisal" every two years by external Islamic Relief staff. At the project level, emergency response funds over 150,000 Euros must be monitored within three months of a project's initiation. Finally, to encourage accountability to donors, Islamic Relief instructs field office staff on how to respond to complaints from beneficiaries. Through these changes in practices, it hoped to alleviate fears about its work, demonstrate its competence, and reinforce legitimacy by becoming an accepted member of the humanitarian community of practice.

The debate about competency in practice was driven not only by a retreating state, accelerating processes of globalization, and a changing strategic environment. It is deeply misleading to see structure alone – in this case, states and international institutions acting as funders – driving accountability into the heart of humanitarian organizations with the sharp point of their spear to change practice. It was not only the competency of humanitarian organizations, but also their failures – or their alleged failures – that pushed forward a language of doing good better.

In withering criticism that grew in the 1990s, analysts who were generally sympathetic to humanitarian purposes began to level shocking allegations about the "harm" that humanitarians were inadvertently doing. They pointed to the shortcomings of humanitarian assistance, to its damaging consequences, to the disruption of local societies and economies, to its capacity to break the social contract on the ground, to the tendency to concentrate on the highly visible emergencies that will "sell in the humanitarian marketplace," and ignore the less visible, the long-lasting, the more difficult to reach.[22] An emphasis on doing was challenged by a discourse of "do no harm," a sense of shared competency was disturbed by rumblings from within and without the community about damage, and the terrain shifted toward a conversation about standards of practice and accountability for outcomes.

In order to identify "harm," humanitarian organizations had to do more than "do"; they had to learn about the broad consequences that flowed from their

---

[22] See De Waal, 1997; Rieff, 2002; Terry, 2002; Eriksson *et al.*, 1996; and Telford, Cosgrave, and Houghton, 2006.

practices. It was no longer sufficient to assert the virtue that flowed from good intentions. If humanitarian leaders were to engage with the critics among them, they had to shift from an ethic of need to a logic of consequences. For some, this was a bridge they could not cross, a trivialization of the moral obligation to help that would be submerged in consequentialist arguments.

Where and how did this debate, a debate that continues to this day, begin? In the aftermath of the Rwandan genocide, it became clear to many humanitarian organizations that their best and "most professional" practices in the management of refugee camps were producing unanticipated and, at times, pernicious consequences, that competency in practice, on the ground, animated by background knowledge, was producing unwanted consequences in a larger context. Comprehensive assessments of the international response to the genocide and to the management of the refugee camps on the Congolese–Rwandan border argued that these camps were filled with refugees who had fled Rwanda, including those who had perpetrated the genocide. Humanitarian organizations consequently found themselves feeding and sustaining genocidaires. This began a jarring conversation.

These negative consequences were not the result of failures in practice, a lack of "professionalism." They were the consequences of operating in a radically changed political context which altered the boundaries of humanitarian space. Groups engaged in violent conflict with one another rejected the sanctity of humanitarian space. On the contrary, they understood that space as explicitly political and treated it as a political arena for action. Humanitarian reiteration of the neutrality and impartiality of their space – deeply embedded principles which had grown out of earlier practice – availed little when humanitarian resources were large in relation to local resources and potentially determining of the political as well as the military outcome of conflict.

Humanitarian organizations have traditionally been very reluctant to acknowledge that through their practices they exercise power and dispose of proportionally very large resources in the contexts in which they operate, that they shape social and economic processes – subtly or unsubtly. The language of power fits very uneasily with the core ethics of service that shape humanitarian culture, with the deep normative commitment to help those who suffer, and with the long-standing traditions of impartiality, neutrality, and independence. The self-image of a moral obligation to provide impartial service to those in need is jarred by an explicit recognition of the significant power and resources that humanitarians command and control in an environment of acute scarcity and insecurity.

Practice was embedded in a complex web, in a normative surround that was fraying both from within and without. Initially practice shaped representation and identity, as humanitarians began by doing and defined themselves largely by what they did. The fundamental principles of the humanitarian community flowed out of the understanding of practice. The shift in power toward humanitarian organizations of the last two decades, however, reshaped practice in ways that posed sharp dilemmas for ethics and politics, and created controversies about standards of practice. The construction of humanitarian space as essentially political, for example, was acknowledged openly by very few humanitarian organizations, even though it was reflected in practices which made accommodations with militias, sought protection from contracted forces, and voiced opposition to the practices of those who abused populations. Practice sat ever more uneasily with principles.

The allergy to "standards for practice" and "accountability for outcomes": competencies at issue

Structures – deepening globalization, retreating states, and changing strategic environments – and agents – increasingly concerned to secure institutional funds on a scale heretofore unknown and yet deeply concerned about the violation of the sanctity of humanitarian space – together pushed background knowledge to the foreground. A heated conversation about standards and competent practice began, and still continues. This discussion within the humanitarian community has been extraordinarily difficult, and notwithstanding the development of charters and codes of conduct, it continues to be so.

Why has the discussion about standards of practice, about competency been so difficult? Why the allergy to this conversation? Perhaps conversations about competencies which bring background knowledge to the foreground are generically uncomfortable within communities of practice. They question what is taken for granted. But these conversations do take place in other communities of practice. They frequently generate conflict, but they are not usually resisted with the same degree of intensity as did the humanitarian community of practice. It is not much of an exaggeration to observe that important leaders within this community fought not to have the discussion.

Conversations around standards and competency are almost always contested in the public and private sectors, but the contest tends to revolve around its particular dimensions, its measures, and the capacity to compensate for political and regulatory deficits. The global financial community, for example, has just been through, yet again, another round of this kind of conversation. The debate is different within the humanitarian community. It is about the appropriateness of having a discussion of competency at all. There is almost a sense of moral outrage among some humanitarians when the subject of competent practice is raised. That the conversation is happening at all strikes deeply at the identity humanitarians have constructed as a community.

Humanitarian organizations approach their work within a historical context of principled action in neutral space. Inheritors of the Dunantist tradition, they are morally committed to provide assistance to all the victims of a conflict and they are self-governed by principles of impartiality and neutrality. These principles served humanitarians reasonably well when combatants followed the rules of war and structured space between them.

War zones in the last three decades do not look much like space that is structured according to shared norms and rules. As civil wars stretched over decades and states were made, unmade, and remade, it became more and more difficult to maintain a restrictive set of parameters for humanitarian work. What assistance should be, where in the chain of transformative logic humanitarian organizations should focus their action, and how humanitarian assistance should be delivered so that it does not create undesirable political consequences, are all now contested. What was once unproblematic is now problematic, in large part because what was once only implicitly political is now explicitly political.

The conversation about standards and competencies is so difficult within the humanitarian community not only because, in exchange for significant new resources, donors are demanding greater control. It is difficult also because the humanitarian community is only reluctantly beginning to grapple seriously with the power and the political roles and responsibilities that flow from their practices. Humanitarians cling to the label of "a-political," a label that fore-closed, for example, a discussion about the political outcomes of their practices. At most, humanitarians could be held accountable for what they did on the ground and the way they did it. Impartiality was not only principled, it was functional; it helped to facilitate access to all sides in a conflict zone, and it avoided explicit discussion of difficult political choices.

That the ground no longer permits impartiality – that humanitarians are now witnesses on behalf of the voiceless, that they intervene in political processes, that their resources are appropriated and misappropriated to shift the terms of the conflict, that humanitarian organizations exercise power through practice – changes the terms of the debate. This discussion of competencies, often tense, speaks to the norms as well as the practices of humanitarians. Some leaders within humanitarian organizations interpret a demand for standards of practice as an implicit allegation of failure – or, even worse, as a charge of immorality in what they do. It is little surprise, then, that some of the large humanitarian organizations were and still are allergic to the conversation.

Competency and logics of practice

Even those humanitarian organizations like MSF that were offended by a donor-led conversation about competency knew that taken-for-granted humanitarian practices could no longer be taken for granted. In the last decade, humanitarian organizations engaged in a discussion about monitoring what they did so that they would "do no harm."[23] This criterion of "do no harm" is

---

[23] Anderson, 1999.

minimalist, yet it involved identifying the consequences of humanitarian practices, specifying chains of logic, and monitoring systems so that harmful trends could be tracked. Here, community members pushed background knowledge to the foreground, made tacit knowledge explicit, and challenged standards of practice. This, too, is not an uncommon story in communities of practice, but within the humanitarian community, the process was fraught with anxiety.

The logic of "do no harm" was deeply consequentialist and engaged practitioners conceptually in the identification and monitoring of outcomes that were closely connected to their work. Concern to do no harm began to shift the logic of humanitarian practice away from an exclusive emphasis on needs and rights to a logic of consequences.

The change in humanitarian language went beyond the inclusion of a logic of consequences in their templates of practice. Rwanda, Bosnia, Kosova, Sudan, and Darfur made clear that humanitarians could save people who were at risk, but as the conflict continued over time, these same people would find themselves at risk again. As James Orbinski famously put it, there were no humanitarian solutions to humanitarian problems.[24] Some organizations now began explicitly to move beyond their "core competencies" to try to change the structural conditions that made people vulnerable. This kind of work is also consequentialist in logic. Any attempt to change structural conditions is, of course, an inescapably and deeply political practice, an exercise of power, irrespective of the official orthodoxies of humanitarian organizations. Not surprisingly, the expansion of practice to change structures was deeply divisive.

We should not exaggerate either the timing or the scope of the broadening of practice. CARE, a humanitarian organization that began by delivering food packages during wartime, broadened its scope fifty years ago to work on reconstruction and conflict resolution. MSF acquired its distinctive identity through its commitment to "témoinage," to stand as witness for those who could not speak for themselves. New organizations reported on human rights violation in war-torn societies and provided educational programming but still considered themselves part of the humanitarian family. Others expanded the continuum from relief to development and worked to make the transition as quick and as seamless as possible. CARE became an important provider of microfinance in Africa. None of this work was without controversy. All of it required an explicit political sensibility to complex interconnections in the societies in which practitioners worked, a willingness to temper a language of needs and rights with a language of consequences, and ongoing iterative movement between principle and practice. Practice was refracting back through humanitarian principles that fitted less and less neatly with what was happening on the ground.

---

[24] Interview by the author with James Orbinski, May 5, 2009. Toronto.

The framing of the discussion of competencies and standards of practice – doing well or doing badly – and outcomes – doing good or doing harm – is itself contested. The narrowest construction looks at whether humanitarian practice achieves the purposes the humanitarian community sets for itself. Critics, from within the community as well as from outside, charged that an evaluation that was limited to the objectives humanitarians set themselves was too narrow, overly subjective and self-referential, and "insufficiently rigorous." Consequently, the current discussion focuses on the more difficult and demanding criterion of the effectiveness of the outcomes of humanitarian practices.

Within this conversation, the meaning of effective practice defined within the conceptual architecture of "outcome" is bitterly contested among humanitarians. It substitutes a logic – and an ethic – of consequence for an ethic of obligation. This is no longer co-habitation of the two logics, but the substitution of one for the other, a significant change in the terrain on which humanitarians both stand and do and a challenge to the fundamentals of humanitarian identity. Arguably, consequentialist ethics always inform decisions about practice when needs are great and resources are inadequate and scarce. Nevertheless, for most humanitarian organizations, needs and rights continue to trump the likely effectiveness of practice in the judgments that they make. The moral obligation to be present, to witness, to give voice to the powerless, for example, is not easily translatable into a language of outcomes and measurement.

How do these fairly abstract arguments translate into operations on the ground? When problems are well structured and context does not matter a great deal, the effectiveness of an outcome can be fairly, easily, and appropriately measured. We can judge the outcomes of inoculating children against polio or smallpox. We can count the number of people receiving anti-retroviral medications, as a proportion of those who need the medication, and measure proportional increases or decreases. As problems and practice become more complex, however, standards of competency and criteria of effectiveness are infused with values and the politics that shape practices.

"Doing good" how? Learning about practice

There is an uneasy fit between the practices of humanitarianism and the conversation humanitarian practitioners are having – among themselves and with donors – about competencies, standards, and accountability. The normative principles of humanitarianism create a framework and template for doing good. The taken-for-granted assumption of many humanitarians and of many who give to humanitarian causes *is* that these organizations are doing good.

Yet some of the best humanitarian organizations want to understand more about the consequences of what they do. They are interrogating their practices, moving background knowledge to the foreground, devoting attention and resources to learning and to sharing what they have learned within the community. This shift in language from competency to learning, to a deeper understanding of the unintended effects of practice in complex environments, helps to ease the conversation and to change practice. Practice is being renegotiated through what members of the community are learning.

The early first response by humanitarian organizations to the awareness of unintended consequences and harmful effects was, as we have seen, to develop voluntary codes of conduct and charters to make the rules explicit for the delivery of humanitarian assistance and to standardize competencies.[25] The standardization of competencies appears to have had some impact on community practices in the field. Nevertheless, there was consensus that these voluntary codes of conduct were a first, partial, and somewhat simplified response to a much larger problem.[26]

In this troubled and contested environment, donor organizations took the lead in creating the Active Learning Network for Accountability and Performance (ALNAP) in 1997, a learning network devoted to practice. Donors certainly wanted better information about the performance of humanitarian organizations but also better information-sharing within the humanitarian community. They wanted to encourage learning about practice to improve performance.[27]

Twenty-three humanitarian agencies are among the sixty members of the network and together they represent the leaders of the humanitarian community.[28] The network was created to provide a sector-wide forum, "owned by all and dominated by none," of donors, international institutions, and humanitarian agencies, which would address learning, accountability, and the quality

---

[25] The Code of Conduct for the International Red Cross and Red Crescent Movement and NGOs in Disaster Relief was adopted at the 26th International Conference of the Red Cross and Red Crescent, Geneva, December 3–7, 1995. The Providence Principles, a set of standardized rules for delivering relief, were followed by SPHERE, a set of minimal standards in delivery of water, sanitation, nutrition, shelter, site planning, and health. These codes of conduct were followed by the Humanitarian Charter which standardized the rules of humanitarian action.

[26] Ramalingam and Barnett, 2010. [27] Stein, 2009.

[28] The twenty-three are humanitarian NGO and NGO umbrella groups: Africa Humanitarian Action (AHA), AIDMI India, CARITAS International, CARE International, Christian Aid, Catholic Relief Services, Danish Refugee Council, GICHD, HAP International, ICVA, IRC, MSF Holland, Norwegian Refugee Council, Oxfam Great Britain, People in Aid, ProVention Consortium, RedR, Save the Children UK, Save the Children USA, SCHR, the SPHERE Project, Voice, and World Vision. These groups represent most of the largest humanitarian NGOs delivering emergency assistance as well as several consortia and groups focused on accountability.

of humanitarian practice. The network has three kinds of core activities. The first – and most important – is information exchange about best practices through biannual meetings, reports, and an annual review series. Program activities include specially commissioned research on key issues of the quality and accountability of humanitarian practice that are of interest to the whole sector. ALNAP has also developed a set of tools that enable meta-evaluation of the evaluations done of humanitarian programs and activities. It seeks to standardize categories of analysis and presentation within reports so that they are more easily compared across the sector. The network has also created an evaluation reports database (ERD) that is searchable on line. The majority of these reports are available publicly, but a minority is confidential and available to full members only through secure access. The Humanitarian Accountability Partnership International (HAP-I), an allied network, was created by a group of humanitarian agencies committed to making humanitarian practice more accountable to its beneficiaries.

At its best, ALNAP approximates "open source learning." Not unlike its counterparts who come together in distributed networks to write computer code, members agree on a set of shared problems, work together to generate information, share practices, compare results, and share what they have learned throughout the network. This kind of learning network privileges a system of continuous feedback and continuous, iterative problem-solving which builds on shared practice and experience.

Symbolic politics and transformation

Practice has always been central to the story of the humanitarian community. Practice constituted the community and helped to establish its core identity. Recently, changes in the structure of global politics and deep unease within the humanitarian community itself about its practices in a changing world came together to provoke a conversation about standards of practice, a conversation that is fraught with doubt, questioning, and tension. Background knowledge, I have argued, was foregrounded, scrutinized, and made explicit. This is not only a story of structures, or of agents, but of both. Nor is it only a story about practice. It is a story of an evoked conversation about standards of practice, led both by those outside and by leaders within the humanitarian community.

The obvious question is how much practice has changed as a consequence of this discussion of competency. What has been learned, and has it fed into practice? The evidence is very thin and mixed. A recent ALNAP review did find slow improvement across the humanitarian sector, but emphasized that a great deal remains to be done.[29] And withering criticisms continue to be leveled at humanitarian practices. Most recently, writing after the relief

---

[29] Harvey *et al.*, 2010.

operation in Haiti, *The Lancet* editorialized that humanitarian organizations continue to be:

> [H]ighly competitive with each other. Polluted by the internal power politics and the unsavory characteristics seen in many big corporations, large aid agencies can be obsessed with raising money through their own appeal efforts. Media coverage as an end in itself is too often an aim of their activities. Marketing and branding have too high a profile. Perhaps worst of all, relief efforts in the field are sometimes competitive with little collaboration between agencies, including smaller, grass-roots charities that may have better networks in affected countries and so are well placed to immediately implement emergency relief.[30]

One of the striking features of this decade-old conversation about competent practice within the humanitarian community is that the knowledge that it has produced seems often to be less important than that the conversation is taking place. Having a conversation about competent practice matters symbolically, both within the humanitarian community and to the large institutional donors that fund its activities. Constructing symbols requires effort and resources, and humanitarian agencies have spent considerable energy trying to develop systems of management, transparency, and accountability to demonstrate their competence. At times these systems do help agencies to learn about what works and to improve how they do what they do. Yet a large part of their value seems to be to convince watching audiences that the willingness of humanitarian agencies to engage in these performative practices is *prima facie* evidence that they are virtuous. Humanitarian organizations try to bridge cultures, religions, and worlds and serve others even while they serve their own. For these kinds of organizations, not only is practice performance, as Adler and Pouliot argue, but performance is necessarily a large part of practice. In that performance, claims to moral standing are foregrounded, often masking the difficult and troubling practices that continue to be reproduced and that sustain communities.

References

Anderson, Mary B., 1999. *Do No Harm: How Aid can Support Peace – Or War*. Boulder: Lynne Rienner.

Barnes, Barry, 2001. Practice as Collective Action. In *The Practice Turn in Contemporary Theory*, edited by Theodore R. Schatzki, Karin Knorr Cetina, and Eike von Savigny, 17–28. New York: Routledge.

Barnett, Michael N., 2008a. Humanitarianism: A Brief History of the Present. In *Humanitarianism in Question: Politics, Power, and Ethics*, edited by Michael N. Barnett and Thomas G. Weiss, 1–48. Ithaca: Cornell University Press.

---

[30] Cited in Ramalingam and Barnett, 2010, 1. See also Polman, 2010.

2008b. Humanitarianism as a Scholarly Vocation. In *Humanitarianism in Question: Politics, Power, and Ethics*, edited by Michael N. Barnett and Thomas G. Weiss, 235–263. Ithaca: Cornell University Press.

2011. *The Empire of Humanity: A History of Humanitarianism*. Ithaca: Cornell University Press.

Bourdieu, Pierre, 1990. *The Logic of Practice*. Stanford: Stanford University Press.

De Waal, Alexander, 1997. *Famine Crimes: Politics and the Disaster Relief Industry in Africa*. Oxford: J. Currey.

Eriksson, John R., Tor Sellström, Howard Adelman, Astri Suhrke, John Borton, Bruce Jones, and Krishna Kumar, 1996. *The International Response to Conflict and Genocide: Lessons from the Rwanda Experience*. Copenhagen: Steering Committee of the Joint Evaluation of Emergency Assistance to Rwanda.

HAP Project, 2001. *Humanitarian Accountability: Key Elements and Operational Framework*. Geneva: HAP. Available at www.hapinternational.org/pool/files/335-final-operational-framework.pdf. Accessed November 9, 2010.

Harvey, Paul, Abby Stoddard, Adele Harmer, and Glyn Taylor, 2010. *The State of the Humanitarian System: Assessing Performance and Progress. A Pilot Study*. London: ALNAP; Overseas Development Institute. Available at www.alnap.org/pool/files/alnap-sohs-final.pdf. Accessed November 9, 2010.

Hopgood, Stephen, 2008. Saying "No" to Wal-Mart? Money and Morality in Professional Humanitarianism. In *Humanitarianism in Question: Politics, Power, and Ethics*, edited by Michael N. Barnett and Thomas G. Weiss, 98–123. Ithaca: Cornell University Press.

International Red Cross and Red Crescent Movement, 1965. *Fundamental Principles*. Available at www.icrc.org/eng/resources/documents/misc/fundamental-principles-commentary-010179.htm. Accessed November 29, 2010.

Islamic Relief, n.d. *Who We Are*. Available at www.islamic-relief.com/Whoweare/Default.aspx?depID=2. Accessed November 29, 2010.

Kirmani, Nida and Ajaz Ahmed Khan, 2008. Does Faith Matter?: An Examination of Islamic Relief's Work with Refugees and Internally Displaced Persons. *Refugee Survey Quarterly* 27 (2): 41–50.

Macrae, Joanna, ed., 2002. *The New Humanitarianisms: A Review of Trends in Global Humanitarian Action*. London: Overseas Development Institute.

Orbinski, James, 1999. Nobel Lecture. Delivered in Oslo, Norway, December 10, 1999. Available at www.nobelprize.org/nobel_prizes/peace/laureates/1999/msf-lecture.html. Accessed November 1, 2010.

People in Aid, 2003. *Code of Good Practice in the Management and Support of Aid Personnel*. London: People in Aid. Available at www.peopleinaid.org/pool/files/code/code-en.pdf. Accessed November 29, 2010.

Polman, Linda, 2010. *War Games: The Story of Aid and War in Modern Times*. New York: Viking.

Ramalingam, Ben and Michael Barnett, 2010. The Humanitarian's Dilemma: Collective Action or Inaction in International Relief? Overseas Development

Institute, Background Note, August. Available at www.odi.org.uk/resources/download/4757.pdf. Accessed November 9, 2010.

Randel, Judith and Tony German, 2002. Trends in the Financing of Humanitarian Assistance. In *The New Humanitarianisms: A Review of Trends in Global Humanitarian Action*, edited by Joanna Macrae, 19–28. London: Overseas Development Institute.

Rieff, David, 2002. *A Bed for the Night: Humanitarianism in Crisis*. London: Vintage.

Rouse, Joseph, 2007. Practice Theory. In *Philosophy of Anthropology and Sociology*, edited by Stephen P. Turner and Mark W. Risjord, 639–681. Amsterdam: Elsevier.

Salih, M. A. Mohamed, 2004. Islamic NGOs in Africa: The Promise and Peril of Islamic Voluntarism. In *Islamism and its Enemies in the Horn of Africa*, edited by Alexander De Waal, 146–181. Bloomington: Indiana University Press.

Searle, John R., 1995. *The Construction of Social Reality*. New York: Free Press.

SPHERE Project, 2004. *Humanitarian Charter and Minimum Standards in Disaster Response*. Available at www.sphereproject.org/content/view/27/84/lang, english/. Accessed November 9, 2010.

Stein, Janice Gross, 2009. The Politics and Power of Networks: The Accountability of Humanitarian Organizations. In *Networked Politics: Agency, Legitimacy, and Power*, edited by Miles Kahler, 151–170. Ithaca: Cornell University Press.

2010. Asset Bubbles, Panic Selling, and Mood Swings in the Global Economy. Manuscript, University of Toronto, Toronto.

Telford, John, John Cosgrave, and Rachel Houghton, 2006. *Joint Evaluation of the International Response to the Indian Ocean Tsunami: Synthesis Report*. London: Tsunami Evaluation Coalition.

Terry, Fiona, 2002. *Condemned to Repeat? The Paradox of Humanitarian Action*. Ithaca: Cornell University Press.

Thaut, Laura, Michael N. Barnett, and Janice Gross Stein, 2011. In Defence of Virtue: Credibility, Legitimacy Dilemmas, and the Case of Islamic Relief. In *Credibility and Transnational NGOs*, edited by Peter Gourevitch, David Lake, and Janice Gross Stein. Cambridge: Cambridge University Press.

UK Charity Commission, n.d. *Register of Charities*. Available at www.charity-commission.gov.uk/ShowCharity/RegisterOfCharities/RegisterHomePage.aspx. Accessed November 29, 2010.

5 | Interactional international law and the practice of legality

JUTTA BRUNNÉE AND STEPHEN J. TOOPE*

Introduction

International law has long struggled to find a place as "real" law. For domestic lawyers, the problem is that international law has few binding enforcement mechanisms, an underdeveloped court system and no international police force. Many International Relations (IR) scholars treat international law as largely irrelevant because they focus primarily on the rational pursuit of material interests to predict behavior. Even international lawyers have found it hard to explain convincingly why states and other actors "obey" legal norms.[1] Although international lawyers have recently turned their attention to compliance,[2] in our view this work has yet to build a compelling argument as to what distinguishes the influence of law from that of other social norms. The question is still properly asked: "Are legal norms distinctive?"[3]

Our answer is an emphatic "yes." Law's distinctiveness rests in the concept and effects of legal obligation. We will show that legal obligation is best explained as resulting from the work of communities of legal practice that uphold specific criteria of legality. It is the fulfillment of these criteria, supported by a continuing practice of legality, that amount to what Adler and Pouliot call "competent performances" of the practice of international law.[4]

At first glance, our focus on legal obligation may seem obvious. But prevailing accounts of international law pay surprisingly little attention to the role of legal obligation, and how it is generated. Many international lawyers see obligation simply as the legal consequence of formal validity or of state consent,[5] or are content to take its existence in international practice for granted.[6] These accounts of international law have reinforced realist and rationalist

---

* This chapter draws from Brunnée and Toope, 2010, but focuses specifically on the role of practice in explaining international legal obligation.
[1] Koh, 1997. [2] Bradford, 2005.
[3] Finnemore, 2000. [4] Adler and Pouliot, Chapter 1 in this volume.
[5] Brownlie, 2003. [6] Brierly, 1968.

theories in IR.[7] If international law is only a formal phenomenon contingent upon state will it is at least initially plausible that states' interests and relative powers will fully determine their conduct. Even constructivist IR scholars, while sympathetic to the notion that norms can shape social interaction, have been remarkably uninterested in looking behind the formal account of law to examine how legal obligation arises and influences actors.[8]

A richer understanding of legal obligation emerges when the focus is shifted from the formal manifestations of law to the interplay between internal markers of legality and the practices that sustain legality. Drawing together insights from constructivist approaches to IR and the legal theory of Lon Fuller, we have developed a comprehensive theory of international legal obligation.[9] Constructivism helps us illuminate how norms emerge and shape social inter-action.[10] Based on a set of criteria of legality identified by Fuller,[11] we argue that legal norms exert a distinctive influence. In Fuller's terminology, norm features such as generality, promulgation, non-retroactivity, clarity, and congruence between rules and official action, inspire "fidelity" of social actors to law. However, law's influence is not explained simply by identifying social norms that meet the criteria of legality. Building on Emanuel Adler's work on "communities of practice,"[12] we suggest that understanding the obligatory effect of international law requires an explicit focus on the practices that sustain legality.[13]

For international lawyers and IR scholars, then, our "interactional" framework provides a novel perspective not only on the concept of legal obligation, but also on the role of practice in international law. Practice, of course, plays an important role in the prevalent accounts of international law. For example, one of the elements necessary for the existence of customary international law is widespread and consistent state practice in conformity with the norm in question. Or, in treaty law, the practice of treaty parties can lead to new interpretations and ultimately modifications of a treaty. However, rather than simply treating state practice as behavioral regularities, or as the day-to-day application of a pre-existing construct called "law," we posit that a distinctive practice of legality is required for law, and legal obligation, to exist and to be sustained over time.

The specificity of legal practice is rooted in the criteria of legality noted above. These criteria are crucial in demarcating "legal" from other "social" norms. They are a very particular "Background," to adopt Searle's terminology; their existence and fulfillment make law possible.[14] However, the criteria are upheld, manipulated, and challenged continuously by actors within legal communities

---

[7] Koskenniemi, 2000. [8] Bederman, 2001. [9] See Brunnée and Toope, 2000 and 2010.
[10] See Finnemore and Sikkink, 1998; Ruggie, 1998; Wendt, 1992 and 1994; and Wiener, 2007 and 2008.
[11] Fuller, 1969. [12] See Adler, 2005 and 2008.
[13] Brunnée and Toope, 2010. [14] Searle, 1995.

of practice. The "Background" is essential for legal norms to arise, but it is not immutable. If the criteria of legality are fundamentally challenged in subsequent practice, legality decays and may be destroyed. As Adler and Pouliot point out, the practice of agents can "simultaneously embody, act out and possibly reify background knowledge."[15] We add that agents can also reshape, challenge, and undermine that background knowledge. Change is the fundamental of social life, mediated through communities of practice that can uphold, question, and destroy knowledge and structures.

Our account does not dismiss as unimportant formal sources of international law like treaty and custom, the creation of courts and tribunals, or better enforcement mechanisms. But rather than treat them as decisive factors in the creation or implementation of international law, it places them in the broader context of international legal practice, so as to better appreciate the roles they play, their potential, and their limitations. Our framework reveals that each of these examples is but a step in the continuing interactions that make, maintain, remake or even unmake international law. The hard work of international law is never done – legal obligation must be built and continuously reinforced by communities of legal practice.

In this chapter, we first provide a detailed description of our interactional theory of international law, focusing especially on its relationship to the notion of foregrounding practices in IR theory, and we explain how it illuminates customary, treaty, and "soft" law-making processes. We then turn to a case study drawn from the global climate regime to illustrate the strengths of our framework in comparison to the prevailing accounts of international law, as well as its implications for the future study of law's influence by IR scholars.

The interactional law framework

Our interactional theory presents a pragmatic view of how international law is made, and maintained or destroyed. We adopt what Kratochwil calls the "generative grammar" of American pragmatism, of which Lon Fuller was the central proponent in legal theory.[16] First, legal norms are social norms and as such they are connected to social practice – they must be grounded in shared understandings, part of what Adler and Pouliot call "background knowledge."[17] Second, what distinguishes law from other types of social ordering is adherence to specific criteria of legality: generality, promulgation, non-retroactivity, clarity, non-contradiction, not asking the impossible, constancy, and congruence between rules and official action. These criteria are a specific form of Searle's "Background."[18] They make legal norms possible. When norm creation meets these criteria of legality and, third, is matched with norm application that

---

[15] Adler and Pouliot, Chapter 1 in this volume.   [16] Kratochwil, Chapter 2 in this volume.
[17] Adler and Pouliot, Chapter 1 in this volume.   [18] Searle, 1995.

also satisfies these requirements – when there exists a "practice of legality" – actors will be able to pursue their purposes and organize their interactions through law. These elements are crucial to generating distinctive legal legitimacy and a sense of commitment among those to whom law is addressed. They create legal obligation. When commitment to law is not sufficiently promoted through these interrelated processes, law is eroded or destroyed.

We now turn to a more detailed exploration of each of the elements of our interactional framework. Although we treat them sequentially here, it will become clear they are in a dynamic relationship, reinforcing or undercutting one another. Shared understandings are needed to ground legal norms. For example, one cannot enact an ambitious environmental regime such as the climate change regime without grounding it in social norms. Conversely, the existence of social norms does not make for international law – in order for legal norms to emerge, social norms must meet the requirements of legality and must be embraced by a community of practice that upholds the criteria of legality in the interpretation, application, and implementation of the norm. In other words, the criteria of legality are not just a check-list that law-makers address as they craft rules and then disregard in subsequent practice. Even when a norm meets the criteria, both the norm and its legality must be maintained in continuing practice. Without that practice, the legal norm will be undermined and eventually destroyed.

Shared understandings

Social norms can emerge only when they are rooted in an underlying set of shared understandings supporting first the need for normativity, and then any particular norms that shape behavior.[19] Shared understandings are collectively held background knowledge, including social norms and practices. But these understandings do not simply exist, or miraculously emerge as agreed among actors. They are *shared* understandings precisely because they are intersubjective – generated and maintained through social interaction.[20] On the one hand, agents generate and promote particular understandings, whether through norm entrepreneurship or through the work of epistemic communities. Shared understandings then emerge, evolve, or fade through processes of social learning.[21] On the other hand, once in existence, shared understandings become "structures" that shape how actors perceive themselves and the world, how they form interests and set priorities, and how they make arguments or evaluate others' arguments.[22]

The central point for our purposes is that shared understandings are inherently interactional, being always at once individual and social.[23] Our

[19] Brunnée and Toope, 2010, Chapter 2.   [20] Stein, Chapter 4 in this volume.
[21] Wendt, 1999.   [22] Adler and Bernstein, 2005.   [23] Finnemore and Sikkink, 2001.

interactional understanding of law is therefore connected to the "structuration" accounts of Bhaskar and Giddens: legal structures constrain social action, but they also enable action, and in turn are affected and potentially altered by the friction of social action against the parameters of the legal structure.[24] Agents and structures both matter and are connected through practice. Practice "weaves together the *discursive and material* worlds," and allows for the mutual constitution of agent and structure.[25] The underlying proposition – that norms are constituted by practice and practices are in turn shaped by norms – does not imply that there can never be relatively stable norms. It merely highlights the fact that such stability, too, is the product of, and contingent upon, practice.[26] While shared understandings, or background knowledge, may be codified or solidified in formal texts, like treaties, they are not created by the text, nor are they necessarily coextensive. Stability may be aided by explicit articulation of a norm in a text, but it is ultimately dependent upon the underlying shared understanding and a continuous practice of legality.

We believe that to be useful in grounding interactional international law, the concept of shared understandings must rest on collective processes of learning. The setting for this interactional learning is furnished by communities of practice, a notion pioneered by social learning theorists Jean Lave and Etienne Wenger, and adapted by Emanuel Adler for the purposes of a constructivist understanding of IR.[27] Wenger has explored social learning through communities of practice in great detail. He shows that learning is not simply a discrete activity through which individuals acquire knowledge, but is part and parcel of everyday life and occurs through continuing social engagement.[28] People's understandings of the world, and of themselves, are produced and reproduced through continuous interactions and negotiation of meanings.[29] Inherent in this account is the proposition that it is through their participation in social practice that actors generate and maintain collective understandings.[30]

Wenger's description of the continuous negotiation of collective meanings leads him to posit the centrality of communities of practice: "Practice resides in a community of people and the relations of mutual engagement by which they can do whatever they do."[31] This concept of "community" has no inherently positive connotations; it can equally "reproduce counterproductive patterns, injustices, prejudices, racism, sexism and abuses of all kinds."[32] Also, while the premise of mutual engagement implies social relationships among members of the community, these relationships can just as easily be conflictual or

---

[24] See Giddens, 1984; and Bhaskar, 1979. See also Adler and Pouliot, Chapter 1 in this volume (practice as both *"explanans* and *explanandum"* – both independent and dependent variable in different circumstances).

[25] Adler and Pouliot, Chapter 1 in this volume. Emphasis in the original.   [26] *Ibid.*

[27] Adler, 2005. Adler traces the concept to Lave and Wenger, 1991, but draws most extensively on Wenger, 1998.

[28] Wenger, 1998.   [29] *Ibid.*   [30] *Ibid.*   [31] *Ibid.*, 73.   [32] *Ibid.*, 132.

competitive as they can be harmonious or cooperative – members can learn to be enemies or friends.[33] Either way, through mutual engagement and sustained practice, members' identities become "interlocked" and are shaped by the practice.[34] This interlocking does not imply, however, that the members of a community of practice must have "a common goal or vision": the only requirement is that members "share collective understandings" of "what they are doing and why."[35] Hence it is possible for communities of legal practice to emerge in the absence of strongly shared substantive values, on the basis only of a shared commitment to the enterprise of legal interaction. This fact is particularly important in the international arena, where law-making takes place under conditions of deep diversity of outlooks, values, and priorities.

Since communities of practice "cut across state boundaries and mediate between states, individuals, and human agency, on the one hand, and social structures and systems, on the other,"[36] we can also appreciate knowledge or norm diffusion as something more than a unidirectional process. It involves the potential expansion of the community of practice to include a broader range of actors. New actors, be they states, international organizations, or non-state actors, draw on the background knowledge already existing within the various communities of practice to which they belong. Yet, it is only when they become actively engaged in a community of practice that its understandings come to be more widely shared (and potentially reshaped as a result of new actors' participation).[37] The same applies to the diffusion of international norms within states' domestic spheres,[38] suggesting that states' propensity to comply with international law is affected in part by the strength and outlooks of domestic communities of practice.[39] Since social recognition of norms, and their meaning, is contingent upon interaction and, therefore, context-specific, it is likely to differ according to domestic experiences with norm-use.[40]

Criteria of legality

Legal norms are rooted in shared social understandings. As we suggested, shared understandings, or background knowledge, may include merely a basic acceptance of the need for law to shape certain social interactions within a society, or may be more substantive and value-laden. However, shared understandings alone do not make law.[41] Many social norms exist that never reach a threshold of legal normativity. What distinguishes legal norms from other types of social norms is not form or pedigree, but adherence to specific "Background" criteria of legality.[42] Lon Fuller set out eight such criteria, which

[33] Wenger, 1998. [34] *Ibid.*, 75–76, 129. [35] *Ibid.*, 22. [36] Adler, 2005, 15.
[37] *Ibid.*, 16. [38] Brunnée and Toope, 2010, Chapter 3.
[39] Cortell and Davis, 2005. [40] Wiener, 2009. [41] Brunnée and Toope, 2010, Chapter 3.
[42] Searle, 1995.

apply to both individual rules and systems of rule-making. Legal norms must be general, prohibiting, requiring or permitting certain conduct. They must also be promulgated, and therefore accessible to the public, enabling citizens to know what the law requires. Law should not be retroactive, but prospective, enabling citizens to take the law into account in their decision-making. Citizens must also be able to understand what is permitted, prohibited, or required by law – the law must be clear. Law should avoid contradiction, not requiring or permitting and prohibiting at the same time. Law must be realistic and not demand the impossible. Its requirements of citizens must remain relatively constant. Finally, there should be congruence between legal norms and the actions of officials operating under the law.[43]

The "congruence thesis" is crucial in understanding Fuller's further point that law is not a unidirectional projection of power.[44] He emphasized the need for reciprocity between officials and citizens in the creation and sustenance of all law.[45] In other words, the criterion of congruence is where the need for analysis of practice becomes most apparent. As we argue elsewhere, congruence is nothing other than a continuous practice of legality that upholds the other criteria of legality.[46] Fuller illustrated that what is often assumed to be a vertical relationship (of authority and subordination) actually has strong horizontal features,[47] a proposition that makes Fuller's work particularly relevant to international law. Reciprocity, in Fuller's conception, means that law-givers must be able to expect that citizens will "accept as law and generally observe" the promulgated body of rules.[48] In order for these rules to be able to guide their actions, they must meet the requirements of legality. Therefore, conversely, citizens must be able to expect that the government will abide by and apply these rules, that the actions of officials will be congruent with posited law, and consonant with the requirements of legality.[49] More than that, law can guide self-directed human interaction only if relatively stable patterns of expectation (or shared understandings) emerge, and if law is anchored in them. Another way of thinking about these processes is that the criteria of legality are crucial in shaping the patterns of a practice of legality. If a practice consists of a "socially meaningful pattern of action,"[50] the criteria of legality provide the meaningful content of legal interaction; they allow for interpretation along similar standards.

The criteria of legality suggested by Fuller are largely uncontroversial. They are themselves a specific "Background" in a community of practice made up of legally trained actors.[51] Few lawyers or legal theorists would argue against promulgation, clarity, or predictability in rules. However, some prominent legal theorists have suggested that the criteria are purely about efficacy.[52]

---

[43] Murphy, 2005, 240–241.   [44] Postema, 1999, 265.   [45] Fuller, 1969.
[46] Brunnée and Toope, 2010, Chapter 1.   [47] Fuller, 1969.   [48] Fuller, 2001, 235.
[49] Fuller, 1969.   [50] Adler and Pouliot, Chapter 1 in this volume.   [51] Searle, 1995.
[52] See Raz, 1979, 223–226; and Hart, 1983, 350.

Rationalist IR scholars, too, are likely to argue that all that the criteria of legality do is to signal clearly how agents should behave. Reciprocity is nothing more than a series of transactions in which interests are traded for advantages. On this reading, law simply enables the efficient functioning of society by sending coherent signals that make interaction predictable. Participation in such a system is rational because an individual agent is benefited by both the possibility of exchange in material interests and predictability in relationships.[53] Indeed, reciprocity in this rationalist sense is also a common explanation given by international lawyers for the existence of legal norms. Rosalyn Higgins argued that there is no point in searching for a single source of obligation. In her view, international law functions purely on the basis of reciprocal obligations rooted in interests.[54] Other legal theorists have looked to a type of systemic reciprocity explained by the long-term interests of states in the predictability provided by law.[55] As part of a recent surge of purely rationalist explanations of international law by American scholars, Jack Goldsmith and Eric Posner have suggested that states may cooperate to uphold a rule of international law if they anticipate long-term interaction on the issue and if the payoffs from defection do not significantly outweigh those from cooperation.[56]

For us, reciprocity is deeper than the exchange flowing from the calculation of material interests. When the eight criteria of legality are met, actors will be able to reason with rules because they will share meaningful standards. One could say, following Adler and Pouliot, that the practice of the actors translates the structural knowledge of the criteria of legality; the reasons for action are structurally supplied. They allow for competent practice to be undertaken.[57] When rules guide decision-making in this fashion, law will tend to attract its own adherence. Fuller called this effect "fidelity" to law.[58] Fidelity is generated and, in our terminology obligation is felt, because adherence to the eight criteria of legality in the creation of norms and in their continuing application (a "practice of legality") produce law that is legitimate in the eyes of the persons to whom it is addressed. Legal obligation, then, is best viewed as an internalized commitment and not as an externally imposed duty matched with a sanction for non-performance. Hence the criteria of legality are not merely signals but are conditions for the existence of law. Only when the conditions of legality are met and when, as we shall suggest shortly, they are upheld by a community of practice, can we imagine agents feeling obliged to shape their behavior in the light of the promulgated rules. In brief, the criteria of legality are directed to the creation of obligation, and obligation is the "value added" of law, distinguishing

---

[53] Simmons, 2000.   [54] Higgins, 1994, 16.
[55] See Henkin, 1979; and Chayes and Chayes, 1995.   [56] Goldsmith and Posner, 2005.
[57] Adler and Pouliot, Chapter 1 in this volume.   [58] Fuller, 1958, 630.

it from social desiderata or the rationalist proposition that "obligation" is a mode of action chosen by actors to signal credible commitment.[59]

In international society, the deeper sense of reciprocity that we just described is even more salient because states are both subjects and law-makers. To the extent that international law is created without adhering to congruence with shared understandings and Fuller's criteria of legality, fidelity to law – the sense of obligation – among states will not be generated. The central insight is that the kind of reciprocity that we are speaking of is created and maintained collectively through continuing practice. Law is not a fixed artifact, a product to be consumed by actors in a system. It is a mutually constituting process of interaction involving a diversity of actors and structures in overlapping communities of legal practice. To be sure, not all members of international society must be engaged in this set of communities at all times. Interactional law can withstand individual defiance so long as a majority of actors works to uphold legality. But when explicit rules are unrelated to how states and other international actors actually behave, fidelity to law is eventually destroyed. The fact that reciprocity requires collective effort also serves to underscore why claims to legal "exceptionalism" by powerful states can be so corrosive. Some states will be actively resentful when confronted with such claims, or with other failures to meet the requirements of legality.

Continuous practice: the hard work of international law

In our description of the lifecycle of legal norms, norms emerge from shared understandings (background knowledge), but must meet the criteria of legality (a specific "Background") to qualify as law. Even then, legal norms, and the reciprocity upon which interactional law relies, require constant reinforcement through a continuing practice of legality if they are not to fall into desuetude or be actively destroyed. If the law deviates from the practices and understandings that prevail within society, it risks being unintelligible to actors – unclear or unreasonable, and impaired in its legality.[60] When the conflict between a society's shared understandings and its legal rules is too stark, legality can come under significant strain. As we have seen, reciprocity is closely connected to all eight legality requirements.

Actors' ability to rely on the law in their decision-making, and their commitment to the law, is fostered by adherence to the requirements of legality, especially congruence between official action and the law. In turn, legality is tethered to broader social practices, in part because actors, to understand law's guidance, must first of all share a basic repertoire of common reference points – "implicit rules" that are embedded in social practice.[61] It follows that interactional obligation must be practiced to maintain its influence. Because obligation

[59] Abbott *et al.*, 2000.   [60] Postema, 1999.
[61] See *ibid.*, 259, 264; and Kratochwil, 2000, 40–41.

depends in large part upon the reciprocity or mutuality of expectations among participants in a legal system – a reciprocity that is collectively built and maintained – it exists only when a society's legal practices are "congruent" with existing norms and the requirements of legality.

The idea of communities of practice rounds out the picture of the relationship between law and shared understandings. One might think of interactional law as a particular type of community of practice, nourished by broader social practices, but distinct from them. As our climate change example will illustrate, interactional law does not arise simply because a community of practice has grown around a given issue or norm. Only when this community is engaged in a practice of legality rooted in the specific "Background" criteria of legality can shared legal understandings, be they procedural or substantive, modest or ambitious, be produced, maintained, or altered. We suggest that there exist multiple, overlapping such communities of legal practice. An overarching community of practice exists that maintains basic substantive (e.g. sovereignty, sovereign equality) and procedural (e.g. rules governing treaty-making) background norms, as well as understandings concerning the requirements of legality that we listed above. Indeed, the 1969 Vienna Convention on the Law of Treaties (VCLT), a universally practiced set of rules on treaty-making and application, reflects, to a very large extent, Fuller's eight criteria of legality and insists upon their application to treaties between states.[62]

International actors draw on this background knowledge as they interact to develop more particularized sets of norms and legal practices, such as treaty regimes pertaining to specific issue areas. Our climate change example will show how the participants in an environmental treaty regime typically draw not only on general rules of treaty law but also on the procedural rules and practices of the UN system, on existing or emerging norms of international environmental law, or on experience gained with the design and implementation of other environmental agreements. This cross-referencing occurs because the norms and practices in question are background knowledge that is shared by participants in the new regime, and because states and other international actors are engaged in multiple communities of legal practice at any one time.

Another important point follows from understanding interactional law as a community of practice: it is not enough to cast socially shared understandings in legal form; they cannot simply be "posited." Positive law may be an element of interactional law, often an important element, but it is not necessarily coextensive with it. The communities of practice concept instructs that positive law is a method of "fixing" legal understandings, or creating "short-cuts" to legal substance or procedure – a function that is particularly important in large, diffuse societies. Again, the example of the climate regime serves to illustrate that positive law may help frame a particular community of practice and its

---

[62] Brunnée and Toope, 2010, Chapter 1.

legal understandings. It may also assist in meeting requirements of legality, such as promulgation, clarity, transparency, or predictability. But without sufficiently dense interactions and participation of its members, positive law will remain, or become, a dead letter. The interactional account, enriched by the concept of communities of practice, thus enables us to appreciate why, as Postema put it, "enacted, pedigree-validated, authoritative norms ('made law') represent only the surface phenomena of law."[63] We stress that our point is not merely that interaction, or continuing practice, is required to give social recognition to a formally valid legal norm.[64] This process is important, of course, to produce and maintain a shared understanding concerning the norm. But, as we have argued, only a distinctive type of interaction – a practice *of legality* – will produce law capable of generating fidelity or an internalized sense of obligation.

For a community of practice around international legal norms to emerge, it is not necessary to imagine the existence of a homogenous "international community." The interactional account reveals that the mere declaration of supposed common values articulated in formal law can be deceptive. Without a community of practice, supposed shared values will remain lofty rhetoric. Yet, communities of practice can actually have an impact without deep shared substantive values. It is not necessary to have a morally cohesive "community" before law-making is possible. In this sense, Fuller's theory differs from Habermas' concept of communicative action, where a "common lifeworld" appears to be a precondition to effective norm-building.[65] Fuller's thin conception of the rule of law is particularly useful in global society. It is congenial to diversity, but permits and encourages the gradual building up of global interaction. Fuller shows us that a community of legal practice can exist with a thin set of substantive commitments; indeed, this is the reality of international law today. That is precisely why it is so important to focus effort on the building up of a more resilient community of legal practice in international society. Our discussion of the evolution of the climate regime will illustrate that, as mutual engagement increases, it is possible even for adversaries to learn from each other; communication and interaction can transform mere behavior into the competent performances of practice, by revealing the "patterned nature of deeds."[66] Over time, with increasing interaction, communities of practice can become more interconnected and value-based, allowing for richer substantive rules.

However, the reality of power imbalances causes pervasive problems in interactions within communities of practice,[67] and therefore within international law. Many commentators, both lawyers and IR theorists, have argued that international law can never be anything more than the expression of the

---

[63] Postema, 1999, 268.   [64] Wiener, 2009, 179.   [65] Habermas, 1996, 80.
[66] Adler and Pouliot, Chapter 1 in this volume.   [67] *Ibid.*

interests of powerful states. At the very least, powerful actors will be dispro-portionately influential in shaping the content of legal regimes, both to protect and advance their interests, and to instantiate and perpetuate their power. What is more, it is argued that any "rules" that do exist in international law are really paper tigers in confronting powerful states; such states can ignore rules at will.[68] Material imbalances, including vast differences in the availability of human resources to monitor, negotiate, or protest, make a mockery of the notions of sovereign equality and consent. Power differentials are exacerbated for devel-oping countries. They operate in an international legal system that is steeped in the history of colonialism, generating continuing bitterness and a sense of disenfranchisement. Some scholars suggest that the existing rules and practices serve only to reinforce the colonial legacy, keeping developing states on the periphery, perpetuating weakness, and assisting in their continuing exploitation by the developed world.[69]

Interactional international law points to a way out of this dilemma. Interactional analysis helps to identify the ways in which the ability of powerful actors to dominate legal relationships can be constrained. Because power is "a relation ... that is both material and symbolic,"[70] power can be constrained through means other than the application of raw material capabilities. Interactional international law reveals that when power is exercised arbitrarily and without the legitimacy generated in part through upholding the criteria of legality, it will not necessarily be effective. Simply asserting control in the absence of shared understandings and a practice of legality is abusive.

By requiring a practice of legality, interactional law also provides a basis for resistance in power relationships. A weaker state within a bilateral treaty regime, for example, can insist upon practices of legality that resist the direct application of greater power; hence the impetus for schemes of third-party dispute resolution in trade treaties. But the strongest insights to be derived from interactional law apply to relations of power within institutions. Although institutions can "represent frozen configurations of privilege and bias,"[71] if the insights of interactional law are taken seriously in negotiations around institutional design and evolution, it may be possible to build a setting that will facilitate a practice of legality and the emergence of communities of practice that can lead to the deepening of social interactions. In our discussion of the climate regime we illustrate that interactional law also undercuts the ability of actors, including powerful actors such as the United States or China, to put forward self-serving normative claims. We suggest that it has this capacity because the claims have to be measured against the eight criteria of legality, and have to fit within shared understandings generated through inclusive participation of all social actors.

---

[68] Byers, 1999. [69] Gathii, 2000. [70] Adler and Pouliot, Chapter 1 in this volume.
[71] Barnett and Duvall, 2005, 52.

An interactional understanding of custom, treaty, and soft law

As we noted at the outset, for most international lawyers and most IR scholars, identifying the distinctive obligatory effect of law has not been a major pre-occupation. Even for Lon Fuller, whose legal theory has been important in our construction of interactional law, identifying the normative distinctiveness of law was not a primary concern. Given his strong pluralism, his interest in the wide variety of mechanisms of normative social ordering outside law, Fuller was never much concerned to trace out a fixed boundary between law and other forms of social normativity.[72] On this point we disagree and share one of positivism's traditional goals: to distinguish between what is legally required and what is socially desirable or acceptable. Our concern is that the way this distinction is typically drawn in contemporary legal theory and international law practice leads us down blind alleys. Legal formalism pervades the contemporary practice of international law – hence the exclusive reliance on sources of law as a means to define the existence of binding rules, the assumption that decisions of the International Court of Justice (ICJ) apply only "positive" law derived from the consent of states, and the desire to define a bright line boundary between law and non-law. We argue that great caution is required in trying to trace out the law and non-law distinction. Legal formalism is inadequate to the task.

We distinguish between "formality" and "formalism."[73] By formalism, we mean a view that treats form as the only indicator of law, and which is close to legalism as described by Judith Shklar.[74] As we noted above, formality is actually an aspect of Fuller's internal criteria of legality. Nonetheless, thinking about the creation of law in purely formal terms provides only limited guidance in analyzing how obligation is created in international society. Although formal indicators provide useful indicia of the existence of binding rules and, of course, "validity" on the terms of the system, they are not enough to identify "law" because formality alone is not strong enough to generate fidelity. What is more, formalism can actually mask the absence of any real sense of obligation. The interactional account instructs that it is crucial not to mistake the formal representation of law for successful law-making. It is continuing practice that upholds the criteria of legality, not formal products of legal structures.

Our explanation of the lifecycle of norms, rooted in the interplay amongst posited norms, shared understandings, the criteria of legality, and the practice of legality makes sense of the most important ways in which international law is created, upheld, changed, and destroyed in contemporary practice: through custom, treaty, and soft law.[75]

---

[72] Fuller, 1969, 131.   [73] Toope, 2007.   [74] Shklar, 1986.
[75] Brunnée and Toope, 2010, Chapter 1.

Interactionalism helps to explain the traditional formulation of customary law as arising from state practice plus *opinio juris*. The latter requirement has always proved to be troublesome for international lawyers, who have difficulty in explaining what is meant by a "belief that [a] practice is rendered obligatory by the existence of a rule of law requiring it."[76] How is one to understand the idea that an abstract entity like a state "believes" something? How is the belief to be proved? Typically, one must resort to extrapolation: when practice is consistent and widespread *enough* then the *opinio juris* can be presumed. But this has never been a fully satisfying explanation.

The interactional theory shows that a social norm, reflecting a shared understanding that meets the criteria of legality, is upheld through practice that is congruent with the norm. This constitutes a "practice of legality." This enriched form of practice is what would traditionally have been called *opinio juris*. Interactional law is not dependent upon practice alone, for that would undermine any distinction between social and legal norms. But neither does it require reference to an artifice – *opinio juris* – that refers to "belief" on the part of a social construct, thereby upholding the fiction of consent. Instead, we are frank that it is practice itself that grounds continuing obligation, but practice rooted in the criteria of legality. Thus, we provide a more objective, less mystical, account of how customary legal norms become binding.

Our account also addresses the temporal problem often noted in the traditional formulation of customary law. How is it that practice "counts" as relevant to the creation of a custom if the practice is not rooted in the belief that the practice is required? In other words, the "first adopters" of any practice cannot believe that they are bound, because the practice is new. How does the tipping point arise at which the practice becomes "required"? One can explain under the traditional theory how custom can be maintained or undermined, but not how it can be created. Interactional law can explain both.[77]

Why have treaties become so important to the evolution of international law? We suggest, very much in keeping with the standard account, that it is in large measure because of the desire for clarity and relative certainty of states in international society. Treaties fulfill important roles, in both creating stability and in promoting normative change. First, they can allow for the crystallization and specification of pre-existing shared understandings. Given the practical challenge of capturing and communicating shared understandings in the international setting, the treaty will often be an important step in interactional lawmaking, generating stability in law. After all, the number of actors in the international arena is so large and their opportunities for direct interaction

---

[76] North Sea Continental Shelf (*Federal Republic of Germany* v. *Denmark and Netherlands*), Judgment, I.C.J. Reports 1969, para. 77.

[77] We are indebted to Professor Beth Simmons for observations that helped us to clarify this point.

are so limited that "snap shots" of the common ground will often be needed to advance the law-making process. Treaties can be important signals of an underlying legality.

Secondly, in the process of treaty negotiation, existing understandings may be pushed or advanced modestly to allow for normative change, as long as the criteria of legality are met. Thirdly, in some cases treaty rules will be posited that are not grounded in shared understandings with the hope that the new "rule" may become a reference point around which new law may coalesce. We argue that such "rules" are not interactional law, but may become so over time if they meet the criteria of legality and become the object of a practice of legality. For example, when diplomats return to their capitals after "successfully" concluding a treaty, we argue that the hard work of international law has often just begun. We must ask if the conditions for the creation of obligation – the existence of shared understandings, and the eight criteria of legality – have been met. Is the treaty rooted in shared understandings reflecting some social consensus that the goals of the treaty are desirable? Alternatively, is it possible to use the treaty as an educative device to work towards shared understandings that can support the transformation of treaty language into real legal obligations? One must then ask whether or not the treaty meets the criteria of legality. Was it concluded through processes that allowed for the genuine participation of relevant actors? Is the language clear enough to be understood in commensurable ways by members of the treaty regime? Does the treaty contradict other international law obligations, or ask the impossible of states? Eventually, one must also confirm the existence of a practice of legality that actually comes to shape the actions of parties. If such a practice has not taken hold, then an individual state party is likely to conclude that there is no congruence between the requirements of the treaty and its application. The treaty will be ignored because it will have inspired no "fidelity."

The VCLT is itself a good example of the interactional processes that we have described. The basic treaty-making rules of the Convention were and continue to be grounded in shared understandings, or background knowledge. These understandings grew into customary law, and were then "codified" or stabilized in treaty form. Other rules pushed the boundaries of the pre-existing law, but were quickly supported by a practice of legality. For example, the rules in Article 20 (4)(b) and Article 21 (3) changed the customary law by requiring that a state could only avoid the effect of a reservation by another state by explicitly declaring that it would treat that state as a non-party.[78] This change has been widely accepted. By contrast, it remains disputed whether or not it is up to treaty parties to determine if another state's reservation is consonant with the object and purpose of the treaty. Arguably, in this respect, the Vienna Convention runs afoul of one of the legality requirements – non-contradiction.

---

[78] *Reservations to the Convention on the Prevention and Punishment of the Crime of Genocide,* Advisory Opinion, I.C.J. Reports 1951.

Article 19 of the Convention states flatly that reservations that are incompatible with object and purpose may not be lodged, whereas Article 20 leaves it to individual parties to accept reservations. Nonetheless, the Vienna Convention confirms that treaty-making is about much more than formality. As we have already noted, virtually all aspects of the Convention reflect Fuller's requirements of legality, and require that they be respected in treaty-making.

Treaty-making is a device for reaching concrete, substantive agreements. But it is also sometimes a means by which parties simply enable particular forms of the practice of legality to play out within a regime. As our climate change example will illustrate, in some environmental regimes initial "framework agreements" are deliberately focused upon the creation of decision-making rules and procedures; they are constitutive, rather than regulatory. In the light of its subsequent evolution, one can view the Vienna Convention in similar terms. Its provisions are designed to create a framework of background rules that enables more particular normative structures to be created. We suggest that it does so in large part because it gives concrete meaning, for the purposes of treaty-making, to the requirements of legality.

Finally, international lawyers regularly grapple with the phenomenon of "soft" law. Some commentators insist that the term is nonsensical or even dangerous.[79] Others would accept that soft law is a relevant category, and matters in some way, but they cannot fit its effects within formal sources doctrine.[80] We argue that "soft" norms may sometimes possess more obligatory force than norms derived from formal sources of law. Interactional international law explains why. When norms are rooted in shared understandings and adhere to the conditions of legality, they generate fidelity, an effect that is hard to attack. Although at first blush soft norms do not figure in the "causes of action" allowed in adjudicative international decision-making, such norms can figure in practical legal reasoning of courts, states, and other international actors.[81] By way of illustration, we detail below how the concept of common but differentiated responsibilities (CBDR), notwithstanding its ambiguous legal status, has been influential in shaping the evolution of the global climate regime. Soft law is an important generator of change in contemporary international law, balancing against the tendency of custom to stabilize past practices.

The global climate regime[82]

For some observers, climate change is the single most important public policy challenge of our time.[83] But describing the "problem" is not actually an easy

---

[79] See Klabbers, 1996; and Weil, 1983.   [80] Dupuy, 1991.   [81] Chinkin, 1989.

[82] In this section, we draw on the detailed analysis of the climate regime undertaken in Brunnée and Toope, 2010, Chapter 4.

[83] King, 2004.

matter. It is dizzying in its complexity, daunting in its implications, and multi-faceted in a way that eludes easy categorization. Beginning with the environ-mental dimension, global warming is a problem of unprecedented scale. It is planetary in scope and intergenerational in its implications. Even more impor-tantly, because climate change implicates virtually all production and con-sumption processes, addressing it is about nothing less than changing the way we do everything that we do, everywhere in the world. Climate change is also a classic collective action problem. It can only be solved if all states, or at least the major greenhouse gas emitters, cooperate. Individual states' material interests are directly affected by any such cooperative effort.

Climate change also raises a series of difficult questions of equity.[84] Historically, emissions of greenhouse gases have been far greater in the industrialized world. The emissions of industrialized countries still significantly exceed those of devel-oping countries, although the emissions of some large developing countries are projected to rise sharply over the next two decades. In 2006, China had surpassed the United States as the largest national emitter of greenhouse gases. Yet, Chinese *per capita* emissions remain far lower than those of the United States or the European Union.[85] The gulf between radically different perceptions of the prob-lem is not easily bridged. Many developing countries see climate politics as part of a larger pattern of historical and economic injustices and so demand that indus-trialized countries bear the primary burden of combating climate change. In turn, many industrialized countries insist on developing country participation as a matter of pragmatic problem-solving, or even economic "fairness."[86] In short, climate change implicates highly charged ideational terrain involving both histor-ical interpretation and current understandings of states' international roles.

The United Nations Framework Convention on Climate Change (UNFCCC) was adopted in 1992, and supplemented through the Kyoto Protocol in 1997. Yet, there are still no globally agreed emission reduction requirements that would meet the regime's objective of averting dangerous climate change. The existing reduction commitments under the Kyoto Protocol are far too modest to accomplish that task, and several of the Kyoto parties are unlikely to comply with even these targets. In the negotiations for a successor to the Kyoto Protocol, developed and developing countries remain deeply divided on the contours of a long-term emissions regime.

At their meeting in Copenhagen in December 2009, parties were unable to agree on the further development of the climate regime. A small group of states, including major emitters like China, India, and the United States, arrived at a political agreement on future actions, dubbed the "Copenhagen Accord." The states that negotiated the Accord had envisaged its subsequent adoption by the plenary body of the UNFCCC, which would have given the Accord the status of a non-binding decision of the parties. But given the resistance of some states,

---

[84] Gardiner, 2004.   [85] Union of Concerned Scientists, 2010.   [86] Roberts and Parks, 2007.

the plenary body merely took note of the Accord, leaving it without clear connection to the regime.[87] Hence, many observers may be inclined to take the climate regime to exemplify international law's weakness. While a set of formally binding norms exists, it is weakly enforced and, at any rate, it reaches only as far as consenting states are prepared to go. States' interests, especially those of powerful states, conventional wisdom might suggest, determine the fate of the regime.[88]

An interactional analysis provides a more nuanced picture of the successes, failures, and prospects of the climate regime. It suggests that a long-term agreement on emission reductions is unlikely to be attainable, and unlikely to have lasting obligatory force, unless it rests on a strong foundation of shared understandings, respects the requirements of legality, and is embedded in a vibrant practice of legality. As the evolution of the global climate regime attests, building up these conditions can be a long and difficult process. The experience with the regime certainly confirms our observation that formal law will often be the starting point for interactional law-making, rather than the end point. Thus, the fact the UNFCCC and the Kyoto Protocol have 194 and 192 parties,[89] respectively, provides *prima facie* evidence of wide support for and commitment to the regime. But membership by virtue of ratification is not enough in an interactional framework. Regime participants must become engaged in a community of legal practice for a sense of obligation, be it procedural or substantive, to arise.

Our assessment is that, notwithstanding deep divisions among the parties on substantive issues, a strong community of practice has evolved under the auspices of the global climate regime. This practice community encompasses state actors that participate formally in the negotiations, governmental organizations and NGOs that observe the negotiations directly and provide "on-site" input, as well as others that follow the developments through internet-based means and provide input from a distance.[90] Epistemic communities, such as the scientists engaged in the work of the Intergovernmental Panel on Climate Change (IPCC), and norm entrepreneurs, including a broad range of NGOs working for or against further climate commitments, are also part of the regime's community of practice. Indeed, within the regime's broader community of practice exist several overlapping, more specialized communities (e.g. relating to science, technical matters, policy questions, or legal matters). Through their members, these communities are connected to one another, and to broader practice communities outside of the climate regime.

The various participants in the practices of the climate regime pursue diverse and often competing objectives, including official government positions,

---

[87] Rajamani, 2010.   [88] See Downs, Danish, and Barsoom, 2000; and Setear, 2001.
[89] See UNFCCC, n.d. a and b.
[90] For a list of accredited organizations, see UNFCCC, n.d. c.

environmental causes, business or commercial priorities, scientific or educational goals, and development or global justice concerns. Still, all participants
share a repertoire of "climate expertise," encompassing the technical and legal
language of the climate regime, at least a working knowledge of the scientific
background information, and an understanding of the main negotiating and
policy issues. In other words, they share a collective understanding of the
enterprise they are engaged in: the maintenance and further development of a
global legal regime to address climate change. They may also share some
conceptions as to why the enterprise is important. But they do not necessarily
have a common outlook concerning all aspects of the problem or common
priorities in addressing it.

What, then, distinguishes the climate regime from the G8 summitry given by
Adler and Pouliot as an example for an international practice?[91] Like G8
summits, the annual meetings of the parties to the climate regime are patterned
performances. They are subject to specific standards of competence and draw
on background knowledge that is bound up in the iterated practices. We suggest
that a central difference between climate meetings and G8 meetings is that the
standards of competence against which performances in the regime are measured include legal standards. These flow not simply from the fact that states
have entered into treaties on climate change. The important point is that the
climate regime's broader community of practice is strengthened by the presence
of a resilient community of legal practice. Its members, be they state negotiators
or representatives of governmental organizations or NGOs, participate in wider
communities of international legal practice. As such they draw the
"Background" of criteria of legality into the climate regime, along with background knowledge on treaty law, on the procedural rules and practices of the
UN system, on norms of international environmental law, and on the design
and implementation of other environmental agreements.

The participants in the climate regime have been successful in cultivating
shared procedural understandings and fostering procedural legality, in terms of
both attention to the criteria of legality, and of the procedural practices within
the regime. For example, the decision-making rules of the regime, such as the
rules of procedure of the Conference of the Parties, or the rules concerning the
adoption of amendments, are a steady staple in the practice within the regime.[92]
Parties pay careful attention to these rules, ensuring that decisions of the treaty
bodies meet the relevant procedural requirements. Indeed, the impetus for the
strong resistance by some developing states to the Copenhagen Accord came
from the failure of the twenty-eight negotiating states to abide by the procedural
conventions of the regime. The high-level negotiations that produced the
Accord did not draw on the negotiating text that was before the Conference
of the Parties. The negotiations were not authorized by the plenary and it was

---

[91] Adler and Pouliot, Chapter 1 in this volume.   [92] Brunnée, 2002.

not informed of their progress. Even the conclusion of the Accord was reported by the media before the plenary of treaty parties had a chance to review it.[93] To be sure, one of the reasons why the high-level negotiations were undertaken in the first place was the slow pace of the negotiations due to the requirement of decision-making by consensus. The negotiation of the Copenhagen Accord presented a pointed challenge to the procedural practices of the regime. Yet, as the Copenhagen meetings and the subsequent developments illustrate, even coalitions of powerful states could not simply bypass, or dislodge, the procedural practices of the regime. These practices have proven to be strong. The treaty parties have resumed negotiations through the established procedural channels, working to develop a negotiating text and incorporate elements of the Copenhagen Accord.[94]

The strong procedural elements of the climate regime illustrate that interactional law can emerge without deep substantive agreement among parties. In the terms used by Sending and Neumann in chapter 9 in this volume, the regime's procedural practices provide "an infrastructure ... for interaction."[95] In adopting the treaty, the parties agreed that climate change was of concern and that it should be addressed on the basis of a legal regime. But in just about every other respect they were deeply divided. In particular, power imbalances between developing and industrialized countries, and a legacy of distrust, were – and continue to be – among the challenges that climate law-making must overcome. Upholding procedural legality is an indispensable part of this process, since parties must first develop a setting in which contentious substantive issues can be legitimately addressed, and in which all parties can participate in the development of shared understandings. The experience with the Copenhagen Accord serves to underscore this point.

We argue that the densely textured procedural practice of legality has given rise to procedural obligations and has helped generate a sense of commitment of the participants to the climate regime and accounts at least in part for its resilience. Procedural legality has also enabled participants to work towards denser substantive understandings, notably regarding the regime's core principle of CBDR. The Convention calls upon parties to protect the climate system "on the basis of equity and in accordance with their common but differentiated responsibilities and respective capabilities."[96] As we have already suggested, enshrining a principle in a treaty text does not necessarily give the norm legal effect. It must be grounded in shared understandings, meet the criteria of legality, and become embedded in a practice of legality. Although the principle has been influential in framing the deliberations among parties and the evolution of the regime over time, our assessment is that it falls short on all of these

[93] Rajamani, 2010.   [94] International Institute for Sustainable Development, 2010.
[95] Sending and Neumann, Chapter 9 in this volume.   [96] Article 3.1, UNFCCC.

requirements of interactional law and still is only a nascent legal norm at this stage.

Specifically, there is broad consensus that states have a common responsibility to address climate change, that their resulting individual responsibilities should be differentiated, and that industrialized countries should lead in climate action. Disagreements remain on whether or not historical and *per capita* emissions are appropriate criteria for differentiation, and whether or not CBDR requires industrialized states to provide financial and technical assistance to developing countries.[97] Meanwhile, it is generally accepted that capacity differentials, especially between developing and industrialized states, are relevant, and there is now growing support for differentiation among industrialized and developing countries, respectively. The latter trend is of particular interest for present purposes. The ongoing negotiations for future emissions reductions provide an interesting window on the evolving background knowledge. The submissions of states and non-governmental participants in the regime reveal a distinct shift in the understanding of the CBDR principle.[98] Developing countries had long resisted differentiation of commitments within their group. While some, notably China and India, continue to insist that differentiation is applicable only as between industrialized and developing countries, a growing number of states (industrialized and developing) now argue that capacity differentials and emissions patterns justify, or even require, differentiation among developing countries.[99]

Turning to the legality of the CBDR principle, it was "promulgated" in the UNFCCC. However, the treaty text masked significant disagreements on the meaning of the articulated proposition and, hence, lacked "clarity." The emergence of legality has been constrained by the fact that only some aspects of the CBDR principle have become shared understandings, while others remain contested. And yet, the principle is routinely invoked by regime participants and has been affirmed in the negotiating mandates for future commitments. Arguably, it is also reflected in the terms of the Copenhagen Accord, which entail commitments for both developed and developing countries, while differentiating between these two groups as well as among developing countries.[100] We conclude that the principle has been woven into the practices of the climate regime. It has given rise to patterned performances and furnishes a central standard of competence for arguments and treaty development. The salience of the principle is beyond question. The rhetorical and drafting practices in the regime indicate that any future commitment regime (generality, non-contradiction) as well as individual parties' commitments (congruence) must be consistent with the principle. To this limited extent, then, the CBDR

---

[97] Rajamani, 2003.   [98] UNFCCC, n.d. d.
[99] See submissions cited in Brunnée and Toope, 2010, Chapter 4, notes 145–154.
[100] Brunnée and Toope, 2010, Chapter 4.

principle provides a legal standard of competence. Still, while parties' practices in the regime serve to reinforce the standard in this basic sense, they have yet to refine it to a point at which it could address other legality requirements such as clarity, not asking the impossible, or constancy.[101] The example of the CBDR principle highlights the dynamic relationship between the emergence of shared understandings and legality, which is shaped by the practices of regime participants while also shaping those practices.

Our brief review of the role played by the CBDR principle in the climate regime also shows that ideas are fundamental to the evolution of legal normativity. Without the enunciation and regular invocation of the CBDR principle, we are not likely to have seen the development of the climate regime that has taken place to date. However, resistance to the principle has been significant, too, with continuing debates over whether or not the required differentiation is only between developed and developing states, or among developing states as well. For a time, some developed states, especially the United States, even challenged the fundamental concept of differentiated obligations, whereas some developing countries, notably China and India, insisted that differentiation meant that only industrialized states were required to take on emissions-related commitments.[102] These positions were based largely on self-evaluations of material interest on the part of key states. The interactional analysis of the climate regime accounts for the role of both ideas and material factors in the evolution of legal norms, showing how the two came to be intertwined in the regime's burden-sharing framework.

Conclusion

Our framework of interactional international law relies upon an understanding of the role played by communities of practice in creating, upholding, and sometimes destroying legal norms. We suggest that legal norms exert an influence that is distinct from that of other social norms, and that that influence is found in the concept of legal obligation. Legal norms must be rooted in shared understandings, or background knowledge, as the role of the CBDR principle in the climate regime illustrates. But they must also meet specific criteria of legality if the norms are to guide self-directed human action and attract adherence. Agents – states and other international actors – matter because they articulate, promote, apply, and work to shift international norms. However, it is only through their collective practice that they develop and uphold norms and their legality. In turn, practices and norms can become structures that facilitate and constrain subsequent interaction.

These interconnected propositions are inherent in the requirement that official practice be congruent with existing norms. If law is to exert its

---

[101] For a more detailed discussion, see Brunnée and Toope, 2010, Chapter 4. [102] *Ibid.*

distinctive influence, participants in a legal system must respect the "Background" criteria of legality as they make law. They must also uphold the criteria as they apply legal norms. If they do not, or if non-compliance with the existing rules becomes widespread, the norms are eroded and eventually destroyed. In short, the interactional account illustrates that legal norms, legal obligations, agents, and collective practices are inextricably linked to one another, and that the concept of communities of practice bridges the agency and structure divide that has long confounded the world of IR theory.

The elements of international legality do not necessarily arise in a specific sequence. Notably, while we suggest that social understandings must support legal norms, legality may in some circumstances assist the development of stronger normative understandings. In other words, our framework of interactional law helps to explain both normative stability and change. As our climate change example has illustrated, states may agree on the need for an international agreement, but not on a particular regulatory scheme. In such a situation, a treaty that sets out procedural rules that meet the requirements of legality, and engender a procedural practice of legality, can provide a setting that facilitates the subsequent development of more ambitious substantive requirements. Similarly, a treaty may spell out a given substantive principle, such as CBDR in the climate regime, in a manner that "papers over" disagreements on the meaning of the norm. Inclusion in the treaty alone does not endow the norm with legality. But it may provide a platform for building up the understandings concerning the norm and developing its legality and obligatory effects.

The interplay among the elements of our interactional account, and the focus on practice, helps us understand the lifecycle of norms, their emergence, diffusion and institutionalization, and potential destruction. The example of the CBDR principle confirms that legal norms cannot simply be posited, nor do they simply exist. Actors must work together to build and maintain social norms and legality. In so doing they draw on background norms and practices, promote new norms, or work to shift existing norms. Crucially, however, they cannot do so in isolation but only as part of a community of practice. Only a community of practice can build and maintain legality because legality is itself a shared understanding ("Background"). However, the concept of legality does not require shared commitment to deep values, only a thin commitment to the criteria of legality and to the need for legal norms in society. The climate change regime illustrates that it is possible to build a normative framework to shape future relations that is almost entirely procedural. A "practice of legality" and "legal obligation" does not require a widespread commitment to fundamental values or to substantive norms. Rather, the growth over time of a procedural framework that requires continuing interaction may facilitate the gradual building up of richer and deeper commitments.

The climate change regime also illustrates the interplay between ideas and material factors. The impact of the CBDR principle demonstrates how even powerful actors can find themselves enmeshed in a legal regime. So far, the United States and major developing countries have been able to resist emission reduction commitments. But neither have they been able to extricate themselves from the procedural legality of the climate regime nor avoid the normative implications of its core principle of CBDR.

Ultimately, then, law is created, maintained, or destroyed through day-to-day interactions in communities of legal practice. Legal obligation cannot be reduced to the existence of fixed rules; it is made real in the continuing practice of communities that reason with and communicate through norms. Although the stock of shared understandings may be relatively limited in international society, law-making is possible. But law-makers may have to be modest in their aspirations if a sustainable community of legal practice is to emerge. To be meaningful, international law may need to track what little common ground there is, even if that ground is confined to a shared sense that future interactions should be *legal*, rather than purely social or political, interactions. As Fuller's account instructs, the hallmark of legal interactions is reciprocity among participants, sustained by adherence to the criteria of legality.

For IR scholars, our account of legal obligation provides a novel explanation of why law "matters," and how it is in fact distinctive. We challenge IR scholars to look beyond the formal indicators of law, and to focus their analytical efforts on the markers and practices of legality. Constructivists have studied how norm entrepreneurs or epistemic communities promote particular understandings, and how norms shape the identities and conduct of international actors. We suggest that the study of communities of legal practice must be added to this research agenda if the phenomenon of legal obligation, and the role of international law in international society, is to be understood. International law is produced and maintained through specific practices that mediate between legal actors (agents) and legal norms (structures). Agreeing with Adler and Pouliot, we suggest further that there exist multiple, overlapping communities of legal practice,[103] notably a global practice community that upholds the basic legality requirements that we describe, and upon which other, more specialized, practice communities draw as they develop international law in particular issue areas. Our theory of international legal obligation also reveals how material interests and ideas interact in the creation and evolution of rules. Finally, the interplay between the elements of our account, and its focus on practices, helps us to bridge between the stabilizing and change-making functions of law, by revealing the elements of the lifecycle of legal norms, their emergence, diffusion and institutionalization, and sometimes their destruction.[104]

---

[103] Adler and Pouliot, Chapter 1 in this volume.   [104] *Ibid.*

References

Abbott, Kenneth W., Robert Keohane, Andrew Moravcsik, Anne-Marie Slaughter, and Duncan Snidal, 2000. The Concept of Legalization. *International Organization* 54 (3): 401–419.

Adler, Emanuel, 2005. *Communitarian International Relations: The Epistemic Foundations of International Relations*. New York: Routledge.

2008. The Spread of Security Communities: Communities of Practice, Self-Restraint, and NATO's Post-Cold War Evolution. *European Journal of International Relations* 14 (2): 195–230.

Adler, Emanuel and Steven Bernstein, 2005. Knowledge in Power: The Epistemic Construction of Global Governance. In *Power in Global Governance*, edited by Michael Barnett and Raymond D. Duvall, 294–318. Cambridge: Cambridge University Press.

Barnett, Michael and Raymond D. Duvall, 2005. Power in International Politics. *International Organization* 59 (1): 39–75.

Bederman, David, 2001. Constructivism, Positivism, and Empiricism in International Law. *Georgetown Law Journal* 89 (2): 469–499.

Bhaskar, Roy, 1979. *The Possibility of Naturalism: A Philosophical Critique of the Contemporary Human Sciences*. New York: Harvester Press.

Bradford, William, 2005. International Legal Compliance: Surveying the Field. *Georgetown Journal of International Law* 36 (2): 495–536.

Brierly, James L., 1968. *The Law of Nations: An Introduction to the International Law of Peace*. 6th edn. Edited by Humphrey Waldock. Oxford: Clarendon Press.

Brownlie, Ian, 2003. *Principles of Public International Law*. 6th edn. Oxford: Oxford University Press.

Brunnée, Jutta, 2002. COPing with Consent: Lawmaking under Multilateral Environmental Agreements. *Leiden Journal of International Law* 15 (1): 1–52.

Brunnée, Jutta and Stephen J. Toope, 2000. International Law and Constructivism: Elements of an Interactional Theory of International Law. *Columbia Journal of Transnational Law* 39 (1): 19–74.

2010. *Legitimacy and Legality in International Law: An Interactional Account*. Cambridge: Cambridge University Press.

Byers, Michael, 1999. *Custom, Power and the Power of Rules*. Cambridge: Cambridge University Press.

Chayes, Abram and Antonia Handler Chayes, 1995. *The New Sovereignty: Compliance with International Regulatory Agreements*. Cambridge, MA: Harvard University Press.

Chinkin, Christine, 1989. The Challenge of Soft Law: Development and Change in International Law. *International and Comparative Law Quarterly* 38 (4): 850–866.

Cortell, Andrew P. and James W. Davis, 2005. When Norms Clash: International Norms, Domestic Practices, and Japan's Internalization of the GATT/WTO. *Review of International Studies* 31 (1): 3–25.

Downs, George W., Kyle W. Danish, and Peter N. Barsoom, 2000. The Transformational Model of International Regime Design: Triumph of Hope or Experience? *Columbia Journal of Transnational Law* 38 (3): 465–514.

Dupuy, Pierre-Marie, 1991. Soft Law and the International Law of the Environment. *Michigan Journal of International Law* 12 (2): 420–435.

Finnemore, Martha, 2000. Are Legal Norms Distinctive? *New York University Journal of International Law and Politics* 32 (3): 699–705.

Finnemore, Martha and Kathryn Sikkink, 1998. International Norm Dynamics and Political Change. *International Organization* 52 (4): 887–917.

2001. Taking Stock: The Constructivist Research Program in International Relations and Comparative Politics. *Annual Review of Political Science* 4 (1): 391–416.

Fuller, Lon L., 1958. Positivism and Fidelity to Law – A Reply to Professor Hart. *Harvard Law Review* 71 (4): 630–672.

1969. *The Morality of Law*. Rev. edn. New Haven: Yale University Press.

2001 [1969]. Human Interaction and the Law. In *The Principles of Social Order: Selected Essays of Lon L. Fuller*, edited by Kenneth I. Winston. Rev. edn. Oxford: Hart.

Gardiner, Stephen M., 2004. Ethics and Global Climate Change. *Ethics* 114 (3): 555–600.

Gathii, James Thuo, 2000. Alternative and Critical: The Contribution of Research and Scholarship on Developing Countries to International Legal Theory. *Harvard International Law Journal* 41 (2): 263–275.

Giddens, Anthony, 1984. *The Constitution of Society: Outline of the Theory of Structuration*. Berkeley: University of California Press.

Goldsmith, Jack L. and Eric A. Posner, 2005. *The Limits of International Law*. Oxford: Oxford University Press.

Habermas, Jürgen, 1996. *Between Facts and Norms: Contributions to a Discourse Theory of Law and Democracy*. Translated by William Rehg. Cambridge, MA: MIT Press.

Hart, H. L. A., 1983. *Essays in Jurisprudence and Philosophy*. Oxford: Clarendon Press.

Henkin, Louis, 1979. *How Nations Behave: Law and Foreign Policy*. 2nd edn. New York: Columbia University Press.

Higgins, Rosalyn, 1994. *Problems and Process: International Law and How We Use It*. Oxford: Clarendon Press.

International Institute for Sustainable Development (IISD), 2010. Summary of the Bonn Climate Talks: August 2–6, 2010. *Earth Negotiations Bulletin* 12 (478). Available at www.iisd.ca/download/pdf/enb12478e.pdf. Accessed November 3, 2010.

King, David A., 2004. Climate Change Science: Adapt, Mitigate or Ignore? *Science* 303 (5655): 176–177.

Klabbers, Jan, 1996. The Redundancy of Soft Law. *Nordic Journal of International Law* 65 (2): 167–182.

Koh, Harold Hongju, 1997. Why Do Nations Obey International Law? *Yale Law Journal* 106 (8): 2599–2659.

Koskenniemi, Martti, 2000. Carl Schmitt, Hans Morgenthau, and the Image of Law in International Relations. In *The Role of Law in International Politics: Essays in International Relations and International Law*, edited by Michael Byers, 17–34. Oxford: Oxford University Press.

Kratochwil, Friedrich V., 2000. How do Norms Matter? In *The Role of Law in International Politics: Essays in International Relations and International Law*, edited by Michael Byers, 35–68. Oxford: Oxford University Press.

Lave, Jean and Etienne Wenger, 1991. *Situated Learning: Legitimate Peripheral Participation*. Cambridge: Cambridge University Press.

Murphy, Colleen, 2005. Lon Fuller and the Moral Value of the Rule of Law. *Law and Philosophy* 24 (3): 239–262.

Postema, Gerald J., 1999 [1994]. Implicit Law. In *Rediscovering Fuller: Essays on Implicit Law and Institutional Design*, edited by Willem J. Witteveen and Wibren van der Burg, 255–276. Amsterdam: Amsterdam University Press.

Rajamani, Lavanya, 2003. From Stockholm to Johannesburg: The Anatomy of Dissonance in the International Environmental Dialogue. *Review of European Community and International Environmental Law* 12 (1): 23–32.

2010. The Making and Unmaking of the Copenhagen Accord. *International and Comparative Law Quarterly* 59 (3): 824–843.

Raz, Joseph, 1979. *The Authority of Law: Essays on Law and Morality*. Oxford: Clarendon Press.

Roberts, J. Timmons and Bradley C. Parks, 2007. *A Climate of Injustice: Global Inequality, North–South Politics, and Climate Policy*. Cambridge, MA: MIT Press.

Ruggie, John G., 1998. What Makes the World Hang Together? Neo-Utilitarianism and the Social Constructivist Challenge. *International Organization* 52 (4): 855–885.

Searle, John R., 1995. *The Construction of Social Reality*. New York: Free Press.

Setear, John K., 2001. Learning to Live with Losing: International Environmental Law in the New Millennium. *Virginia Environmental Law Journal* 20 (1): 139–167.

Shklar, Judith, 1986. *Legalism: Law, Morals, and Political Trials*. Cambridge, MA: Harvard University Press.

Simmons, Beth A., 2000. The Legalization of International Monetary Affairs. *International Organization* 54 (3): 573–602.

Toope, Stephen J., 2007. Formality and Informality. In *Oxford Handbook on International Environmental Law*, edited by Daniel Bodansky, Jutta Brunnée, and Ellen Hey, 107–124. Oxford: Oxford University Press.

Union of Concerned Scientists, 2010. Each Country's Share of CO_2 Emissions. Available at www.ucsusa.org/global_warming/science_and_impacts/science/ each-countrys-share-of-co2.html. Accessed November 29, 2010.

United Nations Framework Convention on Climate Change, n.d. a. Status of Ratification of the Convention. Available at http://unfccc.int/essential_background/convention/status_of_ratification/items/2631.php. Accessed November 29, 2010.

n.d. b. Status of Ratification of the Kyoto Protocol. Available at http://unfccc.int/ kyoto_protocol/status_of_ratification/items/2613.php. Accessed November 29, 2010.

n.d. c. Civil Society and the Climate Change Process. Available at http://unfccc.int/ parties_and_observers/ngo/items/3667.php. Accessed November 29, 2010.

n.d. d. Submissions to the Ad Hoc Working Group on Long-Time Cooperative Action Under the Convention (AWG-LCA). Available at http://unfccc.int/ meetings/ad_hoc_working_groups/lca/items/4918.php. Accessed November 29, 2010.

Weil, Prosper, 1983. Towards Relative Normativity in International Law? *American Journal of International Law* 77 (3): 413–442.

Wendt, Alexander, 1992. Anarchy is What States Make of it: The Social Construction of Power Politics. *International Organization* 46 (2): 391–425.

1994. Collective Identity Formation and the International State. *American Political Science Review* 88 (2): 384–396.

1999. *Social Theory of International Politics.* New York: Cambridge University Press.

Wenger, Etienne, 1998. *Communities of Practice: Learning, Meaning and Identity.* New York: Cambridge University Press.

Wiener, Antje, 2007. The Dual Quality of Norms and Governance beyond the State: Sociological and Normative Approaches to "Interaction." *Critical Review of International Social and Political Philosophy* 10 (1): 47–69.

2008. *The Invisible Constitution of Politics: Contested Norms and International Encounters.* Cambridge: Cambridge University Press.

2009. Enacting Meaning-in-Use: Qualitative Research on Norms and International Relations. *Review of International Studies* 35 (1): 175–193.

PART III

The evolution of practices

6 | *The practice of deterrence*

PATRICK M. MORGAN

It is often suggested that deterrence has changed since the Cold War.[1] As to how, commonly mentioned is that how the targets think has changed in many instances – the opponent may be irrational or rational in ways hard for a would-be deterrer to appreciate. Also suggested is that the opponent's motivation is now often such that threats of grave harm will not deter, or that he has too few "assets" to hold at risk for effective deterrence.

In this chapter, I suggest that while these explanations may be correct they are too narrow and can be enriched by emphasizing that deterrence is always shaped by the political and cultural context in which it operates, as well as by the participants involved and the patterns of behavior they display, that is by practice. It is lodged within and conducted with reference to:

- The nature, dimensions, and motivations of the actors involved in the relevant conflicts
- The behavioral patterns displayed, deriving in part from participants' typical prior experiences
- The practices which go into shaping deterrence in theory and application, and how they evolve over time
- The nature of what officials and military personnel have to work with – equipment, technology, doctrine – in pursuing deterrence.

During the early Cold War, deterrence was primarily explored and explained by development of a comprehensive theoretical approach.[2] This approach initially reflected abstract analysis and only later drew on empirical studies. It was eventually refined and critiqued by examinations of the decision-making, dynamics, and outcomes in various cases of either deterrence or comparable behavior in compellence and other forms of coercive diplomacy.[3] However, as it

---

[1] Paul, Morgan, and Wirtz, 2009.
[2] See Brodie, 1946; Borden, 1946; Wohlstetter, 1959; Schelling, 1960 and 1966; Kahn, 1968; and Snyder, 1961.
[3] See George and Smoke, 1974; Huth, 1988; Huth and Russett, 1984 and 1990; Russett, 1967; Lebow, 1981 and 1989; Tetlock, McGuire, and Mitchell, 1991; and Lebow and Stein, 1994. Deterrence and compellence are conceptually distinct but so overlapping that the distinction is often not useful; "coercive diplomacy" is a broader term for these and other ways of using harm and threats of it to try to shape another actor's behavior.

is a complex social activity, understanding deterrence is enhanced by treating major sustained instances as somewhat distinctive phenomena historically, socially, and culturally – by considering deterrence as varying from case to case. Hence the conception and application of deterrence during the Cold War is necessarily not comprehensively applicable to other deterrence relationships. Practice varies, changes, evolves.

Identifying variable aspects of cases of deterrence activity applying the perspective of this volume, which foregrounds international practices, offers intriguing perspectives.[4] Deterrence was, after all, a well-established practice in international politics. At the outset of the Cold War there was a foundation on which to build both deterrence theory and operational Cold War deterrence. This foundation played a role during the emergence and initial conduct of Cold War deterrence, especially nuclear deterrence. But Cold War deterrence soon developed well beyond that, being reconfigured into a comprehensive strategy in an evolution which continued during the Cold War. Large new clusters of practices had to be rapidly developed and installed to get Cold War deterrence up and running, drawing on theoretical analyses and the experience with severe early crises. The Cold War therefore offers a distinctive, nicely bounded, case of the emergence, conduct, and retreat of a truly important version of deterrence in practice, as practice. Examinations of the period since the Cold War have already helped shed light on what was distinctive about that era's version of deterrence, and how deterrence is now undergoing significant alterations. On this basis some things can be said about:

- Prior practices that helped shape the nature of Cold War deterrence
- How a large constellation of practices in international politics, combined with innovative elements of practice that the Cold War environment and the nature of its key actors generated, gave that era's deterrence its specific character
- Unique aspects of Cold War deterrence practice in terms of:
  - Conducting international life peacefully in the *absence* of community
  - Being pursued intently and with grave purpose despite the absence of a clear way to ascertain when and how it worked, was actually necessary, and had effect
  - Being creatively adjusted – intellectually and in operation – to meet a deeply felt need for, and resulting conversion into, a community-building and community-enhancing component of system security management.
- The simultaneous marginalization in the current era of central features of Cold War deterrence alongside the persistence of many of its aspects – the lingering of practice.

---

[4] Adler and Pouliot, Chapter 1 in this volume.

Preliminary comments

Deterrence is a broad phenomenon. Our concern is its use for security purposes in international politics. That involves using threats of harm, usually to be inflicted by force, to convince others not to use force to do designated harmful things.[5] It has a physical dimension – the means to deliberately inflict harm – and a psychological dimension – the impact of the threats on the target's perceptions and decisions. A deterrence posture involves developing and maintaining military forces, and frequently involves their heightened deployment in connection with, or as a way of, issuing threats, particularly in a crisis/confrontation. It also involves using those forces when deterrence fails in hopes of thereby deterring the target or other actors in the future.

Deterrence is used to manipulate the perceptions, emotions, and cognition of other actors: not just opponents but friends and others who might be future opponents or friends. It is meant to alter or reinforce various behaviors of other actors. It is also used to convey a notion, the deterrer's or more broadly held, of what is acceptable and unacceptable behavior. It is often practiced in a highly routinized, semi-continuous fashion – called "general deterrence" – by having a standing military posture, some set of security-related commitments, and broad proclamations of readiness and determination to respond to threats to those commitments with force if necessary. It shifts into intensive use, frequently in a somewhat ad hoc fashion, when a serious threat of imminent military harm arises. At that point it may be a last resort for warding off that harm. Deterrence theory was developed in the Cold War to make this a rigorous and disciplined strategy, refining deterrence practice so as to maximize its effectiveness and therefore its utility.

"Cold War deterrence" refers to the central security relationship between the East and West, and particularly the United States and the Soviet Union, during and because of the Cold War. It included both nuclear deterrence, its most prominent element, and deterrence via threats from lower-level military capabilities. It also included practicing deterrence on behalf of numerous third parties, i.e. "extended" deterrence.

Over the history of international politics deterrence had been a relatively straightforward *tactic*, used to manage conflicts in which non-conflictual elements were weak or on the verge of being overwhelmed by conflictual ones, when a political relationship could turn violent, verged on violence, or was apt to escalate its existing level of violence. Political relationships experiencing serious conflicts were usually deficient in elements of community, something

---

[5] See Morgan, 1983 and 2003. Technically, the threatened harm could involve sanctions, an embargo, or some other step; but deterrence in international politics normally refers to a threatened use of military force. But the harm to be precluded is not always military, such as when threats have been used to try to deter a political/diplomatic action (Hungary's withdrawal from the Soviet bloc in 1956) or the *development* of nuclear weapons.

quite common in international politics. Deterrence was necessary because other possible constraints were not present or not working, but was often used also to make other influence efforts more effective. Technically, it was not for *resolving* conflicts but for containing their possible outcomes and effects, and in a crude way. It was for escalation control, and that remains its essence.

A conflict situation with deterrence being employed can evolve to where deterrence is increasingly needed or is of diminished importance. Mechanisms for changes of this sort include:

- The way that even successful deterrence does not resolve a conflict, just stabilize it, often only temporarily. This can leave one or more parties frustrated and intent on finding other ways to change that situation. Or, with the conflict stalemated, the intensity of the dispute could mellow.
- The way that deterrence threats, sometimes blatant, can incite escalatory feelings and pressures. Thus it can work against itself, leading to a desire to try something else; accumulated experience might stimulate recourse to other methods.
- The probability that *mutual* deterrence will lead over time to a degree of symmetry in the parties' deterrence efforts.
- The possibility that mutual deterrence can generate appreciation in the parties of their security interdependence.
- Possible appreciation of the need to adapt to the conflict as too well established to dispel.

Origins of Cold War deterrence

As of 1945 deterrence was a well-established practice that, as the Cold War emerged, began to be sharply elevated in importance, reconceptualized, and provided with some theoretical scaffolding. Cold War deterrence as practiced by the superpowers and their alliances involved substantial innovations almost from its inception, with major departures from past practice. Yet it is important to appreciate things about it that were not new, to better understand what was innovative and what was not.

Coming into the twentieth century, international politics was rich in established practices. One was that the participating states saw themselves as constituting a rudimentary community, one readily distinguished from other sorts of political entities.[6] Elements of this community included sovereignty, elaborate diplomatic behavior patterns, various forms of power balancing particularly through expanding military capabilities and making/unmaking alliances, the pursuit and maintenance of empire, the operation of complex war-making capabilities plus associated norms on conducting wars, and practices associated with state creation

---

[6] Bull, 2002.

and state-building, particularly on the basis of nationalism. A notable element of community was the sharp reduction in outright warfare among great powers and associated middle powers for a long period after 1815. Even so, warfare had played such a crucial role in Europe's international affairs that there was great concern about it, with many states constantly engaged in military preparations. Combined with power balancing behavior and elaborate diplomatic efforts, this provided a modicum of security management of international politics. Deterrence was a standard component of power balancing and the periodic use of war.

That security management collapsed on the way into, during, and after the First World War, resulting in an extraordinarily violent twentieth century. For future Cold War deterrence, the most important developments from the Great War period were the initial foray (the League of Nations) into making deterrence the dominant security management practice for the system, and the eventual rise of globalist ideological perspectives that ultimately drove great powers into further profound competition and an even larger war. In the decades before 1914 deterrence had been associated with alliances, arms racing, and semi-pre-emptive war fighting strategies, all conducted on an unprecedented scale. But it was accorded little recognition as a *strategy*. It was the collapse of security management into a war of terrifying proportions that first invited making deterrence the core of security management, as a *collective, community-oriented, institutionalized* practice via the League of Nations. The League was meant to bring overpowering deterrence threats to bear to prevent warfare, without the pernicious consequences of the deterrence in normal power balancing.

Initial groundwork for Cold War deterrence was laid in the First World War in reaction to, first, a drastic alteration in warfare practices and, second, certain emerging scientific and technological changes with anticipated effects on warfare, a kind of relevant "background knowledge." The former had to do with the First World War's stupendous lethality and exhausting effects that threatened to collapse national actors. The latter involved the brief city bombing from planes that seemed terrifying at the time. Analysts incorrectly concluded that the social disruptions and psychological effects from city bombing would determine the winners in future wars, and correctly expected it to be on a much larger scale with much better planes that would readily penetrate national defenses. Starting with H. G. Wells, there was also speculation that those wars would include the use of nuclear weapons. This also led to preliminary suggestions that deterrence of wars might be possible because these prospective terrible effects could be threatened to prevent actors from starting wars. Included were explicit references to deterrence by threats of *retaliation*, not just on the battlefield but against cities and societies.

Also relevant to Cold War deterrence, as an extension of the League, were practices[7] that eventually surfaced in modern arms control. The best example

---

[7] The first such efforts were the Hague Conventions in 1899 and 1906.

was stripping the defeated powers in the First World War of capacities to mount pre-emptive attacks, a forerunner of steps in the Cold War to inhibit first-strike capabilities. Another was the effort to set limits for some or all great powers on selected major weapons systems.

For real success in the League's efforts and these related endeavors a massive elevation in the level of community, particularly among the great powers, was required. This proved to be excessively ambitious. As a result, all of what the League had been designed to accomplish was obliterated in the Second World War. It arose out of the emergence within major states in and after the First World War of profound ideological differences, rooted in globalist worldviews linked to but carried well beyond standard nationalism. The revolutionary great power seeking to transform the international system – relatively rare in the history of international politics – now became almost commonplace: such governments eventually arose in the Soviet Union, Italy, Germany, Japan and, after 1945, the United States. Standard practices in power balancing, diplomacy, empire-building, nationalist state-building, and war were radically altered as a result. The Second World War was therefore a struggle for system dominance in a far broader and deeper sense than in the past, among actors seeking not just physical expansion but thorough ideological and cultural domination. In this immensely intense and destructive war, practices emerged that were central to Cold War deterrence.

It has often been suggested that the Cold War was a continuation of traditional international politics, but that was a misperception, as leading realists suggested.[8] Traditional international politics was certainly not highly ideological, operated in a highly flexible fashion in terms of participants' alignments, and normally utilized war in a limited way. It was not oriented toward vast warfare intending complete defeat and possibly total destruction of opponents. The notion of totalitarianism, which dominated Western Cold War conceptions of the enemy, and communist perceptions of the capitalist–imperialist threat as the continuation of fascism, were alien to standard international politics. Those black-and-white views derived from the Second World War shaped the political environment for the development of Cold War deterrence.

A resulting practice was to be politically operating constantly within a profound and extended conflict with enormous stakes, a conflict considered so serious that the opponent was assumed to be poised to attack should an occasion ever arise, not only in a technical sense but because the opponent was *inherently* evil and aggressive. While international politics had been born out of such a conflict (the wars of religion), and the Napoleonic era had elements of it, displays of this phenomenon in the twentieth century was one source of the Cold War.

---

[8] Scheuerman, 2009.

The Second World War also established, as a core wartime practice of great powers, targeting enemy populations indiscriminately on a huge scale. When carried over into the Cold War as one basis for deterrence-related targeting, it created a peacetime equivalent of the *total war* approach in the Second World War. As in that war, a nation-wide effort was sought in support of security as the main claimant on national resources. The resulting national effort was taken as a partial justification for treating the entire nation as a plausible military target for retaliatory attacks. This strongly conditioned how deterrence in practice developed as it was becoming the dominant Cold War strategy, and was important in shaping the concept of retaliation in early Cold War deterrence and deterrence theory.

Cold War deterrence practice was also influenced by evidence in the world wars that a major-power enemy could withstand extreme punishment. The main participants demonstrated immense staying power, so estimates on the level and kind of retaliation necessary for deterrence threats escalated accordingly. Early post-war American plans for another European war envisioned using numerous atomic bombs to help weaken Soviet industrial, especially war-related, capabilities and attack Soviet forces. Until the H-bomb, military planners and many officials assumed nuclear weapons could and would be used – they were not all that different from conventional weapons, just more efficient. Deterrence by threats of obliteration was fully understood only with the appearance of thermonuclear weapons.

A matching component was certain practices embedded via mastery of new destructive technologies in the world wars. This included conducting "standard" warfare by ever more modern means, eventually through immense firepower coordinated on a continental scale via forces sustained and operated through unprecedented levels of intelligence, communications, industrial production, and logistics. This was accompanied by eventual wartime suppression of past practices on matters like discrimination in targeting and respect for civilians.[9] Crucial here was the emergence of the capacity to inflict significant death and destruction from the air, by bombers and then missiles, combined with indiscriminate targeting – beginning with Guernica, extending through the extended bombing of cities, then the fire raids, and on to Hiroshima and Nagasaki.

Out of this came the initial conception, in deterrence theory and the first enunciated Cold War deterrence strategy, of massive retaliation along the same lines as the ultimate basis of deterrence.[10] While the superpowers eventually disavowed the strategy, they retained the capacity for it as the ultimate threat of their nuclear deterrence postures, and for a number of smaller nuclear powers it was to be the only strategy. Nuclear arsenals were constructed accordingly.

---

[9] This returned later in the Cold War (see p. 148) but with very modest impact.
[10] See Freedman, 1981; and Wenger, 1997.

Another factor contributed significantly to making deterrence so central after 1945. From Napoleon on, much consideration had been given to employing emerging technologies along with very large forces in huge initial battles intended to shatter the opponent's forces and will and achieve rapid, relatively cheap, decisive victories. With nuclear weapons shattering pre-emptive strategies became more plausible, even critical, due to states' vulnerability to an initial nuclear attack. That vulnerability made deterrence vital and *retaliation* the natural function assigned to forces to make deterrence work. This kind of thinking came somewhat naturally after 1945 and was reflected in the earliest post-war theoretical analyses about the future use of force.[11]

In the Soviet Union, and eventually China, after-effects of Second World War practices were apparent in the emphasis, well into the Cold War, on deterrence via vast land forces focused on theater/regional strategies that included using nuclear weapons. Power projection for deterrence purposes was mainly along the lines of controlling border areas and other territory that had provided invasion avenues in the past – Eastern Europe, northern Korea, northern Iran, Tibet, etc., with massive ground forces maintained, as in the past, to offset outsiders' technological superiority. Building on prior experience, deterrence was based mainly on threatening a dense defense in depth that would begin by taking the war to the enemy if possible. This was embraced long after the two governments acquired nuclear weapons, differing from the US approach to deterrence via their quite different experience in the Second World War.

We can imagine alternative paths to deterrence that might have appeared after the Second World War experience. In a more settled and safe post-war environment, cooperative steps to inhibit intense international conflicts and foster active suppression of nuclear weapons would have been a sensible reaction to the war and the new possibility of national, even human, extinction. Alternatively, those conditions could have generated reliance by major states on a recessed deterrence based on readily mobilizable but normally non-deployed nuclear forces, or on deployed but limited nuclear arsenals – a minimum-nuclear deterrence-dominated system. Either approach would have involved complex but not unacceptable adjustments. They were ignored or discarded mainly because the working conceptions behind national security policies emphasized intense political conflict involving totally vicious opponents and the danger of a shattering initial attack much as in the Second World War. Despite relying on new weapons, the response resembled the old adage about generals preparing to fight the last war.

The intensity of the Cold War, amplified by early Soviet post-war behavior, interfered with the emergence of such less ferocious approaches to deterrence. Deterrence theory would eventually be employed to moderate what did develop

[11] Brodie, 1946.

somewhat, but by then the basic features of Cold War deterrence were entrenched: very large arsenals, large peacetime military deployments on high alert, readiness to introduce nuclear weapons into combat at various levels, massive retaliation as the ultimate threat, etc.[12] Even with more great-power cooperation, not uncommon initially after system-wide wars, the depth of the underlying conflict would probably have made the cooperation unsustainable fairly quickly.

Without the carryover of various important practices from the Second World War, it is hard to see how superpower decision-makers would have come to take it as absolutely necessary to hold whole societies at risk of nearly instant obliteration in order to deter their governments, instead of treating threats of something far less catastrophic as quite *enough* to deter.

Cold War deterrence

The decade after the start of the Korean War illustrates how rapidly a complex set of practices in international politics can be put in place when the felt need demands it. Examples include NATO and the Warsaw Pact as alliances with extraordinary peacetime levels of cooperation/integration under centralized superpower command, high concentrations of forces on relatively high alert levels along many areas[13] of the East–West divide in Europe, huge strategic nuclear forces poised to go on high alert, and elaborate early warning systems, all up and running within the decade. A highly innovative new practice was systematic exploration of deterrence in the United States by organized theoretical efforts reflecting perspectives quite detached from standard military practices on strategy and operations, with the results providing major inputs on shaping deterrence practices. Similar though less extensive and often less influential clusters of analysts were created by the other nuclear powers, with some interaction among all of them.

When deterrence theory emerged, primarily in the United States, it did so via application of a broadly rational decision approach including game theory. This was an offshoot of an intellectual framework utilized in the Second World War, refined and extended after the war, which employed systems analysis. Now it was used to help manage American national security affairs in general, and as an extension of a larger philosophical and ideological approach to competing with communism and the Soviet Union. Developed primarily at RAND, it was consciously in opposition to traditional philosophical, professional (military, bureaucratic), organizational, and political modes of analysis.[14] Deterrence theory was therefore a major shift in thinking, and it helped push the US strategic affairs community into an innovative approach to deterrence.

---

[12] See Wenger, 1997; Kaplan, 1983; and Freedman, 1981.
[13] Similar arrangements were set up in and for South Korea.   [14] Amadae, 2003.

Development of deterrence theory paralleled, and was driven by, the emergence of serious issues and difficulties in practicing deterrence in the 1950s and early 1960s. In Washington and London, and presumably in Moscow, officials wrestled with concerns about credibility, stability, the security dilemma, preemptive attack possibilities, and extended deterrence just like deterrence theorists. Some permanent officials came to have considerable familiarity with basic concepts in deterrence theory and their implications.[15] The resulting interplay between practice and theory was facilitated by direct interactions between government officials and military officers with analysts in think tanks, academic institutions, and consulting outfits. Deterrence analysts either worked in the government or contributed important analyses and recommendations on major security issues and particularly deterrence. Development of this huge new cluster of practices was facilitated by extensive wartime experience in government/military cooperation with civilian sector organizations and the creation of special civilian organizations to serve as contract intellectual resources for research.

Deterrence theory constructed analyses on the basis of models of rational decision for depicting national actors in contentious and dangerous international conflicts, extending the assumption of rationality beyond officials to national actors.[16] There was no necessity to construct the theory in this fashion. Occasionally, early notions of deterrence assessed what would be rational for dealing with somewhat irrational opponents, but this was not the main road taken. Thus deterrence in theory, and somewhat in practice, emerged looking like it did in part because of the impact of the particular corner of American intellectual life, especially in the social sciences, which took up the subject.

Accumulating practice

Preparations for deterrence and possible wars among the major powers initially looked much like plans for the Second World War or the fighting it had eventually involved: huge nuclear and conventional forces primed for almost instant use, ready to inflict death and destruction relatively indiscriminately, against the totally despicable enemy, most readily from the air.[17] (The term "Cold War" was wonderfully apt.) Practicing deterrence in peacetime was associated with domestic endeavors normal in wars but new to peacetime: isolating the enemy and cutting oneself off from him – communication, trade, and other exchanges sharply restricted, heightened fears of ideological and espionage penetration (the equivalent of wartime sabotage), constant alert for those who were soft, weak, or secret enemy sympathizers – all part of building (it was hoped) seamless national unity. This was another way in

[15] Wenger, 1997.   [16] See Morgan, 1983 and 2003.   [17] Rosenberg, 1983.

which "background knowledge"[18] shared by practitioners played an important role in notable practices.

Like a true war, Cold War deterrence had an immense physical presence and impact – actual and potential.[19] Among the many material things or artifacts[20] that were involved in deterrence practices were the major powers' sprawling military installations, the incessant presence or movement of highly complex weapons, as well as the huge military research and development institutions. The environmental impact was substantial, and is much more evident now in the extensive cleanup problems on once off-limits bases, nuclear weapons facilities, and even cities (some still off limits in Russia) with long histories of downwind and downstream (or groundwater) pollution. As for the potential physical impact, resources for conducting deterrence constituted a threat of comprehensive devastation to the environment in a war, from either something like "nuclear winter" or the vast devastation anticipated in a non-nuclear Third World War. Traces and effects of pursuing Cold War deterrence showed up in space, the oceans, deep underground, and in many layers of the participants' political, economic, and social systems.

The ideological conflict made the international situation highly uneasy and potentially very unstable. The conflict repeatedly incited frustration with the status quo and resentment toward the opponent on each side. And the threats associated with deterrence were inherently aggravating and thus another source of frustration and resentment. There were constant problems associated with the natural competitive progress of the relevant technologies, provoking fear or ambition on one side or the other. In effect, Cold War deterrence, especially nuclear deterrence, displayed numerous facets of a security dilemma. It therefore seems likely that, once it had begun to emerge, the way Cold War deterrence developed was fairly path dependent, largely unavoidable.

It was soon clear that the intense conflict was extremely difficult to maintain in a stable peacetime mode; it was too inclined toward deteriorating into war. In the early decades crises repeatedly arose that carried considerable potential for escalating into war, while others culminated in limited fighting that intensified East–West political conflict, aroused considerable frustration, and also posed serious threats of escalation. Within this environment early post-war thinking about the nuclear age had begun to grasp basic elements of what became deterrence in theory and practice.[21]

But development and elaboration of the theory and strategy was really powered by "instability" tendencies (the high possibility of major war, even a

---

[18] Adler and Pouliot, Chapter 1 in this volume.
[19] See Schwartz, 1998; Cochran, Arkin, and Hoenig, 1989; Cochran, Arkin, Norris, and Sands, 1989; Norris, Burrows, and Fieldhouse, 1994; and Polmar and Norris, 2009.
[20] Adler and Pouliot, Chapter 1 in this volume.
[21] See Brodie, 1946; Borden, 1946; Viner, 1946; Blackett, 1948; and Freedman, 1981.

nuclear war)[22] inherent in the intense conflict and, it began to be evident, in the ways the conflict was being handled. Deterrence theory was initially devised primarily to improve crisis management and prevention of crisis escalation. But it only vaguely resembled the practice of crisis management descending from the Concert of Europe in the nineteenth century through the great-power crises leading up to the First World War and similar crises prior to the Second World War. The intensity of the Cold War, combined with nuclear weapons, provided the impetus for elevating deterrence as a practice into an elaborate strategy and generating an elaborate theory to go with it. The likelihood of war seemed so high, the stakes so vast, and the level of destruction that could result so apocalyptic, that deterrence for preventing it was installed as the cornerstone of the superpowers' national security policies. It was also to be woven over time into the security structure of the global system, and into the comparable structures of several regional systems not just through direct East–West/US–Soviet competition and occasional confrontation but through many aspects of extended deterrence.

Intense efforts to develop a theory were particularly driven by the practical experience accumulated in, and the evident necessity of, coping with a recurring "stability problem," thereby reflecting a heightened sensitivity to that problem not just in the Cold War but especially in nuclear deterrence itself.[23] The driving concern was that deterrence, in practice, might fail, that war would break out despite it. The stability problem became the core concern in theory and practice, and it persisted throughout the Cold War. (It was one reason theoretical analyses often started by positing an intense crisis, with deterrence being employed to manage it and prevent its escalation.)

Efforts to cope with it were behind the development of a cluster of practices central to Cold War deterrence. There were several variations of the stability problem, some which emerged from theoretical analyses and others reflecting adaptations to accumulated experience. The first version to attract serious attention was fear of the step-level effect on international politics and warfare that using nuclear weapons could have. Approaching the Hiroshima attack participants in developing the atom bomb realized that using one would invite others to imitate the Manhattan Project, setting off arms racing and possibly nuclear surprise attacks thereafter.[24] In the context of the Second World War, the central argument within this community of the scientists, military officers, and civilian officials involved was less over the morality of using nuclear

---

[22] "Stability" here refers to deterrence successfully preventing wars from occurring, or from seriously escalating once they start. The underlying conception is of deterrence as the ultimate escalation control system.

[23] Morgan, 2003. Here theory was more advanced than practice – decision-makers were slow to fully embrace the view that a successful nuclear war was not very feasible, as were adherents of a subordinate version of deterrence theory discussed on pp. 154–156.

[24] See Sherwin, 1975; Kaplan, 1983; and Rhodes, 1986.

weapons (the war had accustomed leaders and others to inflicting mass indiscriminate devastation) than over the specter of future nuclear arms races. The debate was, in itself, the first serious arms control effort in the nuclear age.

In line with the first conception of the stability problem, and as an effort to keep that version from being fully realized, the second version emphasized preventing nuclear proliferation. This was the basis for initiating the broad policy, developed out of similar, lower-level, American efforts during the war, to seize control of available and future supplies of nuclear materials and to restrict the spread of the knowledge and technology needed for creating nuclear weapons. One result was the Baruch Plan for multilaterally halting, then undoing, the development and existence of nuclear weapons by preventing nuclear proliferation and rolling back the first (US) nuclear arsenal. This initiated what eventually became a major line of arms control efforts, and non-proliferation is a core element in American national security efforts to this day. Here practice preceded theory by about a decade – modern arms control thinking as an extension of deterrence theory, with preventing proliferation a major concern, would not blossom until the late 1950s.

Once nuclear weapons had spread (1949), arguments about using them returned in another version of the stability problem. During the Korean War proposals to use nuclear weapons were rejected by President Truman, with strong support from the British.[25] Not using nuclear weapons was seen as a way to contain nuclear proliferation and avoid escalating the war. Deterrence stability was pursued through what became the practice of not using nuclear weapons, even if that meant not winning a war. The practice has existed ever since with rising resonance, leading eventually to more elaborate justification for it in deterrence theory followed by speculation about and then theoretical explanations for the "nuclear taboo" or the "tradition of non-use."[26] Here as well, practice preceded theory, and the later interaction of practice and theoretical analysis contributed to making non-use an ever-more prominent and profound feature of nuclear deterrence. In fact, while some analyses of deterrence, and military reactions to nuclear weapons, assumed they could readily be used, the statesmen involved were, from their unique experience, perspectives, and responsibilities, very reluctant to depart from non-use.

The fourth version of the stability problem, emerging on the heels of the earlier ones, was an appreciation of the stability–instability paradox. Considerable past experience with alliances had made statesmen aware of how an alliance could incite some beneficiaries to behave, in the view of their protectors, irresponsibly.[27] Now a new aspect of this was emphasized. States in a mutual nuclear deterrence relationship that seemed stable, or their clients, might feel free to initiate, pursue, or escalate conflicts below the nuclear level,

---

[25] Strueck, 1995.   [26] See Paul, 2009; and Tannenwald, 2007.
[27] This is now labeled the "moral hazard problem." Crawford, 2003.

confident that mutual nuclear deterrence barred any disastrous escalation. Stable nuclear deterrence could thereby stimulate deterrence failures at lower levels.[28] This was one reason for suggestions by the early 1960s that mutual nuclear deterrence, or unilateral nuclear deterrence where the deterrer was reluctant to use nuclear weapons first, must be supplemented by maintaining large conventional forces in a high state of readiness, probably deployed right where attacks could be expected.[29] Otherwise, after an attack pressure to escalate to the nuclear level might be too great to resist.

A fifth version of the "stability problem," the one that gave rise to the term, had analogs in earlier eras but now seemed uniquely relevant. This was concern that nuclear-armed states in a confrontation might be so vulnerable to initial nuclear attacks on their retaliatory capabilities that each would have an enormous incentive to attack first. A mutual deterrence arrangement of this sort would therefore tend to provoke, not prevent, a war, precisely in situations where it was supposed to stave one off.[30]

Reflecting this version, the theoretical assessment of mutual superpower deterrence or mutual deterrence involving other nuclear powers called for, at a minimum, achieving and sustaining stability on the basis of actors maintaining the capacity to do unacceptable damage to any opponent even after the opponent had delivered his most damaging attack.[31] Unacceptable damage was described as either destruction of the attacker's society, which nuclear weapons made quite possible, or doing far more damage to that nation in other ways than an attack would be worth. Deterrence stability could be achieved in several ways:

- threatening unacceptable damage via effectively *defending* against enemy forces
- threatening to escalate to huge strategic-level destruction after an attack
- not being able to guarantee that such escalation would not occur after an attack.

A crucial contribution to stability, noted above, would be not allowing the emergence of a situation in which one or both parties had a pre-emptive attack capability. That would reinforce stability even in extreme crises by canceling, for any participant, any incentive for a war, or for escalating a war, and restraining any incentive to seek to unilaterally evade mutual deterrence by developing a first-strike capability.[32] This prescription for how to practice Cold War deterrence was devised mainly by analysis.

---

[28] Snyder, 1961.   [29] Wenger, 1997.
[30] See Wohlstetter, 1959; Freedman, 1981; and Morgan, 2003.
[31] This is technically referred to as a "second-strike capability."
[32] A "first-strike" capability is the ability to attack first so effectively that the opponent then lacks the military resources for an effective retaliation.

A cluster of practices emerged, at least in part, from this analysis. Some were focused on making a devastating retaliation impossible to prevent, including steady expansion of nuclear arsenals and pursuit of variations in delivery systems and their deployments, as discussed below. There were efforts to protect retaliatory capabilities from pre-emptive attack by defenses, hiding, and hardening. Elaborate protections for command and control systems, plus redundancies in those systems, were designed as well, along with provisions for shifting command and control responsibilities during attacks or replacing control arrangements destroyed by an attack with semi-automatic substitutes.[33] Gigantic early-warning systems were constructed, which reduced vulnerability to pre-emption when combined with putting a large portion of a great power's deterrence forces, for decades, on a hair trigger – for use on a moment's notice. In short, the stability problem contributed greatly to converting the concept of deterrence into accumulating vast piles of weapons and installing complicated networks of related activities.

Thus theory and analysis often preceded and directed the practices developed. Superpower military forces were slow to appreciate the vulnerabilities at the heart of the stability problem, typically assuming instead, for example, that technical or political warning of a possible attack would lead to appropriate alerts in advance. Theorists and other analysts led the way in forcing adjustments in practice, often by pointing to specific instances of the danger.[34]

Ultimately, intellectual appreciation of the many facets of the stability problem led the superpowers and others to seek agreements to mitigate and contain it, and to obtain other benefits such as containing the cost of deterrence postures.[35] This was a startling achievement in that the Cold War opponents remained deeply hostile and suspicious. The suspicion continued in part because mutual deterrence in practice had built-in tensions (discussed below) between accumulating more weapons for various purposes and pursuing arms limitations. In the same way there was tension between acting tough so as to keep deterrence working and the appeal of negotiations and détente to seek reductions in conflict that could help make deterrence more stable.

Conflicting views on these matters appeared within the two blocs as well, the Europeans typically more enthusiastic about détente efforts than the Americans, while the Chinese frequently charged the Soviets with being too soft on the imperialists. This made both mutual and extended deterrence more complicated, and provoked some alterations in deterrence practices over time. So did the impact of technological developments that repeatedly opened prospects of new advantages and vulnerabilities for one side or the other, in particular because their rates of technological advancement were uneven. Thus using deterrence to stabilize the Cold War was simultaneously accompanied by fears on each side that the opponent was making dangerous military

---

[33] Blair, 1985.   [34] Wohlstetter, 1959.   [35] Morgan, 2003.

improvements, spurring strong efforts to match or exceed those threats. This repeatedly made the mutual deterrence relationship appear fluid and unstable.

On the other hand, that relationship gradually evolved over time in an offsetting direction that was potentially transformative. There was a gradual rise in similarity in the superpowers' behavior on deterrence, easing one source of uneasiness. Their strategic postures came to be more alike. They became more aware of their interdependence in terms of security, and the implications of that. They also became more resigned to the political conflict as basically immovable, and adapted accordingly.

What often crippled responses to the reciprocal fear of surprise attack as posing a stability problem was a competing practice, linked to a different understanding of deterrence, simultaneously at work. It involved an alternative reaction to the stability problem, focused on selectively limiting the consequences of a deterrence failure. From early in the Cold War, first in the United States and later in the Soviet Union, the two military forces were designed and operated in ways designed to give them as close to a first-strike capability as possible.[36] This included acquiring nuclear weapons and delivery systems on a scale vastly greater than needed to inflict unacceptable damage, with the weapons mainly aimed at the other side's weapons, command and communications systems, etc. It even included efforts to put the missile-carrying submarines, the best second-strike forces, at risk of destruction while at sea by elaborately tracking the submarines (the US approach, with the Soviets doing their best to imitate it)[37] or stealing the codes used in communication with them (which the Soviets did). It meant subscribing to the initial agreements limiting ballistic missiles only when each was about to introduce MIRVs[38] to massively expand the number of warheads on each missile, and pursuing missile defense not just to defend against an initial attack but to thwart the opponent's retaliation after being severely attacked. It meant maintaining huge conventional forces for fighting and winning lesser wars with plans for extensive use of tactical nuclear weapons, including pre-emptive strikes, in those wars. It meant subscribing to arms control agreements setting limits on strategic weapons so high that major increases in the weapons could be made before reaching them.

---

[36] See Wenger, 1997; Ball, 1974; Rosenberg, 1986; Nolan, 1999; Kaplan, 1983; McDonough, 2006; Jones, 2008; and Bluth, 2008. With the exception of Israel which sought both nuclear and conventional first-strike capabilities, other nuclear powers avoided such efforts on the grounds that achieving a first-strike capability against the opponent of greatest concern was financially and technologically infeasible.

[37] After US tracking forced Soviet missile submarines to stay in Soviet waters under cover of surface fleets, the United States planned to sneak into those waters to attack them.

[38] Multiple Independently Targeted Re-entry Vehicles, i.e. warheads (for carrying nuclear weapons).

The Soviets put considerable effort into conventional military capabilities *vis-à-vis* NATO and China with extensive pre-emptive possibilities, the goal being to win very rapidly and hopefully preclude any full American conventional military response while nuclear deterrence precluded a nuclear response. (Even though they had no great confidence that this was how a major war in Europe would actually go.)

These were attempts to gain security via achieving *unilateral* survival and victory. Military practice called for limiting the harm the enemy could do if deterrence failed and warfare ensued. The best way to do this was obviously to defeat the opponent. Thus, instead of having fear of total devastation lead to a stable and modest level of nuclear weapons and, at lower levels, modest forces due to fears of escalation in any war, Cold War deterrence in practice brought consistent arms build-ups or enhancements at nearly all levels. It eventually became clear that this was not due just to reciprocal reactions by each to the other's arms adjustments – an arms race. Often it was due to each implementing an internally generated arms program seeking *unilateral* safety, with modest regard to what the other was doing and to the stability of mutual deterrence. What the other side was doing was frequently cited mainly as a useful justification.

This was presented as contributing to deterrence. The simplest version was that the ability to survive and win a war was the best way to prevent anyone else from starting it. Another version was an official US strategy of not deliberately aiming at Soviet population centers (to limit the awful effects of a nuclear war) but rather at Soviet weapons but only to an extent short of a first-strike capability. (This facilitated the armed forces' ability to define the required nuclear weapons in terms of the opponent's weapons they wanted to target and on a scale more suitable to a pre-emptive strike.)

Designing to win made considerable sense at the conventional level, but no sense when each side pursued a war-winning nuclear capability since that incited fear that deterrence would fail: the other side might gain a sudden technological edge that gave it a first-strike capability, or a crisis might lead either or both sides to attack first to maximize damage limitation. This was reinforced by how each superpower readily suspected the other of seeking just such advantages. There were recurring fears of technological breakthroughs on nuclear weapons, or in accumulating conventional forces that could steamroll to victory, or in deploying forces in highly offensive configurations for major breakthroughs at the outset of a war, etc. Such enemy-controlled war-winning configurations and strategies, or fears about them, generated expensive countermeasures alongside each superpower's search for its own versions.

Thus at the strategic level the desire to effectively target the opponent's forces for a pre-emptive attack invited the situation deterrence theory stressed was the most dangerous – a strong mutual incentive in a crisis to attack first. The practice of deterrence was generating the worst form of the stability problem. In the United States, this occurred even before theorists had fully grasped the problem and how to deal with it. As one student of the period puts it: "the work of strategic theorists . . . who engaged in critical and speculative inquiry into the possibilities and dangers of the nuclear era . . . was important in shaping public perceptions, and occasionally influencing the thinking of high policymakers or strategic planners . . . [but] had little relevance in the 1945–1960 period to the pragmatic concerns of operational planners."[39] And practice never really yielded on this point for the remainder of the Cold War.

Why? One factor was the influence of the two military establishments. This was hardly surprising given the priority national security had and the crucial expertise the armed forces offered about both the threat – current and prospective – from the other side and how best to offset it. Military perspectives counted heavily in debates on security policies in part because they were bound to be cited in political struggles or political campaigns designed to damage the career prospects of high officials.

Another factor was the modern practice of civilian control on overall national security policy but not over the armed forces' sphere of professional competence. The planning and conduct of war was held to be too important to be dictated by civilians. When civilian interference was nonetheless periodically attempted during the Cold War on military preparations pertaining to deterrence it was vigorously resisted, usually successfully. Civilian leaders had limited control over the civilian and military bureaucracies generating nuclear weapons and forces. Military requests drove the "requirements" for nuclear (and conventional) weapons and forces, and early on those requirements outran the production capabilities and provoked major expansions in them. Later, when production rose sharply the services found uses for the weapons turned out – production drove deployments.[40] The armed forces dominated targeting, strongly resisting efforts by civilians to control it. Specific targeting plans were tightly held, with access denied to all but the very highest officials – who typically did not attempt to seriously understand their implications.

Military practice understandably dictated crippling opponents' military capabilities as soon and completely as possible once a war seemed likely or had begun. This had been of rising appeal for over a century in response to the growing potential destructiveness of warfare, and numerous approaches to achieving it were developed. With the coming of air power and a corresponding air power theory, attention shifted to ways to deliver pre-emptive or other decisive attacks by air. Putting nuclear weapons in bombers and especially on

---

[39] Rosenberg, 1986, 37.

[40] Wenger, 1997. This seems to have been true in the Soviet Union as well. Once fully geared up, Soviet production capabilities churned out an enormous number of nuclear weapons, with requests from the armed forces having driven the build-up and the armed forces then struggling to figure what to do with all of them. Figures on the costs of the armed forces, particularly in nuclear weapons matters, were very tightly held. Hoffman, 2009.

ballistic missiles made pre-emption highly feasible technologically – prior to or supplementing battlefield combat. While deterrence theory cited the stabilizing effects for mutual deterrence of vulnerabilities to retaliation, military leaders naturally sought a counterforce strategy to escape that vulnerability, in keeping with their fundamental mission of safeguarding the nation.

Was the stability problem ever successfully confronted? Or was the theory incorrect in stressing the problem because it turned out not to matter? The best answer now appears to be as follows. Theoretical work on arms control, and the impetus to pursue it in the superpowers, came to implant standard practices in the conduct of the overall superpower *relationship*. Arms control thinking induced a string of agreements resulting from extensive contacts, negotiations, and exchanges of information on strategic arsenals. These efforts moderated the design and deployment of strategic nuclear forces to only a modest extent, but contributed greatly to some relaxation in the US–Soviet/East–West relationship. One result was that it became easier, after the frightening Cuban Missile Crisis, for the two sides to *avoid getting into such confrontations*. The most serious theoretical concern was a major confrontation with the two parties poised to strike first. Preventing this by trying to alter the deployment patterns and attack plans did not work – the deployments and plans were too deeply rooted in military practice reflecting military responsibilities. The better solution was, instead, to moderate the *conduct of the political conflict* so another Cuban Missile Crisis never occurred. The most harmful consequences were avoided because the political context was altered.

As a result, US revival of the intensity in the Cold War in the 1980s was quite a shock. US allies generally disapproved. One Soviet response was a profound suspicion at the highest level that the United States was actually planning a nuclear attack.[41] Another was a tough initial response politically to the Reagan military build-up. Fortunately, a later response was Gorbachev's denigration of reliance so heavily on mutual, especially nuclear, deterrence and his effort to escalate engagement and cooperation. This fundamentally changed the political context within which Cold War deterrence as an elaborate theory and strategy had flourished.

There is evidence that Gorbachev and his entourage were influenced by Western critiques of the nuclear arms situation and the Cold War, particularly in coming to understand how Soviet behavior often helped provoke dangerous Western policies. This helped them to design steps that eventually persuaded Western officials that Gorbachev was serious about taming the Cold War.[42] Gorbachev particularly emphasized that in the nuclear age security was necessarily interdependent, expanding on a fundamental principle of modern deterrence theory.

---

[41] Hoffman, 2009.   [42] Stein, 1995.

This interplay between one intellectual understanding of mutual deterrence and the innovations introduced eventually into the politics of the Cold War had already led to the US–Soviet, and East–West, deterrence relationship accumulating numerous elements of a *cooperative community*. This included the appreciation of various shared objectives, some agreed-on constraints on the parties' behavior, overlapping perspectives on various issues, enlarged transparency about superpower (and some other) deterrence forces and policies, and rising exchanges of sensitive military information for arms control purposes. Deterrence had come to be a joint enterprise between the antagonists.

A superpower preoccupation emerged with curbing strategic defenses, limiting nuclear proliferation, improving crisis management, enhancing their formal and informal communications, controlling accidents, improved control over unauthorized access to and use of nuclear weapons that could undermine deterrence stability, even planning to prevent irrational leaders or other people with access to nuclear weapons from being able to use them without authorization.[43] It was not just that deterrence led to a preoccupation with stability that led to arms control. Deterrence itself, in its fundamental objective, was a version of arms control. It was primarily for stabilizing conflicts at a point short of outright warfare, just as the activities actually labeled "arms control" were mainly about stabilizing mutual deterrence.

Focusing just on deterrence in theory or alternatively in practice cannot do justice to what took place. As noted above, disturbing anomalies and dilemmas associated with practicing deterrence stimulated intellectual appreciation of the underlying dynamics at work that led, in turn, to adjustments in practice, often after strenuous debate inside the superpowers and other nuclear powers or among them. The efforts which came to fruition primarily in the late 1950s and early 1960s to develop deterrence/arms control theory[44] were directly informed by experience accumulated in conducting the Cold War to that point, and then helped in shaping national security policies thereafter. The effect was to adjust policies and practices to evade some rigidities in Cold War behavior, leading to refinements of deterrence in practice *at the political level* embodied in numerous cooperative endeavors jointly or independently installed.

Clearly the intellectual, political, and administrative practices that constituted mutual deterrence accumulated many characteristics of cooperation so that mutual deterrence became a crude form of community for maintaining a degree of regional and global security management. Mutual deterrence became a regime. Special status was accorded the key major states and important elements of the regime encompassed many other states through extended deterrence or arrangements like the non-proliferation treaty. Practice included accumulated mutual understandings, some typically observed rules of conduct (for instance, US and Soviet forces never openly attacked each other), and

[43] George, Farley, and Dallin, 1988.   [44] Schelling and Halperin, 1961.

self-restraint in upholding them. Mutual deterrence helped create, and was in turn adjusted by, this limited security community that included friends and some enemies.

Two other important points should be mentioned. First, the rudimentary community only partly contained other dangerous tendencies. Superpower nuclear arsenals, particularly the strategic arsenals, continued growing or being refined for the rest of the Cold War. (Other nuclear powers settled for small strategic forces relatively fixed in size.) One reason was a bizarre additional solution to the stability problem that emerged early in the Cold War, due in large part to bureaucratic competition in the US armed forces. The solution, adopted by both superpowers, was to have multiple versions of a strategic nuclear force (with three versions it was called a triad), each capable *by itself* of inflicting a devastating retaliation after an attack. This certainly reduced vulnerability to a pre-emptive attack – attacking one leg by surprise would interfere with doing so for one or both of the others. But it also meant each superpower had enormously redundant strategic nuclear stockpiles. Eventually they were so large that no pre-emptive attack could destroy the retaliatory capacity – just a small surviving fraction would suffice to do unacceptable damage.[45] Chances an attack would produce mutual suicide remained very high. But critics charged that a disastrous deterrence breakdown could still readily result from accidents, miscalculations, hubris, or error, in part because the arsenals were so vast.

The second point is that neither theory nor practice contained destabilizing elements inherent in domestic politics. Worst-case analysis about the enemy's threat was always an effective domestic political weapon and was used liberally. It was therefore attractive politically to expand arsenals, defense research and development (R&D), and missile defense. It was politically wise to look "tough" so as to make one's deterrence threats (supposedly) more potent. Behavior of this sort by one party invited miscalculations by others as to underlying intentions and the threat posed.

Political considerations frequently overrode those suggested by deterrence theory. In alliance relations Europeans were often uneasy about American efforts to reduce reliance on nuclear weapons for dealing with a Soviet attack in Europe – they preferred that the superpowers faced threats of complete catastrophe from a war there – and the United States was disturbed by the possible political ramifications of the European concern. A similar and appropriate Soviet caution about risking a nuclear war over the Taiwan Straits in the 1950s incited Chinese charges of weakness and betrayal of world revolution. There were repeated complications for each superpower from the domestic political effects and alliance reverberations of appearing "inferior" in numbers of nuclear weapons or level of technical advancement. On the Soviet side, this

---

[45] Hence the term "overkill."

contributed to the onset of the Cuban Missile Crisis[46] and repeatedly drove decisions, like the huge US missile and nuclear warhead build-up in the 1960s, that were theoretically unnecessary and unwise.

Domestic and alliance political tradeoffs often skewed arms control and related efforts. Building up one's military posture and talking tough abroad were frequently a prerequisite for, or carried out in exchange for, getting a sufficiently broad coalition behind conciliatory steps to promote détente or get arms control agreements ratified. The price would be increases in defense spending or approval for controversial defense measures backed by the armed forces or steps to mollify important allies.

Political considerations contributed significantly to the way deterrence was deeply affected by the *credibility problem*. Preoccupation with credibility in deterrence threats became something of a compulsion, particularly in the United States. One reason was that the Munich Crisis of 1938, constantly cited on conciliation, had damaged British and French deterrence credibility when they later challenged Hitler's expansionism. This was held to demonstrate the absolute necessity to attend to credibility if deterrence was to work, and as showing how *actions* were the most important factor determining credibility.[47] Concern about American credibility emerged virtually at the outset of the Cold War and was important in creating NATO because American promises were considered, based on the initial US neutrality in the world wars, very suspect.

This was reinforced in the United States by the outbreak of the Korean War in 1950, ascribed to a failure to construct a credible American commitment to South Korea. A major justification for entering the war, therefore, was to reinforce the credibility of the US commitments elsewhere, particularly NATO – one reason the US shipped some five divisions to Western Europe while fighting in Korea. Another response to the Korean War was entering into numerous additional alliances to clarify American commitments around the world and enhance their credibility.

Of course, proliferating allies multiplied the governments needing reassurance about those commitments, and the commitments subject to challenge. Deterrence theory highlighted the critical role of credibility, but in a flawed fashion. The standard view had been that credibility depended on the intrinsic importance of one's interests at stake in a particular case. However, deterrence theory asserted that commitments were interdependent in terms of credibility: how one was upheld (or not), regardless of its intrinsic importance, had a major impact on the credibility of the others in the eyes of friends or enemies.[48] Hence virtually

---

[46] Wenger, 1997.

[47] On the powerful impact of the Munich analogy, and others, on American decision-making during the Vietnam War, see Khong, 1992.

[48] See Schelling, 1960 and 1966.

every commitment was important to the credibility of the overall deterrence posture and had to be upheld, which became a costly and dangerous practice.

This pushed credibility concerns beyond material military *capabilities* into the political/psychological dimension of *will*. Credibility required both the capability and the will to punish an opponent for an attack. Will seemed particularly important under mutual nuclear deterrence, because a rational government ought to be very reluctant to engage in even a small nuclear war – a vigorous defense or an enormously destructive retaliation against the nuclear-armed opponent could invite one's own destruction. It was hard to explain how a deterrence threat, particularly on behalf of an ally when only the ally was attacked, could be credible. Deterrence of nuclear and even non-nuclear powers by nuclear threats had an ineluctable credibility problem.[49]

In response, an array of steps to sustain or enhance deterrence credibility was devised, primarily by the United States, despite uneven evidence of success, developing a potent set of significant practices. In operating general deterrence, credibility was seen as possibly endangered by a myriad of things. Policy-makers could be criticized for all sorts of actions (and inactions) as eroding US credibility. The shorthand for this allegation was that they were "soft" or "weak" on opponents in things like rhetoric, the size of defense budgets or the weapons acquisitions approved, spending on military R&D programs, the specific stationing of forces, the attitude on arms control talks or other negotiations with opponents, responses to allied requests for arms and other support, and much more.

There was little evidence to support all this, or even the assertion that commitments were interdependent. Empirical studies eventually questioned the latter and tended to support the notion that credibility was linked to the deterrer's interests at stake. Studies found that opponents often tended to take a deterrer at his word, making credibility much less of a concern.[50] Thus the "solutions" to the credibility problem were largely a variation on grasping at straws.

Since sustaining credibility was burdensome, expensive, and complicated, why carry it to such lengths? One reason was domestic political necessity – the need to fend off charges of being "soft." This was political hedging. Another was the bipolar context. Under multipolarity state commitments – including security agreements – are necessarily dubious in credibility but bipolarity was assumed to link everything in superpower relations to everything else. Also important was constant concern about the stability problem. If credibility, particularly in nuclear deterrence, was uncertain, deterrence stability was questionable, too. This led to military hedging, such as in Vietnam.

The credibility problem could not be solved except by making retaliation after a failure of deterrence virtually automatic, which policy-makers refused to do. The only recourse was to note, correctly, that nuclear deterrence threats had

[49] See Morgan, 1983 and 2003.
[50] See Maxwell, 1968; Hopf, 1994; Mercer, 1996; and Press, 2005.

an existential credibility; however unlikely it was, they might be implemented and then disaster would result.[51] That was the real threat.

It was not comforting that credibility remained a matter of chance. Even so, deterrence was pursued anyway, periodically by extreme persistence on a particular commitment – in Vietnam, for example, or (for the Soviet Union) Afghanistan. As the Vietnam War indicated, the cost could be so high as to make it very unlikely the deterrer would readily repeat such a venture. This meant eroding the credibility of one's commitments by the efforts mounted to strengthen it. Various allies drew exactly that conclusion (which the Nixon Doctrine encouraged) and sharply expanded their own forces or instituted nuclear weapons programs in response.

From the perspective of this volume, the efforts to understand and deal with the credibility problem collectively illustrated the tenuous grasp of governments and analysts – intellectually, politically, and in action – on the essence and character of deterrence that could serve to properly develop the necessary cluster of practices. Empirical studies were not much help; in looking at cases it was difficult to accurately detect either successes or failures – in many instances, one could not say for sure whether deterrence had worked or failed. Most cases were of conventional, not nuclear, deterrence and who knew if they were comparable? On top of that, studies of decision-making in deterrence situations often questioned the rational decision-maker model at the core of the theory and employed in practicing deterrence. Without access to the opponent's cognitive processes, there was no way to know for sure whether deterrence was really necessary, was really working, or why.

This helped make the Cold War atmosphere one of unevenly controlled insecurity. It was often asserted that the arms racing, the deterrence on the edge of a cliff, the reciprocal threats and recrimination, were inertial. The Cold War was depicted as self-sustaining, a reciprocal imposition of semi-permanent insecurity in the name of security. The inertia seemed palpable in the huge and intricate production, design, and maintenance of complexes for nuclear and other forces, the elaborate training of thousands of people involved, the logistical and other components of weapons deployments and (in conventional conflicts) forces, the detection, monitoring, and warning systems, and the elaborate communications webs – an incredible cluster of practices.

Interrelated national organizational efforts on a vast scale operated for decades to sustain deterrence as the cornerstone of security management. It was evident that the superpower networks of deterrence-related resources were strongly interrelated. For instance, reactions to perceived threats in one national warning system would almost instantly reverberate in the other.[52] Shifts in military deployments or in weapons development and acquisition had similar, though slower, action–reaction patterns. The inertia extended

[51] See Bundy, 1984; and Waltz, 1981 and 1990.   [52] Bracken, 1983.

deeply into international politics. The superpowers swept numerous governments into alliances and patron–client relationships, elaborate blocs, and
deeply penetrating intrusions into friendly societies and political systems
via subsidies, intelligence activities, arms transfers, ideological splits linked to
the great powers, propaganda, etc. These deeply interactive practices helped
make the blocs far more durable and cohesive than alliance arrangements in the
past.

Innovation arising from practice

Despite this inertia, the most important aspect of Cold War deterrence was the
significant innovations that emerged from analysis of and actually operating
deterrence, with effects beyond deterrence itself. Already discussed is how
deterrence in practice, like the theory, led to only modest alterations in preparing and deploying the military forces for deterrence. However, this was not true
across the board. In arms control, innovation resulted from both theoretical
analysis and practical experience.[53]

An example was the development of "hot lines" among the great powers to
facilitate rapid communications at a critical juncture such as the accidental
firing of a missile, lest such situations permit or promote dangerous misper-
ceptions or alarm. Another example was rising concern about accidents and
accident prevention. Experience accumulated with warning systems that issued
false alarms, planes carrying nuclear weapons that crashed, planes that acci-
dentally dropped nuclear weapons, explosions that widely spewed radioactive
materials, etc. Efforts were made in bomb design to contain such incidents and
their consequences. Concern about unauthorized use of nuclear weapons, such
as by terrorists, led to the development of Permissive Action Links in the United
States to strengthen the negative control of national command authorities.[54]
Some of these concerns, responses, and technologies were shared among
nuclear powers to enhance deterrence stability.

Over time, innovation steadily altered verification. Improvements resulted
partially from failures in surveillance, such as Pakistan's proliferation programs
that evaded detection for years, or India's nuclear tests in which the advance
preparations went undetected. One verification breakthrough was the
US–Soviet agreement to make "national technical means" an authorized form
of spying[55] for maintaining confidence in strategic arms limitation agreements.
This was later augmented by provisions in agreements barring the parties from
making serious efforts to evade the satellite or other technical reconnaissance

---

[53] On arms control efforts, see Goldblat, 2002.
[54] Negative control is the ability to prevent use of nuclear weapons when use has not been
authorized.
[55] This referred to satellite intelligence gathering.

involved, or even agreeing to open selected weapons systems for satellite inspection. Another was establishing a requirement that parties to weapons limitation agreements supply figures on their weapons in each specified category, with regular updates, as a baseline for the opponent's verification efforts and making it harder to cheat. A clever adjustment on details about an opponent's weapons systems, where direct access was necessary for verification but impossible to agree on, involved treating each weapon system in a particular category as the ideal version of it. For instance, each missile of a particular type would count as carrying the maximum number of warheads with which that missile had ever been tested (or was tested in the future), to determine when that government had reached the limit on the number of warheads allowed for its missile forces. Quite startling was the US–Soviet agreement to station representatives of each outside the other's production complex for a banned missile system to examine products leaving that facility and ensure that none were the prohibited missiles.

A different sort of innovation has had extensive after-effects. Each side in the Cold War developed alliances as a major aspect of its deterrence activities, in part due to concerns about the stability problem, such as clarifying commitments and reassuring the members. They were also important for containing imprudent behavior by the client states – provocations, nuclear proliferation, etc.

The real innovation lay in constructing not only standard alliances but, as noted earlier, what were meant to become, over time, *communities*. Classically, alliances were the most pragmatic of cooperative arrangements, readily dissolving when the members' interests diverged. Both Washington and Moscow, however, sought to embed extended and collective deterrence in various alliances described as close associations based on common norms, principles, values, and objectives. The members were supposed to conduct relations in ways that departed markedly from standard international politics, resting on and promoting high levels of cooperation, integrated sacrifices, and shared information (like intelligence), all reflecting how the members had minimized fear among themselves. In short, in transforming the practices involved, the alliances were to transcend traditional international politics.

Evolution in this direction was strongly pursued even when an alliance was initially very traditional, like the US–Republic of Korea (ROK) alliance. The goal, in deterrence, was a coherent, politically uniform bloc constituting larger total forces and displaying greater solidarity. One result was that many allies ended up accepting, even welcoming, long-term deployment of "their" superpower's forces – even its nuclear weapons – on their soil, something very rare in the past. The United States even arranged that the stored tactical nuclear weapons in Europe were to be given to the allies for their use once a war started (instant nuclear proliferation!), an arrangement that still exists today. Particularly important was a determined superpower effort to somewhat homogenize their allies: turn non-democracies into democracies and market economies, or non-socialist systems into Soviet-version socialist political and economic systems. This was a radical approach.

Impact on the post-Cold War world

Cold War deterrence had a lifecycle of sorts. The initial circumstances within which it was generated had a major impact. Over time the American version of deterrence, particularly nuclear deterrence, diffused somewhat to the other great powers. In its heyday this version was inconsistently institutionalized due to the impact of important clashing practices plus limitations on the utility of the theory and strategy. Ultimately, practicing deterrence as a somewhat joint enterprise contributed to undoing the Cold War itself. However, while the Cold War ended abruptly, its deterrence has faded more slowly. Important aspects of its practices remain.

The end of the Cold War was a massive watershed. Its demise had never been consistently envisioned in deterrence thinking. Few analysts, most notably George Kennan, anticipated that deterrence and the containment strategy it served could culminate in the decay and disintegration of the Soviet Union. It seemed more like the basis for a moderately stable military stalemate that could endure indefinitely. (Bipolarity was considered particularly likely to endure.) The end of the Cold War was therefore a considerable surprise, in large part because it required leaders to depart significantly from some significant deterrence practices. In what ways did that event alter deterrence, and what elements of it survive?

Taking the latter first, it was somewhat apparent at the time and became very evident since that the American/Western version of deterrence via building pluralistic security communities of allies was far more successful and durable than the Soviet version. Despite the long French effort to turn NATO into a traditional alliance, the allure of the Western version helped undermine the Soviet bloc and end the Cold War. The American-orchestrated web of alliances has remained intact and has expanded considerably, though most new members have far to go to fully adjust to it.[56] What has changed is a shift in focus of the alliances on deterrence. Members now face few enemies to justify preoccupation with deterrence. While remaining exercises in collective deterrence, and extended deterrence, the alliances perform other functions for which deterrence is relevant. NATO is now the regional security manager in Europe and an out-of-area contributor to security management elsewhere, and it has helped stimulate the enlargement and deepening of the European Union. The Western alliance-based communities also exemplify the democratic peace.

[56] There were numerous American informal allies as well that remain so – Israel, Saudi Arabia, Sweden, etc.

European and other allies now provide support to the United States in places like Afghanistan.

Also impressive, less easily explained, and somewhat uncomfortable is why many component practices of Cold War deterrence survive. They are certainly durable. One example is Russian uneasiness – in some quarters, alarm – over Western military superiority and NATO enlargement. Russia's retention of thousands of tactical nuclear weapons is apparently, in part, for deterring a (most unlikely) Western invasion.[57] US and Russian deployed strategic forces are still roughly based on each other's nuclear deployments, with some primed for immediate reaction to the other launching an attack, even though their recent nuclear arms reduction agreements have been based on the premise that they are not enemies.

There is the continuing American extended nuclear deterrence for allies that face no plausible threats (the extended deterrence via conventional forces is somewhat more understandable). Some 200 US nuclear weapons remain in Europe because of opposition by some allies to their removal on grounds that they help sustain confidence in an American extended deterrence that seems unnecessary.

Other core elements of nuclear and (for the United States) conventional deterrence postures have proven quite durable.[58] Cold War nuclear powers retain their nuclear deterrence capabilities, mostly on a smaller scale. For some this reflects possible threats (Israel, Russia, China), a hedge against the return of intense great-power conflicts, or concern about troublesome states that have, or aim to get, weapons of mass destruction (WMD).[59] The United States retains its nuclear counterforce strategy and capabilities for achieving damage limitation to the greatest extent possible, targeting Russian forces in particular.[60] It also maintains smaller, more refined, conventional global power projection capabilities for numerous deterrence/compellence objectives. The other major nuclear powers have significant numbers of strategic nuclear weapons and still rest nuclear deterrence primarily on threats of massive retaliation. Their nuclear forces seem to have been miniaturized, then frozen. Some of this is hedging against worst-possible cases, some is bureaucratic inertia and survival motives at work, some is the power of routines, some is catering to those looking to play the security card in domestic politics. It is widely accepted that a major non-deterrence rationale for keeping or seeking nuclear weapons is prestige and stature. Virtually all the nuclear powers are modestly modernizing their nuclear forces, evidently expecting them to continue.

Deterrence theory says nothing about deterring non-opponents, and is imprecise on deterring actors with no serious inclination or intent toward

[57] Congressional Commission on the Strategic Posture of the United States, 2009.
[58] Cirincione, Wolfsthal, and Rajkumar, 2005.
[59] See Goldstein, 2000; and Alagappa, 2009.   [60] Lieber and Press, 2006.

preparing an attack. There is no real link between theory or lessons of the past and the scale and alert level of Russian and American strategic forces today, given the political state of their relationship. While Israel faces significant threats, India and Pakistan have a rationale for nuclear weapons in view of their past behavior, and North Korea is understandably concerned about its security, none seems likely to use nuclear weapons soon. Nor do the P-5 countries. Few seem well prepared for a major conventional war on short notice, just the United States, Israel, India and Pakistan, Iran, the two Koreas, perhaps China.

As for what else has changed, with far less need for deterrence as the pre-eminent recourse for security, it has shifted back toward being more tactic than strategy. With a sharp reduction in the stakes and the scale of military responses credibly threatened, the effectiveness and reliability of today's deterrence efforts are at traditional levels and the potential or actual targets have become more varied. Cold War deterrence seems mostly irrelevant, as the Bush Administration recognized.

Deterrence is therefore different as its context has shifted. There is no intense political conflict among the great powers; none has a constant pressing concern about an attack by another. As a result, deterrence is less salient in their relations and security policies. The incidence of war among all states is very low, so deterrence preoccupies governments much less.

Alongside the general reduction in serious interstate conflicts, and in combination with the revolution in military affairs that invites a more selective and precise approach to warfare, tolerance for deliberately inflicted casualties in interstate war, particularly civilian casualties, has markedly declined. This is a remarkable development and was virtually unanticipated.[61] States now conduct deterrence within much narrower limits on the kind and scale of harm that can be deliberately inflicted and thus credibly threatened. This is testimony to the impact of norms and of a broad normative shift. Massively destructive technologies are still with us but cannot readily be used. The United States, for example, focuses on inflicting precise, crippling harm in a military action. This has led to efforts to tailor deterrence so that threatened harm pertains more specifically to leaders, elites, and their specific interests, or is designed with their particular cultures and societies in mind.[62] Deterrence practices have been significantly altered.

China and India claim to be uninterested in the deterrence associated with the Cold War. Like others, they reject treating nuclear weapons as useful for war fighting, say they will avoid having huge nuclear arsenals, and support the concept of minimal deterrence and no-first-use policies (with some reservations).[63] This is a retreat not from deterrence but from one version of it.

---

[61] A sharp drop in tolerance for taking casualties was predicted correctly; the reduced tolerance for inflicting them is surprising; Morgan, 2003.

[62] See Bunn, 2007; and Kamp and Yost, 2009.   [63] Basrur, 2006.

Another change is how deterrence is now applied to forestall behavior well short of interstate war, including state-sponsored terrorism, proliferation, and – internally – human rights violations and civil war. This is often undertaken by collective actors on behalf of the international community, often with *internal* developments in states in mind. This is a far different arena, with very different social, cultural, and military dimensions, for using deterrence, and the nature of the deterrer is very different as well.

The conception of what constitutes rationality and a rational actor in deterrence is also undergoing re-examination. Conceptions of the impact of rational and irrational elements on behavior in deterrence situations have been changing, with emphasis on such things as how culture shapes what is deemed rational or the "appropriate" role of rationality in decision-making.[64] Debates proliferate about the rationality of an actor like North Korea, and more room is made for actors deemed irrational.

It is more difficult now to encompass the many elements of deterrence within any overall strategy, making its use considerably more complex. Perhaps culture affects the intensity in international conflicts, dampening or exacerbating tendencies to carry it to the level of massive warfare. Perhaps deterrence is influenced, in how it works or fails, by the degree to which the parties have shared perspectives, norms, and practices, elements of a community. Thus it is difficult to readily deter opponents outside that community, and difficult to understand and explain this for people within it. Within the community deterrence should be much less necessary – other means for containing disagreements are far more suitable.[65] Deterrence seems more appropriate to use against those internally or externally beyond the community and the shared culture. This would make a universal theory of deterrence impractical. Deterrence becomes something widely practiced but varying from place to place, over time, in meaning and effect, depending on the nature of its practitioners and their targets.

Conclusion

Where do practices come from and how does competent performance come into devising necessary adaptations over time? This is an important question, and examining Cold War deterrence can tell us a good deal about this – about the interplay of ideas, stability, change, structure, inertia, and politics involved, particularly in developing a community of practice among antagonists and thereby coming to have a notable impact on our world. Applying the perspective offered by this volume offers new ways of pulling the relevant factors together to reinvigorate our understanding of what Cold War deterrence was and how it was operated. With it, deterrence can be seen as an elaborate social

---

[64] Stein, 2009.   [65] Freedman, 2004.

endeavor rather than a set of very limited and very hostile relationships of greatly detached actors. We see how deterrence practices brought some regularity and order in and through themselves, and not just as ways the parties forcefully constricted each other's behavior.

The lifecycle of Cold War deterrence was initiated by applying it alone, then mutual deterrence, against "others" deemed so crude, brutal, and vicious as to be beyond relating to in normal social terms. It involved a major modification of traditional deterrence in international politics, was strongly affected by practices derived from the world wars while being a child of the shockingly rapid development of nuclear and thermonuclear weapons and delivery vehicle technology. This new deterrence was somewhat shaped and modified by the determined efforts of analysts preoccupied with identifying and institutionalizing practices identified as crucial for deterrence effectiveness and stability, who worked in tandem with policy-makers immersed in the practice of the emerging deterrence through high levels of tension, several major East–West crises, and various limited wars.

Keeping mutual deterrence stable was no mean feat, not least because of the perpetuation of standing military and political practices and perspectives which were understandably intent on being ready to fight not just deter, partly from the desire to survive a grievous failure of deterrence if possible. Struggles to contain and manage the dilemmas and other difficulties in Cold War deterrence, associated in particular with the nuclear revolution, did not always find analysts and decision-makers at their best.

However, the evolving analysis and practice they generated slowly nudged the Cold War relationship into behavior and interactions that had the trappings and components of a modest community. As part of this, the nature of deterrence itself shifted somewhat, becoming less mindlessly vicious in possible effects, more cooperative, and then less obviously necessary to the parties. In the end it began to look somewhat superfluous, one reason it did not block the unraveling of the Cold War. Ultimately it seems to have been the practitioners in the politics of the Cold War, at first gradually and then abruptly, who worked out the true solution to the main version of the stability problem and found ways to live with the credibility problem so as to get through the Cold War, and who then seized an opportunity to abandon the political context that had made deterrence so essential. That era passed and we live now, in our security efforts, amidst the shadows and echoes of its unique deterrence.

References

Alagappa, Muthiah, ed., 2009. *The Long Shadow: Nuclear Weapons and Security in 21st Century Asia*. Singapore: National University of Singapore Press.

Amadae, Sonja M., 2003. *Rationalizing Capitalist Democracy: The Cold War Origins of Rational Choice Liberalism*. Chicago: University of Chicago Press.

Ball, Desmond, 1974. *Déjà vu: The Return to Counterforce in the Nixon Administration.* Santa Monica: California Seminar in Arms Control and Foreign Policy.

Basrur, Rajesh M., 2006. *Minimum Deterrence and India's Nuclear Security.* Stanford: Stanford University Press.

Blackett, Patrick M. S., 1948. *Military and Political Consequences of Atomic Energy.* London: Turnstile Press.

Blair, Bruce G., 1985. *Strategic Command and Control: Redefining the Nuclear Threat.* Washington: Brookings Institution Press.

Bluth, Christoph, 2008. Toward Nuclear Superiority: US Strategic Nuclear Power in the Twenty-First Century. *Korean Journal of Defense Analysis* 20 (2): 125–139.

Borden, William L., 1946. *There Will Be No Time: The Revolution in Strategy.* New York: Macmillan.

Bracken, Paul J., 1983. *The Command and Control of Nuclear Forces.* New Haven: Yale University Press.

Brodie, Bernard, 1946. *The Absolute Weapon: Atomic Power and World Order.* New York: Harcourt, Brace.

Bull, Hedley, 2002. *The Anarchical Society: A Study of Order in World Politics.* 3rd edn. New York: Columbia University Press.

Bundy, McGeorge, 1984. Existential Deterrence and its Consequences. In *The Security Gamble: Deterrence Dilemmas in the Nuclear Age,* edited by Douglas MacLean, 3–13. Totowa: Rowman & Allenheld.

Bunn, M. Elaine, 2007. Can Deterrence Be Tailored? *Strategic Forum* No. 225. Washington: Institute for National Strategic Studies, National Defense University.

Cirincione, Joseph, Jon B. Wolfsthal, and Miriam Rajkumar, 2005. *Deadly Arsenals: Nuclear, Biological, and Chemical Threats.* 2nd edn. Washington: Carnegie Endowment for International Peace.

Cochran, Thomas B., William M. Arkin, and Milton M. Hoenig, 1989. *Nuclear Weapons Databook.* Vol. 1, *US Nuclear Forces and Capabilities.* Rev. edn. Cambridge, MA: Ballinger.

Cochran, Thomas B., William M. Arkin, Robert S. Norris, and Jeffrey I. Sands, 1989. *Nuclear Weapons Databook.* Vol. 4, *Soviet Nuclear Weapons.* Cambridge, MA: Ballinger.

Congressional Commission on the Strategic Posture of the United States, 2009. *America's Strategic Posture: Final Report.* Washington: United States Institute of Peace Press.

Crawford, Timothy W., 2003. *Pivotal Deterrence: Third-Party Statecraft and the Pursuit of Peace.* Ithaca: Cornell University Press.

Freedman, Lawrence, 1981. *The Evolution of Nuclear Strategy.* New York: St. Martin's Press.

  2004. *Deterrence.* Cambridge: Polity Press.

George, Alexander L., Philip J. Farley, and Alexander Dallin, eds., 1988. *US–Soviet Security Cooperation.* Oxford: Oxford University Press.

George, Alexander L. and Richard Smoke, 1974. *Deterrence and American Foreign Policy: Theory and Practice*. New York: Columbia University Press.

Goldblat, Jozef, 2002. *Arms Control: The New Guide to Negotiations and Agreements*. Thousand Oaks: Sage.

Goldstein, Avery, 2000. *Deterrence and Security in the 21st Century: China, Britain, France, and the Enduring Legacy of the Nuclear Revolution*. Stanford: Stanford University Press.

Hoffman, David E., 2009. *The Dead Hand: The Untold Story of the Cold War Arms Race and its Dangerous Legacy*. New York: Anchor Books.

Hopf, Ted, 1994. *Peripheral Visions: American Foreign Policy in the Third World, 1965–1990*. Ann Arbor: University of Michigan Press.

Huth, Paul K., 1988. *Extended Deterrence and the Prevention of War*. New Haven: Yale University Press.

Huth, Paul K. and Bruce Russett, 1984. What Makes Deterrence Work? Cases from 1900 to 1980. *World Politics* 36 (4): 496–526.

1990. Testing Deterrence Theory: Rigor Makes a Difference. *World Politics* 42 (4): 466–501.

Jones, Matthew, 2008. Targeting China: US Nuclear Planning and "Massive Retaliation" in East Asia, 1953–1955. *Journal of Cold War Studies* 10 (4): 37–65.

Kahn, Herman, 1968. *On Escalation: Metaphors and Scenarios*. Baltimore: Penguin.

Kamp, Karl-Heinz and David S. Yost, 2009. *NATO and 21st Century Deterrence*. Rome: NATO Defense College.

Kaplan, Fred, 1983. *The Wizards of Armageddon*. New York: Simon & Schuster.

Khong, Yuen Foong, 1992. *Analogies at War: Korea, Munich, Dien Bien Phu, and the Vietnam Decisions of 1965*. Princeton: Princeton University Press.

Lebow, Richard Ned, 1981. *Between Peace and War: The Nature of International Crises*. Baltimore: Johns Hopkins University Press.

1989. Deterrence: A Political and Psychological Critique. In *Perspectives on Deterrence*, edited by Paul C. Stern, Robert Axelrod, Robert Jervis, and Roy Radner, 25–51. New York: Oxford University Press.

Lebow, Richard Ned and Janice Gross Stein, 1994. *We All Lost the Cold War*. Princeton: Princeton University Press.

Lieber, Kier A. and Daryl G. Press, 2006. The Rise of US Nuclear Primacy. *Foreign Affairs* 85 (2): 42–54.

Maxwell, Stephen, 1968. Rationality in Deterrence. *Adelphi Papers* 8 (50): 1–19.

McDonough, David S., 2006. Nuclear Superiority: The "New Triad" and the Evolution of Nuclear Strategy. *Adelphi Papers* 46 (383): 7–92.

Mercer, Jonathan, 1996. *Reputation and International Politics*. Ithaca: Cornell University Press.

Morgan, Patrick M., 1983. *Deterrence: A Conceptual Analysis*. 2nd edn. Beverly Hills: Sage.

2003. *Deterrence Now*. Cambridge: Cambridge University Press.

Nolan, Janne E., 1999. *An Elusive Consensus: Nuclear Weapons and American Security After the Cold War*. Washington: Brookings Institution Press.

Norris, Robert S., Andrew S. Burrows, and Richard W Fieldhouse, 1994. *Nuclear Weapons Databook*. Vol. 5, *British, French and Chinese Nuclear Weapons*. Boulder: Westview Press.

Paul, T. V., 2009. *The Tradition of Non-Use of Nuclear Weapons*. Stanford: Stanford University Press.

Paul, T. V., Patrick M. Morgan, and James J. Wirtz, eds., 2009. *Complex Deterrence: Strategy in the Global Age*. Chicago: University of Chicago Press.

Polmar, Norman and Robert S. Norris, 2009. *US Nuclear Arsenal: A History of Weapons and Delivery Systems Since 1945*. Annapolis: Naval Institute Press.

Press, Daryl G., 2005. *Calculating Credibility: How Military Leaders Assess Military Threats*. Ithaca: Cornell University Press.

Rhodes, Richard, 1986. *The Making of the Atomic Bomb*. New York: Simon & Schuster.

Rosenberg, David A., 1983. The Origins of Overkill: Nuclear Weapons and American Strategy, 1945–1960. *International Security* 7 (4): 3–71.

    1986. US Nuclear War Planning, 1945–1960. In *Strategic Nuclear Targeting*, edited by Desmond Ball and Jeffrey Richelson, 35–56. Ithaca: Cornell University Press.

Russett, Bruce, 1967. Pearl Harbor: Deterrence Theory and Decision Theory. *Journal of Peace Research* 4 (2): 89–105.

Schelling, Thomas C., 1960. *The Strategy of Conflict*. Cambridge, MA: Harvard University Press.

    1966. *Arms and Influence*. New Haven: Yale University Press.

Schelling, Thomas C. and Morton H. Halperin, 1961. *Strategy and Arms Control*. New York: Twentieth Century Fund.

Scheuerman, William, 2009. *Hans Morgenthau: Realism and Beyond*. Cambridge: Polity Press.

Schwartz, Stephen I., ed., 1998. *Atomic Audit: The Costs and Consequences of US Nuclear Weapons Since 1940*. Washington: Brookings Institution Press.

Sherwin, Martin J., 1975. *A World Destroyed*. New York: Knopf.

Snyder, Glenn, 1961. *Deterrence and Defense: Toward a Theory of National Security*. Princeton: Princeton University Press.

Stein, Janice Gross, 1995. Political Learning by Doing: Gorbachev as Uncommitted Thinker and Motivated Learner. In *International Relations Theory and the End of the Cold War*, edited by Richard Ned Lebow and Thomas Risse-Kappen, 223–258. New York: Columbia University Press.

    2009. Rational Deterrence Against "Irrational" Adversaries? No Common Knowledge. In *Complex Deterrence: Strategy for the Global Age*, edited by T. V. Paul, Patrick M. Morgan, and James J. Wirtz, 58–82. Chicago: University of Chicago Press.

Strueck, William, 1995. *The Korean War: An International History*. Princeton: Princeton University Press.

Tannenwald, Nina, 2007. *The Nuclear Taboo*. Cambridge: Cambridge University Press.

Tetlock, Philip E., Charles B. McGuire, and Gregory Mitchell, 1991. Psychological Perspectives on Nuclear Deterrence. *Annual Review of Psychology* 42 (1): 239–276.

Viner, Jacob, 1946. The Implications of the Atomic Bomb for International Relations. *Proceedings of the American Philosophical Society* 90 (1): 53–58.

Waltz, Kenneth N., 1981. The Spread of Nuclear Weapons: More May be Better. *Adelphi Papers* 21 (171): 1–32.

  1990. Nuclear Myths and Political Realities. *American Political Science Review* 84 (3): 731–745.

Wenger, Andreas, 1997. *Living With Peril: Eisenhower, Kennedy, and Nuclear Weapons*. Lanham: Rowman Littlefield.

Wohlstetter, Albert, 1959. The Delicate Balance of Terror. *Foreign Affairs* 37 (2): 211–234.

7 | Britain's response to the Spanish Civil War: investigating the implications of foregrounding practice for English School thinking

RICHARD LITTLE

At first sight, it might seem that taking practices seriously has little that is new to offer members of the English School because they have habitually acknowledged the centrality of practice in International Relations (IR) and attacked any attempt to establish a categorical distinction between theory and practice. Instead, they have worked on the hermeneutic assumption that to develop a theoretical understanding of IR it is necessary to start from the premise that we need to explore "the thought already embodied and at work in practice."[1] Not only has the English School always acknowledged the centrality of institutional practices in the constitution of international society,[2] but there is now also a growing interest in how the specific practices that constitute the international society have formed and evolved over time.[3] At the same time, however, there is now an emerging recognition that the foregrounding of practices in IR is drawing attention to an expanding body of theoretical literature on the nature of practice that reveals how much the English School has tended to take the idea of practice for granted. By drawing more explicitly on this literature, the English School can clarify the distinctive nature of its approach as well as rendering its theoretical underpinnings more robust.[4] Although English School thinking can be viewed as part of the turn to practice that is now taking place in IR, as Adler and Pouliot argue in Chapter 1 in this volume, it is possible and indeed perhaps even essential to view this notion from a much wider and more ambitious perspective. The aim of this volume is to show that taking international practices seriously can be used to provide an interparadigmatic framework that can then be drawn upon by all the disparate approaches that have developed across the multidimensional field of IR. However, from Adler and Pouliot's perspective, the intention is not thereby to eliminate the differences

---

[1] Keens-Soper, 1978, 40.   [2] Bull, 2002.   [3] See Bain, 2003; and Fabry, 2010.

[4] For a clear exposition of the English School's approach to practice, see Navari, Forthcoming. See also Koivisto's 2010 discussion of how English School thinking can benefit from the explicit use of practice theory.

generated by these competing approaches but rather to find a way of ensuring that their adherents can all engage in a common and meaningful conversation.

In the first instance, I failed to appreciate this broader ambition and indeed my initial aim was primarily to argue that the English School's approach is inherently more pluralistic than is often appreciated. I intended to develop this argument by focusing on the familiar distinction made by some English School theorists between an international system and an international society, and I hoped to draw on the Spanish Civil War to show how and why societal practices are sometimes overridden by systemic pressures, thereby demonstrating that English School thinking can operate outside of the idea of practice. I also hoped to show, therefore, that despite the importance that the English School attaches to societal practices, they also acknowledge the need to accommodate the significance attached by neorealists, among others, to systemic pressures.

So this chapter was originally not only designed to demonstrate the importance of the idea of practice within English School thinking, but was also intended to make a contribution to the ongoing debate within the English School about the salience of the system/society distinction. On one side of the debate, Bull and Watson, for example, insist on the heuristic value of the distinction and they argue that states behave differently when operating under systemic rather than societal conditions.[5] By contrast, critics, like Berridge and James, also operating within the English School perspective, assert that it is not possible to identify any meaningful difference between a system and a society and that certainly Bull failed to do so when he first made the distinction.[6]

The chapter, therefore, was originally going to adopt the former position and use the Spanish Civil War to illustrate that the system/society distinction does usefully draw attention to coexisting dimensions of interstate behavior, with the international society focusing on rule-governed practices and the international system concentrating on the systemic or structural pressures generated by material power relations. It was hoped that the chapter would show that although the British response to the Civil War was intended to follow long-standing institutional practices, pressures exerted through the international system had a significant impact on the implementation of established normative practices so that instead of being reinforced, the international society started to unravel. In terms of Adler and Pouliot's cross-cutting axes, therefore, English School advocates of the distinction view both system and society from a structural perspective with systems operating at the material end of the horizontal axis and society operating at the meaningful end.

The more ambitious view of foregrounding international practices promulgated in this volume, however, has encouraged me to focus more extensively on the Adler and Pouliot approach by suggesting that the idea of practice can be

---

[5] Bull and Watson, 1984.   [6] See Berridge, 1980; James, 1993; and Bull, 2002.

drawn on in a way that helps to reassess the distinction between society and system and thereby, potentially, to resolve the debate that has gone on within the English School. At the heart of this reassessment is the acknowledgment that, contrary to the view of Bull and Watson that the international society is underpinned by a pre-existing international system, it is essential to privilege the idea of international society and to recognize that the international system is in fact endogenous to that society.[7] System and society, however can, under certain circumstances, give rise to divergent practices and what the Spanish Civil War case study does is to illustrate how the existence of these practices can give rise to disagreement and uncertainty among decision-makers about which set of practices should be implemented.

The chapter is divided into five sections. The first looks more closely at the system/society distinction as it has been formulated in the English School and demonstrates that when examined through the lens provided by practice theory, the distinction can be reconfigured in terms of competing sets of practices, and it goes on to show that the reconfiguration is already latent in English School thinking and what practice theory does is to render the reconfiguration manifest. The rest of the chapter then applies this thinking to the Spanish Civil War and the second section sets the scene for the war and then looks at the competing explanations of the British policy towards it. In fact, these explanations have overwhelmingly been supplied by diplomatic historians because the war has been almost entirely ignored by IR theorists. The third section argues that the problem with these historical explanations is that they fail to acknowledge that the British response was to some extent influenced by evolving historical practices that are associated with regime recognition and non-intervention and it goes on to discuss how English School thinkers are now beginning to open up how these practices emerged and evolved across time. The fourth section then looks in more detail at the disagreements and uncertainty among British decision-makers about how to respond to the Spanish Civil War. Finally, the concluding section explores the implications of taking international practices seriously for the debate over the merits of distinguishing between a system and a society within the English School.

Practice theory and the system/society distinction

Although the English School has tended not to discuss the idea of practice directly, at least until recently, preferring instead to focus on the idea of institutions, there is now general agreement that the idea of institutions and practices can be considered to be broadly synonymous. Therefore, although Bull argues in his seminal discussion that the international society is constituted

---

[7] Retrospectively I have realized that this is essentially the move that I made in the conclusion to my book on the balance of power: Little, 2007a.

by five major institutions (the balance of power, war, diplomacy, international law, and great-power management) his analysis of these institutions reveals that they can legitimately be viewed as complex sets of practices.[8] It is significant, therefore, that Buzan has argued that if all the English School literature is surveyed then it becomes possible to extend the list of these institutions.[9] So, for example, some English School theorists want to extend the list to embrace further institutions such as trade, sovereignty, and non-intervention. Buzan wants to label all these as "primary" institutions to distinguish them from "secondary institutions," such as arms control and environmental regimes, and he wants to make this distinction because he accepts Keohane's argument that we need to distinguish between "specific institutions" that can be identified as "related complexes of rules and norms, identifiable in space and time" and "more fundamental practices" that provide "institutionalized" constraints that operate at a deeper level.[10] Buzan then goes on to define primary institutions as "durable and recognized patterns of shared practices rooted in values held commonly by the members of interstate societies, and embodying a mix of norms, rules and principles."[11]

Navari, however, has gone much further in articulating what the concept of a practice means for the English School.[12] Although she accepts that most theorists in the School have failed to expand on what is meant by a practice, she acknowledges that considerable progress has been made in contemporary social science to unpack the meaning and implications of the concept. In pursuing this line of thought, she also focuses very explicitly on the idea of practice as a competent performance, as Adler and Pouliot do in Chapter 1 in this volume. Navari suggests in the process that diplomacy, for example, is "defined by a particular attitude and a particular range of language. It is not spying, shouting, threatening or 'whacking.'"[13] She goes on to argue that the theorist whose views most effectively capture what the English School mean by practice is Schatzki.[14] From his perspective, the identification of a practice requires, first, practical understanding and this involves "knowing how to X, knowing how to identify X-ings and knowing how to prompt as well as to respond to X-ings."[15] Second, a practice involves rules which are the "principles, instructions, and formulations that people adhere to or take into account when they act or speak."[16] Navari argues, however, that, in contrast to Schatzki, for the English School, rules do not have to be explicit. They can be tacit or implicit and, therefore, there is no clear boundary between practical and habitual behavior. Finally, a practice involves "teleoaffectivities," by which Schatzki means not only that a practice must be goal-directed, but also that the goal matters to the community where the practice takes place. From

[8] Bull, 2002. [9] Buzan, 2004. [10] Keohane, 1988, 383–385.
[11] Buzan, 2004, 180. [12] Navari, Forthcoming. [13] Navari, 2008, 2.
[14] Schatzki, 1996. [15] *Ibid.*, 78. [16] Navari, 2008, 4.

Navari's perspective, Bull's conception of an institution is identical to Schatzki's conception of a practice and this helps to confirm, for her, the centrality and importance of practice theory for the English School approach. This conclusion, however, is premised on the assumption that the English School approach is focused on the idea of an international society that is constituted by a number of primary institutions/practices. Such an assessment inevitably raises questions about the status of an international system from the perspective of practice theory and, as a consequence, the basis of the distinction that Bull and other English School theorists have drawn between an international system and an international society. Is it possible to argue that the international system is also constituted by a set of practices?

An international system, according to Bull, identifies states that are "in regular contact with one another, and where in addition there is interaction between them sufficient to make the behaviour of each a necessary element in the calculations of the other."[17] By contrast, an international society presupposes that states are, on the one hand, "conscious of certain common interests and common values" and, on the other, that they "conceive themselves to be bound by a common set of rules in their relations with one another, and share in the working of common institutions."[18] The distinction is frequently referred to whenever Bull's work is discussed and, as Vigezzi makes clear, the distinction is one that had long exercised Bull in his discussions with the other members of the British Committee on the Theory of International Politics – the precursor of the English School.[19]

Before trying to clarify if the international system can also be seen to be constituted by a set of practices, it is worth noting that there is widespread agreement among contemporary theorists working from an English School perspective that the distinction between system and society is unhelpful, and should be dispensed with. The agreement is significant, moreover, because it extends across the very diverse analytical perspectives that are now embraced by the School. James, who was one of the first theorists to initiate an attack on the distinction, insisted that it is simply not possible to conceive of an international system that does not embrace the features that Bull associates with the existence of an international society.[20] By the same token, any meaningful conception of an international society must make the systemic assumption that its members will take each other's behavior into account. It follows, according to James, that Bull has set up a false dichotomy and the most practical step is to discard the idea of an international system because it is the societal dimension that needs attention.

Jackson, on the other hand, accepts that the two terms point up a useful distinction, but he argues that distinguishing between instrumental and

---

[17] Bull, 2002, 9–10.   [18] *Ibid.*, 13.   [19] Vigezzi, 2005.   [20] James, 1993.

non-instrumental behavior is preferable to the system/society distinction.[21] Instrumental (systemic) behavior is based on strategic conceptions of self-interest that necessarily take the actions of other actors into consideration. Failure to take account of others will all too easily give rise to self-defeating strategies. By contrast, non-instrumental (societal) behavior is based on legal and moral obligations that necessarily embrace the legitimate interests of others who will be affected by this behavior. Jackson accepts that both forms of behavior need to be accommodated in any analysis of international society, but he objects to the use of international systems terminology because it too easily gives rise to a mechanistic view of behavior that encourages what Jackson considers to be the utterly mistaken notion that human beings can be pushed around by social structures. However, he insists that when Bull refers to the international system he is not suggesting that human behavior can be structurally determined. Jackson's assessment suggests, therefore, that there is some scope for assuming that the international system might be constituted by a distinctive type of practice.

Buzan provides a third significant discussion of the distinction.[22] He acknowledges Jackson's view that Bull is endeavoring to capture two distinctive types of social behavior, but he insists, nevertheless, that Jackson fails to get at the essence of Bull's position on the international system which does represent a "physical mode of interaction typical of the mechanistic, realist-style analyses of the balance of power as an automatic process rooted in the relative material capabilities of states."[23] From Buzan's perspective, therefore, Bull's view of the international system corresponds almost exactly with the one adopted by Waltz.[24] But if this is how Bull thought about an international system then it is ironic that he anticipated Waltz's approach because he has been credited with promoting a form of analysis that eschews and undermines Waltzian thinking. Nevertheless, there are obvious similarities between how Waltz and Bull viewed the international system, although the nature of the underlying logic becomes much clearer in the wake of Waltz's *Theory of International Politics*. Rather paradoxically, therefore, Buzan concludes that Bull's view of an international system can be captured perfectly well as a type of international society, thereby rendering the need for a system/society divide redundant.[25] He reaches this conclusion by equating Bull's international system with an a-social society, which is located at one end of a spectrum of international societies.

Despite extensive support for Buzan's position, it is still contested.[26] What Buzan's move tends to gloss over is that behavior in an a-social society may operate on the basis of a different kind of logic to the behavior observed in any of the "social" societies identified further along his spectrum of international societies and even more important that these logics may coexist, as Jackson

---

[21] Jackson, 2000, 113–116.   [22] Buzan, 2004, 98–108.   [23] *Ibid.*, 99.
[24] Waltz, 1979.   [25] Buzan, 2004, 190–195.   [26] See Dunne, 2005; and Little, 2007a.

presupposes when he distinguishes between instrumental and non-instrumental behavior. March and Olsen make the same assumption in their very similar distinction between the logic of appropriateness and the logic of expected consequences.[27] Although Bull presupposes that an international system can, in theory, exist in the absence of an international society, he also asserts that every international society is necessarily underpinned by an international system. He wants to establish a framework that helps to make sense of the last few centuries in international politics and at the heart of his position is the belief that the essentially power political orientation associated with the international system, and institutional orientation associated with international society, coexist, and that both exert a significant influence on decision-makers who are responsible for managing international relations. It is very apparent, therefore, that Bull is not just conceiving of the international system as hypothetical, akin to the state of nature; on the contrary, he presupposes that an international society invariably coexists with or is underpinned by an international system. From this perspective, then, the system/society distinction is more akin to Jackson's distinction between instrumental and non-instrumental behavior than Buzan's typology of international societies.

Bull insists that international politics is constituted by a mix of divergent and sometimes competing practices that contribute to a complex and multidimensional reality. He argues, moreover that there are theorists who have captured the essential elements of the practices that he associates with an international system and the practices that he associates with an international society. So "the element of war and struggle for power among states" that he associates with an international system needs to be distinguished from "the element of co-operation and regulated intercourse among states" that he associates with an international society.[28] The thinking of theorists associated with both of these two traditions of thought is seen to have evolved over the past five hundred years and helps to capture the essence of the changing reality of world politics that has gone on during this period. Bull insists, therefore, that it is important not to reify either of these elements and he insists that "it is always erroneous to interpret events as if international society were the sole or the dominant element."[29] From this perspective, then, there is a clear presumption that the international system and the international society need to be defined by different sets of practices.

The difficulty, therefore, with Buzan's decision to relabel the international system as an a-social international society and locate it within a typology of international societies is that the move fails to accommodate the coexistence of system and society. But it also compounds a fundamental problem with Bull's

---

[27] March and Olsen, 1998. Nalbandov, 2009 draws on March and Olsen's distinction in his discussion of the Russian interventions in Georgia between 1992 and 2008.
[28] Bull, 2002, 39.   [29] *Ibid.*, 49.

own position that emerges from his assumption that international societies developed from within or were imposed upon pre-existing international systems. This assumption presupposes that states formed autonomously in the absence of any broader social network. Taking a long historical view of the emergence of states, this does not seem to have happened[30] and unquestionably the modern European states were consolidated within the context of the pre-existing medieval society and these states and the modern European international society were co-constituted. Rather than treating the international system as some kind of alien international society, therefore, it is more in line with the overall spirit of Bull's analysis to associate the international system with a set of practices that coexist with, but can be distinguished in kind from, practices associated with the international society.

The assumption made in this chapter is that societal practices will come under pressure when there is evidence that the international society itself is under threat, and this will become most evident when the established practices associated with great-power management begin to break down with the emergence of great powers that appear to threaten the existing international order. At this juncture, the logic associated with ongoing societal practices will come into question and decision-makers will need to contemplate operating on the basis of a very different logic that will require them to focus primarily on the actions being taken by other states and to recognize that these other states will be responding in a similar fashion. This is discussed in terms of a move from societal practices through to systemic practices. The chapter focuses specifically on the British response to the Spanish Civil War because the case reveals so clearly that despite the flagrant disregard of societal practices by the revisionist states, a status quo state, such as Britain, did not find it easy to move from societal to systemic practices.

Competing accounts of Britain and the Spanish Civil War

The Spanish Civil War was the bloody outcome of a long-standing political struggle between right and left; indeed this struggle had been a perennial feature of modern history in Spain. Although the history could be taken back much further, with an earlier civil war (touched on later in the chapter) taking place in the 1820s, it is worth noting that the first Spanish Republic was brought to an end by the army in 1875 and it was over fifty years before the Republicans regained control in Spain. A second republic was established peacefully in April 1931, largely because the king had lost the support of the army. But the new Republican government still confronted insuperable problems. Right-wing elements were prepared to tolerate the Republic provided their privileges were untouched, whereas left-wing elements saw it as the first stage in the

---

[30] Buzan and Little, 2000.

overthrow of the established social and political order. The center-right government, confronted by growing violence and unable to exercise effective power, held an election on February 16, 1936. A Popular Front coalition, linking left and center parties, established a new government, but it was unable to stem rising disorder. In July, the army mutinied in Morocco. The mutiny quickly spread to mainland Spain and was successful almost everywhere apart from Madrid and Barcelona, but this resistance was sufficient to ensure the survival of the republican government and a military coup was transformed into a civil war between republican forces and the nationalist forces under General Franco that was to persist until 1939. The speed with which Britain announced a policy of non-intervention has been extensively debated by diplomatic historians. In practice, the war was soon internationalized, with Franco receiving support from Germany and Italy and the Soviets supplying aid to the Republicans. Nevertheless, because British policy worked against the incumbent Republican government, there is a widespread presupposition that the British government covertly favored the Franco forces, primarily because of his hostility to communism and, as a consequence, British policy was characterized in the British Parliament at the time as "malevolent neutrality" and has on many occasions subsequently been couched in similar terms.[31]

For most of the twentieth century, Spain played a minor role in world politics but, as E.H. Carr noted, for the duration of the civil war the country became "a center of prime interest and concern in the capitals of Europe."[32] Carr was in a good position to make this judgment because in 1936 he was still a member of the British Foreign Office and Spain was part of his brief. But it is also not difficult to identify evidence that confirms his assessment. For example, during the first two years of the civil war the conflict was on the agenda of three-quarters of the British Cabinet meetings. Moreover, even in the last year of the war, when the outcome seemed a forgone conclusion, Spain was still discussed at half of the Cabinet meetings. Interest in the Spanish Civil War has certainly not waned in subsequent years. There have now been over fifteen thousand books written on the civil war which, as Graham observes, represents a "textual epitaph that puts it on a par with the Second World War."[33]

Despite the ongoing fascination with the Spanish Civil War in other areas of study, the conflict has not played a significant role in the study of IR. There are very few references to the conflict in contemporary IR literature. At first sight, this general lack of interest is odd, because the conflict was so rapidly internationalized – in ways, moreover, that appear, at least superficially, remarkably similar to the internationalization of civil wars during the Cold War era. So, just as the Spanish Civil War was rapidly internationalized, with the Soviet Union supporting the incumbent Republican Government and Italy and Germany

[31] This position has been forcefully presented by Douglas Little, 1985 and 1988.
[32] Carr, 1984, 22.   [33] Graham, 2005, Preface.

supporting Franco's Nationalist forces, so the United States and the Soviet Union can be regularly observed giving some level of support to opposing sides in civil wars throughout the Cold War. Nevertheless, despite the important and often deadly consequences for the indigenous population that flow from this internationalization of civil wars, the issue was never studied, or at any rate theorized, in a sustained and systematic fashion during the Cold War. Perhaps the most obvious reasons to account for this persistent low level of interest is because, first, the study of IR was so state-centric in orientation during the Cold War era, when the foundations of the discipline were laid down, thereby making it difficult to accommodate the idea of a civil war; but, second, civil unrest was also generally ignored because there was a preoccupation with what was happening at the center of the international system rather than in the third-world periphery where the civil wars were almost invariably taking place.

Although clearly there were occasions during the Cold War when intervention in domestic conflict moved to the top of the international agenda, for example, US intervention in Vietnam or Soviet Union intervention in Afghanistan, theorists had difficulty accommodating these developments. So Morgenthau argued, for example, that it was not possible to account for American intervention in terms of his rational theory of international politics and it would be necessary, as a consequence, to formulate a theory of irrationality to account for the US policy in Vietnam.[34] By the same token, Waltz insisted that there were no systemic pressures on either the United States or the Soviet Union to intervene in peripheral areas of the globe and so intervention could only be accounted for at some other level of theory.[35] Given this kind of orientation, therefore, it becomes less surprising that the study of IR in the Cold War did not often display any particular interest in either civil war in general or, more specifically, civil wars where external intervention has taken place.

It would not, of course, be true to suggest that there was no interest in the internationalization of civil wars, but often the interest was displayed by theorists, such as Rosenau, who wished to challenge the state-centric orientation of the field, or Bull who was interested in the normative implications of international intervention.[36] Since the end of the Cold War, however, attitudes towards intervention have changed very substantially. In particular, a growing preoccupation with humanitarian intervention has reinforced an interest in the normative dimensions of intervention and non-intervention.[37] But this shift in orientation has certainly not given rise to any interest in the Spanish Civil War.

---

[34] Morgenthau, 1973.   [35] Waltz, 1979.

[36] See Rosenau, 1964; and Bull, 1984. For a review of the literature on intervention in the Cold War era see Little, 1987 and 1993.

[37] See, for example, Wheeler's 2000 text that charts the reorientation in thinking about intervention.

By contrast, diplomatic historians have made numerous attempts to under-stand the international responses to the Spanish Civil War, particularly since the 1970s when the relevant public records began to open up. However, there is very little consensus among these historians about how to assess the broader significance of the conflict. Although it is often acknowledged that the civil war needs to be treated as "both the dress rehearsal for and the prelude to the approaching Great Contest,"[38] it is insisted that all too often the war is still simply treated as "an irrelevant side show"[39] and, from this perspective, the events of central importance are seen to lie elsewhere. However, now the more usual line of argument is that the Spanish Civil War must be seen as a crucial element in the growing instability that developed in Europe across the 1930s. In particular, the conflict needs to be examined in the context of the appeasement strategy implemented by the Western democracies. There are, of course, diver-gent schools of thought relating to appeasement. The traditional interpretation, often identified as the "guilty men" thesis, that dominated thinking for several decades after the Spanish Civil War, viewed the incumbent leaders in the Western democracies as somehow negligent or incompetent, pursuing strat-egies that promoted rather than inhibited instability. Viewed through this prism of appeasement, the Spanish Civil War can be seen as "one of the earliest and most notorious examples of the British and American diplomatic myopia," leading them to throw away "one of the last opportunities to sidetrack the aggressive designs of Nazi Germany and Fascist Italy."[40] But as the archives opened up, this perspective began to give way to a revisionist line of argument, sometimes characterized as the "terrible times" thesis, that focused attention on the intractable problems that these decision-makers confronted. Further research and reflection, however, encouraged the development of a post-revisionist position that reasserted the culpability of Western decision-makers. So, in the context of the Spanish Civil War, Alpert argues that these decision-makers treated the war as an internal struggle precipitated by the backwardness of Spanish social and economic conditions.[41] As a consequence, the British, in particular, chose to keep their distance from the conflict. But this is not a new line of argument; even at the time, it was insisted that the main aim of the great powers was to "localize" the conflict.[42] But Alpert insists that this view was myopic because it was clear that the effects of the civil war would not be local and, without doubt, Franco's victory had a substantial impact on European instability with the policies pursued by the Western democracies inadvertently fostering German and Italian power.

It is doubtful if diplomatic historians will ever come to an agreement about why the British, in particular, pursued an appeasement policy. Schroeder, therefore, has argued in favor of coming at the issue from a very different

---

[38] Deutscher, 1984, xvii–xviii.   [39] Finney, 1997, 375.   [40] Little, 1985, 10.
[41] Alpert, 1997.   [42] Wilcox, 1938.

direction.[43] For many years now, Schroeder has endeavored to move diplomatic history beyond a study of the minutiae of diplomatic exchanges. He has constantly endeavored to engage with political science and the importance of this endeavor is increasingly acknowledged.[44] What Schroeder is interested in doing is coming to terms with the "rules and understandings underlying the practice of international politics."[45] So, in the context of appeasement, Schroeder argues that he is not interested in the causal factors associated with British appeasement policy in the late 1930s, rather he is interested in "what kind of policy it was," and he wishes to understand this policy in a "generic rather than a genetic sense."[46] At the heart of his argument is the assertion that the appeasement policy pursued by Britain in the context of Austria and Czechoslovakia did not represent a new departure for Britain, but reflected a line of policy that the British had followed throughout the nineteenth century in this region. Although the policy had proved successful in the previous century, what the British failed to realize, either at the time or subsequently, was that the success was due to the local international practices that were in operation in the region at that time. These practices, moreover, presupposed the existence of the Austrian Hungarian Empire. With the elimination of the Empire, the restraint that had characterized relations in the region was also eliminated. There was, therefore, no possibility that the traditional British policy could preserve stability in the region, because it had never been the source of stability and, consequently, the 1930s appeasement policy was bound to fail.

Schroeder's thesis focuses on Central and Eastern Europe and so it cannot be extended to Britain's relations with Spain. Nevertheless, the analysis in this chapter works from a rather similar premise, because it argues that, when the Spanish Civil War broke out, Britain responded initially by endeavoring to implement the generic practices relating to civil wars that had evolved over time in the international society.

Civil wars and the recognition of new states

Although members of the English School have always acknowledged the centrality of institutional practices in the constitution of the international society, it is only very recently that there have been any detailed studies of how the specific practices that constitute the international society have formed and evolved over time. This section draws heavily on Fabry's analysis of the institutional practices associated with the formation of new states because these practices, it is suggested here, are frequently closely entwined with the practices that are related to how civil wars are handled in the international society.[47] Although Fabry makes reference to civil wars, this is not the focal point of his interest.

---

[43] Schroeder, 1976.   [44] See, for example, *International Security*, 1997.
[45] Schroeder, 1994, xii.   [46] Schroeder, 1976, 223.   [47] Fabry, 2010.

What Fabry attempts to do is to demonstrate that establishing the statehood or sovereignty of a new state in the contemporary international society necessarily involves the practice of recognition on the part of the established sovereign states in the society. Fabry, moreover, traces the origins of this practice back to the end of the eighteenth century and the start of the nineteenth century. It can be argued, therefore, that from this perspective these practices are very closely associated with the constitution of the contemporary international society.

In advocating the study of state practice, Fabry self-consciously employs what Hedley Bull identified as a "classical approach" to the study of international relations. Although Fabry does not use this terminology, he essentially adopts a hermeneutic approach that draws in the main on primary documentation in order to investigate how practitioners have dealt with the task of managing interstate relations. In contrast to mainstream social scientists, he is not interested in trying to establish causal models; what he wants to do is to show that practitioners have managed to formulate established and agreed procedures that essentially legitimize their ongoing practices. These practices, however, have evolved across time and reflect the fact that IR, contrary to the views of contemporary realists such as John Mearsheimer, takes place within embedded normative structures. At the same time, Fabry is well aware that international decision-making occurs in complex circumstances and so although he is primarily interested in examining the norms and reasoning associated with international practice, he also acknowledges that practitioners have to take into account the wider political concerns and consequences of these practices. There is, therefore, an implicit appreciation that it is necessary to take account of systemic as well as societal pressures.

According to Fabry, the state practices that linked recognition to the establishment of new states began to emerge once European states began to acknowledge that they were part of a larger international society of sovereign states. More specifically, this development is inextricably linked to the point in time when positive law began to overtake natural law as a defining institution of this nascent international society. This development occurred in the eighteenth century and Fabry accepts Alexandrowicz's argument that the issue of recognition became salient because the legitimacy of dynasticism gradually came under challenge at that time.[48] During the dynastic era, a new state could only legitimately come into existence with the acquiescence of the dynastic owner of the territory. The recognition of the United States is interesting in this context because although the emergence of this revolutionary state clearly posed a fundamental challenge to the very idea of dynastic legitimacy France, still a dynastic state, nevertheless provided the revolutionaries with assistance. No doubt the assistance reflected the importance of systemic practices that played a crucial role even or, from Schroeder's perspective,[49] especially, in the dynastic

---

[48] Alexandrowicz, 1958.   [49] Schroeder, 1994.

era, but established societal practices still remained essentially intact and recognition of the United States by France and most of the other European states was only forthcoming after the British acknowledgment of the new revolutionary state and so established dynastic practices were not undermined by its emergence. Moreover, despite the subsequent threat to dynastic legitimacy posed by the emergence of the French revolutionary state as well as the challenge to the idea of an international society of sovereign states raised by Napoleonic expansion, dynastic legitimacy was essentially reconfirmed in 1815 at the Congress of Vienna but, albeit at the expense of some inconsistency, within the agreed framework of an international society of states.

Fabry's thesis rests on the dual assertion that not only can contemporary thinking about the practice of state recognition be traced back for over two hundred years but also that the practices have throughout this period been indivisibly linked to the idea of self-determination. State recognition and self-determination are, as Fabry puts it, two sides of the same coin. From this perspective, then, the practice of recognition is closely associated with the emergence of a liberal international order and, therefore, Anglo-American thinking played a crucial role in establishing this practice and helping to shape its evolution. Fabry's thesis, therefore, reinforces the argument advanced by a range of very different theorists, such as Morgenthau, Schroeder, Osiander, and Teschke who all argue that the modern international arena dates back to the start of the nineteenth century rather than to 1648 and the Treaty of Westphalia.[50]

Although the emergence of the United States posed a long-term challenge to established recognition practices, Fabry argues that dynastic legitimacy was most seriously undermined, in the first instance, in Latin America. By the mid-1830s, twelve new states, all but Brazil constituted as democratic republics, had emerged as fully fledged members of the international society. This significant development was associated with a substantial transformation in recognition practices as spearheaded by the United States and Britain. Both states explicitly repudiated the practices associated with dynastic legitimacy that were being promoted at that time in Europe and which Spain and Portugal wished to extend to their overseas possessions in Latin America. However, the United States and Britain successfully brought into play a very different set of practices that were then to provide the foundations for recognition of new states over the next two hundred years. By contrast, the practices associated with dynastic legitimacy atrophied and had essentially disappeared by the start of the twentieth century. But the Latin American cases are also important because the British and Americans also operated on the basis of common practices about how to respond to civil wars.

---

[50] See Morgenthau, 1973; Schroeder, 1994; Osiander, 1994; and Teschke, 2003.

In the aftermath of the Congress of Vienna, the dynastic European states were agreed that if they came under challenge from internal revolutionary forces then they had a right to expect intervention from other dynastic powers in order to suppress the revolution. But Britain and the United States challenged the existence of this right and argued, instead, that external intervention into what constituted a civil war in another state was not admissible. When the Latin American territories of Spain and Portugal demanded their independence, therefore, the British and the Americans operated on the basis of very similar assumptions and practices. Both accepted that the struggles for independence in Latin America constituted civil war and that Spain and Portugal had the right to demand respect for their territorial sovereignty. But at the same time, both Britain and the United States were clear that these states had no right to expect intervention by others to help them to suppress these demands for independence. On the contrary, they acknowledged that there was a right to self-determination on the part of the peoples of Latin America. The appropriate response for third parties, therefore, was identified as one of non-intervention and neutrality, thereby defending both the sovereign rights of the parent state and the right to self-determination on the part of a community. There was, however, a desire to establish some continuity with the dynastic era. So, for example, when the British decision was being made to recognize the new states in Latin America, the dispatches from Paris to London that were sent from between 1774 and 1778 were examined to ascertain "the different steps by which France and Spain advanced successively to a recognition of our American colonies and our cooperation with them." The dispatches revealed that neither France nor Spain established official relations with the Americans "until after the treaties of amity."[51] But Britain and the United States were clear that sovereignty could not indefinitely trump self-determination. It was argued that if those seeking self-determination established a *de facto* state, then both countries considered the community to have earned the right to recognition to sovereign status but only over the territory that they controlled and subject to a willingness to satisfy conditions that were considered to be in the general interest of the international society. What Fabry then goes on to show is that while the commitment to self-determination persisted, the other practices associated with the recognition of new states were substantially modified or even overturned during the course of the nineteenth and twentieth centuries.

By contrast, the practices relating to international responses to civil war remained largely intact up to the Cold War, having been firmly entrenched during the era when the Latin American states were formed and recognized. However, it was not only in Latin America where these practices were being institutionalized. The British were also attempting to bring identical practices into play within Europe. But in this context, however, the endeavor brought

[51] Stapleton, 1887, 95–96.

them much more directly into confrontation with the dynastic states that were determined to maintain and exercise the right to intervene in support of any European dynasty being challenged by revolutionary forces. Viscount Castlereagh wrote a robust rejoinder to the 1820 Troppau Protocol issued by Prussia and Russia along with Austria. The Protocol endeavored to legitimize the ubiquitous right to suppress revolution; Castlereagh argued that it was objectionable in principle and unworkable in practice. Nevertheless, the 1823 French intervention in Spain in order to consolidate the position of the Bourbon dynasty was sanctioned by the Congress of Verona in 1822, despite strong British objections. However, the threat of a joint intervention by France and Spain to restore Latin America to Europe encouraged Britain to approach the United States in an attempt to present a united front against this potential intervention. The United States, however, preferred to make an independent declaration which was presented in the President's Annual Message to Congress on December 2, 1823 and is now known as the Monroe Doctrine. Nevertheless, Britain and the United States agreed in principle that when confronted by a civil war, other states in the international society should observe the norm of non-intervention and pursue a policy of neutrality. Although this was broadly the policy that Britain pursued during the American Civil War, the North always denied that the conflict was a civil war. Nevertheless, after the war, the United States acknowledged the legitimacy of the British position, but it then demanded compensation for what were deemed to be breaches by the British of their own position of neutrality.[52] The British disputed the US position but agreed to send the issue to international arbitration where the American position was upheld and compensation was duly paid. When we turn to the British response to the Spanish Civil War, however, a much more complex picture emerges.

Competing British practices during the Spanish Civil War

A detailed analysis of the primary sources provides evidence that the British decision-makers were aware throughout the Spanish Civil War of the societal practices that had been established in the nineteenth century for responding to civil wars. From this perspective, the right to self-determination overrides sovereignty rights once it is established that there is a civil war taking place. As it happens, it did not take long for the British to define the situation in Spain in terms of a civil war. News of an attempted army coup in Spain was received on July 17, 1936 and it was acknowledged that "fighting is widespread and that the issue of the struggle between rebel military forces and Government forces is still uncertain."[53] The following month, the conflict was being identified in the

---

[52] Little, 2007b.   [53] 23.7.1936, FO/371/20525/W7223.

Foreign Office as a "civil war."[54] Reports that the Nationalists had consolidated
their hold in Northern Spain led the Foreign Office to predict a "long drawn-out
conflict."[55] What I show in this section, however, is that despite the fact that the
British acknowledged that there was a civil war going on in Spain and that a
long-standing tradition indicated that they should promote an international
consensus in favor of practices linked to non-intervention, concerns about the
balance of power turning against them on the continent had a profound effect
on the practices pursued by the British.

From an early stage there were concerns in Britain that the civil war could
result in a fragmented Spain. A Foreign Office official insisted, however, that the
"maintenance of the integrity of Spain is certainly a British interest in the
present circumstances, because if Spain were to disintegrate, the separate
parts might very well fall under the control of one or other foreign country."[56]
But there were other concerns voiced almost immediately in Cabinet. Eden, the
Foreign Secretary, suggested that the Nationalists seemed to be gaining the
upper hand and that there was "some danger that the civil war might end with a
Government in power somewhat resentful of our attitude."[57] It was also pointed
out that the Italians would regard the conflict in Spain "not only as a struggle
between Communism and Fascism but also and primarily as a field in which
she might find herself able to strengthen her own influence and weaken
Britain's sea power in the Western Mediterranean."[58] The military were clear
that in the event of a future war, it was essential to maintain friendly links with
Spain, or at the very least secure her neutrality. It was argued that if Spain
became an enemy of Britain and permitted hostile forces to operate from Spain
then it would make Britain's position very precarious because of the crucial role
played by Gibraltar in maintaining the imperial links that depended on access
to the Mediterranean. By the same token, if the harbors on the Spanish Atlantic
seaboard were in enemy hands, then Britain's communications with the
Americas would also be rendered vulnerable. Under these circumstances, the
British considered that they had no alternative but to follow practices that
would preserve the existing balance of power.

The fact that the civil war in Spain was so quickly seen to have wider
international and systemic ramifications made it much more difficult to determine how to respond to the conflict. Nevertheless, from an early stage it was
agreed by the military as well as the Foreign Office that the British should abide
by their long-established policy of non-intervention. Lord Cranborne, an
Under Secretary of State, acknowledged that the 1820 White Paper written by
the Foreign Secretary, Lord Castlereagh, in response to the Troppau Protocol,

[54] 8.14.1936, Pollock memo, FO/20530/W8509.
[55] 8.6.1936, Leigh Smith memo, FO/20526/W8509.
[56] 1.11.1937, Sargent memo, FO/371/21285/W3322.   [57] 10.28.1936, *Cabinet Papers*, 23/86.
[58] 8.31.1936, *Cabinet Papers*, 24/264.

established non-intervention as a basic tenet of British foreign policy.[59] Although the British favored a policy of non-intervention Eden, the Foreign Secretary, argued initially that the British were also in a strong position to act as a mediator because the "victory of either extreme would be most unwelcome to us so that we must be up and doing in favor of compromise whenever opportunity affords."[60] By this time, however, the British were already heavily involved in the attempt to implement the French suggestion of a collaborative policy to prevent arms from reaching either side in the Spanish Civil War.[61]

Initially, the Foreign Office reaction to the French proposal was rather cool. Mounsey argued that it would be a mistake to "*tie our hands* to any agreement which is not practically universal."[62] Another Foreign Office official noted that the British should remain "completely impartial and free to pursue the policy of nonintervention."[63] As a consequence, the French plan was soon being given serious consideration. One official commented that while there were "several possible courses of action . . . assistance to the rebels must of course be ruled out as contrary to all our principles of correctness and justice."[64] The British initially suggested informal conversations among the major powers. The Italians, however, called for a commission. Although the Germans rejected this suggestion, the British set up an internal interdepartmental committee to handle the issue of non-intervention and then within a few days succeeded in getting general international agreement on a Non-Intervention Committee that would meet in London.[65] The aim of the committee was to establish and police an arms embargo.

Although the British initiated the standard practice for dealing with civil wars, by adopting a policy of non-intervention and endeavoring to ensure that all other states complied with this practice, they quickly began to diverge from established procedures. Soon after the military insurrection, for example, the Republican government indicated that they were going to establish a blockade. Shuckburgh argued that an effective blockade amounted to a recognition by the

---

[59] Northedge, 1966, 441.

[60] 9.3.1936, Eden memo, FO/371/20537/W10351 5/22. It is worth noting that the British were also anxious to pursue a policy of mediation in the context of the American Civil War. See Little, 2007b; and Brauer, 1972.

[61] For decades after the civil war, there was a significant debate about who first proposed a policy of non-intervention. As Carlton argued, those on the left presupposed that the Popular Front Government in France only went along with the policy "under pressure from the right-wing British Government." Carlton, 1971, 40. It is now generally accepted that the French acted on their own initiative. See also Gallagher, 1971; and Warner, 1962. For a more recent account endorsing this position, see Stone, 2005.

[62] 8.2.1936, FO/371/20526/W7504 5/23. Emphasis in the original.

[63] 8.2.1936, Mounsey to Halifax, FO/371/ 20526/W7504.

[64] 8.19.1936, Mounsey to Cadogan, FO/371/20573/W9717.

[65] See 9.3.1936, FO/371/20575/W10587 5/27, 5/26; and Kleine-Ahlbrandt, 1962, 13.

Republicans of the belligerent status of the Nationalists.[66] A direct parallel then existed with the American Civil War and it was acknowledged that this was the leading precedent.[67] In the American Civil War, in the wake of the Northern states implementing a blockade of the Southern States, the British argued that this was tantamount to a declaration of war and a recognition by the North that they were engaged in a civil war, and on this basis they accorded the Southern States belligerent status. In the context of Spain, however, the British insisted that the legality of the blockade could only be established after the insurgents had been granted belligerent status by the British.[68] But the government proved unwilling to take this step. Although the need to grant belligerent status to the Nationalist Government was discussed throughout the civil war, the time was never considered appropriate and so the move was always pushed into the future. The Cabinet failed to respond to the blockade because it wanted a more dramatic development to justify the decision.

In mid-October, for example, the Cabinet decided to recognize the insurgents as belligerents when they captured Madrid,[69] but the Republicans managed to hold Madrid at this time. In the meantime, Germany and Italy announced on November 18 that they were granting the Nationalist Government *de jure* status. But this move was certainly not in line with established practice. Therefore, Eden was forced to rethink the existing policy. He decided to delay granting belligerent status because it would leave the Government open to the charge that Britain was following in the wake of the dictators' policy. But the Government was also constrained by domestic factors. As Prime Minister Chamberlain argued the following year, if Franco was granted belligerent status, at that juncture, then the government's opponents would argue that the move "revealed the Government's policy in its true light, which they had always claimed was support for Franco."[70] The failure to give *de facto* recognition to the Nationalist Government was a source of persistent irritation within the Foreign Office. One official noted in frustration that "ever since September 1936, by our whole course of action we have admitted and could not deny that there was a war and that Franco was a party."[71] Towards the end of the civil war a member of the Foreign Office suggested that if belligerent rights were eventually to be accorded, then it would represent the "crowning illogicality of the whole treatment of the Spanish Civil War" because it would occur "at that moment when the war seems likely to end by the defeat of one side."[72]

The British failure to grant belligerent status to the Nationalists was inconsistent with their policy of defending the Non-Intervention Committee which

[66] 8.13.1936, FO/371/20530/W8554 3/39.   [67] 8.10.1936, FO/371/20529/W8234 3/40.
[68] 8.13.1936, FO/371/20530/W8554 3/41.   [69] 10.21.1936, *Cabinet Papers*, 23/85.
[70] 6.30.1937, *Cabinet Papers*, 23/88 6/109.
[71] 2.17.1938, Beckett memo, FO/371/22635/W738.
[72] 3.22.1938, Beckett memo, FO/371/22641/W4211.

presupposed that the incumbent Republican Government was confronting an insurgent Nationalist Government, which had been recognized by the international society as a belligerent. Under these circumstances, external parties were required to pursue a policy of neutrality. But the issue was complicated by the fact that the Germans and Italians, and then the Russians, were violating the arms embargo. It was clear that they had no interest in working within the normative framework provided by the international society. Unsurprisingly, the Republican Government complained that the British arms embargo had much larger consequences for them, because of the external military support being given to the Nationalists. A Foreign Office official accepted that it was difficult to respond to this argument, except to indicate that "the political consequences of giving the legal government the facilities to which it is undoubtedly entitled would have been far too great to have been risked."[73] British Cabinet members endeavored to justify the position by portraying the Soviet Union as the main violator of the non-intervention policy. After Eden made this argument in the House of Commons, the War Office expressed surprise because it was not consistent with their evidence. There was also concern that Eden's statement would be used by Germany and Italy to justify their policies.[74] When Eden was informed that the Foreign Office was also keeping a record of the infringements of the non-intervention agreement, he noted, "Glad, for I may have to justify my scarcely veiled allusions to the House today."[75] But over time, the reluctance to recognize the Franco regime grew. It was argued that by "granting belligerent rights to Franco under pressure we should undoubtedly be regarded in Europe as recognizing the success not of him, but of Italy and Germany."[76] It was argued that only after the German and Italian troops had been removed could Franco's belligerent status be recognized.

As the conflict in Spain persisted, however, and the general situation in Europe deteriorated, doubts emerged about the prevailing policy within the Cabinet. The societal implications of policy were subordinated to systemic considerations. By the start of 1937, Eden argued that Spain had become an international battleground and that "the character of the future Government of Spain has now become less important to the peace of Europe than that the dictators should not be victorious in that country."[77] By contrast, Lord Halifax reduced Spain to a "tactical situation" where it was important not to "lose sight of the main *desideratum* of not allowing our relations with Italy and Germany to deteriorate."[78] Eden disagreed and argued that future relations with Germany would be conducted "with very much greater advantage to ourselves

[73] 9.7.1936, FO/371/20575/W10779 3/43.   [74] 11.23.1936, FO/371/20586/W16391 7/72.
[75] 11.18.1936, FO/371/20585/W15880 7/73.   [76] 7.6.1937, FO/371/21296/W13036 7/83.
[77] 1.8.1937, *Cabinet Papers*, 24/267 9/150.
[78] 6.30.1937, FO/371/21296/W12187 9/151.

if we had demonstrated beyond all possible doubt that in the Mediterranean there is a point beyond which the United Kingdom cannot be drawn by sapping and mining or by bluster and threats."[79] Throughout 1937, it is clear from Eden's comments on Foreign Office documents that he is becoming increasingly disenchanted with and isolated from the prevailing British position. A Foreign Office official, for example, complains that "instead of trying to wean General Franco away from the increasing German and Italian influence they [the Russians] have under the cover of non-intervention thrown him more into their arms." Eden notes, "There are others who think that the democracies should have done more to help the Government, thus obviating this danger."[80] By the start of 1938, Eden's position had become untenable and he resigned in February.[81]

Although the Non-Intervention Committee failed to prevent foreign intervention in the Spanish Civil War, it did pose an effective barrier to the establishment of an Anglo-Italian agreement. Despite the general consensus that an agreement could not be put in place prior to a settlement in Spain, there was no consensus about what would constitute a settlement. In May 1937, Eden had argued that the objective of the Non-Intervention Committee would only be realized when the "last foreigner" had been withdrawn and "that unhappy country has been allowed to settle her own destiny in her own way."[82] Some Foreign Office officials argued, however, that Britain should threaten to leave the Committee if Germany and Italy failed to accept British proposals that were being put forward. But Lord Cranborne argued that "[t]o take the initiative in breaking an agreement which has the overwhelming support of public opinion in this country and has after all fulfilled its main purpose of stabilizing a dangerous situation would be a great gamble."[83] This position held through 1937, but after Eden's resignation the Prime Minister argued that he had never assumed that the elimination of foreign troops from Spain was the *sine qua non* for an agreement with Italy.[84] The agreement with Italy was established in April 1938, pending a settlement of the Spanish question. But the British decision-makers were unable to agree on the definition of such a settlement. By the start of 1939, Cadogan was expressing irritation that the French would not let the Spanish War "fizzle out." Since it was clear that Franco was going to win, French policy "merely prolongs the fighting – allowing Mussolini to dig further in."[85]

But within weeks the war did come to an end; however, British systemic concerns about the balance of power persisted. With the onset of the Second World War, Britain's main concern was to ensure that Franco pursued a policy of neutrality and did not side with Germany and Italy. For Franco, the

[79] 12.14.1936, *Cabinet Papers*, 24/265 9/152.
[80] 12.23.1937, FO/371/21302/W22043 9/155.   [81] 2.20.1938, *Cabinet Papers*, 23/92 9/156.
[82] 7.19.1938, FO/371/22651/W10243 9/144.   [83] 6.7.1937, FO/371/21335/W11004 9/147.
[84] 3.2.1938, *Cabinet Papers*, 23/92 9/143.   [85] 1.25.1939, FO/371/24115/W1471 9/168.

continuation of the alliance forged during the civil war depended on the willingness of Germany and Italy to sanction Spanish imperial expansion. Franco's imperial ambitions led to an unprompted offer to enter the war on the side of the Axis powers. But Hitler was unwilling to satisfy Franco's ambitions. As Rees notes, "far from playing a canny game to stay out of the war, Franco only avoided a disastrous intervention because of the reluctance of the Germans and Italians to accept Spain as a co-belligerent."[86]

Conclusion

Viewing the Spanish Civil War from the perspective of international practices suggests that the way that some English School theorists like Bull and Watson distinguish between an international system and an international society is problematic.[87] They presuppose that an international society can only develop in the wake of a fully formed international system and that only then will system and society coexist. What the analysis of the case study suggests here, however, is that it is only possible to identify systemic practices in the context of an international society. So, for example, as soon as the British recognized that Spain was engulfed by civil war, their immediate response was to fall back on the societal practice of non-intervention, using the British response to the American Civil War as the exemplar. Following the British and French, the Germans, Italians, and Soviets all agreed to participate in the Non-Intervention Committee but in contrast to the British and the French, they were, at the same time, pursuing a very different practice, violating the terms of non-intervention by supplying one side in the civil war with arms. Rather than following a normative practice, therefore, these states were pursuing a practice based on purely instrumental or systemic thinking. But these states were also well aware that their actions were deviant because they insisted in public that they were abiding by non-intervention rules.

Because the British were unprepared for war, they needed to establish some kind of *modus vivendi* with these states. But they were also torn between trying to sustain international normative practices, thereby maintaining some distance between themselves and the deviating practices of the authoritarian continental powers, without jeopardizing their future security. So, for example, the British wished to establish a military alliance with Italy, in an effort to move the balance of power in Britain's favor, but they refused to do so until the disagreements over Spain had been resolved. Krasner, who has looked closely at the issue of norm deviance and conformity, cannot account for the British

---

[86] Rees, 2003, 639. For a detailed account of Britain's relations with Spain at this time, see Smyth, 1986. See also Goda, 1993 for an intriguing account of Hitler's interest in Gibraltar in 1940.

[87] Bull and Watson, 1984.

position. He insists that systemic or instrumental practices always take precedence over normative or societal practices. Therefore, he associates international norms with "organized hypocrisy" because of the persistent decoupling
between principles and practices:[88] the decoupling takes place when political
leaders find that it is in their interests to do so. Norms are followed, but only
when they do not interfere with state interests. From Krasner's perspective,
interests always trump norms. However, Krasner accepts that states do not wish
to be seen to be violating norms and so will almost invariably maintain that they
are not violating them. The difficulty with this line of argument is that it fails to
provide an adequate account for the durability of normative practices. By
contrast, members of the English School argue that the norms associated with
primary institutions such as sovereignty and non-intervention are so firmly
embedded that they play a crucial role in constituting a society of states.

   The case study provides more support for the English School than for
Krasner. British decision-makers do seem to have been socialized into accepting
the institutional and constitutive status of non-intervention, reflecting a deep-
seated preoccupation with the practices associated with it. Moreover, Krasner's
assumption that political leaders will simply ignore these rules when it is in their
interests to do so fails to recognize how profoundly the practices are implicated
in the process of defining the situation that the decision-makers find themselves
in. The systemic or deviant practices pursued by Russia, Italy, and Germany are
only identified as "deviant" in the context of an existing international society.
Even if societal practices start to break down, as they did in the 1930s, and to
give way to systemic practices, Bull is surely right when he stresses that these
systemic practices will certainly not eliminate the memory of practices that can
sustain an international society.[89] Nevertheless, it remains useful to draw a
distinction between normative practices that sustain and systemic practices that
undermine the existence of an established international society. The Spanish
Civil War case study demonstrates that it is extraordinarily difficult for a
country like Britain, confronted by deviant states, to pursue a coherent and
consistent set of practices. Ultimately, they also have no alternative but to adopt
systemic practices in an effort to survive.

References

Alexandrowicz, C. H., 1958. The Theory of Recognition *In Fieri. The British Year
    Book of International Law* 34: 176–198.
Alpert, Michael, 1997. *A New International History of the Spanish Civil War.*
    Basingstoke: Macmillan.
Bain, William, 2003. *Between Anarchy and Society: Trusteeship and the Obligation of
    Power.* Oxford: Oxford University Press.

---

[88] Krasner, 1999, 220, 226.   [89] Bull, 2002.

Berridge, Geoffrey, 1980. The Political Theory and Institutional History of States Systems. *British Journal of International Studies* 6 (1): 82–92.

Brauer, Kinley J., 1972. British Mediation and the American Civil War: A Reconsideration. *The Journal of Southern History* 38 (1): 49–64.

Bull, Hedley, 1984. *Intervention in World Politics*. Oxford: Clarendon Press.

2002 [1977]. *The Anarchical Society: A Study of Order in World Politics*. 3rd edn. New York: Columbia University Press.

Bull, Hedley and Adam Watson, eds., 1984. *The Expansion of International Society*. Oxford: Clarendon Press.

Buzan, Barry, 2004. *From International to World Society? English School Theory and the Social Structure of Globalization*. Cambridge: Cambridge University Press.

Buzan, Barry and Richard Little, 2000. *International Systems in World History: Remaking the Study of International Relations*. Oxford: Oxford University Press.

Carlton, David, 1971. Eden, Blum and the Origins of Non-Intervention. *Journal of Contemporary History* 6 (3): 40–55.

Carr, E. H., 1984. *The Comintern and the Spanish Civil War*. London: Macmillan.

Deutscher, Tamara, 1984. Introduction. In *The Comintern and the Spanish Civil War* by E. H. Carr, edited by Tamara Deutscher. London: Macmillan.

Dunne, Tim, 2005. System, State and Society: How Does it All Hang Together? *Millennium* 34 (1): 157–170.

Fabry, Mikulas, 2010. *Recognizing States: International Society and the Establishment of New States Since 1776*. Oxford: Oxford University Press.

Finney, Patrick, ed., 1997. *The Origins of the Second World War*. London: Arnold.

Gallagher, M. D., 1971. Leon Blum and the Spanish Civil War. *Journal of Contemporary History* 6 (3): 56–64.

Goda, Norman J. W., 1993. The Riddle of the Rock: A Reassessment of German Motives for the Capture of Gibraltar in the Second World War. *Journal of Contemporary History* 28 (2): 297–314.

Graham, Helen, 2005. *The Spanish Civil War: A Very Short Introduction*. Oxford: Oxford University Press.

International Security, 1997. Symposium: History and Theory 22 (1): 5–85.

Jackson, Robert, 2000. *The Global Covenant: Human Conduct in a World of States*. Oxford: Oxford University Press.

James, Alan, 1993. System or Society? *Review of International Studies* 19 (3): 269–288.

Keens-Soper, Maurice, 1978. The Practice of a States-System. In *The Reason of States: A Study in International Political Theory*, edited by Michael D. Donelan, 25–44. London: Allen & Unwin.

Keohane, Robert O., 1988. International Institutions: Two Approaches. *International Studies Quarterly* 32 (4): 379–396.

Kleine-Ahlbrandt, William L., 1962. *The Policy of Simmering: A Study of British Policy During the Spanish Civil War, 1936–1939*. The Hague: Martinus Nijhoff.

Koivisto, Marjo, 2010. Practices of Liberal World Order: Internationalism and Imperialism in International Society. Paper presented at the Annual Meeting of the Standing Group in International Relations, September, Stockholm.

Krasner, Stephen D., 1999. *Sovereignty: Organized Hypocrisy*. Princeton: Princeton University Press.

Little, Douglas, 1985. *Malevolent Neutrality: The United States, Great Britain, and the Origins of the Spanish Civil War*. Ithaca: Cornell University Press.

1988. Red Scare, 1936: Anti-Bolshevism and the Origins of British Non-Intervention in the Spanish Civil War. *Journal of Contemporary History* 23 (2): 291–311.

Little, Richard, 1987. Revisiting Intervention: A Survey of Recent Developments. *Review of International Studies* 13 (1): 49–60.

1993. Recent Literature on Intervention and Non-Intervention. In *Political Theory, International Relations, and the Ethics of Intervention*, edited by Ian Forbes and Mark Hoffman, 13–31. Basingstoke: Macmillan.

2007a. *The Balance of Power in International Relations: Metaphors, Myths and Models*. Cambridge: Cambridge University Press.

2007b. British Neutrality versus Offshore Balancing in the American Civil War: The English School Strikes Back. *Security Studies* 16 (1): 68–95.

March, James G. and Johan P. Olsen, 1998. The Institutional Dynamics of International Political Orders. *International Organization* 52 (4): 943–969.

Morgenthau, Hans J., 1973 [1948]. *Politics Among Nations: The Struggle for Power and Peace*. 5th edn. New York: Alfred A. Knopf.

Nalbandov, Robert, 2009. Battle of Two Logics: Appropriateness and Consequentiality in Russian Interventions in Georgia. *Caucasian Review of International Affairs* 3 (1): 20–36.

Navari, Cornelia, 2008. The Concept of Practice in the English School. Paper presented at the 2nd Global International Studies Conference of the World International Studies Committee, July, Ljubljana.

Forthcoming. The Concept of Practice in the English School. *European Journal of International Relations*.

Northedge, Frederick S., 1966. *The Troubled Giant: Britain Among the Great Powers, 1916–1939*. London: Bell.

Osiander, Andreas, 1994. *The States System of Europe, 1640–1990: Peacemaking and the Conditions of International Stability*. Oxford: Oxford University Press.

Rees, Tim, 2003. Between the Rock and a Hard Place: Spain's International Relations in the Twentieth and Twenty-First Centuries. *Journal of Contemporary History* 38 (4): 633–646.

Rosenau, James N., ed., 1964. *International Aspects of Civil Strife*. Princeton: Princeton University Press.

Schatzki, Theodore R., 1996. *Social Practices: A Wittgensteinian Approach to Human Activity and the Social*. New York: Cambridge University Press.

Schroeder, Paul W., 1976. Munich and the British Tradition. *The Historical Journal* 19 (1): 223–243.

1994. *The Transformation of European Politics: 1763–1848*. Oxford: Clarendon Press.

Smyth, Denis, 1986. *Diplomacy and Strategy of Survival: British Policy and Franco's Spain, 1940–41*. Cambridge: Cambridge University Press.

Stapleton, Edward J., ed., 1887. *Some Official Correspondence of George Canning*. Vol. 1. London: Longmans, Green & Co.

Stone, Glyn, 2005. *Spain, Portugal and the Great Powers 1931–1941*. Basingstoke: Palgrave Macmillan.

Teschke, Benno, 2003. *The Myth of 1648: Class, Geopolitics and the Making of Modern International Relations*. London: Verso.

Vigezzi, Brunello, 2005. *The British Committee on the Theory of International Politics (1954–1985): The Rediscovery of History*. Milan: Edizioli Unicopoli.

Waltz, Kenneth N., 1979. *Theory of International Politics*. Reading, MA: Addison-Wesley.

Warner, Geoffrey, 1962. France and Non-Intervention in Spain, July–August 1936. *International Affairs* 38 (2): 203–220.

Wheeler, Nicholas J., 2000. *Saving Strangers: Humanitarian Intervention in International Society*. Oxford: Oxford University Press.

Wilcox, Francis O., 1938. The Localization of the Spanish War. *The American Political Science Review* 32 (2): 237–260.

8 | Domestic practices and balancing: integrating practice into neoclassical realism

NORRIN M. RIPSMAN*

Can the concept of practice contribute to a realist analysis of world politics? All realists privilege the causal impact of the international system and its structural constraints as the principal drivers of international politics. The dominant group of realists, the structural realists, contend that the explanatory power to explain all that matters in international politics – principally international security competition and war – resides almost exclusively in the external structure. They deride theorists who pay attention to agency, by examining the role of leaders and other domestic actors, as reductionist and counterproductive. Recently, neoclassical realists have enriched realism, not by refuting the primacy of the international system, but by incorporating unit and subunit level variables to explain how structural constraints and opportunities get transmitted to state policy-makers and how policy responses are formulated. This has been an important theoretical advance, paying attention to both agency and structure, which can explain variations in the way different states respond to similar external challenges and anomalous foreign policy responses clearly at odds with systemic pressures. The focus on practice advocated in this volume offers an opportunity to increase the explanatory power of neoclassical realism by focusing on an important area that has as yet remained outside its purview: the space between agency and structure constituted by domestic political and international practices.

In this chapter, I shall overview the neoclassical realist challenge to structural realism and explain how attention to domestic political practices can sharpen that challenge and improve neoclassical realist theory. I argue that national foreign policy practitioners can often have an important impact on whether and how particular states balance against threats by using their background systemic and cultural knowledge to determine what constitutes appropriate and competent foreign policy behavior and, consequently, to establish practices that shape policy

* I wish to thank Emanuel Adler, Lilach Gilady, Vincent Pouliot, and participants at the conference on "The Practice Turn in International Relations" at the Munk Centre, University of Toronto, November 2008, for comments on an earlier draft of this chapter. In addition, I thank Shaun Cavaliere and David McKay for their research assistance.

responses. In line with Emanuel Adler and Vincent Pouliot's Chapter 1 in this volume, I argue that paying attention to domestic practices can explain some policy choices – even in the national security issue area – that a focus solely on external structures, domestic institutions, and domestic actors would not. To demonstrate this, I shall present an illustrative case study of the impact of the practice of non-partisanship, or bipartisanship, in American national security policy from 1945 to 1950. Bipartisanship stemmed from the recognition by the Administration and a core group in Congress, for a time, that competent foreign policy performance required both executive consultation with the legislature and congressional support for the Administration's foreign policy agenda which resulted from consultation. This practice enabled a significant proportion of the Republican opposition to support a move away from isolationism after the Second World War toward anti-Soviet balancing, provided it occurred within an agreed-upon context of nascent international institutions such as the United Nations, the Economic Recovery Program, and the North Atlantic Treaty Organization (NATO). Without attention to this consequential practice, it would be difficult to explain why American domestic institutional constraints prevented an activist foreign policy agenda after the First World War, but not after the Second World War. In addition, without reference to the practice of bipartisanship, it would be difficult to explain why Washington engaged in balancing against the Soviet Union within that particular institutional context.

Neoclassical realism, domestic practices, and balancing

According to structural realists, the driving force of international politics is differential growth rates, which change the relative distribution of capabilities between states.[1] Rising states pose a challenge to others and lead them, almost automatically, to balance against the challenger either through armament (internal balancing) or alliances (external balancing). In addition, states are compelled to anticipate power shifts and forestall them through policies such as preventive war.[2] While Kenneth Waltz, for example, acknowledges that states do not always behave as the international system requires them to, he contends that, because those that defy systemic imperatives are frequently defeated and eliminated, states are socialized over time to balance against rising great powers.[3] Thus, regardless of their regime type or other domestic political differences between them, neorealists expect states to balance against rising challengers in a predictable and unproblematic manner.[4]

---

[1] See Waltz, 1979; Organski and Kugler, 1980; and Gilpin, 1981.
[2] See, for example, Levy, 1987; and Copeland, 2000.   [3] Waltz, 1979, 118–128.
[4] See, for example, Waltz, 1967, esp. 306–311, where he argues that the domestic differences between Great Britain and the United States had little impact on their foreign policy behavior.

A group of realist scholars, whom Gideon Rose has labeled "neoclassical realists," challenges this fluid and automatic neorealist conception of balancing, on two grounds.[5] First, domestic politics and the personalities of individual leaders can have a significant effect on foreign policy and occasionally interfere with the state's ability to respond correctly to systemic imperatives. Thus, according to Jack Snyder, while the international system rarely rewards expansionism and usually punishes it, and while most states avoid expansionism for that reason, states governed by imperialistic cartels and militaristic general staffs frequently ignore these constraints at their own peril.[6] More significantly, Randall Schweller observes that while, on average, states tend to balance against rising powers, "underbalancing" is more common than Waltz and neorealists would expect. He explains these deviations in terms of elite and societal divisions that prevent the state from mobilizing adequate societal resources to balance effectively.[7] Furthermore, leaders may misperceive the balance of power, which may lead them to respond to challenges inappropriately.[8] According to these neoclassical realists, therefore, domestic political constraints can explain suboptimal or dysfunctional balancing behavior (i.e. behavior that deviates from systemic requirements). In other words, they contend that most of the time balancing is rather fluid and automatic; only in unusual circumstances do domestic political realities interfere with rational national security responses.

More recent neoclassical realist scholarship provides an even broader scope for domestic politics, which opens up a second challenge to the fluidity of neorealist balance of power theory.[9] Although on rare occasions the systemic imperatives provide adequate information on the appropriate response to a rising challenger or threatening state (e.g. in 1967, when a pre-emptive strike was the only reasonable option available to Israel when faced with an Egyptian mobilization and blockade of the Straits of Tiran, coupled with the withdrawal of the UN peacekeeping force in the Sinai[10]), more frequently a range of policy responses are all plausible. Thus, for example, there is room for domestic debate about whether containment or engagement is the appropriate American strategy to deal with the rise of China.[11] Under these more relaxed circumstances, domestic actors and institutions have far greater scope to determine whether and how a state will respond to a rising adversary. States and domestic actors still construct policies in reference to the international challenges and opportunities they face. Therefore, domestic groups that seek to maximize their interests by directing foreign policy in a manner disconnected from the international environment the

---

[5] Rose, 1998.   [6] Snyder, 1991.   [7] See Schweller, 2004 and 2006.

[8] Wohlforth, 1993.

[9] See Taliaferro, Lobell, and Ripsman, 2009; and Ripsman, Taliaferro, and Lobell, 2009.

[10] Oren, 2002.

[11] For competing positions on how to treat the rise of China, see Friedberg, 2005; and Ross and Feng, 2008.

state faces are likely to be unsuccessful. Thus the international system still conditions the foreign policy response, although the shape it will take will be tailored by the domestic arena.[12] In this vein, Mark Brawley demonstrates that in the 1920s and early 1930s, Great Britain, France, and the Soviet Union all identified impending German recovery as the leading threat to their security, but because of their particular domestic political circumstances, they adopted distinctly different strategies to respond to the threat.[13]

The implication of these neoclassical realist insights is that balancing – and foreign policy responses more broadly – is less automatic than structural realists assume and is more dependent on domestic political arrangements. To this point, however, most neoclassical realists have focused on either domestic political institutions, domestic actors – such as interest groups – or state leaders. Thus, in the former camp, Jack Snyder explains overexpansion in terms of the political institutions that govern grand strategy.[14] In a similar vein, Miriam Fendius Elman and Susan Peterson argue that presidential and parliamentary democracies respond differently to systemic incentives due to institutional differences between them.[15]

In the domestic actors' camp, some argue that interest groups and societal sectors compete to define international threats and opportunities consistently with their own interests.[16] Others observe that state leaders can also have an impact on policy choices independently of their underlying societal coalition, either through the attitudes and beliefs they bring to office, or their political preferences. For example, building on the work of Robert Jervis, William Wohlforth observes that "if power influences the course of international politics, it must do so largely through the perceptions of the people who make decisions on behalf of the states."[17] Therefore, the psychological make-up of leaders is important. Moreover, as Daniel Byman and Kenneth Pollack argue, in the right circumstances skillful leaders may be able to impose their own policy preferences on the state, thereby personalizing its foreign policy response.[18] Finally, some neoclassical realists incorporate both domestic institutions and actors into their explanatory framework. In this regard, Schweller's model incorporates institutional variables affecting governmental and regime stability, as well as actor variables relating to the degree of elite and societal consensus and cohesion.[19]

---

[12] For this reason, the approach remains realist and distinct from a liberal, *Innenpolitik* approach. Rose, 1998.
[13] Brawley, 2009.   [14] Snyder, 1991.
[15] See Elman, 2000; and Peterson, 1995 and 1996. As I indicate below, my own work begins with an institutional approach similar to theirs, but includes procedural and normative influences, as well: Ripsman, 2002.
[16] See Lobell, 2003; and Brawley, 1993.
[17] See Wohlforth, 1993, 2; and Jervis, 1976, 18–19, 28–31.   [18] Byman and Pollack, 2001.
[19] Schweller, 2006.

My own neoclassical realist approach to foreign policy-making in democratic states also goes beyond merely the effect of domestic political institutions. I argue that the foreign policy choices that states make are influenced by the degree of autonomy they have from public opinion, societal groups, or the legislature. At core, autonomy derives from the formal institutional structure of the state, which defines the scope of executive authority to govern and construct foreign policy. Thus, for example, Westminster-style parliamentary regimes, with plurality voting in single-member constituencies, tend to afford more foreign policy autonomy than parliamentary regimes with proportional voting, since the latter tend to encourage large, multiparty coalitions, where the executive must bargain with different parties to enact policies. Yet, what actors do within the scope of authority delineated by institutional structures is moderated by domestic political procedures and the procedural norms that inform them. Thus, for example, the procedure of party discipline in Great Britain enhances executive autonomy by stifling dissent and discouraging legislators from using their constitutional power to oversee foreign policy.[20] States that are structurally autonomous from public opinion, societal groups, and the legislature can respond to international challenges as they see fit. Less autonomous states, however, must bargain with domestic groups to enact policy and mobilize adequate societal resources to implement it, unless they have the capacity or legitimacy to buy off, coerce, or coopt domestic opponents.[21] Therefore, whether and how states balance against rising adversaries will vary based on national attitudes, domestic political institutions, procedures, and norms.[22]

While these unidimensional and multidimensional neoclassical realist theories have added depth to structural realist analyses, paying attention to the role of domestic political practices can add even more explanatory power. Indeed, within the confines of an existing domestic institutional structure, the nature of policy-making is influenced by more than merely procedures – which institutionalize behavior and, therefore, may be understood as institutions in and of themselves – and the norms that inspire them. Practices, understood as appropriate and competent performances by a temporally constituted community of practitioners, can also affect policy choices.[23] Although these practices may be less enduring, may be restricted only to a portion of the entire community of practitioners, and may affect only a limited range of issues, they may also shape policy choices and outcomes in a manner akin to institutions and procedures. For example, the practice of bipartisanship in American government after the Second World War, which I will discuss

---

[20] Ripsman, 2002.
[21] Blanchard and Ripsman, 2008. On the state's need to bargain with domestic groups to secure the resources to implement national security policy, see Barnett, 1992, Chapters 1–2; and Taliaferro, 2009.
[22] See, for example, the contributions in Katzenstein, 1996.
[23] Adler and Pouliot, Chapter 1 in this volume.

in greater depth later, also affected US behavior in the post-war world. The practice allowed for more decisive action by the executive, which could overcome what could otherwise be insuperable domestic hurdles, by engaging in limited consultation with the congressional opposition in return for broad-based policy support. By the same token, until 1967, societal dissent over national security was largely stifled in Israel because Israeli society, as a whole, recognized that the importance of national security policy and the need for decisive governmental action in this field made restraint a sound and competent practice.[24] In contrast, during the French Fourth Republic, legislators and domestic interests followed the reverse practice of obstruction and interference in foreign affairs, utilizing all their institutionally granted foreign policy powers to the maximum. Thus, domestic practices can affect the way different states respond to systemic imperatives.

Taken together, neoclassical realists view the policy process as a bargaining process between the foreign policy executive (the state) and societal groups, mediated by the domestic institutional, procedural, and normative context within which policy is forged. Practices also mediate that bargaining process in the manner discussed above. Where institutions, procedures, and practices insulate the executive and procedural norms stifle dissent, the more autonomous national security executives are freer to respond to systemic demands as structural realists would expect; more constraining institutions, procedures, and practices that empower domestic actors lead the state to construct foreign policy with greater attention to the internal environment. In a more complex domestic environment, many of the structural realist assumptions about national security policy – i.e. that states will always prefer internal balancing to external balancing, that states will always prefer to balance rather than to bandwagon, that states can mobilize national resources as necessary to counter geopolitical rivals – may all fall victim to the preferences of domestic veto players and dominant societal coalitions.[25] Differences in domestic decision-making environments can also explain variations in state motivations, such as whether they are minimalist defensive realist states (which strive for what Waltz calls "an appropriate amount of power" to maintain their security) or maximalist offensive realist states (which seek security through expansion and maximization of their power), whether they are revisionist or status quo states, or whether they are opportunist jackals in response to the misfortune of others.[26]

---

[24] Hermann, 1993.

[25] On the superiority of internal balancing, see Waltz, 1979, Chapter 8. On balancing versus bandwagoning, see Walt, 1987; and Christensen and Snyder, 1990. On veto players, see Tsebelis, 2002.

[26] Most structural realists are defensive realists, including Snyder, 1991; Waltz, 1979; Posen, 1984; Van Evera, 1999; and Taliaferro, 2000/2001. Offensive realists include Mearsheimer, 2001; and Layne, 2006. On the link between domestic politics and the choice between offensive realist and defensive realist strategies, see Lobell, 2002. On status quo vs. revisionist and opportunist states, see Schweller, 1994; and Morgenthau, 1985, 52–85.

A state's domestic foreign policy-making institutions, procedures, and practices affect not only national balancing behavior, but also the behavior of other states – insofar as other states respond to that state's practice-mediated actions – and resultant international outcomes. Therefore, *contra* neorealists, the structure of the international system does not, on its own, determine either the foreign policy responses of states or international outcomes. Attention to practice, in addition to domestic political institutions and actors, can thus help to resolve disagreements between structural realists. For example, it can resolve the debate over the likely consequences of hegemony. Waltz and balance of power theorists argue that unipolarity is unstable and leads to balancing coalitions. Hegemonic stability theorists and power transition theorists, in contrast, maintain that hegemony promotes stability and cooperation. The key to this disagreement may be the domestic political context, including the content of what constitutes competent political practices, within the hegemon. When domestic institutions, procedures, and practices in the hegemon encourage domestic scrutiny of policy and allow domestic groups to voice their concerns over policy openly, that can serve as a moderating influence on hegemonic behavior. This is reinforced when practitioners and the dominant societal coalition favor less costly burden-sharing and multilateral enforcement of global rules.[27] In consequence, the hegemon may appear less threatening to other states and, as a result, may be more likely to elicit cooperative, rather than balancing, responses internationally. In contrast, a less domestically constrained hegemon, equipped with practices that inhibit domestic actors from using their power to limit executive supremacy over foreign affairs, may pose more of a threat to others and provoke balancing.

Thus, John Owen links the absence of balancing against the United States in the 1990s not to the fact of hegemony, but to the liberal character of American hegemony and its high degree of consultation and cooperation with its allies.[28] He argues that, as a result of the restrained American hegemony, "[l]iberal elites the world over tend to perceive a relatively broad coincidence of interest between their country and other liberal countries. They tend to interpret the United States as benign and devote few resources to counterbalancing it."[29] T.V. Paul similarly argues that the prevalence of soft (frequently diplomatic) balancing, rather than traditional military-oriented balancing, against US power was inspired in part by the fact that American domestic political practices prevent overly aggressive behavior that challenges the sovereignty of other states. He writes, "U.S. power seems to be limited by a multitude of internal and external factors, thus making the United States a 'constrained

---

[27] Thus, to some extent practitioners determine the nature of balancing. Similarly, as Patrick Morgan's Chapter 6 in this volume indicates, practitioners determined the nature and content of nuclear deterrence.

[28] Owen, 2001/2002.   [29] *Ibid.*, 121.

hegemon.'"[30] Yet, in the aftermath of the September 11 terrorist attacks, the institutional restraints on American national security policy have evaporated. The Patriot Act, the Bush Doctrine, and norms discouraging interference with executive efforts to secure the United States from the scourge of terrorism have created a climate in which the American Government has been able to flex its military might at will. A noteworthy feature of this context is that, due to the enhanced threat perception, even President George W. Bush's congressional opponents during the early years of his presidency were reluctant to be too critical of his security policies because they felt that would constitute improper practice. A consequence has been decreased cooperation from Washington's allies in the Western world – witness French, German, and Belgian efforts to stymie American efforts to build a coalition against Iraq – and increasing challenges from China and Russia.[31] Clearly, the content of what constitutes competent foreign policy performance in a state can affect the manner in which other states perceive and respond to its behavior internationally. Thus, the nature of domestic foreign policy practices can affect not only national behavior, but also the policy responses of other states and, consequently, the character of the international system.

It follows, then, that international politics is shaped, at least in part, by domestic practices and their evolution over time. Yet the relationship is not static or unidirectional. The definition of competent behavior itself evolves over time and is also affected not only by national culture but also by external circumstances. Thus, for example, the greater security Israel experienced after the 1967 Six Day War, together with the perception that Israeli leaders had failed the country in the build-up to the Egyptian and Syrian surprise attack in 1973, led Israeli society to define competent performance in terms of greater scrutiny in the policy process and greater activism. This led the Israeli public, legislators, and media commentators to become more critical and active in opposition to government policy, even in the face of the significant national security challenges posed by two *intifadas* and the Iranian nuclear weapons program.

Similarly, the foreign policy failures of the French Third Republic, which resulted in defeat by Germany and occupation, conditioned the foreign policy practices of the Fourth Republic. Members of the legislature, key societal interests, and the public at large concluded that foreign policy was far too important to allow the executive unfettered authority; therefore, the understanding of competence evolved to encourage domestic actors to utilize whatever institutional power they had to scrutinize and intervene in the foreign policy process.[32] In the context of the French Fourth Republic's fragmentary multiparty system based on the enshrined principle of parliamentary

---

[30] Paul, 2005, 53.   [31] See, for example, Pape, 2005.
[32] See, for example, Macridis, 1952; and Immergut, 1992, 69.

sovereignty, with large and cumbersome coalition governments, practices of scrutiny and interference complicated policy-making considerably and brought down many a government. In this context, although three successive French premiers believed that rearming German military units within the context of the French-inspired European Defence Community initiative was an urgent necessity for France, they were unwilling to submit the plan to the legislature for fear of defeat; consequently, they delayed (and ultimately defeated) a measure that the governments of France, Great Britain, and the United States believed was required by the realities of the post-Second World War balance of power.[33]

Not only practices, of course but, in a similar manner, national institutions are also partly shaped by the international environment that states face at a founding institutional moment.[34] Necessity is frequently the mother of invention and it is often in moments of crisis or unprecedented circumstances that states are able to overcome domestic inertia and build a coalition in support of new institutions or meaningful changes to existing ones.[35] Thus, for example, the heightened threat situation of the post-Second World War security environment led the US Government to pass the National Security Act of 1947, which established national foreign policy institutions, including the Central Intelligence Agency (CIA), the Joint Chiefs of Staff (JCS), and the National Security Council (NSC), which were responsible to the executive with only minimal congressional oversight.[36] These institutions would then continue to discourage and/or thwart attempts by congressional leaders to monitor and constrain American national security policy for decades to come – at least until the failures of the Vietnam War and the excesses of Watergate led a push to rein in executive authority over foreign affairs.

Political practices, which are more temporal, and which depend on practitioners' evolving sense of what constitutes competent behavior at a given historical moment, should not be tied as closely to a particular historical set of circumstances as institutions. Nonetheless, as the political culture and national history become part of the background knowledge that practitioners internalize, they, too, may interpret competent behavior in terms of enduring national images.

We can, therefore, witness the recursivity that Emanuel Adler and Vincent Pouliot identify in Chapter 1 in this volume. States do not merely respond to objective requirements of the balance of power in a uniform and unproblematic way, as structural realists assume. Instead, national policy responses to international challenges are negotiated between the foreign policy executive and key societal actors within the context of existing domestic institutions and

---

[33] See Ripsman, 2000/2001 and 2002; McGeehan, 1971; and Large, 1996.
[34] See, for example, Gourevitch, 1978; Thelen, 1999; and Pierson, 2002.
[35] See, for example, Olson, 1982; Trimberger, 1978; and Skocpol, 1985, 9–11.
[36] See Zegart, 1999; and Stuart, 2003.

prevailing procedures, procedural norms, and political practices. These negotiations determine whether to respond to a threat or opportunity, what resources to devote to policy, and whether and how to coordinate with other states. The resulting balancing decisions will affect other states' judgments of the responder and, therefore, their subsequent balancing behavior, which will shape the balancing outcome. The outcome will influence the security environment that the state faces subsequently. In this manner, the international legacy of previous national policy choices may have a long-term feedback effect, conditioning the international environment within which future balancing decisions are taken and, possibly, influencing the development of domestic norms, practices, procedures, and institutions. As a result, balancing behavior in subsequent periods may differ considerably, as practitioners draw upon an evolved set of institutions, procedures, norms, and practices.

In the next section, I explore the importance of practices in determining the national security behavior of states by examining the practice of bipartisanship in American foreign policy in the late 1940s and the impact it had on American security policy.[37]

Bipartisanship and American foreign policy, 1945–1950

At the end of the Second World War, US policy-makers were faced with a dilemma similar to that which the country confronted in 1919: should the United States play an active and engaged role in world affairs, or should it retreat into relative isolation, except where direct American interests were concerned? President Franklin Delano Roosevelt and his successor, Harry Truman, concluded that American power was necessary to stabilize a much more dangerous world and that isolationist sentiment was outmoded. To overcome isolationist opposition in Congress they utilized the practice of non-partisanship or bipartisanship to generate a broad-based consensus for post-war American involvement in world affairs.

The practice of bipartisanship entailed two key components. The executive was expected to consult with the leadership of both factions in Congress. In return for this consultation, even members of the opposition were supposed to support the government's foreign policy. The community of practice, however, did not extend to the entire Congress, nor did the practice of bipartisanship endure for more than a few years from the mid- to late 1940s. In fact, bipartisanship succeeded when it did due to the behavior of the Secretary of State and a small group of Republican senators and Congressmen, who until 1949 routinely broke party ranks and voted with the Democrats on foreign

---

[37] In evaluating the nature, origins, community of practice, scope, limits, and reason for the demise of a practice, this case study shares similarities with Richard Little's Chapter 7 in this volume on the practice of non-intervention.

policy votes. We shall examine their reasons for practicing bipartisanship, the key issues over which it prevailed, the impact it had on US foreign policy, and the reasons for the demise of the practice.

The reasons for the practice can be traced, in part, to the novel strategic situation that the United States faced after the Second World War.[38] Prior to the war, the security buffers provided by the Atlantic and Pacific Oceans meant that the United States could be largely indifferent to international affairs and pursue a policy of isolationism. The development of the aircraft carrier, utilized widely during the war in the Pacific, and the impending advent of missile technology meant that the United States was no longer invulnerable and could no longer afford to remain aloof from global security competition. This was especially true since the United States was unlikely to retain its monopoly over the possession of atomic weapons, meaning that Washington faced an impending threat of the highest order from the Soviet Union, a great-power rival that had both the will and capability to harm the United States.[39] Furthermore, the collapse of the European great powers as a result of the Second World War meant that the United States was not only in a unique position to act as a global leader, but also had a responsibility to assume the mantle of leadership in containing the power of the Soviet Union. Agreement on the need for containment, therefore, forged the limited sphere of bipartisan consensus that enabled bipartisan foreign policy to occur.[40]

Under these new circumstances, key individuals in Congress, most notably Senator Arthur H. Vandenberg, who was the high priest of bipartisanship, recognized the need for unity to counter the more challenging international environment. As Malcolm Jewell notes, "[t]he argument for a bipartisan foreign policy has always been a simple one – the need for unity. Senator Vandenberg

---

[38] By explaining bipartisanship primarily in terms of the strategic situation, I take issue with Peter Trubowitz and Nicole Mellow's (2005) contention that the resort to bipartisanship is determined primarily by domestic political factors, such as the presence of divided government. Indeed, as we shall see, the heyday of bipartisanship began prior to the end of the Second World War, before the 1946 congressional election led to a brief period of divided government.

[39] Collier, 1991, 19. Senator Arthur H. Vandenberg, an instrumental figure in the practice of bipartisanship, for example, commented: "My attitude toward international affairs in general and toward collective security for our own national defense was sharply altered by WWII. Prior to WWII, the oceans were virtual moats around our continental bastions. All this changed progressively at Pearl Harbor and thereafter. It became very obvious to me that this was a different world in which we had to sustain our own freedoms. The climax in this trend was demonstrated this past week in a continuous Atlantic flight in something like four hours and thirty seven minutes from England to America. Meanwhile, the atom bomb sharply altered the problem of national defense. These things – and all their related circumstances – rendered obsolete ... our prior thinking regarding our own national security. In other words, I believe I have only been keeping abreast realistically with the progress of our times." Vandenberg, 1952, 577.

[40] See, for example, Briggs, 1994.

emphasized that 'it permits our democracy to speak with a degree of unity at critical moments when swift decision is vital and when we face totalitarian opponents who can command their own instant unity by police decree.'"[41] Unity was essential given the constitutional division of foreign relations power between the executive and the Congress, which amounts to "an invitation to struggle for the privilege of directing American foreign policy."[42] Especially during the period from 1946 to 1948, when Republicans controlled both houses of Congress while a Democratic president held power, a lack of unity would have paralyzed US foreign policy at a critical time. Thus, Vandenberg justified bipartisanship as "a mutual effort, under our indispensable two-party system, to unite our official voice at the water's edge so that America speaks with maximum authority against those who would divide and conquer us and the free world."[43]

To this end, several minority legislators – notably Vandenberg, H. Alexander Smith, and Henry Cabot Lodge, II – voted to support the Administration's foreign policy to give it a sense of legitimacy and create a degree of national unity, which would lay the groundwork for continuity in foreign policy even if elections were to bring another party to the White House or shift control of the Congress. Furthermore, they worked closely with the Administration to forge policy and "functioned as the administration's congressional watchdogs" on foreign policy matters, building consensus within Congress and highlighting any potential problems in advance so as to overcome likely obstacles.[44] In addition, they also committed to eschewing making foreign policy a partisan issue in election campaigns. Thus, for example, Democratic Secretary of State Cordell Hull and Republican foreign policy specialist John Foster Dulles agreed in 1944 to leave the United Nations issue out of the November 1944 presidential election campaign in order not to jeopardize the project.[45] Similarly, when Vandenberg ran for re-election in Michigan in 1946, he passed up an opportunity to criticize the Administration's unpopular $3.75 billion loan to Great Britain (which many advised him to do), or at least distance himself from it; instead, "he took to the Senate floor to support the loan in a speech that was credited by the Administration and the press as an important factor in winning the close fight."[46]

In return, the Administration consulted with opposition politicians to a great extent and genuinely made an effort to compromise when necessary to create a bipartisan consensus. Jewell goes so far as to assert that, during the high water mark of bipartisanship, "the ranking member of the [Senate Foreign Relations Committee] from the administration party – whether chairman or not – was usually less influential than the opposition leader on the committee."[47]

---

[41] Jewell, 1962, 3.   [42] Corwin, 1957, 171.   [43] Vandenberg, 1952, 552.
[44] Johnson, 2006, 17–18.   [45] Hoopes and Brinkley, 1997, 162.   [46] *Ibid.*, 305.
[47] Jewell, 1962, 111.

Moreover, the White House also restrained itself from seeking partisan advantage on foreign policy matters. This was clearly illustrated when, in the lead-up to the 1946 congressional elections, Commerce Secretary Henry A. Wallace publicly attacked the Republican Party as pursuing an anachronistic foreign policy "of economic nationalism and political isolation," charging that bipartisanship had caused the Democratic Administration to surrender "too much to isolationism masquerading as tough realism in international affairs."[48] In response to Vandenberg's complaints, supported by Secretary of State James F. Byrnes, Truman asked Wallace for his resignation, rather than undermine the spirit of bipartisanship that had been forged.[49]

The community of practice that sustained bipartisanship, then, was this cadre of Republican legislators who edged away from obstructionism of an active foreign policy agenda,[50] and the key Democratic Administration officials who directed American foreign policy under Truman. The community formed due to the entrepreneurial leadership of US Secretary of State Cordell Hull – who, as we shall see, inaugurated the practice and inculcated it through his bipartisan consultations over the Dumbarton Oaks conference and the United Nations – and Vandenberg, who sold and reinforced its logic to a small group of Republican senators and congressmen. The spirit of bipartisanship was easiest to maintain when the State Department was presided over by individuals who considered themselves to be above partisanship. Toward the end of the war, Secretaries of State Hull (until November 1944) and Edward R. Stettinius (from December 1944 to June 1945) both viewed foreign policy issues as of too much importance to allow political bickering to derail the national interest. As Hull commented in his memoirs, he had always believed that bipartisanship suited the foreign policy area because of its critical importance, but he was especially committed to it in the wake of war:

> [E]ver since my entry into the State Department in 1933, I had taken numerous steps to prevent politics from coming into the Department and our foreign policies ... I had also gone out of my way to maintain friendly relations with the Legislative Branch of the Government, to consult with Senators, Representatives, and other leading members of both major parties, as well as with editors and writers, and to keep them as fully informed as possible. Following the outbreak of war in Europe on September 1, 1939, I intensified this practice, and I heightened it still more following Pearl Harbor ... Then in 1944 I determined to bring our nonpartisan practice to a head.[51]

For his part, Stettinius was appointed interim Secretary of State precisely because he viewed himself as a statesman rather than a politician and "[h]e

---

[48] Vandenberg, 1952, 300–301.   [49] *Ibid.*, 302.
[50] Malsberger, 2000 refers to them as the "new conservatives."   [51] Hull, 1948, 1656.

did not have strong party identification, an advantage when the administration was attempting to construct a bipartisan foreign policy."[52]

The first post-war American Secretary of State, James F. Byrnes, who had joined a congressional delegation to the Paris Peace Conference of 1918 and had been impressed by the absence of opposition legislators, was adamant that the post-Second World War peace would also fail unless opposition leaders were consulted. He concluded that "we must have a foreign policy that is bipartisan in its origin and development; that is national rather than political in its conduct and its character; and that, consequently, is a continuing policy worthy of the confidence of other nations."[53] He elaborated further on his reasons for concluding that consultation with the opposition in Congress was the only competent executive practice in a dangerous world:

> The political party in power cannot ask the opposition party to share responsibility for the conduct of our foreign relations unless the leaders of the opposition are fully advised of our policies. This is true when the Congress and President are of the same party. It is particularly true when a majority of the Congress and the Chief Executive are not of the same political party. The executive branch of the government cannot announce a policy of importance requiring congressional action and then inform the leaders of the opposition. Even if the opposition leaders think the proposal unwise they must support it or create abroad the impression of dissension. A policy of bypassing the Congress would make impossible a bipartisan policy.[54]

Byrnes' successor, George C. Marshall, a career military officer, similarly viewed himself as a servant of the United States, rather than of the Democratic Party, during his tenure as Secretary of State, from 1947 to 1949. As he commented upon taking office: "I am assuming that the office of secretary of state, at least under present conditions, is nonpolitical and I am going to govern myself accordingly. I will never become involved in political matters."[55] True to his word, he was a firm advocate of bringing Republican leaders with him to key international conferences, such as the 1947 Moscow Conference, and holding private conferences with Republican leaders to build consensus, as he did while drafting the Marshall Plan.[56]

Although he was more skeptical of bipartisanship and was at least partly responsible for its decline, Truman's Secretary of State from 1949 to 1953, Dean Acheson, understood bipartisan cooperation as a necessary political bargain under divided government, which was essential to navigating this new strategic reality:

---

[52] See Campbell and Herring, 1975, xxiv; and Stettinius, 1949, 15.
[53] Byrnes, 1947, 233–234.   [54] *Ibid.*, 235.   [55] Cray, 1990, 586–587.
[56] On the former, see Payne, 1951, 291. On the latter, see p. 216.

> The idea of a nonpartisan foreign policy was the holy water sprinkled on a political necessity. The perhaps apocryphal sign in the Wild West saloon – "Don't shoot the Piano Player" – was the basic idea of nonpolitical foreign policy. Foreign policy has no lobby, no vested interest to support it, and no constituents. It must be built on a broad conception of the national interest, which lacks the attraction and support that can be generated by, say, a tax reduction, a tariff increase, or an agricultural subsidy. The Constitution makes the President the piano player of foreign policy, but unless his immunity from assault with intent to kill is extended to members of either party who work with him in the legislative branch, no consistent foreign policy is possible under the separation of powers. The doctrine, of course, aids the Administration, but its immediate beneficiaries are in the Congress.[57]

Thus successive Secretaries of State sacrificed foreign policy privilege at the altar of consensus-building in order to overcome the constitutional division of powers and forge an American-led post-war Western order. The community of practice was constituted in large part by their beliefs in the competency of consultation and compromise in the face of the great challenges that faced the United States in the post-war world. As we shall see, the practice of bipartisanship consequently eroded when executive beliefs began to shift.

Bipartisanship did not extend to all US foreign policy issue areas, though, only to major programmatic initiatives that helped define an active American involvement in the post-war world and efforts to contain the spread of communism. The first issue in which bipartisanship played a part was the ratification of the United Nations (UN) Charter in 1945. This was a significant issue in US politics because of the Senate's post-First World War failure to ratify Woodrow Wilson's League of Nations project. A key reason for Wilson's failure to achieve the ratification of the Versailles Treaty ending the First World War and his pet project of the League of Nations was his excessive partisanship. Instead of working with Republican legislatures, who controlled the Senate – whose supermajority vote was required to ratify treaties – Wilson pursued "the politics of confrontation," excluding high-profile Republicans from the five-man delegation to Versailles and berating opponents of the treaty publicly.[58]

In contrast, Franklin Roosevelt and his successor, Harry Truman, reached across party lines to secure a broad coalition of support for a new international organization (IO) to foster post-war cooperation. Indeed, as Ole Holsti observes, "the agreement between Secretary of State Cordell Hull and [John Foster] Dulles, the foreign policy adviser to Republican candidate Thomas Dewey, to keep the United Nations issue out of the 1944 campaign is often cited as the genesis of

---

[57] Acheson, 1969, 95.
[58] For a more recent account of Wilson's belligerent approach, see Ripsman, 2004/2005.

'bipartisanship' in foreign policy."[59] Hull initiated the bipartisan process by consulting with a select senatorial committee comprised of senators from both parties, beginning on April 25, 1944.[60] He maintained contact with opposition politicians throughout his involvement on this issue. Perhaps more significantly, at Stettinius' instigation, Roosevelt appointed Vandenberg, whom the President personally disliked, together with two other Republicans (Congressman Charles A. Eaton and former Minnesota Governor Harold Stassen) to the US delegation to the Dumbarton Oaks conference. Vandenberg agreed on the condition that he was free to act independently on the delegation and depart from the President's official policy if he felt obliged to do so; Roosevelt reluctantly consented.[61] After Roosevelt's death, Truman followed the bipartisan path with a lunch consultation with several influential Republicans (including Vandenberg and Republican House Leader Joseph Martin) on April 13, 1945, in which he heard their concerns about the new IO. This departure from previous practice went a good way to bridge the interparty hostility that could have interfered with American support for the United Nations.[62]

This unprecedented level of consultation had a notable effect on the congressional opposition. Vandenberg and other key Republicans used the consultation process and their input into the US delegation to request modifications of the treaty that advanced their own pet concerns, as well as those that would overcome the key concerns of Republican senators and enable them to bring them on board.[63] Vandenberg and Democratic Senator Tom Connally, together, subsequently shepherded the treaty through Congress, heading off challenges that could have prevented ratification or alterations that could have undermined its spirit, such as a suggestion by Senator Eugene Milliken that Congress be consulted each time the UN Security Council required American armed force deployments.[64] The result was a resounding 89–2 vote in favor of the new United Nations Charter.[65]

Bipartisanship was also instrumental in forging the Truman Doctrine to assist indigenous forces fighting communist insurgents in Greece and Turkey and the Marshall Plan to provide economic assistance to war-ravaged Western Europe. Regarding the former, as Greek communist insurgents threatened to overthrow the Greek Government and consequently isolate Turkey in a sphere

---

[59] Holsti, 1996, 18. Others date it from the appointment of Senators Arthur Vandenberg and Tom Connally as delegates to the 1945 San Francisco Conference that led to the United Nations: Berger, 1975, 222.

[60] Hilderbrand, 1990, 57.   [61] Schlesinger, 2003, 62–63.

[62] Vandenberg noted in his diary, "Truman came back to the Senate this noon for lunch with a few of us. It shattered all tradition. But it was both wise and smart. It means the days of executive contempt for Congress are ended; that we are returning to a government in which Congress will take its rightful place." Vandenberg, 1952, 167. On the significance of this meeting for bipartisanship, see Troy, 2008, 127.

[63] See, for example, Schlesinger, 2003, 167–168.   [64] *Ibid.*, 270–271.

[65] Collier, 1991, 20–21.

of communist regimes, Truman and Marshall decided that American military assistance was critical to prevent losing these and other countries to Soviet-inspired insurgencies, especially as British economic difficulties forced London to stop underwriting security initiatives in the Eastern Mediterranean.[66] To sell this expensive and potentially expansive program to Congress – which controlled the purse strings – Truman invited the ranking members of the Senate and House Foreign Relations Committees (Vandenberg and Connally in the Senate, Charles A. Eaton and Sol Bloom in the House), Martin (Speaker of the House), the Republican Chairman of the Senate Foreign Relations Committee (Styles Bridges) and others to a private White House briefing by Marshall and then-Undersecretary of State Acheson. While the Republicans were reluctant to commit money abroad at a time when they wanted to reduce taxes, they were persuaded by Acheson's appeal, stressing the urgency of the mission and the stakes involved.[67] Consequently, when Vandenberg briefed his Republican caucus on the Truman Doctrine, he stressed that "this is a matter which transcends politics. There is nothing partisan about it. It is national policy at the highest degree."[68] The Administration further secured congressional goodwill by agreeing in principle to accept the Vandenberg–Connally amendment linking Truman Doctrine aid to the United Nations.[69] Consequently, as a result both of being brought on board in the consultation session and of having secured key concessions, leaders of both parties supported the Truman Doctrine aid program in the legislature and, although some in both parties opposed the principle, the measure passed with no alterations.

The Marshall Plan responded to the persistent post-war economic crisis in Europe, which Marshall believed the Soviet Union was helping to perpetuate and capitalize on by preventing Big Three decisions that would inspire post-war recovery.[70] Although the Marshall Plan asked Congress for something it was most averse to – a large foreign aid program, which amounted to over half of the entire 1948 federal budget[71] – Marshall was able to make the effort succeed by inviting Vandenberg to confidential consultations, at which he stressed its importance in containing communism. He won Vandenberg and the group of Republicans he represented over by stressing that "[n]ow as never before national unity depended upon a truly nonpartisan policy in the year of a presidential election . . . The security of the country itself was the supreme consideration."[72] Vandenberg, of course, bargained with the executive and received key concessions, including making the plan administrator independent of the State Department, reducing the total amount requested for Fiscal Year 1949 from

---

[66] Price, 1955, 3.   [67] Jones, 1955, 137–143.   [68] *Ibid.*, 169.   [69] Hartmann, 1971, 64.

[70] Price, 1955, 21–23. John Gimbel (1976, 6–17) argues that the plan was also designed to overcome French opposition to German recovery by making both French and German recovery contingent on each other and on a broader European economic revival.

[71] Bonds, 2002, 123.   [72] Cray, 1990, 610.

$6.8 billion to $5.3 billion, and avoiding mention of an expected $17 billion total figure for the program in the draft legislation.[73] Having secured these concessions in consultation with the Administration, Vandenberg became one of the plan's principal cheerleaders, cajoling reluctant senators to back it without further alteration.[74] Notably, in the congressional votes for both the Truman Doctrine and the Marshall Plan, the degree of support for the Administration's policy was comparable in both parties. In the Senate, the Democrats voted 34–7 in favor of aid to Greece and Turkey and 38–4 in favor of the Marshall Plan; the Republicans supported these measures by margins of 35–16 and 31–13, respectively.[75] This is not to say that bipartisanship was solely responsible for their passage; certainly the growing fear of communism in the wake of Soviet challenges in Greece, Turkey, and Finland, the increasing strength of communist parties in France and Italy, and the Soviet coup in Czechoslovakia made legislators from both parties fear the consequences of inaction. Nonetheless, the practice of bipartisan consultation and concessions smoothed the way.

One final major success for bipartisanship was the establishment of NATO. Although the North Atlantic Treaty was signed in April 1949, after the heyday of bipartisanship had already passed (see pp. 218–221), Congress had already approved the pact in principle by passing the so-called Vandenberg Resolution authorizing regional peacekeeping operations under Article 51 of the UN Charter. Thus, despite the Republicans' well-known reluctance to commit the United States to entangling alliances, they had in fact handed the president the authority to do just that.[76] The resolution itself was cooked up by Undersecretary of State Robert A. Lovett and Vandenberg as a way to overcome senatorial opposition to closer military cooperation between the United States and Western Europe.[77] Following the passage of the Vandenberg Resolution, Vandenberg and Connally used their private consultations with the State Department to make two changes to the North Atlantic Treaty being negotiated. First, they altered the wording of Article 5 to leave to each signatory the right to judge whether force was required in response to an attack on another NATO member, rather than making that responsibility automatic. Second, they insisted on a clause in Article 11 that would respect the role of Congress in making war by providing that the treaty be "carried out by the parties in accordance with their respective constitutional processes."[78] With these concessions from the Administration, which together with the Vandenberg Resolution ensured that the Senate would get some of the credit for the alliance

---

[73] See Hartmann, 1971, 160–161; and Arkes, 1972, 139–141.
[74] See Price, 1955, 63–65; and Cray, 1990, 625.
[75] There was bipartisan support for both measures in the House of Representatives, as well, but Republican support was considerably smaller. Collier, 1991, 14.
[76] Sundquist, 1981, 106.   [77] Robinson, 1969, 44–46.
[78] See Vandenberg, 1952, 475–477; and Donovan, 1982, 47–48.

and share in the Administration's foreign policy prestige, Vandenberg and Connally, his successor as Senate Foreign Relations Committee Chairman following the Democratic Party's victory in the November 1948 elections, heartily endorsed the pact and won an 82–13 vote of support from the Senate.[79]

While bipartisanship was practiced with regard to these and, to some extent, a few other issue areas of foreign policy, it did not extend to all areas of foreign affairs. Indeed, as James McCormick and Eugene Wittkopf point out, bipartisanship coexisted with partisanship and ideology throughout this period.[80] The issue of China, in particular, was the subject of considerable partisan debate during the early post-war period. The executive did not consult with opposition members in Congress about its China policy and partisan bickering prevailed over whether the Democratic Administration had "lost China" to communist takeover, or whether the United States had had little power to influence the outcome of the Chinese civil war.[81]

That the practice was limited in this manner to most, but not all, foreign policy issue areas is illuminating. To begin with, it helps clarify that bipartisanship was indeed a practice – tied to the choices and judgments of foreign policy practitioners about appropriateness and competence – rather than a rigidly defined institution that routinized congressional support for the Administration's foreign policy. Where practitioners judged that consultation and cooperation were justified, they followed bipartisanship; in areas where it was judged illegitimate or unwise, partisanship prevailed. Furthermore, the nature of issue areas, such as China or Palestine, where partisanship continued, suggests that bipartisanship was linked to a distinction between vital and peripheral security interests. On matters understood to be of paramount geopolitical importance to US interests, such as European security, global security, and the global economy, practitioners comprising the bipartisanship community of practice believed it would be incompetent to undermine the unified voice of the executive with partisan wrangling.[82] In areas less vitally important, where there appeared to be more policy leeway, however, eschewing partisan advantage would have been understood as politically incompetent.[83] In this vein, Arthur Schlesinger observed that "the bipartisan foreign policy was not a good idea. It was only a necessity. At least it was a necessity for those who believed that the American national interest enjoined resistance to the Stabilization [*sic*] of western Europe."[84]

By 1949, the practice of bipartisanship began to wear thin, for several reasons. To begin with, the Democratic Party regained the House and the Senate in the

---

[79] See Kaplan, 2007, 92–96; and Collier, 1991, 24.   [80] McCormick and Wittkopf, 1990.

[81] Collier, 1991, 25–26.   [82] See, for example, Jewell, 1962, 6.

[83] For this reason, Vandenberg emphatically pointed out that "bipartisan policy has been confined within relatively narrow limits. It has applied to the UN. It has applied to the peace treaties in Europe. It has applied to nothing else." Vandenberg, 1952, 351.

[84] Schlesinger, 1973, 129.

November 1948 elections. Since the Democratic Administration now had greater leeway within Congress, it could go it alone more frequently and reduce the extent of consultation it engaged in. Furthermore, the incoming Democratic majority in the Congress used its newfound muscles to tread on the sensibilities of the Republican minority, which undermined the goodwill required for bipartisanship. Particularly vexing for the Republicans was the change the Democrats made to the composition of the pivotal Senate Foreign Relations Committee. The Democrats claimed eight seats on the thirteen-seat committee, a departure from the seven:six ratio the Republicans maintained when they had a similar majority in the Senate. To the Republicans, this action was "implicit with hostility" and made it "plain that the Democrats propose to play politics with war and peace," which was inconsistent with the spirit of bipartisanship.[85] Subsequently, the outbreak of the Korean War in June 1950 led to a more formal rupture in bipartisanship, as Truman ordered US military assistance to South Korea without prior consultation with Congress. Immediately thereafter, Republicans in Congress blamed the Administration for the North Korean invasion because Acheson had not included South Korea within the publicly declared American security perimeter.[86]

For their parts, the Democrats in Congress accused the Republicans of questioning the legitimacy of the war for partisan purpose, a charge that is also credible.[87] The Republicans who had jumped aboard the bipartisanship train had done so in part because they believed a Republican candidate would win the presidential election in 1948 and that it would be useful to establish the basis for congressional support for a new Republican Administration's foreign policy through the instrument of bipartisanship.[88] Truman's surprising defeat of Thomas E. Dewey in 1948 made the prospect of four more years of supporting a Democratic Administration unappealing, especially as many believed restraint from partisan attacks had hamstrung Dewey against the vulnerable incumbent.[89]

Perhaps the greatest impetus for the collapse of bipartisanship, however, was personnel change in both the Administration and the Republican leadership. Notably, the new Secretary of State installed for Truman's first full term as president, Acheson, was rather skeptical of bipartisanship, which he felt served the interests of the opposition more than it did the Administration.[90]

---

[85] Vandenberg, 1952, 468.   [86] Collier, 1991, 26–27.
[87] See, for example, Connally, 1954, 350–351.   [88] Kepley, 1988, 17.   [89] *Ibid.*, 17–18.
[90] See, for example, Acheson, 1969, 95. Acheson complained of the Administration's experiences with bipartisan consultations: "We were learning again – although we hardly needed to – what everyone in the executive branch since President Washington's day had learned, that to advise and consult with the Congress is next to impossible. One can learn its uninformed opinion or one can try to inform the opinion of a few key members by long, patient, secret talks, as Lovett had done with Vandenberg leading up to the Vandenberg Resolution of 1948; but to devise a joint approach to a complicated and delicate matter of foreign policy is not within the range of normally available time and people. Here the separation of powers really separates." *Ibid.*, 318.

Consequently, he enacted policy more unilaterally, at the expense of the good-
natured consultation that had been the rule since the Second World War. As a
journalist observed at the time: "The bipartisan relationship as to foreign affairs
has undergone a subtle but unmistakable change since Acheson took over as
Secretary of State. Senator Vandenberg has been consulted often enough, but
always in an atmosphere of restraint and stiff formality – in marked distinction
to his easy and friendly contacts with the two previous Secretaries of State,
Byrnes and Marshall."[91]

Indeed, Republican Senator Robert Taft placed the blame for the breakdown
of bipartisanship squarely on Acheson, complaining: "'There isn't any bipartisan foreign policy and there has not been any for the last year.' The Republicans,
he brusquely informed a radio audience, 'are not consulted any more and they
have not been consulted since Mr. Acheson became Secretary of State. Nobody
can imagine anything that is called a bipartisan foreign policy. There isn't any
such thing.'"[92]

Of equal significance was Vandenberg's gradual withdrawal from the scene
due to deteriorating health. In each of the major successes of bipartisanship,
Vandenberg had played the key role in bridging the gap between the
Administration and key Republicans in the Congress. He appeared to consult
with the Administration in good faith and then played an instrumental role in
selling the consensus policy to the legislature. After his departure, more impla-
cable Republicans, such as Taft, exerted greater influence within the Republican
Party, which made bipartisanship far more difficult an endeavor, especially with
a less consultative, more unilateral Secretary of State directing policy.[93] Thus, as
the individuals who constituted the community of practice were replaced with
different policy-makers/agents with different attitudes and conceptions of
competent performance of foreign policy-making, practices changed, too.

During this critical period of American foreign policy, bipartisanship constituted an important domestic political practice that had profound implications for the nature of US foreign policy and for global politics. Before
explaining this impact, however, it is important to justify the assertion that
bipartisanship constituted a practice, rather than an institution or an institutionalized procedure. Bipartisan cooperation over foreign affairs operated for a
very short time period, over a rather restricted scope of issues (those concerning
the containment of communism and American involvement in the post-war
order), with a very limited and fluid community of practice, consisting of the
president, the Secretary of State, and a small group of opposition legislators. It
was not routinized behavior, expected of all legislators, but the product of both
the worldviews of the practitioners and a bargain over each specific policy
initiative. The demise of the practice in the early 1950s, under the tenure of a

[91] Vandenberg, 1952, 533.   [92] Berger, 1975, 234.
[93] See, for example, Berger, 1975, 233–234; and Troy, 2008, 133.

new Secretary of State (Acheson) and after Vandenberg's retirement, indicates that bipartisanship was never institutionalized, but depended more on the behavior of specific individuals within a specific community of practice based on their own conceptions of appropriate and competent behavior in a specific set of circumstances.[94]

As a result of the short-lived practice of bipartisanship, the United States was able to overcome institutional constraints on US foreign policy and the American tradition of isolation from global affairs. Bipartisanship thus paved the way for resolute American leadership of the Western bloc after the Second World War, which had several noteworthy consequences for world affairs. To begin with, it allowed for the creation of political, economic, and military institutions, such as the World Bank, the International Monetary Fund (IMF), the General Agreement on Tariffs and Trade (GATT), and the North Atlantic Treaty Organization (NATO), which would institutionalize active American leadership of the post-war Western world. This was a significant change from American attempts at leadership after the First World War, which foundered due to partisan bickering between Woodrow Wilson and Republicans in Congress.

Bipartisanship had longer-term domestic and international consequences, as well. Domestically, it allowed for the creation of a national security state that would allow unprecedented authority for the executive in the conduct of foreign policy. Since key figures of both parties agreed on the need for resolute action in the security theater, there was comparatively little resistance when Truman began to centralize control over security with the National Security Act of 1947.[95] As a result, it created the possibility of future excesses, such as US involvement in the Vietnam War, where the executive was able to circumvent potentially prudent domestic opposition and pursue its own policy. Internationally, bipartisanship enabled the multilateral balancing effort by assuring other Western allies that the United States would not abandon them and by inspiring them to contribute to the institutions of Western security, such as NATO. The American activism that bipartisanship enabled, however, also worried the Soviet Union and may have led it to greater risk-taking in an effort to avoid encirclement. Thus the domestic practice of bipartisanship helped to shape broader patterns of international politics.

Conclusion: practice makes perfect?

If we did not pay attention to the practice of bipartisanship, we would not be able to explain several key puzzles of post-Second World War American

---

[94] To reinforce this point, it would be helpful to explore in depth exactly how this community of practice constituted itself, learned the practice, and viewed itself in light of the practice. To do this effectively would take more space than is available here and go beyond the scope of this chapter. I therefore leave these important questions for future research.

[95] See, for example, Zegart, 1999.

national security policy. In particular, why was the US Government able to
break with its tradition of isolationism after the Second World War, whereas
Woodrow Wilson, a committed internationalist, could not after the First World
War? In both cases, the president lacked sufficient partisan support in Congress
and required the support of opposition members of the Senate and the House of
Representatives to commit the United States to international institutions and
alliances. Given the well-known division of foreign relations powers in the
United States and the long and cherished history of avoiding entangling
commitments, a traditional neoclassical realist approach focusing on the
domestic institutional context or the influence of key societal interest groups
would be at a loss to explain the ease with which the Truman Administration
assumed an active global role. Without the community of practice constituted
by a small group of opposition legislators and the Secretary of State, who
believed that consultation and compromise served the national interest, the
Truman Administration's post-war program should have met the same fate as
Wilson's grandiose plans, regardless of the new threats the United States faced
in the post-war era.

It would also be difficult for structural realists or traditional neoclassical
realists to understand the nature of the post-war American involvement, relying on multilateral institutions, such as the United Nations, NATO, the Bretton
Woods institutions, and others, rather than more overtly unilateral measures
that might ordinarily have been more successful in a Congress that feared
entangling alliances.

We can conclude, then, that although neoclassical realism adds considerable
explanatory power to structural realism, incorporating attention to practices
and practitioners would enhance neoclassical realism further. While domestic
institutions, actors, decision-making procedures, and norms clearly have a
profound effect on whether and how states respond to international challenges,
political practices, such as the practice of bipartisanship discussed in this
chapter or non-intervention, as discussed by Richard Little's Chapter 7 in this
volume, can lead states to behave in ways that defy behavioral expectations
based simply on institutional setting or the constellation of domestic interests.
In this regard, the practice shift that Adler and Pouliot call for in Chapter 1 in
this volume does not revolutionize neoclassical realist theory, but it can add
considerable value to neoclassical realist approaches to foreign security policy.

There are, of course, certain methodological challenges of including practices. As critics of neoclassical realism correctly point out, a structural theory of
international politics is more parsimonious than those, such as neoclassical
realist approaches, which include a range of domestic political variables.[96] In
addition, the level of contextual information required about each individual
case in order to determine the nature of domestic institutions, decision-making

---

[96] See, for example, Walt, 2002; and Legro and Moravcsik, 1999.

procedures, and political practices complicates case research and discourages broad generalizations. Nonetheless, as I have argued elsewhere, while parsimony is helpful, explanatory power is critical. Sacrificing parsimony for theories that explain more and resolve critical puzzles is more useful for our understanding of international politics.[97] Furthermore, the generalizations yielded by more parsimonious theories, such as neorealists', amount to gross oversimplifications that consequently misrepresent the cases they study.[98] The value added of including practices, therefore, justifies the demands their inclusion places on researchers.

References

Acheson, Dean, 1969. *Present at the Creation*. New York: Norton.

Arkes, Hadley, 1972. *Bureaucracy, the Marshall Plan, and the National Interest.* Princeton: Princeton University Press.

Barnett, Michael N., 1992. *Confronting the Costs of War: Military Power, State, and Society in Egypt and Israel.* Princeton: Princeton University Press.

Berger, Henry W., 1975. Bipartisanship, Senator Taft, and the Truman Administration. *Political Science Quarterly* 90 (2): 221–237.

Blanchard, Jean-Marc F. and Norrin M. Ripsman, 2008. A Political Theory of Economic Statecraft. *Foreign Policy Analysis* 4 (4): 373–400.

Bonds, John Bledsoe, 2002. *Bipartisan Strategy: Selling the Marshall Plan.* Westport: Praeger.

Brawley, Mark R., 1993. *Liberal Leadership: Great Powers and Their Challengers in Peace and War.* Ithaca: Cornell University Press.

2009. Neoclassical Realism and Strategic Calculations: Explaining Divergent British, French, and Soviet Strategies Toward Germany Between the World Wars (1919–1939). In *Neoclassical Realism, the State, and Foreign Policy*, edited by Steven E. Lobell, Norrin M. Ripsman, and Jeffrey W. Taliaferro, 75–98. Cambridge: Cambridge University Press.

Briggs, Philip J., 1994. *Making American Foreign Policy: President–Congress Relations from the Second World War to the Post-Cold War Era.* Lanham: Rowman & Littlefield.

Byman, Daniel L. and Kenneth M. Pollack, 2001. Let Us Now Praise Great Men: Bringing the Statesman Back In. *International Security* 25 (4): 107–146.

Byrnes, James F., 1947. *Speaking Frankly*. Kingsport: Kingsport Press.

Campbell, Thomas M. and George C. Herring, eds., 1975. *The Diaries of Edward R. Stettinius, Jr.: 1943–1946*. New York: New Viewpoints.

Christensen, Thomas J. and Jack Snyder, 1990. Chain Gangs and Passed Bucks: Predicting Alliance Patterns in Multipolarity. *International Organization* 44 (2): 138–168.

---

[97] Taliaferro, Lobell, and Ripsman, 2009, 23.   [98] Ripsman and Blanchard, 2000.

Collier, Ellen C., 1991. *Bipartisanship and the Making of Foreign Policy: A Historical Survey.* Boulder: Westview Press.

Connally, Tom, 1954. *My Name Is Tom Connally.* New York: Crowell.

Copeland, Dale C., 2000. *The Origins of Major War.* Ithaca: Cornell University Press.

Corwin, Edward S., 1957. *The President: Office and Powers, 1787–1957.* New York: New York University Press.

Cray, Ed., 1990. *General of the Army: George C. Marshall – Soldier and Statesman.* New York: W.W. Norton.

Donovan, Robert J., 1982. *Tumultuous Years: The Presidency of Harry S Truman, 1949–1953.* New York: Norton.

Elman, Miriam Fendius, 2000. Unpacking Democracy: Presidentialism, Parliamentarism, and Theories of Democratic Peace. *Security Studies* 9 (4): 91–126.

Friedberg, Aaron L., 2005. The Future of US–China Relations: Is Conflict Inevitable? *International Security* 30 (2): 7–45.

Gilpin, Robert, 1981. *War and Change in World Politics.* Cambridge: Cambridge University Press.

Gimbel, John, 1976. *The Origins of the Marshall Plan.* Stanford: Stanford University Press.

Gourevitch, Peter, 1978. The Second Image Reversed: The International Sources of Domestic Politics. *International Organization* 32 (4): 881–912.

Hartmann, Susan M., 1971. *Truman and the 80th Congress.* Columbia: University of Missouri Press.

Hermann, Tamar, 1993. Grassroots Activism as a Factor in Foreign Policy-Making: The Case of the Israeli Peace Movement. In *The Limits of State Autonomy: Societal Groups and Foreign Policy Formulation,* edited by David Skidmore and Valerie M. Hudson, 127–147. Boulder: Westview.

Hilderbrand, Robert C., 1990. *Dumbarton Oaks: The Origins of the United Nations and the Search for Postwar Security.* Chapel Hill: University of North Carolina Press.

Holsti, Ole R., 1996. *Public Opinion and American Foreign Policy.* Ann Arbor: Michigan University Press.

Hoopes, Townsend and Douglas Brinkley, 1997. *FDR and the Creation of the UN.* New Haven: Yale University Press.

Hull, Cordell, 1948. *The Memoirs of Cordell Hull.* Vol. 2. New York: Macmillan.

Immergut, Ellen M., 1992. The Rules of the Game: The Logic of Health Policy-Making in France, Switzerland, and Sweden. In *Structuring Politics: Historical Institutionalism in Comparative Analysis,* edited by Sven Steinmo, Kathleen Thelen, and Frank Longstreth, 57–89. Cambridge: Cambridge University Press.

Jervis, Robert, 1976. *Perception and Misperception in International Politics.* Princeton: Princeton University Press.

Jewell, Malcolm, 1962. *Senatorial Politics and Foreign Policy.* Lexington: University of Kentucky Press.

Johnson, Robert David, 2006. *Congress and the Cold War*. Cambridge: Cambridge University Press.

Jones, Joseph M., 1955. *The Fifteen Weeks*. New York: Viking Press.

Kaplan, Lawrence S., 2007. *NATO 1948: The Birth of the Transatlantic Alliance*. Lanham: Rowman & Littlefield.

Katzenstein, Peter J., ed., 1996. *The Culture of National Security: Norms and Identity in World Politics*. New York: Columbia University Press.

Kepley, David R., 1988. *The Collapse of the Middle Way: Senate Republicans and the Bipartisan Foreign Policy, 1948-1952*. New York: Greenwood Press.

Large, David Clay, 1996. *Germans to the Front: West German Rearmament in the Adenauer Era*. Chapel Hill: University of North Carolina Press.

Layne, Christopher A, *The Peace of Illusions: American Grand Strategy from 1940 to the Present*. Ithaca: Cornell University Press.

Legro, Jeffrey W. and Andrew Moravcsik, 1999. Is Anyone Still a Realist? *International Security* 24 (2): 5-55.

Levy, Jack S., 1987. Declining Power and the Preventive Motivation for War. *World Politics* 40 (1): 82-107.

Lobell Steven E., 2002. War is Politics: Offensive Realism, Domestic Politics, and Security Strategies. *Security Studies* 12 (2): 165-195.

2003. *The Challenge of Hegemony: Grand Strategy, Trade, and Domestic Politics*. Ann Arbor: University of Michigan Press.

Macridis, Roy C., 1952. Cabinet Instability in the Fourth Republic (1946-1951). *Journal of Politics* 14 (4): 643-658.

Malsberger, John W., 2000. *From Obstructionism to Moderation: The Transformation of Senate Conservatism*. Selinsgrove: Susquehanna State University.

McCormick, James M. and Eugene R. Wittkopf, 1990. Bipartisanship, Partisanship, and Ideology in Congressional-Executive Foreign Policy Relations, 1947-1988. *Journal of Politics* 52 (4): 1077-1100.

McGeehan, Robert, 1971. *The German Rearmament Question*. Urbana: University of Illinois Press.

Mearsheimer, John J., 2001. *The Tragedy of Great Power Politics*. New York: W. W. Norton.

Morgenthau, Hans J., 1985 [1948]. *Politics Among Nations: The Struggle for Power and Peace*. 6th edn. New York: McGraw-Hill.

Olson, Mancur, 1982. *The Rise and Decline of Nations: Economic Growth, Stagflation, and Social Rigidities*. New Haven: Yale University Press.

Oren, Michael B., 2002. *Six Days of War: June 1967 and the Making of the Modern Middle East*. Oxford: Oxford University Press.

Organski, A. F. K. and Jacek Kugler, 1980. *The War Ledger*. Chicago: University of Chicago Press.

Owen, John M., IV, 2001/2002. Transnational Liberalism and US Primacy. *International Security* 26 (3): 117-152.

Pape, Robert A., 2005. Soft Balancing Against the United States. *International Security* 30 (1): 7-45.

Paul, T. V., 2005. Soft Balancing in the Age of US Primacy. *International Security* 30 (1): 46–71.

Payne, Robert, 1951. *The Marshall Story: A Biography of George C. Marshall*. New York: Prentice Hall.

Peterson, Susan, 1995. How Democracies Differ: Public Opinion, State Structure, and the Lessons of the Fashoda Crisis. *Security Studies* 5 (1): 3–37.

    1996. *Crisis Bargaining and the State*. Ann Arbor: University of Michigan Press.

Pierson, Paul, 2002. The Limits of Design: Explaining Institutional Origins and Change. *Governance* 13 (4): 475–499.

Posen, Barry R., 1984. *The Sources of Military Doctrine: France, Britain, and Germany Between the World Wars*. Ithaca: Cornell University Press.

Price, Harry Bayard, 1955. *The Marshall Plan and Its Meaning*. Ithaca: Cornell University Press.

Ripsman, Norrin M., 2000/2001. The Curious Case of German Rearmament: Democracy, Structural Autonomy, and Foreign Security Policy. *Security Studies* 10 (2): 1–47.

    2002. *Peacemaking by Democracies: The Effect of Structural Autonomy on the Post-World-War Settlements*. University Park: Pennsylvania State University Press.

    2004/2005. The Politics of Deception: Forging Peace Treaties in the Face of Domestic Opposition. *International Journal* 60 (1): 189–216.

Ripsman, Norrin M. and Jean-Marc F. Blanchard, 2000. Contextual Information and the Study of Trade and Conflict: The Utility of an Interdisciplinary Approach. In *Beyond Boundaries? Disciplines, Paradigms, and Theoretical Integration in International Studies*, edited by Rudra Sil and Eileen M. Doherty, 57–85. Albany: State University of New York Press.

Ripsman, Norrin M., Jeffrey W. Taliaferro, and Steven E. Lobell, 2009. Conclusion: The State of Neoclassical Realism. In *Neoclassical Realism, the State, and Foreign Policy*, edited by Steven E. Lobell, Norrin M. Ripsman, and Jeffrey W. Taliaferro, 280–299. Cambridge: Cambridge University Press.

Robinson, James A., 1969. *Congress and Foreign Policy-Making: A Study in Legislative Influence and Initiative*. Homewood: The Dorsey Press.

Rose, Gideon, 1998. Neoclassical Realism and Theories of Foreign Policy. *World Politics* 51 (1): 144–172.

Ross, Robert S. and Zhu Feng, 2008. The Rise of China: Theoretical and Policy Perspectives. In *China's Ascent: Power, Security, and the Future of International Politics*, edited by Robert S. Ross and Zhu Feng, 293–316. Ithaca: Cornell University Press.

Schlesinger, Arthur M., Jr., 1973. *The Imperial Presidency*. New York: Houghton-Mifflin.

Schlesinger, Stephen C., 2003. *Act of Creation: The Founding of the United Nations*. Boulder: Westview.

Schweller, Randall L., 1994. Bandwagoning for Profit: Bringing the Revisionist State Back In. *International Security* 19 (1): 72–107.

    2004. Unanswered Threats: A Neoclassical Realist Theory of Underbalancing. *International Security* 29 (2): 159–201.

2006. *Unanswered Threats: Political Constraints on the Balance of Power.* Princeton: Princeton University Press.

Skocpol, Theda, 1985. Bringing the State Back, in Strategies of Analysis in Current Research. In *Bringing the State Back In*, edited by Peter B. Evans, Dietrich Rueschemeyer, and Theda Skocpol, 3–37. Cambridge: Cambridge University Press.

Snyder, Jack, 1991. *Myths of Empire.* Ithaca: Cornell University Press.

Stettinius, Edward R., 1949. *Roosevelt and the Russians: The Yalta Conference.* New York: Doubleday.

Stuart, Douglas T., 2003. Ministry of Fear: The 1947 National Security Act in Historical and Institutional Context. *International Studies Perspective* 4 (3): 293–313.

Sundquist, James L., 1981. *The Decline and Resurgence of Congress.* Washington: The Brookings Institution.

Taliaferro, Jeffrey W., 2000/2001. Security Seeking Under Anarchy: Defensive Realism Reconsidered. *International Security* 25 (3): 152–186.

2009. Neoclassical Realism and Resource Extraction: State Building for Future War. In *Neoclassical Realism, the State, and Foreign Policy*, edited by Steven E. Lobell, Norrin M. Ripsman, and Jeffrey W. Taliaferro, 194–226. Cambridge: Cambridge University Press.

Taliaferro, Jeffrey W., Steven E. Lobell, and Norrin M. Ripsman, 2009. Introduction: Neoclassical Realism, the State, and Foreign Policy. In *Neoclassical Realism, the State, and Foreign Policy*, edited by Steven E. Lobell, Norrin M. Ripsman, and Jeffrey W. Taliaferro, 1–41. Cambridge: Cambridge University Press.

Thelen, Kathleen, 1999. Historical Institutionalism in Comparative Politics. *Annual Review of Political Science* 2 (1): 369–404.

Trimberger, Ellen Kay, 1978. *Revolution from Above: Military Bureaucrats and Development in Japan, Turkey, Egypt, and Peru.* New Brunswick: Transaction Books.

Troy, Gil, 2008. *Leading From the Centre: Why Moderates Make the Best Presidents.* New York: Perseus.

Trubowitz, Peter and Nicole Mellow, 2005. "Going Bipartisan": Politics by Other Means. *Political Science Quarterly* 120 (3): 433–453.

Tsebelis, George, 2002. *Veto Players: How Political Institutions Work.* Princeton: Princeton University Press.

Vandenberg, Arthur H., Jr., ed., 1952. *The Private Papers of Senator Vandenberg.* Boston: Houghton-Mifflin.

Van Evera, Stephen, 1999. *Causes of War: Power and the Roots of Conflict.* Ithaca: Cornell University Press.

Walt, Stephen M., 1987. *The Origins of Alliances.* Ithaca: Cornell University Press.

2002. The Enduring Relevance of the Realist Tradition. In *Political Science: State of the Discipline*, edited by Ira Katznelson and Helen V. Milner, 197–230. New York: W. W. Norton.

Waltz, Kenneth N., 1967. *Foreign Policy and Democratic Politics: The American and British Experience.* Boston: Little, Brown.

1979. *Theory of International Politics*. Reading, MA: Addison-Wesley.

Wohlforth, William C., 1993. *The Elusive Balance: Power and Perceptions During the Cold War*. Ithaca: Cornell University Press.

Zegart, Amy B., 1999. *Flawed by Design: The Evolution of the CIA, JCS, and NSC*. Stanford: Stanford University Press.

PART IV

Practices in practice

9 | Banking on power: how some practices in an international organization anchor others

OLE JACOB SENDING AND IVER B. NEUMANN

Introduction

Students of world politics take different positions on the role of international organizations (IOs). For realists, IOs have little or no independent power as they are seen as epiphenomenal of the underlying distribution of material interests between great powers.[1] For rationalists, IOs are central arenas that can help states institutionalize mechanisms to deter cheating and reduce transaction costs, thus changing state behavior and furthering cooperation between states.[2] IOs are said to structure the interest-driven bargaining between states, thereby constraining state behavior and, partly, state interest. But rationalists stop short of ascribing agency sufficient to IOs being in a situation of power *vis-à-vis* states.[3] For constructivists, however, IOs can be powerful actors in their own right, with the capacity to shape and transform state interests.[4] Constructivists argue that IOs are actors by virtue of the expertise and normative ideals that they embed. Despite their different views on the character of IOs, however, realists, rationalists, and constructivists all draw an analytical boundary between the inside and the outside of IOs.

In this chapter, we seek to bypass the problem of how to determine the boundary of IOs and their environment by looking instead at the practices through which states and IOs interact. By focusing on the practices that structure state–IO relations, we want to capture the situated and contextualized character of how states operate within IOs, and how IOs operate *vis-à-vis* states. Crucially, the question of possible IO authority and autonomy may then be analyzed as the *effects* of concrete practices rather than as emanating from *a priori* defined features of IOs and/or states.[5] We focus on the role and power of expertise in IOs, as this has been a central issue in studies highlighting their relative autonomy and authority.[6] We argue that the link between expertise and the power of IOs may be better understood in terms of the concrete practices

---

[1] Mearsheimer, 1994/1995.   [2] Keohane, 1984.   [3] Drezner, 2007.
[4] See Barnett and Finnemore, 2004; and Finnemore, 1996.   [5] Mitchell, 1991.
[6] See Barnett and Finnemore, 2004; Woods, 2006; and Weaver, 2008.

through which that expertise is organized in and brought to bear by IOs, and the effects thereof.

We also have some practice theory fish to fry. Drawing on Ann Swidler's concept of "anchoring practice" and on the more general argument that cultural factors are tool-kits, we see expert knowledge produced and used by IOs as defining an infrastructure or reference-point for interaction.[7] This infrastructure renders some "strategies for action" available, and closes off others. Specifically, we analyze World Bank practices in order to demonstrate how such a focus on practices may provide some counterintuitive insights. The Bank's expertise is embedded in a set of key practices that structure its relation with states. Key among these is the Country Policy and Institutional Assessment (CPIA), which is the Bank's annual assessment of the "performance" of client countries according to a set of Bank-defined criteria for good policies and institutions. The CPIA is an anchoring practice – a bundle of interwoven practices making possible other, more specific practices.[8] One such specific practice is the Bank's Performance Based Allocation system (PBA), which structures negotiations and debate between Bank Management and member states over how to allocate funds and over what constitutes good policy.

In the first section, we describe in more detail why a turn to practice provides a good handle on the study of IOs and their relations to member states. In so doing, we lean on a relational view of the social, where what should be studied are what Abbott calls "things of boundaries," i.e. phenomena producing boundaries, rather than the boundaries of already taken-for-granted things.[9] Our things of boundaries are practices, which in and of themselves define where the inside of an IO stops and the outside begins. In the second section we discuss in more detail our conception of practice and how it relates to the editors' modular framework. In employing the concept of anchoring practice in the third section, we highlight the hierarchy between practices, arguing that some practices are more fundamental than others. The bulk of this section is devoted to a discussion of how practices can be seen to embody knowledge and related cultural factors that structure the actors themselves by shaping their available strategies (as opposed to the ends that they pursue). The empirical analysis in the fourth and fifth sections centers on the World Bank and on the practice of annually assessing client countries' policy and institutional "performance" through the CPIA. The CPIA wields little power on its own, but becomes a powerful anchoring practice by rendering possible and defining the criteria used in a more specific practice of central importance to the identity of the Bank – the so-called PBA. Together, the anchoring practice (CPIA) and the specific practice

---

[7] See Swidler, 2001a and 2001b; and Vaisey, 2009.
[8] See also Lene Hansen's discussion of general vs. specific practices. Hansen, Chapter 11 in this volume.
[9] Abbott, 1995.

(PBA) make up a "thing of boundary," i.e. that which defines the boundary between the World Bank and its member states. The sixth section draws some brief conclusions.

States, IOs, and the boundaries between them

The question of delineating the boundaries between entities under scrutiny is a vexed one in the social sciences. In his path-breaking critique of state-centered and society-centered theories, Timothy Mitchell argued that social scientists had been "unable to fix the elusive boundary" between state and society, and that it was better to take the uncertain boundary between the two as the point of departure for analysis. "How is the effect created that certain aspects of what occurs pertain to society, while others stand apart as the state?" Mitchell asked.[10] Andrew Abbott has similarly suggested – at a more general level – that we study things of boundaries rather than boundaries of things.[11] Bracketing discussions of relational ontology for now, we concur that boundaries are elusive, and that trying to pin them down rather than taking them for granted is very important, not least for the study of IOs.

We may of course identify and distinguish an IO from its environment by focusing on the organization's physical location, its internal characteristics, the fact that a staff member of an IO is hired by and responsible to that organization rather than to that individual's home country, etc. We incur a price by following that route, however. To pick but one example, at the United Nations, it is established practice that hiring decisions are not purely meritocratic and determined autonomously by the bureaucracy. They are not merely internal to the IO. On the contrary, country quotas are a central element, and politicization of hiring is not uncommon. So, when a key work like Barnett and Finnemore's bypasses this problem of boundaries by focusing squarely on the internal characteristics of IOs as bureaucratic organizations, they generate new insights, but there is a price to pay. They simply assume that the environment in which IOs operate is *not* significant either for the IO's internal characteristics or for the authority and autonomy of states. They assert that they do not want to "create a mythical world of IO omnipotence to replace a mythical world of IO obsequiousness" and that the key strength of their conceptualization of IOs as bureaucracies is that it "puts the interactive relationship between states and IOs at the center of analysis rather than presuming that the relationship is a one-way street in which states simply dictate to IOs."[12] But in order to put this "interactive relationship" at the center of analysis, a focus on the internal, bureaucratic features of IOs is incomplete.

In making a case for the power of IOs by virtue of these bureaucratic features, notably the rules they formulate and the expertise they embed, Barnett and

[10] Mitchell, 1991, 89.   [11] Abbott, 1995.   [12] Barnett and Finnemore, 2004, 12.

Finnemore adopt a broad view of power that includes both causal and constitutive dimensions.[13] They include the working of "productive power," operating through mechanisms of constitution in distant social relations, in the power of IOs. If we turn this broad definition of power around and direct it at IOs, however, it becomes clear that just as state understandings of the world and their attendant governing practices are shaped by IOs, so IOs are shaped by their environment and notably by the sovereign states that are their constitutive members. IOs are not only international *bureaucracies*, but also *international* bureaucracies. Our focus is, accordingly, on anchoring practices and more specific practices that structure the interaction between states and the World Bank. In this way, we hope to get a better handle on the role of expertise in constituting and defining IOs' power in world politics.

Knowledge, discourse, practices

We define practices in keeping with Adler and Pouliot's Chapter 1 in this volume, thus stressing that practices are meaningful and patterned actions that are performed more or less competently and which both reflect and render manifest culturally established knowledge and understandings.[14] Employing Ann Swidler's concept of "anchoring practices," we focus on what Adler and Pouliot refer to as "subordination"– how some practices are dominant and organize others. For Swidler, practices are anchoring by virtue of enacting constitutive rules and principles. We broaden this conceptualization by also considering how – as the editors highlight – practices can be anchoring also in other ways – for example, by making other practices possible.

What, then, do we gain by adopting a practice perspective on IOs? Beyond focusing on IOs as "things of boundaries" through a focus on the practices that structure state–IO interaction, what is the added value of a focus on practices? Three issues stand out. First, thinking in terms of anchoring practices specifies the object of study and so makes it more amenable to empirical analysis. Had we adopted a typical constructivist stance of privileging the power of norms, ideas, or knowledge in shaping actors' identities and interests, we would have missed out on the specific context in which such ideational factors may causally or constitutively affect actors and their doings. By analyzing IOs and the role of expert knowledge therein through a focus on practices, we can specify and assess how "context" matters. This is so because knowledge is produced, used, and has effects in and through already patterned activities – that is, practices. When, for example, the World Bank started to highlight good governance as a *sine qua non* for growth and aid effectiveness in the late 1990s, it did so on the basis of studies produced within the Bank, notably by Craig Burnside and David Dollar, which argued that aid is more effective in countries with good policies

[13] *Ibid.*, 25.   [14] Adler and Pouliot, Chapter 1 in this volume.

and institutions.[15] To understand the effects of this knowledge on Bank operations, and on donor and recipient countries, we must be attentive to which practices were already in place and how such practices structured and conditioned the reception, use, and effects of this knowledge. The Bank has considerable in-house economic expertise, and Bank research staff are encouraged to publish research papers in academic journals. This practice helps account for the more direct relation between expertise and Bank policy than in, say, the United Nations Development Programme (UNDP), which does not have its own research department. Such attention to the institutional setting within which ideational factors emerge and gain purchase is, we believe, an important advance on extant constructivist scholarship.

Second, a turn to practices allows us to explore how different forms of power can be at work simultaneously.[16] Discourse is typically defined as "systems of signification" that define what is normal, appropriate, possible, and so on. By analytically privileging practices over discourse and looking at the hierarchies between practices, we can specify the locus of power, and so improve on poststructuralist work that tends to see discourse as omnipresent and determinative of outcomes.[17] We thus move beyond the idea that one form of power – whether it is compulsory, institutional, structural, or productive – is causally or constitutively efficacious in explaining or accounting for particular outcomes. Our focus here is thus on anchoring practices (*explanans*) as determinants of other practices (*explanandum*). This is not to say that we see practices overall as an isolated "cause" of something else. Rather, we see practices as performing discourse, acting to organize, redirect, and not least specify the functioning of discourse that IOs enact and partake in producing. We thus follow Barnett and Duvall's call for analyses that are agnostic as to what type of power is involved or is most significant. We seek to show that one way in which the CPIA is anchoring is to render possible other practices, such as the practice of allocating funds according to a given set of criteria about what constitutes good policies, where the CPIA both defines the standard and assesses countries against that same standard. In this sense, the CPIA makes possible a direct form of compulsory power that comes with allocating funds according to the PBA system. But it also helps establish less direct forms of power, as when the ratings produced by the CPIA allow Bank Country Teams to engage in policy dialogue

---

[15] See Burnside and Dollar, 1997 and 2000.

[16] Throughout, we employ the typology of power suggested by Barnett and Duvall. They define compulsory power as "direct control over others" that operates through interaction of actors in specific social relations. Institutional power is "control over socially distant others" that operates through interaction of specific actors but through diffuse social relations. Structural power is "direct and mutual constitution of the capacities of actors" operating through direct social relations of constitution. Productive power is distinguished from structural power by the fact that the social relations of constitution are diffuse rather than direct. Barnett and Duvall, 2005, 12–22.

[17] See Adler and Pouliot, Chapter 1 in this volume; and Neumann, 2002.

with client countries where Bank staff speak from a position of authority based not only on the general presumption that the Bank houses experts in an area but also through the specific ratings and scores produced by the CPIA.

Third, a central claim found in extant International Relations (IR) accounts of the power of expert knowledge is that it "constitute[s] the world, creating new interests, actors and social activities."[18] More specifically, expert knowledge is held to be central to IO power as it is key in forging "intersubjective agreement" among states.[19] We think that this is too strong a claim if such intersubjectivity is meant to denote a set of shared beliefs and attendant interests. As laid out in the constructivist literature, a prolonged period of persuasion, learning, and socialization based on certain knowledge and norms produces new under-standings, identities/interests, and behavior. We are not convinced by this argument, and have taken our stand against it at length elsewhere.[20] We argue instead that the interplay of, and hierarchical relations between, practices may account for the differentiated impact and role of different forms of knowl-edge. The CPIA assesses developing countries, activates Bank expertise, and produces "facts" that shape what is discussed and how. It does not create new interests or produce intersubjective agreement. There is little or no overt persuasion, learning, and socialization in evidence. Rather, the CPIA is an anchoring practice because it provides a common reference-point, an infra-structure for interaction that allows actors to engage in other, non-anchoring practices – a point also emphasized by Brunnée and Toope's Chapter 5 in this volume. Indeed, a distinct feature of anchoring practices is that they are strengthened, not weakened, by criticism and contestation. Power feeds on resistance. Although we should not stretch the metaphor, the practice of diplomacy, anchoring for other practices in world politics, is taken for granted and it derives its strength in part from allowing disagreement and contestation, also over the appropriate form and content of diplomacy in different situa-tions.[21] The CPIA operates in much the same way, being a constant topic for discussion and criticism by Bank member states. But this criticism concerns *how* the CPIA and the PBA are designed and organized; it does not challenge them as such. In short, stability in the policies and practices of IOs, in this case the World Bank, does not necessitate self-reflective intersubjective agreement. It is enough that agents act in accordance with anchoring practice(s) as they engage in other practices, such as following the PBA or criticizing the CPIA.

Anchoring practices

Swidler sees anchoring practices as "enactments of 'constitutive rules,' [that acquire] their power to structure related discourses and patterns of activity

---

[18] Barnett and Finnemore, 2004, 7.   [19] *Ibid.*, 69.   [20] Neumann and Sending, 2010.
[21] Pouliot, 2010.

because they implicitly define the basic entities or agents in the relative domain of social action."[22] For Swidler, anchoring practices are concrete manifestations of constitutive rules, which in turn define basic entities and so structure discourse. This view challenges constructivist theories in IR that privilege "ideational factors" as central explanatory variables, and also the idea that discourses structure practices.[23] Swidler argues that her account "acknowledges the omnipresence of discourses," but that it "sees discourses largely as commentaries on concrete realities which are culturally constituted in and through practices." In this sense, practices make up "the unspoken realities upon which more directly symbolic or linguistically mediated activities are based."[24]

It seems to us that Swidler's reaction to a problematic privileging of discourse over practice is an equally problematic privileging of practice over discourse. As laid out by Swidler, anchoring practices become a single locus of power radiating through discourse. They also assume an ontic status. We retain the idea of anchoring – that some practices structure others – but we do not see this anchoring as stemming from the enactment of constitutive rules. Rather, all practices enact and embody constitutive rules and principles in that they are *social* practices. The question of which practices the analyst singles out as anchoring and structuring for others hangs, not least, on what that analyst wants to study. We see anchoring as a mechanism having to do with rendering other practices possible, as laid out by the editors in Chapter 1 in this volume. But we also see anchoring practices as being determined by which practices enact and embody defining rules and principles for a broader universe or set of practices. We further specify practices as providing and structuring the *practically important tools and resources* that actors need to "go on" and engage in other practices. This last aspect of anchoring practices we lift from Swidler herself, who suggests that practices provide "the infrastructure for repeated interactional patterns": "They remain stable not only because habit ingrains standard ways of doing things, but because the *need to engage one another forces people to return to common structures.* Indeed, antagonistic interchanges may reproduce common structures more precisely than friendly alliances do."[25]

This conceptualization acknowledges the power of discourse, but does so in a way that specifies how and why seeming stability does not presume strong intersubjective agreements. Note that such a conceptualization of anchoring does *not* in fact presuppose Swidler's own contention that anchoring practices enact constitutive rules. Rather, we see the enactment of constitutive principles to be a generic feature of all social practices. The point of this little exercise in reconceptualization is to provide an analytical framework that is better suited to grasp how the boundaries between IOs and their environment emerge. IOs are

[22] Swidler, 2001b, 95.
[23] For an authoritative statement of this view, see Jepperson, Wendt, and Katzenstein, 1996.
[24] Swidler, 2001b, 94.   [25] *Ibid.* Emphasis added.

at the same time bureaucratic organization with a degree of autonomy and authority that hails from their expertise, and arenas where (particularly powerful) states rein in, dictate, and shape what IOs do. That makes the question of how the boundary between IO as actor and IO as arena is drawn a central issue in world politics. Practice theory offers a way to study the drawing of such boundaries empirically. IOs may be powerful not because they produce intersubjective agreement, but because of their imbrication in specific practices, and that imbrication may be unpacked by means of practice theory. How these practices are organized and defined cannot be accounted for solely by referring to IOs as bureaucratic organizations, since any bureaucracy is only as authoritative as its environment determines. As are all organizations, bureaucracies are dependent on support and legitimacy in their environment.

The content of the practices that structure how IOs operate and interact with member states render some forms of actions possible, while others are deemed impractical, unnecessary, and inappropriate. As a corollary, practices may become powerful not because actors consciously or unconsciously conform to them, but because they define an infrastructure, a set of tools for actors to use and deploy in their interaction with each other. It follows that some practices are anchoring because they define one set of strategies for action rather than others. We lean on the pragmatist tradition's view of practices as always involving a performative and reflexive aspect here, as emphasized in Kratochwil's discussion of pragmatism in Chapter 2 in this volume. In our case, one key to understanding the relationship between the Bank and its environment – of how the boundary between the two is structured – is found in how the CPIA enacts and builds on principles concerning the role of science and truth in modern forms of governing. This in turn renders possible the PBA, which enacts and specifies how the principle of sovereign equality is to translate into equitable aid allocations and thus a "rules-based" and bureaucratic system. The combination of these two practices, with CPIA rendering the PBA possible and specifying the content of what counts as "performance," did not happen as a result of a process internal to the Bank. It is due to what happened both inside and outside of it. It is a thing of boundary, and it structures the micro-practices through which Bank management interacts with donors as well as how donors debate and negotiate in the context of Bank meetings.

The practice of producing knowledge about the world may be seen as anchoring for governing. Distinctively modern forms of governance rest on knowledge about society. Models, categories, and explanations are used not only to make sense of the social world but also to render it legible and concrete.[26] In Bob Jessop's formulation, the economy can be seen as a "narrated system that is accorded specific boundaries, conditions of existence, typical economic agents, tendencies and countertendencies, and a distinctive overall

---

[26] See Hacking, 2002; and Wagner, 2001.

dynamics."[27] The economy, in other words, is not simply there to be governed, but assumes its distinct form, boundaries, and actionable indicators through knowledge-generated models, categories, and indicators. The power of the economics profession in the governing of the economy can be understood in terms of the active work of the profession to establish a universal language of analysis and control.[28] As such, the profession has been heavily involved in "attempts in numerous countries to reformat the economy as a whole, in programs of neoliberal economic structuring."[29]

At a general level, the practice of relating knowledge production with governing can be seen as an enactment of the constitutive rules of modernity: the historical evolution of the social sciences is intimately tied to concerns of society's governability.[30] In this interpretation, the CPIA, understood as a central mode of producing knowledge that feeds directly into how the Bank seeks to shape, guide, and govern client countries, can be regarded as an anchoring practice as defined by Swidler. The CPIA certainly draws its strength and position from this constitutive rule, but its specific direction, organization, and purpose only makes sense within the broader context of the discourse on development, and on the more specific arguments within it that accord a privileged position to certain causal factors to foster development. It does anchor and shape other practices, but not in a strong and singularly constitutive manner, as if its power radiated from a center and throughout a broader discourse.[31] While there is a constitutive rule that defines modern governing as resting on specific bodies of knowledge, it does not say which bodies of knowledge, or how it ought to be organized. For this reason, we opt for a more flexible conceptualization of hierarchy between practices and hence of the concept of anchoring than that suggested by Ann Swidler.

The CPIA is anchoring in large part because it serves as "a tool for governing and a tool for truth."[32] Desrosières notes that there is strong socio-political pressure for experts to "furnish something to lean on, or at least a common language of reference, around which the famous 'democratic debate' can be organized."[33] The CPIA fills such a function within the Bank as the indicators and rankings it produces – even when they are disputed and negotiated – serve as the common framework where it is possible to agree and disagree about how to guide, assist, and help developing countries. Anchoring practices, in this interpretation, draw their strength from how they produce stable signposts and resources for a plethora of actors, those involved in direct tasks of governing, those that formulate the direction of policies, and even those for whom it has not been naturalized and who may in principle oppose it (such as critics of the "Washington consensus").[34]

---

[27] Jessop, 1999, 379.   [28] Fourcade, 2006.   [29] Mitchell, 2005, 297.   [30] Toulmin, 1990.
[31] See Adler and Pouliot, Chapter 1 in this volume; and Neumann, 2002.
[32] Desrosières, 2004, 1. See also Desrosières, 1998.   [33] Desrosières, 2004, 1.
[34] A case in point being Powell, 2004.

Note that the preceding discussion does not assume that expert knowledge is a source of power because it redefines actors' identities or interests. We thus seek to move out of the logic of constructivist literature on norms and knowledge, summed up by Risse as follows: "Socially shared ideas – be it norms (collective expectations about proper behavior of a given identity) or social knowledge about cause-and-effect relationships – not only regulate behavior but also constitute the identity of actors."[35] It is this view of socio-cultural factors that seems to underwrite Barnett and Finnemore's argument that IOs are in part powerful by virtue of how they are able to forge "intersubjective agreement" as it denotes a set of beliefs, understandings, and attendant interests that actors agree on. In this model, expert knowledge produced and used by IOs affects states' understandings and also their identities and interests – they can teach states their interests.[36] But even the most institutionalized bodies of knowledge advanced by IOs are contested and continually criticized. More generally, socio-cultural factors – whether it be norms, values, ideologies, or knowledge – are far too heterogenous and also contradictory to bring about consensus or a convergence of interests.[37] As DiMaggio has argued, actors know much more culture than they use, and since culture is also contradictory, it cannot serve as a motive for action in the way implied in constructivist theory.[38] DiMaggio goes on to argue, in cadences that dovetail nicely with Swidler's argument, that we should focus on how and why different physical and social environments facilitate or trigger the use of different schemata and strategies for action. As laid out in Chapter 1 in this volume, practice theory also insists that culture is "not only in people's minds, discourse, and interactions" but also in the "performance of practices."[39] We take this argument one step further, advancing the notion that knowledge, as a cultural factor, is central to IOs' power but that it is so by being embedded in practices that define and provide strategies for action and vehicles for advancing certain positions rather than others.[40]

The World Bank

The World Bank has two parts, the International Bank for Reconstruction and Development (IBRD) and the International Development Association (IDA).

---

[35] Risse, 2000, 5.   [36] Finnemore, 1996.   [37] Swidler, 2001a.   [38] DiMaggio, 1997, 267.
[39] Adler and Pouliot, Chapter 1 in this volume.
[40] This position is similar to that advanced by Krebs and Jackson. Critiquing constructivist work on norms and deliberation, they argue that "whether or not a social actor has internalized a particular set of normative principles is not causally relevant." And note, as an illustration of their model of "rhetorical coercion," that "[a] ruler pursuing policies incapable of public justification would find her path strewn with numerous practical obstacles. This lack of rhetorical resources might even compel her to alter her course of action"; Krebs and Jackson, 2007, 57.

Established in 1960, the IDA gives loans and grants to countries that do not qualify for IBRD loans from the Bank. Its purpose is to "promote economic development, increase productivity and thus raise standards of living in the less developed areas of the world [by providing finance] on terms which are more flexible and bear less heavily ... than conventional loans."[41] For 2010, IDA commitments totaled US$ 14.5 billion. For Fiscal Year 2011, there are seventy-nine IDA eligible countries. This eligibility is defined by an income *per capita* of less than $1,165.[42]

The World Bank has 185 member states, with a staff of more than 10,000 in more than a hundred country offices. Its central role as an authority on development matters stems in large part from the fact that it houses the world's largest research center on development issues, located in the Development Economics Vice Presidency (DEC). For critics of the Bank, the DEC is central for maintaining the neoliberal paradigm. One study notes, for example, how research aimed at identifying and discussing alternatives to the so-called neoliberal paradigm is marginalized through a host of mechanisms, including hiring procedures and promotions. Also, the process of internal review of papers is such that "[i]f you are a respected neoclassical economist, then [approval] only needs one sign-off, that of your boss. If it's critical, then you go through endless reviews, until the author gives up."[43]

The World Bank is not just any type of IO. It is a bank, and since its inception it has enjoyed a greater degree of authority and autonomy *vis-à-vis* member states than most other IOs.[44] The World Bank's highest organ is the Board of Governors, comprising Finance and Development ministers of member states. The Board of Governors typically meets twice a year. The more hands-on governing and oversight of the Bank is done by twenty-four Executive Directors (EDs). Crucially, while EDs are elected by member states and are to represent them, they are *also* to represent the Bank *vis-à-vis* member states. In marked contrast to member states' permanent missions to the United Nations, EDs have their offices inside the World Bank building in Washington, DC, and are on the payroll of the World Bank, not of the member states.[45] This is but one illustration of the importance of focusing on the specific practices that structure the interaction between states and the Bank.

The main forum for debates about Bank policies and operations is IDA Replenishments, where donors meet every third year to contribute funds to the IDA. Initially, Bank policies were considered to be within the purview of the EDs of the Bank who, as noted in the preceding paragraph, reside permanently in Washington, DC, are on the Bank's payroll, have offices inside the Bank, and fulfill the dual function of representing member states *and* the Bank. During the

---

[41] International Development Association, 1960, Article 1.
[42] International Development Association, n.d.   [43] Broad, 2006.   [44] Woods, 2006.
[45] Woods, 2006, 19.

Ninth Replenishment (IDA 9) – we are currently in IDA 16 – IDA Deputies, who represent donor governments, called for a greater say on matters of policy. This has remained established practice since then, with policy matters being central to the IDA Deputies' reports. Once approved by the Board of Governors, these reports form the basis for Bank policy and operations.[46]

The CPIA and the PBA

While the Bank's EDs are key to the workings of the Bank, so are the member states. We see the relationship between the CPIA and the PBA practices as central to grasping how the boundary between IOs and member states is constituted. The CPIA is anchoring for PBA in making it possible, and both practices enact and feed on constitutive rules in their environment. As a constellation of practices, they constitute the specificity of the boundary between the Bank and member states.

CPIA and PBA: overview

The CPIA is produced each year and is organized by the Operations Policy and Country Services (OPCS). The exercise involves not only the OPCS and all Bank country offices, but also the Regions (six in total), thematic Departments, and Networks. It entails two distinct phases, one that selects typical poor-, medium-, and low-performers for a benchmarking phase, and another that entails actual assessments of all countries, using the fixed ratings for the bench-mark countries as a standard. This is to ensure that the criteria are used consistently and that Bank staff in each country set the ratings right on each criterion.[47] The second stage involves Bank staff assessment and scoring of the countries. This is done by Bank staff in the country concerned. Bank staff are guided in this work by an "Assessment Questionnaire" that provides detailed descriptions of how to rate countries according to different criteria. According to the Bank, the CPIA ratings are "staff assessments" or expert opinions of client countries' policies and institutions. The fact that the CPIA is carried out each year, is structured by a set of detailed instructions, involves a large segment of Bank staff, and is central to a range of other Bank practices, warrants, we believe, our reading of it as an anchoring practice.

The CPIA contains sixteen indicators that are used to rank a country's performance in four thematic areas – namely, economic management, structural policies, policies for social inclusion and equity, and public sector management and institutions. For each of the sixteen indicators (down from twenty in 2005), countries are ranked on a scale from 1 to 6, where 1 is defined as "very weak performance" and 6 as "very strong performance." The guidelines for the

---

[46] World Bank, 2001b.   [47] World Bank, 2005.

exercise assert that in rating countries on the different criteria, the scores "should reflect a variety of indicators, observations, and judgments that are based on country knowledge originated in the Bank, analytic work or policy dialogue, or work done by partners, and relevant publicly available indicators."[48] The guidelines for the CPIA are highly detailed. For example, criterion 12, "Property Rights and Rule-based Governance," comprises three dimensions: (a) legal basis for property rights, (b) predictability, transparency, impartiality and enforcement of laws regulating economic activity, (c) crime and violence as impediment to economic activity. The assessment of the performance on this criterion is, moreover, guided by a description for each score.[49]

The criteria are supposed to capture factors that are within a country's control (as opposed to outcomes) and to measure actual actions rather than plans and intentions. Moreover, Bank staff are to rate countries "on their current status in relation to the criteria and to the benchmark countries," where ratings for benchmark countries are prepared in advance and given to country teams to use in performing their part of the CPIA. Importantly, ratings are to reflect the level of a country's performance against benchmark ratings, *not* on the improvements from the previous year. Alongside each score on all the sixteen indicators, country staff are to produce so-called "write-ups," which justify the score and provide examples. While the Bank since 2004 has published the rankings of all countries on the different indicators, it does *not* publish the write-ups and justifications for the rankings.

The CPIA's core function is to provide the key input to the PBA system. The PBA factors in country needs, measured by gross national income (GNI) *per capita* and population size. But the key determinant of aid allocations is – as the name suggests – performance. The CPIA is the central element of the total Country Performance Rating (CPR) that is used in the PBA. The CPR, moreover, combines the four different CPIA clusters (A–D). The CPR accords, in keeping with prevailing development thinking in the Bank, a much higher weight to the governance aspects of the CPIA (Cluster D). The current CPR is calculated as follows:[50] Country Performance Rating = $(0.24 * CPIA_{A-C} + 0.68 * CPIA_D + 0.08 * Portfolio)$. It gives a 68 percent weight to the governance factor, 24 percent to the other CPIA clusters, and 8 percent to the portfolio assessment (Advanced Reform and Restructuring Program, ARRP). To arrive at the final International Development Association (IDA) allocation, the CPR is given a weight of 5 and combined with population size and poverty levels, as measured by GNI *per capita*, as follows: IDA country allocation = f (Country performance rating$^{5.0}$, Population$^{1.0}$, GNI/capita$^{-0.125}$).[51]

---

[48] *Ibid.*, 4.   [49] World Bank, 2008a, 32.
[50] The formula is subject to triennial discussions, i.e. in the event of IDA Replenishment.
[51] World Bank, 2008b.

CPIA–PBA: evolution over time and the power of Bank expertise

If we hold the external environment fixed and accord it little significance in the analytical framework, we run the risk of not appreciating how IOs are special types of bureaucracies that operate in an international realm. If we accord too much weight to the IOs' environment, however, we may deny agency to their internal functioning; focusing on the constellation of the PBA and the CPIA is helpful. The principle of sovereign equality is central to IOs' identity and mode of operation: IOs must retain legitimacy from states. To do so, they typically seek to formulate rules and principles for how funds are to be allocated so that the system appears equitable, transparent, and predictable in the eyes of both donors and recipient countries. Here, the CPIA and the PBA together perform a vital function in specifying these rules and principles.

The PBA system is conceived as a substitute for political negotiations about how much aid is to be allocated to each country. The practice of allocating funds according to a set of defined rules is an example of how the Bank operates as a bureaucratic organization. So is the Bank's insistence that this happens according to "objective criteria."[52] *How* that practice for an "objective" rules-based system of aid allocations has been defined, however, is derivative of some method to assess what constitutes "good" and "poor" performance. This is where the CPIA comes in as a method to produce robust factual claims. The CPIA makes the PBA possible, anchors it, by defining a set of given criteria for what constitutes performance, and by assessing countries' actual policies and institutions against those criteria. More concretely, the CPIA specifies the contents of the criteria to be about so-called "aid effectiveness," the idea that one should allocate funds to those countries that can make most effective use of aid. The contents of the criteria have evolved over time, from being about a limited set of fiduciary concerns in the 1970s to today's comprehensive standard for development.

The precursor to the current CPIA focused primarily on countries' economic management and poverty alleviation efforts.[53] Over time, both the scope and content of the CPIA criteria have changed – a process that signifies the power of Bank expertise. During the first two decades of the CPIA, the specific contents of the CPIA and its weight in the PBA formula was *not* discussed with member states, but were authoritatively defined by the Bank bureaucracy. However, actual IDA allocations were on numerous occasions subject to political and "arbitrary" priorities of key member states – notably the United States (see pp. 250–251). But as a rule, IDA allocations are determined through the PBA – with specific allocations to each country being made public only to IDA Deputies at the end of each fiscal year – precisely to safeguard against efforts to open the process up to political negotiations. The definition of "performance," however,

---

[52] Steets, 2008, 7.   [53] World Bank, 1992.

has been expanded considerably during the last decade or so. In 1997, governance was explicitly introduced through a new criterion on the legal and regulatory framework. Here, concern with corruption was central, as evidenced by the reference to the importance of paying attention "to the implications for corruption of public sector administration" in assessing all elements – tax reforms, volume and composition of expenditures, public expenditure management, and civil administration."[54] The following year, the CPIA was again changed, in no small part as a response to Burnside and Dollar's influential study, "Aid, Policies, and Growth."[55] This change in the CPIA is significant, as it now came to reflect "an agreed set of Bank wide criteria for promoting growth and poverty reduction."[56]

These developments reflect important features of the evolution of general development thinking, but they also reflect an important feature of the position of the CPIA in the Bank's operations. When it was first established, it was focused on a set of core economic issues addressed to the IDA's concern with fiduciary risks. At present, the CPIA covers a country's policies and institutional characteristics on a comprehensive scale. It defines a standard of "good" policies and institutions that the Bank sees as conducive to sustainable growth, poverty reduction, and the effective use of development assistance.[57] Beyond anchoring the PBA system, the CPIA has come to define a standard for the types of policies and institutions that IDA encourages and advances through its general policies and country operations, notably through its policy dialogue with client countries and in the Bank's country-specific operational strategy, the Country Assistance Strategy (CAS).

The expansion over time in how performance is to be measured and how the CPIA is weighted and used in the PBA looks, at first sight, like an evolution defined largely by Bank expertise and Bank management: they dovetail with evolution in development thinking over time within the Bank, as evidenced, for example, by the higher emphasis on governance issues since the late 1990s following the studies produced by the Bank on aid effectiveness. But a closer look at key documents from successive IDA Replenishment negotiations shows that the relationship between the Bank and member states is much more complex and nuanced.

CPIA–PBA as a frame for policy debates and negotiations

The Bank has recognized that precisely because of its highly technical character, the CPIA is "not well understood by countries (and others)" and that there is a need for the Bank to be "more proactive . . . in explaining to country counterparts" both the organization of the CPIA as well as how the results on the

---

[54] World Bank, 2001a, 9.   [55] Burnside and Dollar, 1997.   [56] World Bank, 2001a, 11.
[57] World Bank, 2008b.

different criteria are produced.[58] One effect of this is to place member states in a disadvantaged position *vis-à-vis* Bank staff and management with respect to the framing and content of central policy debates. While member states are effectively dependent on Bank knowledge and expertise in evaluating and providing the necessary background knowledge for how to amend and reform the CPIA and/or the PBA, they are still actively engaged in shaping its contents. One review notes that the PBA system has "evolved to *reflect new knowledge* and specific IDA *replenishment recommendations* directed to tightening and revising its design and implementation . . . The IDA 12 Replenishment Agreement also calls for an opening of the performance-based allocation system to more public scrutiny."[59] A background paper from 2004 reported that "[s]ome Executive Directors questioned the robustness of the [CPIA] ratings. At their request management assembled an external panel of experts to review CPIA process and methodology."[60]

Here we encounter a paradox: while the practice of the PBA reflects and embodies a key principle for any IO – namely, to treat members according to given, transparent rules – this very practice also positions Bank management in a position of expertise-induced authority to determine when and how that principle is in danger of being diluted. Different member states have continually been skeptical about the balance between needs and performance in the PBA. Responding to a request from member states to review the PBA in this light, Bank management responded by saying: "On balance management's recommendation is to maintain the current formula. [While] research demonstrates the importance of strong support for very poor countries implementing good policies, capturing this insight through further refinements of IDA's allocation formula introduces other undesirable effects, particularly in *diluting the focus on performance*."[61]

Indeed, there has been considerable debate on whether and how the CPIA can better capture country-specific features beyond the role of "needs" relative to "performance." The concern from many Deputies is that an undue "one-size-fits-all" approach is being imposed. The CPIA does factor in country context, as Bank staff are instructed to take account of a country's "stage of development" in their ratings. While the Bank readily acknowledges the importance of grasping country context in understanding what generates economic growth,[62] these principles run against the PBA as a rules-based system: the more country context is factored into the CPIA assessments, the less equitable the PBA system becomes. If one country – Bangladesh being the most frequently referred-to example, as it has a very poor CPIA rating on governance yet has rather spectacular economic growth rates – is rewarded and rated for its performance on

---

[58] World Bank, 2004, 13.   [59] World Bank, 2001a, iv. Emphasis added.
[60] World Bank, 2004, 1.   [61] World Bank, 2001a, 5. Emphasis added.
[62] Kanbur, 2005, 12.

outcomes, the integrity of the PBA falls apart. This is because outcome variables – and, ultimately, success in achieving the Bank's stated objectives – conflict with the logic of the PBA as being about those factors that fall within the purview of a government's control.

Hence, calls for sensitizing the CPIA to country context have been rejected on the basis of a concern for upholding a rules-based system of allocations. Here, debates about the criteria and methods used in the CPIA are structured not only by the "evolution" of expert knowledge within the Bank, but also by the externally imposed principle of upholding a rules-based allocation system. This helps explain why IOs – despite their claims to the contrary – always operate with one-size-fits-all approaches in some form: in order to adhere to the procedural, administrative principle of unbiased and equal treatment of states, IOs rely on elaborate techniques and mechanisms to create a rule, a standard, from which to make decisions and to allocate funds. At the Bank, this standard for decision-making is produced and anchored by the CPIA, and its effects are visible through the PBA. But this practice also enables governing at a distance by virtue of establishing standards that apply to all. In this sense, the power of IOs to produce "global best practices" inheres in IOs as bureaucracies, but it is something that – as expressed in the CPIA and PBA – is very much a product of the power of states to shape IOs' mode of operations. Paradoxically this externally imposed practice, enacting a principle of "equal" treatment according to given rules, also puts IOs in a position of power over these very same states by defining the content of these (universal) rules. In this sense, the donor countries are hoisted with their own petard. Here we have a very clear example of the primacy of practice over discourse. Development discourse encourages the formulation of custom-made plans for specific groups: countries, regions, segment of a population (women, children, landmine victims, etc.). Practice, however, dictates a one size fits all that trumps all that, at least on the overall level that we are concerned with here (tailor-made programs do occur, but they remain exceptions). If the anchoring practice of the CPIA were to be followed, there would be no infrastructure for the donors to work within. Allowing tailor-made programs, therefore, would potentially destroy the very possibility for immediate action.[63]

The power of IOs does not inhere in certain discourses or practices assuming a "doxic" character. Rather, the CPIA and the PBA together furnish something to lean on. Together, these two practices define the parameters and the attendant symbolic tools available to member states and the Bank about what to discuss and how to discuss it. They define the infrastructure for interaction and, as such, the CPIA renders possible the workings of direct forms of power through the PBA. The CPIA itself is the locus for more indirect forms of

---

[63] Alternatively, one could argue that discourse, by encouraging tailor-made programs, holds out narratives that will form the basis of new practices. There are always two stories to tell; whether to privilege discourse or practice is an analytical question.

power by defining the terrains on which Bank staff and states interact. Review and criticism actually confirm and reinforce those functions, for critics of the Bank typically do not challenge the existence of the CPIA and the PBA, but rather their specific contents, calling for reforms and amendments. As Jeff Powell of the Bretton Woods Project argues: "While most of the governance criteria reward behavior which is lauded across the political spectrum, there is a bias toward such factors as stringent private property rights and low regulation of business."[64] Similar criticisms against the CPIA and the PBA have been formulated by different donor governments (including the United Kingdom, Germany, and Norway). These critics accord the Bank considerable authority to determine how to assess reform proposals, how to respond to them, and how to frame emerging issues in the context of the existing practices of the CPIA and PBA. When criticism was waged regarding the transparency and publication of CPIA ratings, the Bank conceded to calls from Deputies to publish CPIA ratings. The Bank noted that "disclosure of the rating system would allow it to benefit from open scrutiny and to serve as a diagnostic tool for strengthening development partnerships."[65] If anything, however, the publication of the ratings has further strengthened the position of the CPIA within the Bank and *vis-à-vis* other actors. The CPIA is used by credit rating agencies (Moody's, Standard and Poor's, for example) in assessing creditworthiness, and by bilateral donors in their bilateral country allocations. To sum up, the CPIA and PBA structure the space for IO–state interaction.

CPIA and the boundaries of political sovereignty

In a highly instructive piece, social anthropologist James Ferguson notes that in the 1990s, civil society was seen as an untainted progressive force, waiting to be released by donor investments in NGOs.[66] In the following decade, the relationship seems to have been reversed, with the state now occupying the role of guardian and driving actor that will build capacity, install skills, and formulate new rules so that the state can be an active agent in molding and fostering society and the economy. Seabrooke notes about the International Monetary Fund (IMF) that following the crisis in legitimacy that ensued in the wake of its failures during the Asian financial crisis, the Fund gradually began to identify and promote global "best practices" that effectively extended its policy advice from strictly economic matters to matters involving governance more broadly.[67] Where the Bank is concerned, its Articles of Agreement state that it is to make decisions solely based on economic considerations. The lifecycle of the CPIA demonstrates that the slide noted by Ferguson and Seabrooke may be traced within the Bank as well.

[64] Powell, 2004, 2.   [65] World Bank, 2002, para. 18.   [66] Ferguson, 2006, Chapter 4.
[67] Seabrooke, 2007.

The CPIA "has evolved well beyond the 'Washington Consensus' to take into account a wider range of policy areas..."[68] The CPIA's catalogue of which elements of the state are considered most appropriate for action serves as a bridge from the economic realm to the state and the political realm. The CPIA furnishes decision-makers with a set of "actionable" indicators that transforms client countries from being primarily economic entities into social and political entities as well. The CPIA also specifies what is "social," what is "political," and what is "administrative" in client countries, as well as what should be such – which is to say that the CPIA defines the boundary of the political sovereignty of recipient countries.

For Barnett and Finnemore the expansion of IO missions (so-called "mission creep") is due in large part to the inherent logic of experts trying to do their job; the "logic of their task dictates that more must be done to accomplish it."[69] We do not think that mission creep is due to bureaucratic rules or the logic of expertise as such. Rather, seen through the lens of the role of the CPIA, that logic spawns narratives that allow the Bank to make claims about what should and should not be done. Although sanctioned by donors, the central drive behind this expansion has been the knowledge-production inside the Bank about the importance of governance and the social (and also environmental) context for aid effectiveness, poverty reduction, and economic growth. As an annual assessment practice, the CPIA is the central vehicle through which the Bank can lay claim to competence to enter recipient countries' non-economic policies. With the weight of the governance cluster of the CPIA at 68 percent in the PBA formula, the Bank rewards those countries that have what the Bank sees as preconditions for success in effective uses of aid and for economic growth in place.

Conclusion

To sum up, IOs may be understood as a series of practices, some of which are anchoring for others. This anchoring does not stem from the enactment of constitutive rules, for that is something all practices have in common. Anchoring has to do with rendering other practices possible, as laid out by the editors in Chapter 1 in this volume. Practices have their lifecycle, and they need to be performed. Practices are constitutive of the social, but for reasons of infinite regress we see no ontic grounds that may determine which practices to study. That becomes an analytical question. Practices are, moreover, a good way to get an empirical handle on boundaries and the patterning of the relations between actors. In this chapter, the IO under study was the World Bank, the anchoring practice was its CPIA, and the practice that it anchored was the PBA.

One key concern for students of IR remains the relationship between IOs and their member states. In extant scholarship, the boundary between IOs and

---

[68] World Bank, 2007, 3.   [69] Barnett and Finnemore, 2004, 72.

member states is treated as a given. Had we opted for a traditional realist or constructivist interpretation of the case at hand, we would either have concluded that given the US preponderance of voting shares in the Bank, they by and large also control it, or that because of the authority of the Bank's expertise, it powerfully shapes development policy and states' interests and behavior. By focusing on a key set of practices that organizes the relations between states and the World Bank, we have told a more nuanced and complex story: the relations between the Bank and states is fundamentally structured by certain key practices, and we looked to their content and interrelations to show that the power of Bank expertise is structured, even determined, by the practices through which it is produced and used. Further, we showed that different forms of power – direct and indirect – are at work simultaneously. Finally, we showed that the principle of sovereignty and its corollary – equitable treatment according to predictable, transparent criteria – gives the Bank power over states, yet it also reduces the Bank's effectiveness in promoting development.

The micro-processes that go into shaping the CPIA and the PBA involve Bank personnel in Washington, DC and at the country level, Bank EDs performing dual roles as state representatives and Bank representatives, and Deputies representing member states. These make up the core of a practice community, where the Bank musters an indispensable resource for the maintenance of the CPIA and the PBA, namely expert knowledge. Member states muster funds. The negotiations over how the constellation of the CPIA and the PBA should be set up determine where the Bank ends and the member states begin (and vice versa). The corollary is that our focus on practices added value by demonstrating in detail how states work through IOs and that – while Bank expertise is powerful in defining the contents of the CPIA – the Bank is not only a bureaucracy, but also an *international* bureaucracy.

By definition, indirect government spells problems of constraints, for if there were no constraints government would not be indirect, but direct. IOs are bureaucratic organizations – namely, their practices tend to be of the one-size-fits-all type (what holds good for Malawi, holds good for Chile, holds good for Bangladesh). The CPIA and the PBA are definitely one-size-fits-all practices. As a consequence, their existence constrains a number of specific initiatives from donor countries. But constraints are relative: the constellation of the CPIA and the PBA does not always override specific interventions. Andersen, Hansen, and Markussen note, for example, that following the US intervention in Afghanistan, World Bank assistance to Pakistan almost quadrupled from US$ 226 million in 2001 to 860 million in 2002.[70] The existence of the CPIA and the PBA are important for outcomes, but they do not determine them. Furthermore, when it comes to the effects of the CPIA and the PBA in recipient states, implementation studies demonstrate that, when these two practices

---

[70] Andersen, Hansen, and Markussen, 2006, 773.

clash, the latter are often more determining of outcome. For example, Ethiopia has had a stable CPIA score of 3.4 between 2005 and 2008 (ranked 38 out of 79 countries, and just above the threshold for being defined as "fragile"). Nonetheless, there has been an increase in IDA funding from US$ 449.9 million to 634.5 million over the same period.[71] Moreover, while the Bank asserts that the CPIA "anchors" (their expression) the Bank's work at the country level through the CAS, a brief look at the CAS for Malawi indicates that this is not so, as the areas for intervention singled out by the Bank (with a prioritization of infrastructure and agriculture) do not reflect the Bank's own assessments as reflected in Malawi's CPIA ratings.[72]

IOs are powerful in part because they embody expertise. There is certainly productive power at work in how the understandings and behavioral patterns of actors are shaped by the expertise and knowledge generated by IOs such as the World Bank. Productive power measures, categorizes, and quantifies the world. It is, nonetheless, an open question whether the governments of recipient states are as shaped by this form of power, as is often suggested. The examples from Ethiopia and Malawi suggest that productive power rather seems to operate *in concreto* and through specific practices that are also infused with *other* forms of both direct and indirect power. Examples abound of how governments of developing countries "enact" or "mimic" definitions of statehood and good governance in order to get access to funds, rather than using funds as stipulated by donors.[73] There is a glitch between speech acts at the negotiation table and acts of implementation here – a fact brought home in Stephen Krasner's description of sovereignty as "organized hypocrisy."[74] Developing countries face conflicting demands from international donors in terms of combating corruption, on the one hand, and engaging in corruption through patron–client relations to stay in power, on the other. The power embedded in Bank practices are easily cancelled out if and when recipients of aid use such funds to secure the hold on power or to cater to important domestic constituencies.[75] Our aim in this chapter was, however, elsewhere, namely on demonstrating that practice theory offers a thoroughgoing relational perspective on IOs and member states as well as an apt tool with which to specify the workings of IO expertise and knowledge *vis-à-vis* member states.

References

Abbott, Andrew, 1995. Things of Boundaries. *Social Research* 62 (4): 857–882.

Andersen, Thomas Barnebeck, Henrik Hansen, and Thomas Markussen, 2006. US Politics and World Bank IDA-Lending. *Journal of Development Studies* 42 (5): 772–794.

[71] See Sending and Lie, 2010; and, for numbers for Ethiopia, World Bank, n.d.
[72] World Bank, 2010.   [73] Meyer and Rowan, 1977.   [74] Krasner, 1999.
[75] This mechanism is captured in Alex de Waal's discussion of the "political marketplace" and its implications for the effectiveness of external actors' interventions: de Waal, 2009.

Barnett, Michael N. and Raymond D. Duvall, eds., 2005. *Power in Global Governance*. Cambridge: Cambridge University Press.

Barnett, Michael N. and Martha Finnemore, 2004. *Rules for the World*. Ithaca: Cornell University Press.

Broad, Robin, 2006. Research, Knowledge, and the Art of "Paradigm Maintenance": The World Bank's Development Economics Vice-Presidency (DEC). *Review of International Political Economy* 13 (3): 387–419.

Burnside, Craig and David Dollar, 1997. Aid, Policies, and Growth. Policy Research Working Paper 1777. Washington: World Bank.

    2000. Aid, Policies, and Growth. *American Economic Review* 90 (4): 847–868.

Desrosières, Alain, 1998. *The Politics of Large Numbers: A History of Statistical Reasoning*. Translated by Camille Naish. Cambridge, MA: Harvard University Press.

    2004. For a Politics of the Tools for Knowledge: The Case of Statistics. Paper presented at the Conference "Politics and Knowledge: Democratizing Knowledge in Times of the Expert," June, Bergen.

De Waal, Alexander, 2009. Mission Without End? Peacekeeping in the African Political Marketplace. *International Affairs* 85 (1): 99–113.

DiMaggio, Paul, 1997. Culture and Cognition. *Annual Review of Sociology* 23 (1): 263–287.

Drezner, Daniel W., 2007. *All Politics is Global: Explaining International Regulatory Regimes*. Princeton: Princeton University Press.

Ferguson, James, 2006. *Global Shadows: Africa in the Neoliberal World Order*. Durham: Duke University Press.

Finnemore, Martha, 1996. *National Interests in International Society*. Ithaca: Cornell University Press.

Fourcade, Marion, 2006. The Construction of a Global Profession: The Transnationalization of Economics. *American Journal of Sociology* 112 (1): 145–194.

Hacking, Ian, 2002. *Historical Ontology*. Cambridge, MA: Harvard University Press.

International Development Association, 1960. *Articles of Agreement*. Available at http://siteresources.worldbank.org/IDA/Resources/ida-articlesofagreement. pdf. Accessed November 22, 2010.

    n.d. What is IDA? Available at http://go.worldbank.org/ZRAOR8IWW0. Accessed November 29, 2010.

Jepperson, Ronald, Alexander Wendt, and Peter J. Katzenstein, 1996. Norms, Identity, and Culture in National Security. In *The Culture of National Security: Norms and Identity in World Politics*, edited by Peter J. Katzenstein, 33–75. New York: Columbia University Press.

Jessop, Bob, 1999. Narrating the Future of the National Economy and the National State: Remarks on Remapping Regulation and Reinventing Governance. In *State/Culture: State-Formation After the Cultural Turn*, edited by George Steinmetz, 378–406. Ithaca: Cornell University Press.

Kanbur, Ravi, 2005. Reforming the Formula: A Modest Proposal for Introducing Development Outcomes in IDA Allocation Procedures. Discussion Paper 4071. London: Centre for Economic Policy Research.

Keohane, Robert O., 1984. *After Hegemony: Cooperation and Discord in the World Political Economy.* Princeton: Princeton University Press.

Krasner, Stephen D., 1999. *Sovereignty: Organized Hypocrisy.* Princeton: Princeton University Press.

Krebs, Ronald and Patrick Thaddeus Jackson, 2007. Twisting Tongues and Twisting Arms: The Power of Political Rhetoric. *European Journal of International Relations* 13 (1): 35–66.

Mearsheimer, John J., 1994/1995. The False Promise of International Institutions. *International Security* 19 (3): 5–49.

Meyer, John and Brian Rowan, 1977. Institutionalized Organizations: Formal Structure as Myth and Ceremony. *American Journal of Sociology* 83 (2): 340–363.

Mitchell, Timothy, 1991. The Limits of the State: Beyond Statist Approaches and Their Critics. *American Political Science Review* 85 (1): 77–94.

2005. The Work of Economics: How a Discipline Makes Its World. *European Journal of Sociology* 46 (2): 297–320.

Neumann, Iver B., 2002. Returning Practice to the Linguistic Turn: The Case of Diplomacy. *Millennium* 31 (3): 627–651.

Neumann, Iver B. and Ole Jacob Sending, 2010. *Governing the Global Polity: Practice, Mentality, Rationality.* Ann Arbor: University of Michigan Press.

Pouliot, Vincent, 2010. *International Security in Practice: The Politics of NATO-Russia Diplomacy.* Cambridge: Cambridge University Press.

Powell, Jeff, 2004. The World Bank Policy Scorecard: The New Conditionality? *Bretton Woods Update* 43. Available at www.brettonwoodsproject.org/art-84455. Accessed November 29, 2010.

Risse, Thomas, 2000. "Let's Argue!": Communicative Action in World Politics. *International Organization* 54 (1): 1–39.

Seabrooke, Leonard, 2007. Legitimacy Gaps in the World Economy: Explaining the Sources of the IMF's Legitimacy Crisis. *International Politics* 44 (2/3): 250–268.

Sending, Ole Jacob and Jon Harald Sande Lie, 2010. The Role of the CPIA and the PBA at the Country Level: Case Studies of Ethiopia and Malawi. Draft. Oslo: Norwegian Institute of International Affairs.

Steets, Julia, 2008. Adaption and Refinement of the World Bank's "Country Policy and Institutional Assessment" (CPIA). Discussion Paper. Eschborn: Deutsche Gesellschaft für Technische Zusammenarbeit.

Swidler, Ann, 2001a. *Talk of Love: How Culture Matters.* Chicago: University of Chicago Press.

2001b. What Anchors Cultural Practices. In *The Practice Turn in Contemporary Theory,* edited by Theodore R. Schatzki, Karin Knorr Cetina, and Eike von Savigny, 83–101. New York: Routledge.

Toulmin, Stephen, 1990. *Cosmopolis: The Hidden Agenda of Modernity*. Chicago: University of Chicago Press.

Vaisey, Stephen, 2009. Motivation and Justification: A Dual-Process Model of Culture in Action. *American Journal of Sociology* 114 (6): 1675–1715.

Wagner, Peter, 2001. *A History and Theory of the Social Sciences*. London: Sage.

Weaver, Catherine, 2008. *Hypocrisy Trap: The World Bank and the Poverty of Reform*. Princeton: Princeton University Press.

Woods, Ngaire, 2006. *The Globalizers: The IMF, the World Bank, and Their Borrowers*. Ithaca: Cornell University Press.

World Bank, 1992. Allocations Revisited. IDA10 Discussion Paper 2. Washington: International Development Association.

2001a. Review of the Performance-Based Allocation System, IDA10–12. Washington: World Bank.

2001b. The IDA Deputies: An Historical Perspective. Washington: International Development Association. Available at http://siteresources.worldbank.org/IDA/Resources/Seminar PDFs/deputS.pdf. Accessed November 20, 2010.

2002. Additions to IDA Resources: Thirteenth Replenishment. Washington: World Bank. Available at http://siteresources.worldbank.org/IDA/Resources/FinaltextIDA13Report.pdf. Accessed November 20, 2010.

2004. Disclosing IDA Country Performance Ratings. Washington: World Bank. Available at http://siteresources.worldbank.org/IDA/Resources/disclosingIDACPR.pdf. Accessed November 22, 2010.

2005. Country Policy and Institutional Assessments. Washington: World Bank. Available at http://siteresources.worldbank.org/IDA/Resources/CPIA2005Questionnaire.pdf. Accessed November 22, 2010.

2007. Selectivity and Performance: IDA's Country Assessment and Development Effectiveness. Washington: International Development Association.

2008a. Country Policy and Institutional Assessments. 2008 Assessment Questionnaire. Washington: World Bank.

2008b. IDA's Performance Based Allocation System for IDA15. Washington: International Development Association. Available at http://siteresources.worldbank.org/IDA/Resources/IDA15Annex1.pdf. Accessed November 29, 2010.

2010. Malawi Country Brief. Available at http://go.worldbank.org/PH14P64710. Accessed November 29, 2010.

n.d. Country Assistance Strategy: Ethiopia. Available at http://go.worldbank.org/ZBCG9IF761. Accessed November 29, 2010.

10 | *The practice of political manipulation*

ERIK VOETEN

Otto von Bismarck is widely credited with keeping Germany on a course for peace from 1871 to 1890 by being a "brilliant diplomatic tactician"[1] who outmaneuvered powerful domestic and international opposition to implement his preferred policies. Many historians believe that Jean Monnet pushed European integration towards his preferred path through the strategic use of rhetoric without ever even holding elective office.[2] Stories abound in which savvy politicians or activists strategically engineer a situation to their own advantage; leaving their less accomplished opponents to lick their wounds. It should not be contentious to suggest that the ability of leaders to skillfully manipulate their environments matters for the outcomes we care about in international politics. It is much trickier to systematically study such political manipulation, coined "heresthetics" by William Riker. As Riker writes:

> Heresthetics is an art, not a science. There is no set of scientific laws that can be more or less mechanically applied to generate successful strategies. Instead, the novice heresthetician must learn by practice how to go about managing and manipulating and maneuvering to get the decisions he or she wants. Practice is, however, difficult to engage in, especially since one must win often enough to become a political leader before one has much opportunity to practice.[3]

This chapter examines the practice of political manipulation (heresthetics) in the context of collective bargaining in international organizations (IOs) and specifically the UN General Assembly (UNGA). The study of heresthetics has focused on domestic legislatures in which agenda control, strategic voting, and the manipulation of dimensions (for example, issue linkage) have been identified as categories of manipulation.[4] Such practices are also prominent in the UNGA and other international organizations, even though the strategic context differs markedly.

There are three advantages to taking international practices seriously in studying the use of political manipulation in global collective bargaining.

---

[1] Byman and Pollack, 2001, 121.   [2] For example, Brinkley and Hackett, 1991.
[3] Riker, 1986, ix.   [4] Riker, 1986.

First, practices create informal norms that structure the collective bargaining process. In virtually any interesting strategic dilemma there are multiple equilibria with vastly differing implications. Formal institutions, such as voting rules and committees, can impose structure that steers the decision-making process towards some solutions rather than others. Yet, in the global context these institutions are generally weak. Shared expectations about how the process of bargaining works, or what rhetoric is acceptable, can focus the bargaining process on particular solutions. It is not novel to suggest that cultural analysis may aid strategic analysis in this regard.[5] The focus on practice is especially useful because of its attention to background knowledge, because it weaves together discursive and material worlds and, most importantly, because it stresses that there are patterns of rhetoric and actions that create path dependency. These patterns shape beliefs that actors have about each other.

Second, an international practices approach highlights that political manipulation can be performed in more or less *competent* ways. The strategic approach dictates that if attempts at political manipulation exhibited obvious regularities and became routine, they could easily be learned and counteracted. In this sense, the transformative potential of political manipulation depends on one side being better at it than their opponents. Gaps in heresthetic abilities are a regular feature of most political settings and are frequently stressed by diplomatic historians and practitioners in accounts of important achievements. Yet, rational choice theorists are traditionally reluctant to attribute explanatory value to superior skill, fearing that such accounts lend themselves to *ex post* rationalizing, even if they often seem reasonable empirically. The practice approach offers a more systematic way to think about this issue by stressing the acquisition of background knowledge and understanding as integral elements of competent performances. For example, it suggests that political manipulation is a practice that can be learned. The self-determination case stresses how the few former colonies with experience in UNGA bargaining strategically redefined the decolonization issue in ways that didn't satisfy many former colonies, but that was more successful than other attempts at dealing with the issue that were not consistent with UNGA practices. Similarly, while many developing countries were outmaneuvered into accepting intellectual property rights (TRIPS) as part of the 1994 WTO agreement, they subsequently learned (with the assistance of Western-based NGO networks) to strategically use agenda-setting and issue linkages in order to curtail the impact of the TRIPS agreement.[6] Thus more or less predictable temporal and cross-sectional variation in competence may help account for outcomes.

Third, understanding practices of political manipulation in given contexts aids the interpretation of collective agreements. Despite the evasiveness of precise

---

[5] See, for example, Greif, 1994.   [6] Sell and Prakash, 2004.

scientific laws about political manipulation, one can discern patterns in the types of practices that skilled herestheticians employ in a given context. The types of agenda or dimensional manipulations that are going to be effective depend on the norms and rules that operate in a given institutional context. The practice of political manipulation in the UNGA constitutes a distinct "community of practice" from other areas of world politics, thus pointing to a "parallel existence of practices."[7] This implies that rhetorical strategies that may work in the UNGA may not be successful elsewhere (and vice versa). Conversely, textual interpretations of UNGA resolutions are often misleading about their actual purpose. For example, there are strong norms of universality in the United Nations. Thus, many resolutions are cloaked in universal language even if their actual purpose is much more limited, leading to frequent accusations of hypocrisy. Understanding the strategic imperatives that led to the universal language can aid our understanding of where and how we can expect consistent application.

These theoretical points are illustrated with an analysis of the political history of the adoption and application of one of the most significant resolutions the UNGA has adopted: the 1960 *Declaration on the Granting of Independence to Colonial Countries and Peoples*. Scholars have tended to view the Declaration and the ensuing UNGA decolonization regime either as a "normative victory"[8] or as "organized hypocrisy."[9] I argue that an understanding of the heresthetics underlying the creation and application of the resolution can shed light on discrepancies between the normative ideals captured by the rhetoric of the resolution and the systematic deviations of those principles in practice. The main herestheticians were representatives from the former colonies that had experience with the UNGA's political process. They skillfully exploited exogenous shocks in order to get an outcome they had long desired but had been unable to achieve. Yet, despite the universal and liberal language of the resolution, its intended area of application was limited to the specific problem of decolonization, not to broader issues of self-determination for minorities. Indeed, while the resolution's principles have been consistently applied to the former problem, their broader application has been wildly inconsistent.

Collective choice and manipulation in IOs

The actors that populate the international system are enormously diverse with respect to their material interests and capabilities, their moral and ethical commitments, their ideological convictions, their political institutions, and their cultural attachments. Yet, the fates of these actors are also inherently interdependent. Hence, conflicts are inevitable and so are demands for coordinating interactions. IOs are in large measure attempts to meet these demands. The theoretical study of collective choice reminds us that aggregating heterogenous individual preferences

[7] Adler and Pouliot, Chapter 1 in this volume.   [8] Jackson, 1993, 124.   [9] Krasner, 1999.

into a collective choice is an arduous process with many possible outcomes even given a set of fixed voting rules and preferences.[10] One interpretation of such results is that collective decision-making produces only transitory results and is in continuous disequilibrium.[11] A more common interpretation is that further structure is needed to induce stable outcomes.[12]

Structure in this context refers to the processes that create transitive social orders.[13] In the domestic politics literature, formal institutions take pride of place as structures that can induce equilibrium. For example, most legislatures have division-of-labor arrangements that delegate agenda control to committees and rules that restrict the introduction of amendments. Structure can also stem from restrictions on preference orderings. For example, the structure of a political situation differs between situations where actors are divided along a single dimension (for example, left–right) and situations where multiple dimensions of contestation are involved. Moreover, there may be informal norms that help structure how outcomes are achieved in a given legislative setting.[14] Similar structures are present in IOs. IOs have committees, procedures for introducing amendments, and may even be dominated by one-dimensional contestation.[15] IOs also tend to develop distinct informal protocols and assumptions that organize the process of reaching collective agreements. For example, it is widely recognized that the United Nations has a unique New York culture[16] that structures how agreements are reached; even warranting an "Insider's Guide to the UN."[17]

Political manipulation is the process of using or shaping the structure of a decision-making environment to one's advantage. Structural features of a collective choice environment are not neutral: they provide some actors with better opportunities than others. Yet, some actors are also better at skillfully manipulating the formal and informal institutions of a collective decision-making environment to get what they want. Riker focused on three ways that actors manipulate outcomes. The first is agenda manipulation: controlling what issues are and are not considered, how the alternatives are framed, how they are and can be amended, and how they are pitted against each other in votes. The importance of agenda manipulation and gate-keeping is widely recognized in

[10] For example, Arrow, 1963. Later theorems that further document the existence of cycles in majority voting mechanisms are commonly referred to as "chaos theorems" (see McKelvey, 1976, 1979, and 1983). The difficulties in aggregating preferences and the existence of cycles have been known at least since Condorcet, who formulated a famous voting paradox associated with majority rule.
[11] This interpretation of the instability of the political process is most commonly associated with Riker, 1980.
[12] See, for example, Shepsle, 1979; and Shepsle and Weingast, 1981.
[13] Morrow, 1988, 77.   [14] See, for example, Asher, 1973; and Helmke and Levitsky, 2004.
[15] Voeten, 2000.   [16] Smith, 2006.   [17] Fasulo, 2004.

the IO literature.[18] It is also generally understood that this activity requires both background knowledge and skill.

Second, actors can vote strategically. Strategic voting means that actors do not vote for their sincerely preferred alternative but for the alternative that is likely to generate the best outcome, given expectations about how others may vote. There is ample evidence for strategic voting in the context of IOs.[19] The ability of actors to vote strategically depends on the information they have about the expected behavior of others, which is likely to come from past practice and skilled leadership.

Third, actors can redefine a situation by manipulating the dimensions of an issue. An example of this is issue linkage, another topic that has received ample attention in the literature.[20] It may also involve reducing the dimensionality of conflict. For example, the framers of the self-determination issue removed the right of former colonies to nationalize industries and moral assessments of colonialism from the resolution. This did not necessarily reflect their preferences but was done to broaden the coalition.

The novelty here is not to suggest that agenda-setting, strategic voting, and manipulation of issue dimensions matter but to study these activities as a practice, a performance that can be executed in more or less competent ways. Many actors try to strategically manipulate agendas but these attempts often fail. For example, the USSR strategically raised the stake on the self-determination issue by having Nikita Khrushchev personally introduce a resolution directly to the plenary session of the Assembly. Yet, the resolution failed. In the narrative, I suggest that this was so because while the language of the resolution was obviously strategically chosen to appeal to the former colonies, it failed to abide by the informal norms of UNGA resolutions. Khrushchev, a UN outsider, did not utilize the structure of the decision-making environment well. Instead, a number of experienced delegates from former colonies skillfully redrafted the bill in UNGA language. They also altered the dimensionality of the situation by removing all language that referred to the Cold War conflict, thus making the issue only about self-determination of former colonies. Moreover, they voted strategically by casting their ballots against amendments to the resolution that condemned colonialism in stronger terms, a decision that was particularly difficult for many former colonies less attuned to the strategic context of the UNGA.

The practice of political manipulation in the UNGA

So far, I have stressed the similarities between domestic legislatures and IOs. Yet there are also notable differences. The most important one is how actors within

[18] See, for example, Pollack, 1997; Sell and Prakash, 2004; and Carpenter, 2007.
[19] See, for example, Frey, 1984; Garrett, 1992; and Voeten, 2001.
[20] See, for example, Tollison and Willett, 1979; Haas, 1980; and Davis, 2004.

IOs relate to their external environments. In domestic legislatures the external environment matters, in that it provides incentives for re-election or possible veto points (for example, the presidency and the courts). Yet, the issues in IOs are typically different. First, decisions in most IOs are not directly enforceable. This is certainly true for the UNGA, which adopts non-binding resolutions. Consequentially, the actual effect of resolutions is thought to be minimal unless they are adopted by near-unanimity, despite the fact that the formal voting rule is majority rule.[21] Second, IOs usually do not have sole jurisdiction over an issue. Generally, other multilateral or unilateral courses of action should be taken into account when discussing alternatives. As such, the literature on collective decision-making in international politics identifies coercion as imposing structure on bargaining processes.[22] For example, Voeten offers a model in which bargaining in the Security Council is structured through formal rules (veto power), coercion (the asymmetric availability of outside options), and the assumption that competition takes place in a one-dimensional policy space.[23]

Such structural constraints shape UNGA decision-making in important ways, but they do not fully determine outcomes. This point is crucial for scholars who wish to make sense of UN resolutions. The analogy with Bourdieu's discussion of the juridical field is useful here.[24] Bourdieu criticizes both *formalists*, who view the law as a self-contained system that is autonomous from its social and political environment, and *instrumentalists*, who conceive of the law as a mere tool in the hands of the powerful. Formalists fail to appropriately acknowledge the influence of those who exercise power outside the legal domain while instrumentalists do not account for the unique qualities that separate legal practice from other social activities.[25] Similar critiques can and have been uttered against scholars of the United Nations. For example, Stanley Hoffmann observed that:

> It has always been a problem that specialists of international politics dealing primarily with the diplomatic and strategic scene dismissed the UN from their analyses, whereas lawyers and political scientists specialized in the study of the UN's political functions tended to lock themselves up, so to speak, within the UN and to look at the world outside only dimly, as it was filtered into and through the UN.[26]

---

[21] Higgins, 1963.
[22] Young (1978) distinguishes three mechanisms that help resolve conflicts of interests in international politics and are thus part of the structure of the international system: institutionalized bargaining, coercive diplomacy, and organized warfare. Morrow (1988) points out that coercion essentially covers the latter two mechanisms since warfare is the result of the failure to achieve goals through coercive diplomacy.
[23] Voeten, 2001.   [24] See also Brunnée and Toope, Chapter 5 in this volume.
[25] Bourdieu, 1987.   [26] Hoffmann, 1998, 179.

This is indeed a serious problem. Outsiders who analyze the effects of UN resolutions without understanding the process by which such resolutions come about are usually quick to dismiss them as ineffective and hypocritical given that the high-sounding principles expressed in the resolutions are frequently violated. Yet, some of the language of UN resolutions is a product of political manipulation that reflects internal UN norms and should be interpreted as such. For example, the UN self-determination regime was based on a political bargain that solely applied to the issue of granting independence to former colonies. Yet, the structure of the situation dictated that the actual text of the resolutions revealed more universal aspirations. Many scholars have pointed to the hypocrisy of the self-determination regime by highlighting how these universal principles were not consistently applied in non-colonial cases.[27] Yet, as I will show, the regime was consistently applied to colonial cases, with important consequences, and thus should not be dismissed as irrelevant. Understanding how to interpret the resolution, however, requires comprehension of the practice of political manipulation that helped create it.

It is also an error to become so caught up in internal processes that one no longer recognizes that the UNGA is but a small part of the international political universe. In the same way that legal insiders "have an easy time convincing themselves that the law provides its own foundation,"[28] UN insiders tend to see a world that is shaped by piles of UN resolutions that build upon each other to logically constitute a body of reference for action. Consequentially, UN insiders are often frustrated that what appears logical from an internal perspective is not accepted in the broader realm of international politics.

It is beyond the scope of this chapter to provide a full anthropological accounting of the habits and routines of UN delegates. I wish to focus here on three characteristics that effective UN resolutions tend to have, that are reasonably well understood, and that help illuminate the disjuncture between the rhetoric of UNGA resolutions and their applicability outside the UN context. The first two, an aspiration to be *neutral* and *universal*, are shared with the juridical field.[29] These aspirations may stem from a broader desire to become a "Parliament of Men," as Paul Kennedy put it.[30] *Neutrality* is a core principle that underlies many UN efforts. For example, scholars have argued that the desire to be perceived as neutral prevents the United Nations from being effective in peacekeeping, which sometimes requires a party to take a stand.[31] *Universality* is also a fundamental founding principle of the United Nations. As I suggested above, at times resolutions are packaged in universalist language even if the actual political coalition that supports a resolution does not support a universalist interpretation of it. Both neutrality and universality are

---

[27] See Krasner, 1999; and Franck, 1988.   [28] Bourdieu, 1987, 819.   [29] *Ibid.*, 820.
[30] Kennedy, 2006.   [31] For example, Barnett, 2003.

also linked with the necessity for near-universal support for resolutions to be effective. Indeed, as the case will illustrate, the UNGA adopts many resolutions that depart from neutral and universal language but those are almost never adopted with near-unanimity and never approximate the status of customary law, as did the self-determination resolution. Thus, for herestheticians who care about the effect of resolutions rather than their symbolic value, universal and neutral language is invaluable.

A third feature is that the language of effective UN resolutions tends to be much more *liberal* than many of the resolution's supporters would accept outside the UN context.[32] This feature caters to the need for support from the United States and other Western states with the ability to affect outcomes outside the UN arena. This was especially important for self-determination, which needed to be accepted by the colonial powers and/or the states that had leverage over those powers. The underlying imperative is that liberal democracies have greater difficulties voting against resolutions that unambiguously advance liberal inter-nationalist principles than similar resolutions that do not. The need for liberal language does, of course, not imply that the actors who advocate these resolutions for other reasons also intend to abide by the liberal language. Indeed, the disjuncture between the liberal nature of many UN resolutions and the illiberal practices that are sometimes maintained in their name frequently invites accu-sations of hypocrisy. Yet, liberal internationalist language can become a powerful symbolic tool for actors to achieve what they want in the UN context.[33]

Skillful diplomats recognize that effective UNGA resolutions have these fea-tures. By skills I do not just mean overall diplomatic skills but an understanding and appreciation of how things work at the United Nations. The narrative contains some anecdotal examples of this but there is also some general (albeit old) research into this matter. For example, Alger showed with a pre-test and a post-test among UNGA delegates that participation in the UNGA changed notions about how the institution actually operates and how a country's goals can be achieved in this institution.[34] Keohane argued that most delegates are aware that "accomplishing their objectives depends on some compatibility with dominant values of the Organization."[35] A more recent example is John Bolton, who was sent to the United Nations with a clear intent to break its culture of decision-making[36] but who, by most accounts, was not particularly successful in achieving US goals.

The processes that reproduce these practices are not immediately obvious. Delegates are diplomats trained and socialized into their national Foreign Service bureaucracies. They are only temporarily assigned to the United

---

[32] Hurd, 2005.   [33] *Ibid.*   [34] Alger, 1963.   [35] Keohane, 1969, 868.

[36] Among others, Bolton argued that: "There is no such thing as the United Nations. There is only the international community, which can only be led by the only remaining superpower, which is the United States." Bolton quoted in "Hawks Sit Out Phoney Peace While War Machine Rolls On," *The Observer*, January 12, 2003.

Nations and usually have little autonomy. As such, the UNGA is an unlikely arena for socialization, and even if socialization occurs it may not matter much. For example in the self-determination case, the US delegation appeared persuaded by the 1960 *Declaration* and publicly applauded its adoption, but President Eisenhower decided against voting in favor of it.[37] Yet, this example also hints at an interesting disconnect between what occurs inside and outside the institution that could reflect a distinct way of doing things inside the UNGA.

Self-determination: ideas, power, and political manipulation

Most of the literature on self-determination falls within a constructivist framework and focuses on understanding the ideational transformations that led to the rejection of colonialism as an acceptable form of rule.[38] For example, Jackson argues that two simultaneous games of sovereignty have emerged within international society.[39] Next to the old, "hardball" game, a new, softer, game evolved that deals exclusively with assigning formal authority and is governed by the rule of law, not by power politics. This game has created sovereign rights for ex-colonies regardless of their level of or prospects for empirical statehood, and has led to the appearance of "quasi-states," states that would not have been able to guarantee their independence in the old hardball game.

According to Jackson, the emergence of this new game represents fundamental institutional change shaped by liberal ideas that originated in the West but quite surprisingly came to benefit the third world. The "final normative victory"[40] came with the adoption of the 1960 *Declaration on the Granting of Independence to Colonial Countries and Peoples*. The *Declaration* is widely regarded to be a constitutive principle of the international system[41] and has been heralded in this literature as the "consummation of the global expansion of the Westphalian constitution of international society,"[42] the "New UN Law of Self-Determination,"[43] and as the "second Charter" of the United Nations.[44] According to Thomas Franck, very few norms have had as dramatic an impact on the international system.[45]

A limitation of this and other accounts of ideational revolutions in sovereignty[46] was that the rules of the "new game of sovereignty" did not match the

---

[37] More generally, members of the US UN mission tend to value the United Nations and the views of the majority in the United Nations more highly than other State Department members (Bleichman, 1968).

[38] See, for example, Crawford, 2002; and Philpott, 2001.

[39] Jackson, 1990, 47–49.   [40] Jackson, 1993, 124.

[41] See Brownlie, 1988, 5; Cassese, 1995, 320; Crawford, 1979, 101; Farer, 1968; Gros Espiell, 1977; and Higgins, 1994.

[42] Philpott, 2001, 153.   [43] Pomerance, 1982, 12.

[44] Jackson, 1990, 70.   [45] Franck, 1988, 743.

[46] See, for example, Crawford, 2002; Philpott, 2001; Reus-Smit, 1997; and Zacher, 2001.

liberal views from which it supposedly stemmed. Just as many Western states had long embraced human rights only as long as these did not apply to colonial peoples, most former colonies now championed human rights with the sole purpose of ridding the world of colonialism. As Louis Henkin put it: "Human rights was being used as a political weapon against colonialism or economic imperialism, not to enhance the rights of all persons against all governments."[47] This led to what Jackson calls an "ironic and unintended outcome" of the rule-based regime: that many peoples are trapped within illiberal regimes that deny or neglect human rights.[48] I argue that labeling this outcome "ironic" and "unintended" follows directly from a failure to understand the process that led to the 1960 *Declaration*. There is no evidence that the architects of the 1960 *Declaration* intended to create a liberal self-determination regime, the text of the resolution notwithstanding.

Critics argue that the process of affirming legitimate rule is better charac-terized as one of "organized hypocrisy," in which deviations from norms are persistent across both time and space.[49] It is certainly true that the self-determination regime has not been consistently applied when evaluated against the lofty principles that it proclaims. As argued above, I claim that it only constrains future actions to the extent that these applications fit the political purposes of the coalition that established it. Thus, we can expect hypocrisy, but in predictable circumstances.

Bargaining over self-determination

Entry onto the international scene

Although the antecedents of the self-determination concept can be traced to the American Declaration of Independence and the French Revolution, its appearance as an operative political principle in the international arena dates from the Bolshevik Revolution and Woodrow Wilson's efforts to reshape Europe at the end of the First World War.[50] The ideals advanced by Lenin and Wilson contained insurmountable disparities. Lenin thought of self-determination as an uncondi-tional right to secession that was logically linked to the socialist revolution: "Just as mankind can achieve the abolition of classes only by passing through the transition period of the dictatorship of the oppressed class, so mankind can achieve the inevitable merging of nations only by passing through the transition period of complete liberation of all the oppressed nations, i.e. their freedom to secede."[51]

To Wilson, self-determination meant the right of a people to freely select a government, stating that "[e]very people has a right to choose the sovereignty

---

[47] Henkin, 1965, 513.   [48] Jackson, 1990, 49.   [49] Krasner, 1999.
[50] See, for example, Crawford, 1979; Carr, 1951; and Hechter and Borland, 2001.
[51] Lenin, 1969.

under which they shall live."[52] He initially referred to it as a right that potentially applies to all peoples but later, under the influence of the British as well as his own Secretary of State Robert Lansing, relegated the idea of self-determination for "underdeveloped peoples" to a rather distant future.[53] Even during the Paris Peace Conferences, Lansing criticized Wilson's conception of self-determination (or, rather, self-government) calling it dangerous and unrealistic:[54]

> It is an evil thing to permit the phrase to continue to dwell in the minds of men as expressing a principle having the apparent sanction of the civilized world, when it has been in fact thoroughly discredited and will always be cast aside whenever it comes in conflict with national safety, with historic political rights or with economic interests affecting the prosperity of a nation.[55]

Indeed, neither the Peace Treaties following the First World War, nor the Covenant of the League of Nations, upheld liberal ideals. The self-determination principle was applied selectively to Central and Eastern Europe, but not to Western Europe, let alone Africa and Asia. The method that Wilson deemed appropriate for self-determination – plebiscites – was also employed selectively. Where the interests of the Allies were likely to be imperiled, populations were not consulted.[56] As a result, before the Second World War, self-determination was neither an international legal standard[57] nor a widely accepted social norm.

This practice changed only slightly during and right after the war. Winston Churchill stated that the provisions regarding self-determination in the Atlantic Charter were restrictively aimed at "the States and nations of Europe under the Nazi yoke."[58] A small breakthrough came when the self-determination of peoples was mentioned in the UN Charter as a principle based on which nations should develop "friendly relations."[59] However, self-determination was formulated as one of the many lofty desiderata of the United Nations and

[52] Wilson, 1927, 187.   [53] Pomerance, 1976, 25.
[54] He referred to it as "a phrase that is simply loaded with dynamite," and argued: "In the end it is bound to be discredited, to be called the dream of an idealist who failed to realize the danger until too late to check those who attempt to put the principle in force. What a calamity that the phrase was ever uttered! What misery it will cause!" Lansing, December 1918, as quoted in Cassese, 1995, 25, n. 32.
[55] Lansing, 1921 quoted in Pomerance, 1976, 10.
[56] See Cassesse, 1995, 26; and Pomerance, 1982. For example, the Treaty of Versailles transferred territories to Poland and Czechoslovakia, the treaty of peace with Austria allocated South Tirol to Italy, and banned Austria from joining Germany, all without a democratic process.
[57] This view was confirmed by the League of Nations committees on the Åland Islands question. Hannum, 1990, 29.
[58] He made this statement in the House of Commons, Session 1940–1941. Quoted in Stettinius, 1949, 244.
[59] Chapter 1, Article 1.2.

did not impose any legal obligations on member states, nor did it imply a right to secession for minorities, independence for colonial countries, or the right to choose leaders through democratic procedures.[60]

The weak formulation of the self-determination concept in the Charter came despite efforts by the Soviet Union to include a fully-fledged right to independence for colonial peoples. The USSR continued its attempts to include such a provision in UN Covenants, but initially failed to assemble broad support. Only three countries outside the Soviet bloc – Yugoslavia, Colombia, and Pakistan – supported a Soviet amendment to the 1948 Universal Declaration of Human Rights (UDHR) that proposed an explicit provision to apply the self-determination principle to colonial peoples.[61] In 1950, the Third Committee rejected a Soviet proposal to the same effect.[62] In 1952, Egypt successfully amended a narrowly phrased proposal by the Soviet Union, and the UNGA adopted an article to be included in international covenants of human rights that used the general phrasing: "all peoples have the right to self-determination."[63] Yet, support was far from universal: the amendment passed with 36 affirmative votes, 11 no votes, and 12 abstentions. The divisions were squarely along Cold War lines. Brazil, for instance, voted against it, and Argentina, Colombia, Costa Rica, Honduras, Uruguay, and Venezuela abstained. All Western countries, except for Greece, voted against the provision, stating that evidence of viable empirical statehood should precede legal independence.

The 1960 Declaration

By the early 1950s, the debate on issues of self-determination had not reached down to fundamental methods and practices but rather clung to "noble utterances on behalf of high-sounding principles which would not be translated into responsible action by any of the states whose delegates make the speeches."[64] During the 1950s, however, an increasing number of colonies gained independence and became members of the United Nations after the end of the Cold War membership deadlock. Total UN membership grew from sixty in 1950 to ninety-nine in 1960. In 1960 alone, seventeen new nations joined. By this time, one-third of the voting members of the UNGA had achieved independence after 1945. The newly established voting power of former colonies, combined with the growing perceived illegitimacy of colonialism in many Western societies, created a window of opportunity to bring the issue of colonialism to

---

[60] See Cassese, 1995, 37–43; and Pomerance, 1982, 9–10.
[61] United Nations General Assembly Official Records 3/930 (A/784), December 10, 1948 (8;34;14).
[62] United Nations Document A/1559, December 4, 1950, 28.
[63] United Nations General Assembly Official Records 6/519, February 5, 1952 (36; 11; 12).
[64] Eagleton, 1953, 88–89.

the forefront in the UNGA. An important additional motivation for the super-powers was that the allegiance of many new nations in the Cold War conflict was still up for grabs.

Nikita Khrushchev seized this opportunity on September 23, 1960, by requesting to add a *Declaration on the Granting of Independence to Colonial Countries and Peoples* on the agenda of the 15th session.[65] Khrushchev person-ally attended much of the session, a highly unusual move. In a tactical maneu-ver, the USSR succeeded in allocating the issue directly to the plenary session, which guaranteed a much larger exposure than the slow and much less visible First Committee.[66] The Soviet draft was not written in the neutral and universal language of the General Assembly and contained unadorned insults to the colonial powers and their motivations, as exemplified by the following excerpt:

> For what purposes do those who refuse to renounce colonial rule wage murderous war against peoples? Why are the freedom-loving aspirations of the enslaved peoples suppressed? Sometimes it is said that this is done in the interest of the "civilization" of the less developed countries to prepare them for self-government. But this is a lie given the guise of truth . . . The main object of the colonial regime is in fact to secure enormous profits for big foreign monopolies, which have seized the key economic positions in the colonies and to extort their wealth by every possible means. Therefore, the entire economy of a colony is one of exploitation.[67]

This language was clearly strategically aimed at swaying new member states towards allegiance with the Soviet bloc. Yet, many of the new states who had assembled in the Afro-Asian caucus feared that the intemperate language of the draft would result in a Cold War vote in which the Western and Latin American countries would vote in opposition to the Soviet draft. The Afro-Asian group therefore decided to form a working group with the thorny task of formulating an alternative draft proposal that would accommodate both the diversity of opinion within their own group and have a broader appeal than the Soviet draft. The committee in charge of drafting the new resolution consisted primarily of experienced UN members.[68] In comparison to the original draft, the new Afro-Asian draft made no mention of specific deadlines for ending colonialism, did not demand the dismantling of foreign bases, and did not include any

---

[65] United Nations Document A/4501, September 23, 1960.

[66] The procedural issue was adopted by common consent on October 13, 1960. It was generally assumed that Western countries would have voted against the proposal had the vote been taken as scheduled on October 12. However, this meeting had to be adjourned prematurely when the Irish Assembly President was so angered by a denigrating comment from the Romanian delegate about Irish independence that he slammed his gavel down so hard that it broke (Kay, 1970, 153, n. 21).

[67] United Nations Document A/4502, September 23, 1960, 5–6.

[68] The committee consisted of Guinea, India, Iran, Indonesia, Nigeria, and Senegal.

allegations against specific countries. These concessions were not equally appreciated by all, but were necessary for broad acceptance. As the Iranian delegate put it:

> [M]any of the co-sponsors of this draft declaration who have suffered greatly from the ravages of colonialism would have preferred a more expressive text, including clauses condemning colonialism in its most culpable aspects. However, in order to rally all currents of opinion in the Assembly in favor of a text acceptable to all the Members of the United Nations, they have, in a spirit of conciliation, accepted phrases of a much more moderate nature.[69]

The *Declaration* was strategically rewritten in general liberal language that implied a broad concern with individual human rights, as suggested by its opening paragraph:

> Mindful of the determination proclaimed by the peoples of the world in the Charter of the United Nations to reaffirm faith in fundamental human rights, in the dignity and worth of the human person, in the equal rights of men and women and of nations large and small and to promote social progress and better standards of life in larger freedom, . . .[70]

The operative articles of the *Declaration*, however, focus on the rights of an undefined "peoples." Best known is Article 2: "2. All peoples have the right to self-determination; by virtue of that right they freely determine their political status and freely pursue their economic, social and cultural development."

Article 7, the last article of the *Declaration*, stresses that none of this grants anyone the right to interfere with the internal affairs of states: "7. All States shall observe faithfully and strictly the provisions of the Charter of the United Nations, the Universal Declaration of Human Rights and the present Declaration on the basis of equality, *non-interference in the internal affairs of all States*, and respect for the sovereign rights of all peoples and their territorial integrity."[71]

On December 14, 1960 the *Declaration* passed with 89 votes in favor, no votes against, and 9 abstentions, including those from the United States, the United Kingdom, and France.[72] The US vote was long uncertain but President Eisenhower decided to abstain, apparently after a personal appeal from British Prime Minister Macmillan.[73] The official reason given by both the British and the Americans was that the *Declaration* failed to mention the constructive

---

[69] United Nations General Assembly Official Records, 15th Session, 926th Meeting, November 28, 1960, para. 75.
[70] United Nations Document A/RES/1514 (XV), December 14, 1960.
[71] *Ibid.* Emphasis added.
[72] *Ibid.* Those abstaining were: Australia, Belgium, Dominican Republic, France, Portugal, Spain, Union of South Africa, United Kingdom, and United States.
[73] Kay, 1970, 169.

aspects of colonialism. Members of the US delegation allegedly stood up to applaud the passage of the resolution.[74]

On the same day, votes were taken on the original Soviet draft in two parts[75] and on two Soviet amendments to the Afro-Asian drafts.[76] All the Soviet proposals failed to get majority support. The final 1960 *Declaration* was not the result of coercive efforts by powerful states. Nor can it be seen as the direct outcome of a moral campaign held by entrepreneurs from developing or developed nations for a norm that cascaded into broad acceptance by international society. Rather, it can only be understood as a strategic attempt by African and Asian countries to formulate the right to self-determination in a way that defined the right in a way that appealed to both camps in the Cold War conflict: the liberal language made it hard to reject for the Western countries and the inclusion of a right to independence anchored its appeal to the Soviet bloc.

Institutionalization

The main obstacles for the "right of all peoples to self-determination" to become an effective constitutive rule were the development of rules of exclusion and the allocation of competency to an institution to determine whether or not the right applies. The adoption of Resolution 1541, the day after the acceptance of the *Declaration*, addressed the first issue.[77] This resolution introduced practical rules that effectively limited the application of the right to self-determination to units that are both "geographically separate" *and* "ethnically and/or culturally distinct" from the country administrating them. This particular definition of a non-self-governing territory is a very specific interpretation of the Charter's original definition: "territories whose peoples have not yet attained a full measure of self-government." The new interpretation, which became known as the theory of "salt-water colonialism," again reflected a compromise position within the developing world, where states were concerned that the self-determination regime would confer rights to ethnic minorities

---

[74] *Ibid.*

[75] The first vote was on the first three paragraphs of the draft that called for the immediate granting of independence to all colonial possessions and the elimination of foreign bases in the territory of other states. The motion was rejected by a narrow margin of 32 to 35, with 30 abstentions. The vote on the remainder of the Soviet draft, which included a vehement denunciation of the colonial powers themselves, was voted down with a slightly larger margin: 25 to 43, with 29 abstentions. All votes were taken on December 14, 1960 during the 15th Session, 947th Meeting of the UNGA.

[76] The first Soviet amendment proposed a 1961 target date for the end of colonialism and was rejected by a vote of 29 to 47, with 22 abstentions. A second amendment to place the question of implementation on the agenda of the Session failed to get the required two-thirds majority (41; 35; 22).

[77] United Nations Document A/RES/1541 (XV), December 15, 1960.

within their borders. It upheld the principle of absolute sovereignty within inherited frontiers, a principle also embodied in the 1963 Charter of the Organization of African Unity.[78] Both the communist bloc as well as most Western nations abstained from voting on the roll call.[79]

The second issue, assigning competency to an institution, was addressed during the 16th Session by the installation of a Special Committee with the task to "make suggestions and recommendations on the progress and extent of the implementation of the Declaration." Only France, the United Kingdom, South Africa, and Spain abstained from the vote to install this Committee.[80] The new US Government, led by President John F. Kennedy, supported the resolution and voiced willingness to actively participate in implementing the 1960 *Declaration.*[81] The Committee was drawn up according to the so-called "troika" formula (another feature of UNGA practice), meaning that it had members from the West, the Soviet bloc, and the non-aligned states. Nevertheless, its make-up guaranteed a solid anti-colonial majority. From 1962 to 1966 the Committee covered no less than sixty non-self-governing territories.[82] Moreover, it introduced a large number of anti-colonial resolutions to the plenary session.

The developing countries succeeded fairly well in consistently applying the rules of exclusion for purposes of agenda control. There were no resolutions on self-determination in Biafra, Kurdistan, Kashmir, or Latvia, but a very large number of resolutions on often tiny islands or groups of islands that obviously satisfied the salt-water criterion. Potential solutions for self-determination claims were also limited, with a strong predisposition towards independence. That non-self-governing territories wished to opt for independence was often taken for granted, even if the prospects for empirical statehood were small.[83]

The inviolability of colonial frontiers was also upheld. There are only two examples where concerns for ethnic divisions overcame the protection of absolute sovereignty within inherited colonial frontiers. First, in separate UN-supervised plebiscites the people of the Southern Cameroons, under British administration, opted for integration into Cameroon, a former French colony, whereas those of the Northern Cameroons voted for a union with Nigeria.[84] Along with the West, twelve African countries did not vote in favor of the implementation of the results of this referendum, partly because Cameroon had

---

[78] Jackson, 1990, 153.
[79] Only 2 nations voted against: Portugal and the Union of South Africa, 21 nations abstained.
[80] Portugal did not participate in the vote. United Nations General Assembly Official Records, 16th Session, 1066th Meeting, November 27, 1961, para. 149.
[81] Kay, 1970, 174–177.   [82] *Ibid.*, 795.   [83] See Cassese, 1995, 74; and Pomerance, 1982.
[84] The initial mandate for the referenda was given on March 13, 1959 (A/4095). The results were approved and implemented on April 21, 1961 (A/4737).

claims to the Northern Cameroons.[85] Second, in 1962 the UNGA allowed Rwanda and Burundi to form separate states, even though they had been one formal colony.[86] In both cases, claims of specific ethnic and linguistic groups within former colonies were honored. Such claims became increasingly less likely to be recognized. For example, the island of Fernando Poo was integrated into Equatorial Guinea, despite the fact that it had a distinct ethnic group, the Bubi, that it had rejected the option in a 1968 plebiscite, and that it had only become part of the formal colony of Equatorial Guinea in 1963.[87] A similar case is the Comorian Island of Mayotte, whose population, in separate referenda and with large majorities, expressed its wish to remain associated with France. The General Assembly condemned the separate referenda conducted by France as violations of the national unity and territorial integrity of the Comoros.[88]

The right to self-determination thus increasingly became a right for sovereigns as opposed to a human right. The most obvious exception to this rule were the numerous resolutions in which the Assembly condemned the apartheid regime as a crime against humanity and a denial of the essential right to self-determination of the people of South Africa.[89]

Countries from both blocs continued to use the self-determination issue for strategic purposes in the Cold War conflict. The West argued that the right to self-determination should also apply to the Baltic States and the Soviet satellite states in Eastern Europe. The USSR continued to attempt to link the issue with the socialist cause. For example in 1962, the USSR introduced an amendment stating that "peoples and nations have the inalienable right to the unobstructed execution of nationalization, expropriation and other essential measures aimed at protecting and strengthening the sovereignty over their national wealth and resources."[90] Similarly, in 1965 Western countries introduced a resolution demanding the cessation of the violation of human rights and the right to self-determination for the people of Tibet.[91] This proved to be one of the more divisive applications of self-determination. The final resolution was adopted with a vote of 43 to 35, with 23 abstentions. The Western and Latin American countries voted in favor of the right of self-determination, and the developing

---

[85] The final vote on the acceptance of the results was: 63;23;11.Togo voted against, Burkina Faso (Upper Volta), Central African Republic, Chad, Congo Brazzaville, Congo Leopoldville, Gabon, Ivory Coast, Madagascar, Niger, and Senegal abstained.

[86] United Nations Document A/RES/1746 (XVI).

[87] Pomerance, 1982, 30. See also United Nations Document A/RES/2230 (XXI), December 20, 1966.

[88] Pomerance, 1982, 31. There have been various General Assembly resolutions. See especially United Nations Document A/RES/31/4, October 21, 1976.

[89] Some resolutions concerning Rhodesia and Namibia also fit this pattern, although they were often directed against the United Kingdom.

[90] United Nations General Assembly Official Records 1131 (XVII), December 14, 1962 (34; 48; 21).

[91] United Nations Document A/RES/2079 (XX), December 18, 1965.

nations abstained or voted against. Clearly, this was a Cold War vote that had more to do with the question of Chinese membership of the United Nations than with an actual attempt to assure self-determination for the people of Tibet. Many African and Asian states expressed their displeasure with these tactics. As the Nigerian delegate put it: "the Africans and Asians who have worn the shoe of colonialism, know best how and when it pinches."[92] Increasingly, both the West and the East left the initiative on the drafting of resolutions considering self-determination to developing nations. The 1960 *Declaration*, as the first major, successful compromise between developing nations, served as the guideline for future resolutions and covenants. For example, the formulation of the *Declaration* was adopted in the 1966 International Covenant on Civil and Political Rights (ICCPR) and in another landmark UNGA resolution: the 1970 *Declaration on Principles of International Law concerning Friendly Relations and Cooperation among States.*[93] Most resolutions that reaffirmed the 1960 *Declaration*, or that more generally referred to the right to self-determination as an inalienable right of peoples without referring to specific applications, were adopted with unanimity or near-unanimity, certainly after 1970. Yet, applications to non-obvious colonial cases continued to be controversial. Perhaps the best example is the Western Sahara.

Self-determination in the Western Sahara

The Western Sahara, previously known as the Spanish Sahara, represents one of the most politically complex cases of self-determination. Both Morocco and Mauritania put forth claims to part of the Spanish colony in which huge phosphate deposits had been discovered. Moreover, an Algerian-supported guerrilla insurgency by the region's indigenous inhabitants, the nomadic Sahrawis, sprang up in the early 1970s. Regardless of its political complexity, the case was relatively straightforward from the standpoint of appropriateness. As affirmed by a series of UNGA resolutions dating back to 1966, the people of the Western Sahara had the right to self-determination, which was to be exercised through the holding of a referendum.[94] The International Court of Justice (ICJ) ruled in 1975 that Morocco and Mauritania had no valid claim on the Spanish Sahara based on historic title and, even if they did, that contemporary international law accorded priority to the Sahrawis' right to self-determination.[95] This interpretation reaffirms practice since 1960.

---

[92] United Nations General Assembly Official Records, 16th Session, 1066th Meeting, November 27, 1961.

[93] United Nations Document A/RES/2625 (XXV), October 14, 1970.

[94] United Nations Document A/RES/2229 (XXI), December 20, 1966 (105;2;8). Only Spain and Portugal voted against; Morocco and Mauritania voted in favor of this resolution.

[95] See Franck, 1976, 711; and McWhinney, 1984, 29.

The day after the publication of the ICJ's advisory opinion, the Moroccan Government nevertheless announced a massive march from Morocco into the Spanish Sahara. The UN Security Council failed in ordering Morocco's king to call off the march, essentially because of opposition from France and the United States.[96] Faced with the Moroccan march in times of domestic uncertainty due to Franco's terminal illness, Spain decided to engage in tripartite negotiations in Madrid with Morocco and Mauritania and eventually sold the Sahara to these states.[97] Spain obtained a 35 percent interest in the Sahara's phosphate industry and gained additional fishing rights off the Saharan and Moroccan coasts. In exchange, the Western Sahara was divided along previously agreed lines between Morocco and Mauritania.

This action changed the politics of the situation. No longer was it a clear colonial case. On December 10, 1975 the UNGA adopted two contradictory resolutions. The first, Resolution 3458A, reaffirmed the Sahrawis' right to self-determination and called upon Spain to arrange a free and genuine act of self-determination under UN supervision. This resolution was adopted by a vote of 88 to 0, with 41 abstentions. The second, Resolution 3458B, basically recognized the tripartite agreement. It was, according to the Moroccan representative, "the only text among us which fully takes into consideration the realities and the specifics of the question of Spanish Sahara." The vote on this resolution was extremely close: 56 to 42, with 34 abstentions. On the latter resolution, nations were faced with a classic conflict between principles and politics. The appropriate rule, as defined by numerous UNGA resolutions and the ICJ ruling, was confirmed by the unanimous finding of a 1975 UN Visiting Mission that called for a UN-administered plebiscite on the question of independence. This unanimity was all the more remarkable because both the Iranian member and the Ivory Coast chairmen were under considerable pressure to report conclusions more favorable to the Moroccan cause.[98]

How, then, did nations line up on the final vote? It would be mistaken to suggest that all Black African states were more willing to tolerate domination by fellow Africans than by white Europeans.[99] Only 9 non-Islamic African states voted in favor of the resolution, 16 voted against, and 5 abstained. Moreover, the annexation of the Western Sahara by Morocco and Mauritania was condemned by fellow African states as a violation of the right to self-determination. As the representative of Benin put it: "The right to self-determination has been weakened, watered down, treated with contempt and made inoperable by the

---

[96] Franck, 1976, 714.
[97] Morocco's march began on November 5, 1975. King Hassan requested the marchers to return to their starting point on November 9. Negotiations began in Madrid on November 11 and agreement was reached on November 14. Franco died on November 20, but before his death he was already no longer capable of ruling due to illness, which created a power vacuum.
[98] Franck, 1976, 709.   [99] See Neuberger, 1986 for this general argument.

developments referred to in the draft resolution."[100] Moreover, POLISARIO, the Sahrawi guerilla movement, declared a government in exile, the Saharan Arab Democratic Republic, which was recognized as a full member of the Organization of African Unity (OAU) in 1984, prompting Morocco to withdraw from the organization.[101] Many African states thus behaved indeed according to the standard for appropriate behavior.

There seem to be two main reasons why states voted in favor of the resolution. The first, and by far the most important, is alliance politics. The United States clearly falls into this category. Spain and Morocco were seen as being of vital strategic importance. Moreover, Morocco's government was generally perceived as pro-American, whereas Algeria's socialist government of President Boumedienne was not. The perceived strategic importance of Morocco is exemplified by the sale of a squadron of jet fighters to the country in February 1976; just three months after Morocco invaded the Western Sahara.[102] Similar considerations were important for France, the United Kingdom, Germany, and the other European countries, which were especially concerned with appeasing Spain in the face of its domestic uncertainty. Alliance with Spain played a role in the decision of a number of, mostly dictatorial, Latin American countries such as Chile, Bolivia, Paraguay, and Uruguay to vote in favor of the resolution. Moreover, almost all Arab countries were aligned with Morocco in this period, and let alliance considerations take precedence over legal standards of appropriateness. Many of these states also left the OAU with Morocco in 1984, thus dealing the organization a severe blow.

Secondly, a number of countries that had territorial claims based on historic title voted in favor of the resolution. These countries hoped that the resolution would set a precedent, or at least provide ammunition for their own claims. Thomas M. Franck expressed these concerns: "The 'settlement' of the Saharan issue in favor of Morocco's claim of historic title and the denial of self-determination to the Sahrawi people radically departs from the norms of decolonization established and consistently applied by the United Nations since 1960. This is bound to have an important significance for numerous other irredentist territorial claims."[103]

So, Guatemala hoped that the resolution would set a precedent for its claims on Belize, Cameroon with respect to parts of Nigeria, Indonesia with respect to East Timor, and Argentina with respect to the Falkland Islands. However, the particular way in which the UNGA dealt with the Western Sahara, and later with East Timor, does not reflect a change of the rules. It merely exemplified the limited applicability of existing rules. The original coalition that established the rules of the game was based on a limited objective: to end Western colonialism. Issues that fall outside of this scope are bound to be decided by the formation of different coalitions.

---

[100] United Nations General Assembly Official Records 2435 (XXX), December 10, 1975, p. 124.
[101] Fowler and Bunck, 1995, 59.   [102] Franck, 1976, 696.   [103] *Ibid.*, 694.

Conclusion

This chapter has accepted the challenge of foregrounding international practices within a strategic choice framework. Strategic approaches analyze how actors with well-defined preferences seek to achieve their goals through purposive actions whose effectiveness is conditional on the actions of others. One of the main problems that plagues studies of strategic choice is that in virtually any interesting strategic dilemma there are multiple equilibria, often with hugely differing implications. For example, in studies of interethnic cooperation there are almost always equilibria in which ethnic groups cooperate and in which all-out violence occurs.[104] It matters greatly which equilibrium prevails. So it is in studies of collective choice, which have long been dominated by theorems about cycling and instability. Game theory provides some guidance in thinking about problems of equilibrium selection, but in the end it is insufficient.

It is not new to suggest that cultural analysis may help in this regard. Yet, most of this has focused on cultural values rather than practices. Chapter 1 in this volume defines practices as patterned actions that are embedded in particular organized contexts and are developed through learning and training. Understanding practices as a way of focusing or structuring complex collective bargaining processes may thus be especially important when bargaining takes place in institutional contexts where past practice exists and can thus shape expectations about how future issues are resolved. The UNGA is an ideal case for this.

Substantively, one of the most important points is that the practice of political manipulation in the UNGA has a distinct logic from political manipulation in other areas of world politics. It reflects a community of practice that is distinct but influenced by other communities of practice. This implies that strategies and strategists that are successful outside the UN arena may not work inside it. Successful UN resolutions reflect universal and liberal aspirations, not because all states that sign off on those resolutions share these aspirations but because resolutions that do not reflect them are unlikely to have any impact in world politics. The self-determination case suggests, however, that such resolutions may well have a more limited purpose and thus real effects. Indeed, there was a coalition that defended these more limited purposes vigorously even while they were inconsistent about the application of the universal principles embedded in the resolution. This is a warning against textual interpretations of UNGA resolutions (common among legal scholars), but it also points to ways in which to analyze how hypocrisy in the application of norms is organized.

A second substantive point is that the transformative potential of the practice of political manipulation depends on the existence of gaps in the heresthetic abilities of actors. Transformation can also occur when new actors learn how an

---

[104] See, for example, Fearon and Laitin, 1996.

institution works and use their new-found skills to (partially) rectify past distributive injustices. The TRIPS example and the self-determination case both give examples of this. Learning is certainly not the only potential cause of gaps in heresthetical abilities. Yet it remains difficult to theorize more systematically about why some actors are simply more skilled in political manipulation than others.

The practice turn requires, almost by definition, attention to micro-level evidence and thick description. It is not always well suited for making *ex ante* predictions or even counterfactual analysis as there are too many moving parts. I cannot with any reasonable plausibility claim to show that the allocation of statehood would have evolved differently if alternative practices had prevailed at the UNGA or if a different institutional venue had been chosen for this purpose. This is a serious limitation of the practice approach that should not be underestimated. Yet, in analytic descriptions of past events (sometimes called "analytic narratives"), there is a natural way in which an international practices approach informs rational choice analyses of collective decision-making. Strategic choice models are centrally concerned with the beliefs actors have about what others are likely to do and what actions are available to them. Better information about such beliefs puts actors at a strategic advantage. In institutionalized contexts, these beliefs are likely shaped by practices, which in turn could help determine who prevails.

References

Alger, Chadwick F., 1963. United Nations Participation as a Learning Experience. *Public Opinion Quarterly* 27 (3): 411–426.

Arrow, Kenneth, 1963. *Social Choice and Individual Values*. 2nd edn. New Haven: Yale University Press.

Asher, Herbert B., 1973. The Learning of Legislative Norms. *American Political Science Review* 68 (2): 499–513.

Barnett, Michael, 2003. Bureaucratizing the Duty to Aid: The United Nations and Rwandan Genocide. In *Just Intervention*, edited by Anthony F. Lang, Jr., 174–191. Washington: Georgetown University Press.

Bleichman, Arnold, 1968. *The "Other" State Department: The United States Mission to the United Nations – Its Role in the Making of Foreign Policy*. New York: Basic Books.

Bourdieu, Pierre, 1987. The Force of Law: Toward a Sociology of the Juridical Field. *Hastings Law Journal* 38 (5): 814–853.

Brinkley, Douglas and Clifford Hackett, eds., 1991. *Jean Monnet: The Path to European Unity*. Basingstoke: Macmillan.

Brownlie, Ian, 1988. The Rights of Peoples in Modern International Law. In *The Rights of Peoples*, edited by James Crawford, 1–16. Oxford: Clarendon Press.

Byman, Daniel L. and Kenneth M. Pollack, 2001. Let Us Now Praise Great Men: Bringing the Statesman Back In. *International Security* 25 (4): 107–146.

Carpenter, R. Charli, 2007. Setting the Advocacy Agenda: Theorizing Issue Emergence and Nonemergence in Transnational Advocacy Networks. *International Studies Quarterly* 51 (1): 99–120.

Carr, E. H., 1951. *The Bolshevik Revolution, 1917–1923.* New York: Macmillan.

Cassese, Antonio, 1995. *Self-Determination of Peoples: A Legal Reappraisal.* Cambridge: Cambridge University Press.

Crawford, James, 1979. *The Creation of States in International Law.* Oxford: Clarendon Press.

Crawford, Neta C., 2002. *Argument and Change in World Politics: Ethics, Decolonization, and Humanitarian Intervention.* Cambridge: Cambridge University Press.

Davis, Christina L., 2004. International Institutions and Issue Linkage: Building Support for Agricultural Trade Liberalization. *American Political Science Review* 98 (1): 153–169.

Eagleton, Clyde, 1953. Self-Determination in the United Nations. *American Journal of International Law* 47 (1): 88–93.

Farer, Tom J., 1968. Problems of an International Law of Intervention. *Stanford Journal of International Studies* 3: 20–26.

Fasulo, Linda, 2004. *An Insider's Guide to the UN.* 1st edn. New Haven: Yale University Press.

Fearon, James D. and David D. Laitin, 1996. Explaining Interethnic Cooperation. *American Political Science Review* 90 (4): 715–735.

Fowler, Michael Ross and Julie Marie Bunck, 1995. *Law, Power, and the Sovereign State: The Evolution and Application of the Concept of Sovereignty.* University Park: Pennsylvania State University Press.

Franck, Thomas M., 1976. The Stealing of the Sahara. *American Journal of International Law* 70 (4): 694–721.

  1988. Legitimacy in the International System. *American Journal of International Law* 82 (4): 705–759.

Frey, Bruno S., 1984. The Public Choice View of International Political Economy. *International Organization* 38 (1): 199–223.

Garrett, Geoffrey, 1992. International Cooperation and Institutional Choice: The European Community's Internal Market. *International Organization* 46 (2): 533–560.

Greif, Avner, 1994. Cultural Beliefs and the Organization of Society: A Historical and Theoretical Reflection on Collectivist and Individualist Societies. *Journal of Political Economy* 102 (5): 912–950.

Gros Espiell, Héctor, 1977. Implementation of United Nations Resolutions Relating to the Right of Peoples under Colonial and Alien Domination to Self-Determination. United Nations Document E/CN.4/Sub.2/390, June 22, 1977.

Haas, Ernst B., 1980. Why Collaborate? Issue-Linkage and International Regimes. *World Politics* 32 (3): 357–405.

Hannum, Hurst, 1990. *Autonomy, Sovereignty, and Self-Determination: The Accommodation of Conflicting Rights.* Philadelphia: University of Pennsylvania Press.

Hechter, Michael and Elizabeth Borland, 2001. National Self-Determination: The Emergence of an International Norm. In *Social Norms*, edited by Michael Hechter and Karl-Dieter Opp, 186–233. New York: Russell Sage.

Helmke, Gretchen and Steven Levitsky, 2004. Informal Institutions and Comparative Politics: A Research Agenda. *Perspectives on Politics* 2 (4): 725–740.

Henkin, Louis, 1965. The United Nations and Human Rights. *International Organization* 19 (3): 504–517.

Higgins, Rosalyn, 1963. *The Development of International Law through the Political Organs of the United Nations.* London: Oxford University Press.

1994. *Problems and Process: International Law and How We Use It.* Oxford: Clarendon Press.

Hoffmann, Stanley, 1998. *World Disorders: Troubled Peace in the Post-Cold War Era.* Lanham: Rowman & Littlefield.

Hurd, Ian, 2005. The Strategic Use of Liberal Internationalism: Libya and the UN Sanctions, 1992–2003. *International Organization* 59 (3): 495–526.

Jackson, Robert H., 1990. *Quasi-States: Sovereignty, International Relations, and the Third World.* Cambridge: Cambridge University Press.

1993. The Weight of Ideas in Decolonization: Normative Change in International Relations. In *Ideas and Foreign Policy: Beliefs, Institutions, and Political Change*, edited by Judith Goldstein and Robert O. Keohane, 111–138. Ithaca: Cornell University Press.

Kay, David A., 1970. *The New Nations in the United Nations, 1960–1967.* New York: Columbia University Press.

Kennedy, Paul, 2006. *The Parliament of Man: The Past, Present, and Future of the United Nations.* New York: Random House.

Keohane, Robert O., 1969. Institutionalization in the United Nations General Assembly. *International Organization* 23 (4): 859–896.

Krasner, Stephen D., 1999. *Sovereignty: Organized Hypocrisy.* Princeton: Princeton University Press.

Lenin, Vladimir I., 1969 [1916]. Theses on the Socialist Revolution and the Right of Nations to Self-Determination. In *Selected Works.* London: Lawrence & Wishart.

McKelvey, Richard D., 1976. Intransitivities in Multidimensional Voting Models: Some Implications for Agenda Control. *Journal of Economic Theory* 12 (3): 472–482.

1979. General Conditions for Global Intransitivities in Formal Voting Models. *Econometrica* 47 (5): 1085–1112.

1983. Constructing Majority Paths Between Arbitrary Points: General Methods of Solution for Quasiconcave Preferences. *Mathematics of Operations Research* 8 (4): 549–556.

McWhinney, Edward, 1984. *United Nations Law Making: Cultural and Ideological Relativism and International Law Making for an Era of Transition.* Paris: UNESCO.

Morrow, James D., 1988. Social Choice and System Structure in World Politics. *World Politics* 41 (1): 75–97.

Neuberger, Ralph B., 1986. *National Self-Determination in Postcolonial Africa.* Boulder: Lynne Rienner.

Philpott, Daniel, 2001. *Revolutions in Sovereignty: How Ideas Shaped Modern International Relations.* Princeton: Princeton University Press.

Pollack, Mark A., 1997. Delegation, Agency, and Agenda Setting in the European Community. *International Organization* 51 (1): 99–134.

Pomerance, Michla, 1976. The United States and Self-Determination: Perspectives on the Wilsonian Conception. *American Journal of International Law* 70 (1): 1–27.

1982. *Self-Determination in Law and Practice: The New Doctrine in the United Nations.* The Hague: Martinus Nijhoff.

Reus-Smit, Christian, 1997. The Constitutional Structure of International Society and the Nature of Fundamental Institutions. *International Organization* 51 (4): 555–589.

Riker, William H., 1980. Implications from the Disequilibrium of Majority Rule for the Study of Institutions. *American Political Science Review* 774 (2): 432–446.

1986. *The Art of Political Manipulation.* New Haven: Yale University Press.

Sell, Susan K. and Aseem Prakash, 2004. Using Ideas Strategically: The Contest Between Business and NGO Networks in Intellectual Property Rights. *International Studies Quarterly* 48 (1): 143–175.

Shepsle, Kenneth A., 1979. Institutional Arrangements and Equilibrium in Multidimensional Voting Models. *American Journal of Political Science* 23 (1): 27–59.

Shepsle, Kenneth A. and Barry R. Weingast, 1981. Structure-Induced Equilibrium and Legislative Choice. *Public Choice* 37 (3): 503–519.

Smith, Courtney B., 2006. *Politics and Process at the United Nations: The Global Dance.* Boulder: Lynne Rienner.

Stettinius, Edward R., Jr., 1949. *Roosevelt and the Russians: The Yalta Conference.* Garden City: Doubleday.

Tollison, Robert D. and Thomas D. Willett, 1979. An Economic Theory of Mutually Advantageous Issue Linkages in International Negotiations. *International Organization* 33 (4): 425–449.

Voeten, Erik, 2000. Clashes in the Assembly. *International Organization* 54 (2): 185–215.

2001. Outside Options and the Logic of Security Council Action. *American Political Science Review* 95 (4): 845–858.

Wilson, Woodrow, 1927. *War and Peace: Presidential Messages, Addresses, and Public Papers (1917–1924),* edited by Ray Stannard Baker and William E. Dodd. New York: Harper.

Young, Oran R., 1978. Anarchy and Social Choice: Reflections on the International Polity. *World Politics* 30 (2): 241–263.

Zacher, Mark W., 2001. The Territorial Integrity Norm: International Boundaries and the Use of Force. *International Organization* 55 (2): 215–250.

11 Performing practices: a poststructuralist analysis of the Muhammad cartoon crisis

LENE HANSEN

This chapter takes the practice framework laid out in Chapter 1 as the starting point for a more in-depth discussion of what a poststructuralist-practice approach might entail and what it could accomplish. In doing so, it suggests a reading of practice through Michel Foucault who is frequently alluded to in works on practice,[1] but who has not yet been systematically explored. Drawing on Foucault as well as poststructuralism more broadly, I start from the view laid out in Chapter 1 that practices are repeated in a manner that makes them "reminiscent of routine."[2] Yet, while the view of international practices as routine performances surely casts important light on phenomena and dynamics that have often been overlooked – or not properly understood – by the discipline of International Relations (IR), I suggest that practices might also not be routine, more precisely that there are instances when specific practices are sought to be performed as if they are routine, when in fact they take place on a terrain that is much more contested and unstable. Our understanding of "routine," a key concept in practice theory as evidenced by Chapter 1, would in short benefit from a poststructuralist emphasis on the inherent instability of discursive practices.

As Chapter 1 also makes clear, poststructuralism and Pierre Bourdieu-inspired approaches have a lot in common: they were the first to introduce the concept of practice to IR and both have pointed to the significance of everyday practices and the need for understanding them as linguistic as well as material. Yet, there are also ways in which the two approaches differ, one of which is how the role of inarticulate, routine background knowledge should be theorized. The Bourdieu-inspired theory developed by Vincent Pouliot, for instance, defines practices as "the result of inarticulate, practical knowledge that makes what is to be done appear 'self-evident' or commonsensical,"[3] while the poststructuralist approach I lay out in this chapter takes practices to be ambiguously situated between the

---

[1] See Adler and Pouliot, Chapter 1 in this volume; Pouliot, 2008, 265; Schatzki, 2001, 1; Swidler, 2001, 84; and Neumann, 2002.
[2] Adler and Pouliot, Chapter 1 in this volume.   [3] Pouliot, 2008, 258.

sedimented and self-evident, on the one hand, and the contested and unstable, on the other.[4] Specifically, I suggest that as "practitioners practice," they perform *specific* practices that are asserted as though they belong to a *general* – perhaps "self-evident" – practice. Even uncontested specific "routine" practices are crucial to the reproduction of general practices, and we should therefore keep the relationship between specific and general practices open and examine the (potential) gap between them. Methodologically, this allows us to build a research design around prominent specific practices, asking which general practices they mobilize and whether a specific practice's claim to a general category of practices is stable or not. Finally, drawing on Foucault, I emphasize how discursive practices constitute a domain with a particular politico-epistemic quality – as, for example, legalistic, political, artistic, religious, ideological, or ethical.

My suggestion to incorporate practices not simply as routines and background knowledge, but as (strategic or unconscious) performances of "routines," might set this chapter apart from the understanding of practice advocated not only by Pouliot, but by *The Practice Turn in Contemporary Theory*, the landmark study to foreground practice in the social sciences. Although the introduction to that volume stated that "there is no unified practice approach,"[5] most authors adopted an understanding of practice as institutionalized, learned, non-articulated knowledge. Barry Barnes defined practices as "socially recognized forms of activity, done on the basis of what members learn from others, and capable of being done well or badly, correctly or incorrectly;"[6] Ann Swidler, following Sewell, as "enacted schemas, schemas which can be transposed from one situation or domain to another and which are expressed in, and can be read from, practices themselves."[7] Even the discussion about whether practices are skills or habits revolves around a shared understanding of practices as deeply embedded. As valuable as this understanding is, when transposed into IR there is a risk that it prevents us from studying foreign policy crisis. In contrast to the often-used examples of practices as riding in formation or cooking, during a crisis the "commonsensical" proves insufficient to counter the challenges in question. This, of course, does not imply that everything is in flux or that known practices are not invoked, but rather that "the end of routine" is introduced. This process is different from the death or birth of a practice in that it points to instability within the practice itself. Picking a more specific question from the larger framework presented in Chapter 1, I seek therefore to develop a poststructuralist-practice perspective that highlights the tension between stability and rupture within practice itself. While I think this perspective is applicable to foreign policy events and international practices more broadly, it seeks to be particularly attuned to those events that "rise" to the

---

[4] For a different use of Bourdieu, see Abrahamsen and Williams, Chapter 12 in this volume.
[5] Schatzki, 2001, 2.   [6] Barnes, 2001, 19.   [7] Swidler, 2001, 80–81.

level of foreign policy crises and the public discourses that come with them. I choose a case study to develop – and illustrate – this perspective, namely that of the 2005–2006 Muhammad cartoon crisis, which is widely believed to be the worst that Denmark has faced since the Second World War.

As laid out in Chapter 1, this volume has been an invitation for authors to use the international practices perspective to facilitate a meta-conversation between IR approaches believed to have little in common. It has also been an invitation to further more specific "practice theories of IR" and to reflect on whether taking international practices seriously allows one to do something better or differently than "prior to practice." From the poststructuralist perspective to be developed in this chapter, taking on board the turn to practice has facilitated a more dynamic analysis, in that poststructuralist accounts of discursive structures might tend to see those "as too static, stable, and coherent,"[8] thus not noticing important shifts, changes, and instabilities. Second, by focusing on how specific, concrete practices constitute subjectivities, knowledge, and authority, and how these are performed in relation to general practices, one gets a design that allows "doings" rather than abstract structures to organize the analysis of unfolding events. This in turn foregrounds the constitution of agency – and agency's reliance upon and constitution of materiality – in a manner that can be downplayed by poststructuralism. Third, by letting practices take the analytical and methodological lead, one can highlight the dynamic way in which foreign policy events are "processed" through a set of specific epistemic domains. Fourth, by coupling a traditional poststructuralist textual methodology with an identification of "practice actions," the space between texts and "doings" is opened up for closer analysis.

To better ground the elaboration of a poststructuralist-practice perspective, I have chosen a soft "inductive" research design that begins with the case study. To further explicate what empirical and theoretical questions a practice perspective should ask – and answer – I then discuss how other IR perspectives have explained the cartoon crisis. Such explanations have come virtually exclusively from Danish scholars and this body of work reveals an interesting coexistence of realist, particularly neoclassical realist, and constructivist perspectives that sometimes intersect. Even if not framed in a practice vocabulary, this micro-cosmos of IR analysis throws interesting light on how neoclassical realism[9] and softer constructivist perspectives might "meta-dialogue." The second section discusses what questions these analyses have been unable to answer and how these questions might be approached from a practice perspective. It also turns to practice analyses that have engaged themes of relevance for the cartoon crisis to see whether they provide a ready-made answer to the cartoon crisis, namely those of diplomacy[10] and the Western security

---

[8] Wæver, 2004, 207.   [9] Ripsman, Chapter 8 in this volume.
[10] See Neumann, 2002, 2005, and 2008; and Adler-Nissen, 2008.

community.[11] I conclude that these works offer valuable insights, but that their focus on diplomats' practices and on tacit background knowledge differs from my concern with the public and discursive "practice performances" of central actors during times of crisis. In the attempt to theorize these, I turn in the third section to the development of a poststructuralist-practice approach which starts from the framework laid out in Chapter 1 while turning some of its components in a more distinct poststructuralist direction. I suggest that specific practices claim to perform general practices and that these always involve a "gap" between specific and general practices. I also hold that practices are constituted within particular politico-epistemic domains that delineate which forms of authority and knowledge are appropriate. The fourth section presents a research design built on this framework and applies it to the cartoon crisis through four sets of practice-event constellations. The conclusion sums up and points to further challenges to be engaged by a poststructuralist-practice approach.

The Muhammad cartoon crisis and its dominant explanations

An introduction to the case study

On September 30, 2005, the Danish daily newspaper *Jyllands-Posten* published a full-page article by the paper's cultural editor-in-chief, Flemming Rose, called "The face of Muhammad." Encircling Rose's text were twelve cartoons produced, Rose explained, in response to *Jyllands-Posten*'s soliciting of drawings from the members of the Danish editorial cartoonists' association.[12] The cartoonists had been asked to draw Muhammad, "as they saw him," thereby defying what Rose identified as a growing fear among visual artists, translators, authors, and cartoonists that engaging satirically with Islam would have repercussions. To draw Muhammad would be to defy such intimidation and to defend free speech and other liberal, Western values. The specter of a Western culture under siege is further brought out by the newspaper's main editorial which, under the headline "The threat from the dark" argues, first, that those who speak on behalf of Islam are articulating a worldview that belongs to "the dark Middle Ages," and second, that many Western actors are too politically correct to counter such voices. To a Danish audience, this rhetoric is not unusual, particularly when coming from *Jyllands-Posten*, which is a right-leaning newspaper. The cartoons are mainly seen as a provocation – or, according to some of the cartoons which

---

[11] See Adler, 2008; Williams, 2007; and Pouliot, 2008.

[12] The name of the association is *Danske Bladtegnere*, the literal translation of "bladtegner" is "one who draws for (news) papers," and its members produce illustrations for newspapers and on-line media as well as editorial cartoons. Given the choice in English between "editorial cartoonists" and "illustrators," *bladtegnere* are best described by the former term.

satirize *Jyllands-Posten*'s project, a media stunt – and Danish Muslim protests and demonstrations are deemed to be fairly limited in scope.[13]

A key event in setting the cartoons on track to becoming "a crisis" was the request for "an urgent meeting" that Prime Minister Anders Fogh Rasmussen received in mid-October. The meeting was requested by eleven diplomats from countries with large Muslim populations through a formal letter which identified the cartoons as one of four recent examples of the "on-going smearing campaign in Danish public circles and media against Islam and Muslims." This letter internationalizes the issue, and Fogh Rasmussen's refusal of the meeting on the grounds that the ambassadors ask him to interfere with *Jyllands-Posten*'s freedom of speech adds fuel to the fire. Over the coming months a heated debate rages over what the diplomats were requesting (the curtailing of free speech or a discussion of the constitution of "the Muslim" in Danish public discourse), whether Fogh Rasmussen was right to decline the meeting, and what the cartoons signify (the freedom of speech or a vilification of "Muslims"). The cartoons attract growing international attention and by the end of 2005 the Danish Government is facing criticism from major countries in the Middle East and Asia, including Bangladesh, Egypt, India, Iran, and Pakistan.[14] Diplomatic relations deteriorate further as the Saudi Arabian ambassador is called home on January 26, 2006 and Danish diplomatic missions are attacked and burned in Beirut, Damascus, Djakarta, and Tehran during the first weeks of February.[15] Up to 250 people are estimated to have died in demonstrations/riots across the world[16] and Danish companies, including the dairy giant Arla Foods, are hit by a massive boycott. According to Minister of Foreign Affairs, Per Stig Møller, these events constitute the biggest crisis since the German occupation during the Second World War, and this crisis interpretation gains widespread hold.[17] The crisis is not only material, but goes to the heart of the idea of Denmark as a humanitarian supporter of the third world. At that point, the UK and US governments come forward with a show of support for Danish interests and condemnation of the attacks, but their support is lukewarm in that they also state that they find the cartoons offensive.

By March 2006, the demonstrations start to wind down, but the cartoons continue to resurface, most noticeably in February 2008 when a "second crisis" erupts as Danish newspapers reprint the cartoons in response to the Danish Security and Intelligence Services' announcement that they have identified a plot to murder Kurt Westergaard, the cartoonist who drew the most famous of the cartoons, that of a man with a bomb in his turban. Until this day, the cartoons have been invoked as the cause of a number of actual or foiled terrorist

[13] "Arrangerede begivenheder," *Weekendavisen*, October 21, 2005.   [14] Larsen, 2007, 55.
[15] See Hove, 2007, 64–68; and Larsen, 2007, 57.   [16] Klausen, 2009, 107.
[17] Rasmussen, 2006, 196. A more detailed account of the events can be found in Larsen, 2007; and Klausen, 2009.

attacks including the one on the Danish Embassy in Islamabad in June 2008 which killed six people, and they continue to resurface in Danish diplomatic relations with "the Muslim world." At the level of personal insecurity, Westergaard escaped an attack in early 2010 by hiding in the safe room of his house. For the purpose of this chapter I will, however, focus on the "first crisis" running from October 2005 to March 2006.

Explaining the crisis: Danish IR traditions

Why did the crisis arise, and why did it unfold in the way that it did? And what were the implications for Danish foreign policy? As a subject of academic analysis, the cartoon crisis has so far attracted interest mainly from the fields of communication,[18] political theory,[19] and theology.[20] The field of IR has shown some interest yet, with the exception of the works addressed below, the cartoons crisis is mentioned only as an example: of "clash of civilization" politics and discourses[21] or the significance of emotion in IR.[22] There have been no journal articles in the higher-ranked European and US-based journals that take the crisis as its main subject or case study, nor have there been monographs or anthologies with a distinct IR approach.[23] Possible explanations for this absence might be that the crisis' Danish origins worked against non-Danish speakers engaging it in full, or it might have been seen as too unruly (too many actors, levels, issues, and constellations) or as too unique to be a case study from which more general insights can be gained. Yet even though our search for existing explanations is confined to Danish IR, we do find a fair range of contemporary perspectives that cast light on how practice-based analysis (here of a more specific poststructuralist kind) is situated on the larger terrain of IR. As many Danish intellectuals became concerned with the cartoon crisis, so did IR scholars, and many wrote shorter pieces, for newspapers, magazines, or journals with a wider readership (*Den Ny Verden, Militært Tidsskrift*). With the partial exception of Petersen, however, none of these foregrounds IR theory; in the account on the following pages the analyses are read through the lens of contemporary IR in order to highlight the theoretical assumptions and arguments that are made.[24]

---

[18] See Kunelius *et al.*, 2007; Peterson, 2007; and Sakr, 2008.
[19] See Modood *et al.*, 2006; Rostbøll, 2009; Lægaard, 2007; and Rytkønen, 2007.
[20] Gregersen, 2009.   [21] See Etzioni, 2006, 373; and Fierke, 2007, 95–97.
[22] Saurette, 2006, 496. On emotion see also Bially Mattern, Chapter 3 in this volume.
[23] I am using the cartoon crisis as a case study in an article that develops a theory of visual securitization: Hansen, 2011. Klausen, 2009 is the first monograph to investigate the crisis, and it provides a detailed and rich account of the events, but it does not set the crisis within a theoretical framework.
[24] Petersen, 2006.

As Henrik Breitenbauch and Anders Wivel point out, Danish IR has a realist as well as a constructivist tradition and the analyses of the cartoon crisis fit this pattern.[25] The former has historically been known as "adaptation theory" and it makes realist assumptions insofar as it sees the state as the primary actor and the international system as dominated by power politics. As in classical and neoclassical realism, the focus is on the interface between foreign policy and international politics.[26] Treating the cartoon crisis in passing, Hans Mouritzen's analysis of the Danish approach to the Iraq War is a telling example of this tradition. Mouritzen stresses the explanatory power of geo-politics and, hence, of states' immediate environment: "proximate power is more important than distant power."[27] Striking a realist balance of power note, he explains Denmark's decision to support the coalition against Iraq as the outcome of Danish balancing against the immediate powers (Germany and France) by allying with a more distant one. Yet the high level of the Danish engagement can only be accounted for by incorporating the moral ideology and belief of Fogh Rasmussen, an ideational factor located at the unit level.[28] Although not offering a full account of the cartoon crisis, Mouritzen sees moral ideology as playing a crucial role in this case as well.

Nikolaj Petersen also sets out from adaptation theory – a theory of which he has been one of the founders[29] – in his analysis of the implications of the cartoon crisis for Danish foreign policy. Starting with a description of Fogh's foreign policy, Petersen points to five features: first, an active, offensive foreign policy indicative of an ambition to constitute Denmark as a middle power; second, a liberal/neoconservative foreign policy focused on the promotion of values; third, a willingness to be a close ally of the United States, a feature that fits with the neoconservative values' promotion, but which is also due to interest and balancing considerations under unipolarity; fourth, a militarization of security policies; and, fifth, a weakened position within the European Union due to the opt-outs on justice and home affairs, military cooperation, and the European Monetary Union (EMU). Although Petersen's primary goal is to assess the consequences of the cartoon crisis, he does point to the following factors that help explain its evolution:

- Fogh's commitment to a neoconservative foreign policy – although, as it turned out, his understanding of the status and application of "freedom of expression" was challenged by the United States, supposedly Denmark's main ideological ally.
- A Danish underestimation of how globalization has weakened the boundaries between foreign and domestic politics. This has enabled

---

[25] Breitenbauch and Wivel, 2004, 429–434.
[26] *Ibid.*, 429–430. On neoclassical realism see also Ripsman, Chapter 8 in this volume.
[27] Mouritzen, 2006, 498.   [28] *Ibid.*, 507.   [29] Petersen, 1977.

transnational and non-Danish actors to mobilize around political issues – for instance, Danish immigration policies.

- A Danish dependency on the European Union and the United States, and an unwillingness particularly of the latter to get involved in the cartoon crisis due to strategic interests in the Middle East and a public sentiment in favor of "religious tolerance" and "self-moderation."

Assessing the implications of the cartoon crisis for Danish foreign policy, Petersen adopts a model of foreign policy room for maneuver as based on (1) the level of foreign policy ambition; (2) domestic constraints and possibilities: these are further defined as the degree of support for a foreign policy in parliament and society, and as capabilities (material and immaterial, soft and hard power); (3) international constraints and possibilities. Given that the level of foreign policy ambition is constant – and high – from the 1990s onwards, Petersen focuses on (2) and (3). In terms of domestic constraints and possibilities, he points out that public opinion was supportive of the stance adopted by *Jyllands-Posten* and the prime minister, but that there was serious criticism from the businesses operating in the Middle East who were hit by the boycotts. As far as capabilities go, material capabilities are deemed relatively constant before and after the crisis, thus the crucial question is how the Muhammad crisis has affected Danish "soft power," more specifically the view of Denmark as a model society domestically and a promoter of "good values" abroad. Although listed under domestic constraints and possibilities, this takes us into international constraints and possibilities, where Petersen holds that Denmark's soft power had been declining prior to the crisis as illiberal policies on immigration and cutbacks in development aid had influenced the perception of the country, particularly in the West. This drop in soft power partially explains why the European Union and the United States were lukewarm in their support of Denmark during the crisis, and the government's handling of the cartoon crisis precipitated a further soft power decline. Although some support was granted, the main allies *did* view the cartoons as offensive and Denmark had as a consequence to spend some of its international goodwill. The outcome, argues Petersen, is that it is less likely that Denmark will be asked to participate in US-led coalitions, particularly in the Arab world. As regards the Muslim world, particularly the Middle East, Denmark's soft power drop appears even steeper, as Petersen holds that "[t]he ability of Denmark to stand as a strong, selfless promoter of democracy in the Arab world has been replaced by suspicion as to what our motives are."[30] In sum, both the internal and particularly the external constraints on Danish foreign policy have grown as a result of the crisis.

Petersen's analysis caused quite a stir. The Danish Parliament's Foreign Policy Committee asked the Minister of Foreign Affairs, Per Stig Møller, to

---

[30] Petersen, 2006, 175. Translation L. H.

make an official comment, and he replied – perhaps not surprisingly – that he disagreed with the view that the room for maneuver had been limited, pointing to Denmark's active use of its membership on the UN Security Council in 2005–2006, to its collaboration with Syrian and Lebanese authorities during the evacuation of Danish citizens from the Lebanon War in 2006, to its contribution to the United Nations Interim Force in Lebanon (UNIFIL), as well as to the continued support in the Middle East for the Ministry's high-profile "Danish–Arab Partnership Program" launched in 2003.[31] Petersen's charges were also refuted by Ulrik Federspiel, Permanent Secretary of State for Foreign Affairs, who in his annual assessment of Danish foreign policy for the *Danish Foreign Policy Yearbook 2007* stated that "other events in 2006 clearly showed that the decline of Danish soft power and Denmark's international standing did not materialise as predicted."[32]

I will return to the debate over whether Denmark had to draw on its "soft power capital" in the fourth section. We should note, however, that while adaption theory has an obvious realist element in that it focuses on state and alliance behavior, power, and capabilities, it also expresses the pragmatism Breitenbauch and Wivel identify as a crucial trait of Danish IR.[33] Petersen's analysis emphasizes soft power, the significance of states' images abroad, and policy-makers' ideologies and beliefs in a way that, though not couched in those terms, echoes a soft constructivist concern with the role of norms, beliefs, and foreign policy identity.

Turning to the other side of Danish IR – constructivism – exemplified in Breitenbauch and Wivel by the Copenhagen School,[34] we do not find a theory-based analysis similar to that of Petersen's. Non-realist contributions have come in the form of shorter articles that usually discuss the inability of state-centric thinking to capture the cartoon crisis. Drawing on James Der Derian's work on diplomacy and "anti-diplomacy," Bjørn Møller held that the late-modern diplomatic system with the state as the linchpin connecting non-state and transstate actors to international politics had been replaced by a post-modern diplomatic system where the state no longer held that privilege.[35] During the cartoon crisis, "informal and decentralized diplomacy took the lead, controlled the events, and the Danish state itself was responsible for the sidelining of official diplomacy."[36] Or, in Ole Wæver's words, "Denmark has not been hit mainly by official responses, but by transnational, unofficial, (pseudo)popular protests. This is not in accordance with the classic account of how diplomacy works."[37] As a consequence classical state-based IR theories were no longer (as) applicable.

---

[31] Larsen, 2007, 80.   [32] See Federspiel, 2007, 16; and Larsen, 2007, 80–82.
[33] Breitenbauch and Wivel, 2004, 431–434.   [34] *Ibid.*
[35] See Møller, 2006; and Der Derian, 1992.   [36] Møller, 2006, 90. Translation L. H.
[37] Wæver, 2006. Translation L. H.

Looking specifically to alliance formation and behavior, Mikkel Vedby Rasmussen argued that the case showed that traditional post-Second World War alliances no longer governed global politics.[38] Taking the view, with Petersen, that the Muhammad crisis *did* leave Denmark isolated, Rasmussen holds that old alliances and institutions like NATO and the European Union offer inadequate protection against new alliances, which unite state and non-state actors, are driven by values rather than interests, and are governed by risks rather than threats. Rasmussen emphasizes that the prominent role played by non-state actors in the cartoon crisis is at odds with traditional state-centric understandings of foreign policy and that interests are insufficient to glue an alliance together. Yet, while Rasmussen holds that values and narratives are imperative to an understanding of how alliances evolve, such values and narratives must also be connected to interests – more specifically how states strike a balance between them if they conflict: the UK and US governments had to distance themselves from the "clash of civilization" narrative argued by *Jyllands-Posten* and the Danish Government because this would undermine their projects in the Middle East.[39] Thus while realist and constructivist explanations of the cartoon crisis differ in the degree to which they incorporate non-state actors, there is much overlap between the two in their emphasis on values, narratives, soft power, and the interests of key allies.

Targeting the blank spots of existing explanations

So, given that explanations of the cartoon crisis are already on offer, what is it that a poststructuralist-practice perspective should contribute? First, while the analyses above point to the role of values and beliefs as motivating specific foreign policies as well as alliance behavior, they do not provide a systematic account of how values become constituted or how they are linked with foreign policy identities. Why, for instance, was the Danish prime minister's articulation of a neoconservative values-based foreign policy discourse which resonated with that of George W. Bush's own Administration, explicitly rejected by the latter? Existing accounts rightly identify this difference, but conclude the explanation by noting that the United States is a multicultural and (multi-) religious society. This however cannot by itself explain *why* these traits came to be significant for the understanding of the crisis itself, unless we hypothesize societal characteristics as causal factors separate from the political processes that grant them significance. We need therefore to dig deeper into the constitution of "values," their content as well as their relevance for foreign policy. The international practices perspective offers a fruitful platform from which to investigate this constitution. It facilitates more precisely an understanding of the way in which actors at key junctures mobilize specific practices in a manner

---

[38] Rasmussen, 2006.   [39] *Ibid.*, 202.

that constitutes collective subjects with identities that embody or differ from the "proper" values to be adopted. "Values" are not, in short, something that societies or actors *have*; they are performed through practices in discourse.

Second, a practice approach can cast valuable light on how practices were significant for forming the epistemic and political terrain on which the cartoons were debated. Why, for instance, did the discussion become pitched between "free speech" and "offensiveness"? Why were the cartoons considered one homogenous "offensive" whole by most of the global media as well as by the Bush and Blair Administrations, when they varied hugely in terms of their compliance with a clash of civilization, anti-Muslim discourse? As I will show in the fourth section, to answer these questions requires that we pay attention not only to the role of values in foreign policy, but also to the more intricate ways in which the performance of specific practices invokes or relies upon general practices and particular politico-epistemic domains.

Third, a practice perspective allows us to rethink two central discussions that can easily reach a dead end, not only in the case of the cartoon crisis but in IR more broadly. To begin with, the question of whether states or non-state actors are more important can be turned into the study of how "practitioners" (broadly conceived) perform within and constitute politico-epistemic domains. This reformulation lets the unfolding of practices, rather than a predetermined definition of who counts as actors, structure the analysis. Also, the question of whether states, in this case Denmark, lose or retain their soft power, prestige, or international reputation as a result of their actions is crucial for scholars and practitioners alike. In the case of the cartoon crisis, scholars like Petersen and Rasmussen identify a loss[40] while others, including the Government, took the opposite view.[41] It is not impossible to construct a research design through which this dispute could be turned into an empirically verifiable question. Yet one of the problems such a study would confront is that those engaged in discussing "soft power loss" in the public realm impact the object – soft power, which is at least in part an ideational factor – which is to be measured. "Soft power" or "international images" are crucial to our understanding of world politics, but they are social constructions whose content and status are performed through practice. From a poststructuralist-practice perspective, the question is thus not whether "Denmark" lost soft power *vis-à-vis* the Middle East and NATO allies, but how the government "practiced" practices that sought to counter those who held that "alliance cohesion" and Denmark's status in the Muslim world had been jeopardized.

I will lay out a poststructuralist-practice framework that facilitates such an analysis on pp. 292–296. First, however, let us briefly consider two bodies of practice analysis of relevance to the cartoon crisis, namely those of diplomacy and the Western security community. Starting with diplomacy, Iver B. Neumann and

---

[40] See Petersen, 2006; and Rasmussen, 2006.   [41] Larsen, 2007, 80.

Rebecca Adler-Nissen have studied the concrete practices that diplomats perform.[42] Neumann's analysis of diplomacy in the High North mixes policy documents and academic analysis with extensive interviews with diplomats, politicians, and other actors involved, concluding that traditional capital-based diplomatic practices were complemented with local ones, thus transforming the practice of diplomacy itself. Adler-Nissen traces the daily diplomatic handling of the Danish and British opt-outs, identifying three different strategies that seek to ameliorate the effects of "being outside." Both studies generate important knowledge about the everyday practices that make diplomacy "work," both link these practices to official foreign policies (Norwegian policies towards Russia; Danish and British policies towards the European Union), and both explain tension or change (changing policies in the High North in response to the ending of the Cold War; maneuvering around the opt-outs as EU treaties are being revised). Thus, while both studies point to the significance of routines, they also identify the transformation of other practices, or the establishment of new ones. Thus not *all* knowledge is background knowledge or follows Bourdieu's "*habitus*" logic defined by Adler-Nissen as "the unconscious overtaking of rules, values and dispositions gained from an individual and collective history."[43]

As an important element in any analysis of the cartoon crisis must be diplomatic conduct – and misconduct – these two analyses are obviously relevant to the study I pursue. Mirroring the research strategy of Adler-Nissen and Neumann I could have interviewed involved diplomats to trace the ways in which they might mobilize routine diplomatic practices or introduce new ones – for instance, related to "public diplomacy."[44] Yet, I choose to focus not on the micro-practices that constitute "diplomacy," but on the way in which "the crisis" came into being and was constituted through public "doings" and discourse. Diplomacy is part of the analysis as it is a general practice performed by key actors, but given my concern with the public unfolding of the crisis it cannot by itself explain the course of events.

As the cartoon crisis evolved around repeated – and competing – constructions of "the West" and raised the specter of intra-alliance tensions, studies of the Western security community are also relevant. Pouliot describes NATO as the institutional embodiment of the Western security community, and his study of NATO "practitioners" concludes that "so long as diplomacy remains the only thinkable or self-evident practice in mutual dealings, one has to

---

[42] See Neumann, 2002, 2005, and 2008; and Adler-Nissen, 2008.
[43] Adler-Nissen, 2008, 669. The concept of "practice" is, however, a bit slippery in both analyses. In Adler-Nissen "practice" and "strategy," which does most of the explanatory work, appear to be the same: Adler-Nissen, 2008, 673, 678. In Neumann, 2002 it is not fully clear if there is a change in diplomatic "practice" itself or "only" in terms of which actors can appropriate it.
[44] Andreasen, 2008.

conclude that the security community is alive and well."[45] As Pouliot demonstrates, there is no longer "anything like a veiled threat of possible violent retaliation among community members."[46] Yet from the perspective of most Danish actors, the way diplomatic practices played themselves out in the cartoon crisis did *not* show a seamless security community, as the United States and the United Kingdom offered reluctant and only partial support. Yet, rather than discuss whether this contravenes Pouliot's assessment of the wellness of "the West," I suggest that we see Danish and allied statements – and silences – as diplomatic performances of what a "security community" entails. The cartoon crisis shows us that we need a framework attuned to the instabilities that practice performances seek to resolve or silence and to the gaps and slippages between specific and general practices – for instance, when performances fail to conform to the general practice of alliance solidarity. It is to the development of such a framework that I now turn.

A poststructuralist-practice approach

The poststructuralist-practice approach I develop in this section draws upon the framework laid out by Emanuel Adler and Vincent Pouliot in Chapter 1, focusing on where poststructuralism might further our understanding of practices. The more specific theoretical contributions that I make are three: (1) I introduce the distinction between specific and general practices (mentioned in Chapter 1); (2) I argue that practices constitute and are constituted within politico-epistemic domains; and (3) I point to a fifth form of relationship between practices called "intersection." These concepts and distinctions are to some extent derived inductively from the cartoon crisis, to be further analyzed in the fourth section, and one might therefore wonder to what extent they are applicable beyond this case. I return to this question in the Conclusion.

From a poststructuralist perspective, the concept of discourse is central, as "practice cannot be thought 'outside of' discourse."[47] This view is seconded by Adler and Pouliot, who hold in Chapter 1 that it is "relevant to conceive of discourse as practice and to understand practice as discourse."[48] Foucault held that one should see "discourse itself as a practice" that produces a set of linguistic structures.[49] Such discursive structures are necessary for our ability "to speak of this or that object," to name, analyze, classify, and explain what happens in the social and material world.[50] Because practices "systematically form the objects of which they speak," they are not solely linguistic, but constitute materiality as well.[51] As the ability – or, rather, inability – of poststructuralism to account for materiality is often at the forefront of discussions of

---

[45] Pouliot, 2008, 280.   [46] *Ibid.*   [47] See Neumann, 2002, 628; and Hansen, 2006.
[48] Adler and Pouliot, Chapter 1 in this volume.   [49] Foucault, 1972, 46.   [50] *Ibid.*
[51] *Ibid.*, 49.

poststructuralism in the social sciences, it might be worth pointing out that Foucault himself conceived of practices as discursive as well as non-discursive. Non-discursive practices were stressed because of "the *function* that the discourse under study must carry out *in a field of non-discursive practices*." For example, the birth and evolution of the discipline of economics was linked to non-discursive practices such as "the circulation of goods, monetary manipulations and their effects, the system of protecting trade and manufactures, fluctuations in the quantity of the metal coined."[52]

Materiality in the form of architectures and technology were also crucial to Foucault's analysis of the prison as a form of governance, or to the birth and evolution of a system of knowledge known as sexuality.[53] Drawing on Foucault, poststructuralists stress that, while the epistemological and methodological focus should be on discursive practices, there is a material character to every discursive structure.[54] To take a discursive approach to the study of warfare is, for example, to examine the constitution of a very "material" set of fighting forces, military hardware, and dead bodies; or, in the case of the cartoon crisis the materiality of boycotts and embassy burnings. Poststructuralism clearly underlines the "structuring" work that discursive practices do, but one should keep in mind that Foucault took issue with structuralist determinism, and this made him stress that while discourses were structures, they were never fully stable. Structures need to be (re)produced through discursive and non-discursive practice and there is always a singular, unique quality that sets a given practice performance aside.[55]

Let me suggest that bringing Foucault's poststructuralist understanding of practices and discourses to the framework laid out in Chapter 1 might allow us to develop three additional "practice concepts." First, poststructuralism agrees that routines, background knowledge, and taken-for-granted-ness is crucial: discourses are dependent upon reiterated – "routine" – performances or else they fade, and because discourses are social rather than properties of free-standing individuals they "function" on a backdrop of shared knowledge or "taken-for-granted-ness." Yet, the instability that poststructuralism identifies in discursive structures implies that specific practices are always performed in relation to a general practice – that is, they appeal to, or draw upon, "given" structures of meaning. Specific practices are performed as exemplars of a general practice, which means that they are measured against the – socially constituted – understanding of what a general practice implies. We might say that the general practice has an epistemic superiority as it is that which the specific practice is performed in reference to. General practices' epistemic superiority also imply that they are "larger" than any specific practice – or, put differently: a specific practice can never exhaust a general one. A

---

[52] *Ibid.*, 68, 175. Emphasis in the original.   [53] Foucault, 1975 and 1978.
[54] Laclau and Mouffe, 1985, 108.   [55] Foucault, 1972, 28.

government might express alliance solidarity through a diplomatic meeting, but this does not exhaust the meaning of the general practices of "alliance solidarity" or "diplomacy." There is as a consequence always a gap between specific and general practices, even as the former are successfully performed.

"Routines" in this respect are thus performances that seek to shore up the gap between the specific and the general practice, and it is through the performance of "routine" that practitioners constitute themselves as competent. "Routine" might also work as a form of justification. Take, for example, the EU practice of returning asylum seekers to the first EU country entered, a practice which can be invoked as "routine" when specific extraditions are challenged. Yet, if general practices – say, diplomacy – have an epistemic superiority, they are also only instantiated through specific performances. General practices "live," in other words, through specific practices that seek to embody them and through discursive accounts of when such specific practices are successful and when not. For example, those who criticized the Danish Government for diplomatic blunders during the cartoon crisis – that is, failure to perform a practice properly – still reproduced an understanding of "diplomacy" as a general practice.

Clearly, the "gap" or tension between specific and general practices is one that varies empirically. We would assume that the tension is higher during times of transition than during continuity, as transitions usually challenge assumed routines and background knowledge. Take, for instance, the introduction of women to the diplomatic profession – an evolution which, as Neumann shows, raises questions about whether "diplomacy" itself might change, for instance by subdividing into gendered diplomatic practices.[56] But specific practices might also "tackle" challenging events in such a way that potential tensions regarding general practices are overcome. Here we might think of how the general practice of states recognizing each other as sovereign equals "survived" the process of decolonization, where "subjects" that had previously been considered inferior to "the West" were to be incorporated as formal equals. Instability between specific and general practices might also occur as specific practices are performed as if they belong to general practices even if their "fit" with the latter is dubious. Whether such "fits" are contested or not is a matter of the audience's response (on competence and audiences, see also Chapter 1). It is tempting to assume that the further a stretch between a specific and a general practice, the more unlikely an audience is to accept it, but that would assume that audiences have full knowledge of what those practices entail. It also assumes that audiences have institutions and resources to challenge "misfits," an assumption that presumes a liberal public sphere. The relationship between specific and general practices is thus discursive and analytically open: specific practices might be constituted as competent or

[56] Neumann, 2008.

incompetent, as "routine" or extraordinary, and they might fit to varying degrees with the general practice they claim. The analysis of the cartoon crisis in the fourth section will show in more detail how specific practices might be performed in relation to general ones.

Second, to see specific practices as performances claiming to instantiate a general practice is to highlight agency. As laid out in Chapter 1, practices are "both *individual (agential)* and *structural*" and, as such, subjects are constituted – and constitute themselves – in discourse.[57] In this respect the relationship between subjects and practices is mutually constitutive: subjects perform practices, and hence (re)produce them, but it is also through practices that subjects are constituted. Diplomats become "diplomats" through practicing diplomacy and "diplomacy" is (re)produced through "diplomats" practicing it. It is also through competent specific practice that "practitioners" gain the authority to speak about the general practice. To practice is thus to draw upon and reinforce authority. Some subject positions are easier to establish as authoritative because they speak from positions that are institutionally sanctioned. Diplomats speak on behalf of "their" country and university professors speak from a platform of knowledge, if not truth. Those who start from less advantageous positions must demonstrate "competent performances" – and usually claim an institutional basis or constituency – to be recognized by other "practitioners" and audiences. At a more concrete level, while all practices must be performed competently – or else authority is eroded – what "competence" entails varies across practices. Those who practice must demonstrate that they "know their practice," but practices are also epistemic in that they constitute events, objects, and phenomena within a particular "knowledge optic." As I will show below, it mattered hugely which practices were brought to bear on the cartoon crisis – for instance, whether they situated the events within a religious, a political, or a legal field of practice (that is, the epistemic domain). Epistemic domains are neither neutral nor derived from the object itself, and because they constitute subjectivities and authority, they are inherently political. We might as a consequence conceptualize practices as constituting – and being constituted within – *politico-epistemic domains*.

It would be impossible to construct a complete list of the politico-epistemic domains through which international practices are performed, but some of the most important ones at a fairly general level would be the political, the legal, the religious, and the ethical. Politico-epistemic domains are essentially socially constituted, they have a historicity, and they are embodied within, and reproduced through, a set of institutions. One might think of (some) politico-epistemic domains as tied to the evolution of academic disciplines and knowledge forms,[58] or one might use the concept to distinguish between

---

[57] Adler and Pouliot, Chapter 1 in this volume. Emphasis in the original.
[58] Foucault, 1970.

practices that are said to be "emotional" or "rational."[59] Zooming in on a concrete case, we might further specify and fine-tune the politico-epistemic domains invoked to capture more subtle variations. In short, the concept of the politico-epistemic domain can be applied at different levels of abstraction and tailored to identify the way in which knowledge and authority forms are constituted in a given case.

Third, the concepts of specific and general practices and politico-epistemic domain lead me to suggest a fifth type of relationship between practices that supplements the four laid out in Chapter 1: parallel existence (with no significant interference between practices), symbiosis, hybridization, and subordination. This fifth relationship could be called *intersection* and defined as the specific and general practices mobilized in the course of a foreign policy "event." As the analysis in the section below will show, the practices that were central to the cartoon crisis intersected in (contested) negotiations of the cartoons and "the crisis," thus they cannot be said to exist in parallel existence. Yet, "symbiosis" does not capture the relationship between these practices either, in that they do not "form a coherent whole" but fight over what the crisis is about. The distinctiveness of the practices implies further that they do not add up to "hybridization." The fourth type of relationship, subordination, comes closer in that one may look at particular instances of practice – one distinct "doing" – as referring to a standard practice – in that sense, in Ann Swidler's terminology, anchoring it.[60] *Jyllands-Posten*'s publication of the twelve cartoons would thus be subordinated to the deeper practice of "editorial cartooning." Yet, this terminology is problematic because it assumes a fit, or "anchor," between the subordinate and the superior practice. As I will show, what characterized the cartoon crisis was rather a series of "misfits" between the specific practices and the general practices they were held to perform. Thus to describe the practices at work as "subordinate" would miss crucial performances across and within specific politico-epistemic domains.

The Muhammad cartoon crisis as intersecting practices

As laid out in Chapter 1, practices can enter the analysis in many different ways. The one I offer below asks how specific practices were key in producing the cartoon crisis. Practices are in this respect "explanations," although the fact that these were chosen and performed by "practitioners" reminds us that "practices" require agency "to explain." In keeping with the theoretical discussion above, I see four constellations of events, general and specific practices, politico-epistemic domains, and practitioners as central to explaining the genesis and form of the crisis. The four constellations are concerned with the practices of publishing, cartooning, diplomacy, law, and alliance solidarity.

---

[59] On emotions, see also Bially Mattern, Chapter 3 in this volume.   [60] Swidler, 2001.

It should be mentioned that the analytical focus is on the interface between Danish and non-Danish actors and that the analysis does not deal with *all* practices or events that could have been included. One could, for example, have devoted more attention to the practice that came to epitomize it, and thus fully bring the "crisis" into being, namely the burning of embassies and Danish flags. This practice has a clear materiality and it works discursively through mobilizing established diplomatic and national symbols. Another "crisis practice" that could have been brought out is boycotting. I have chosen, however, to focus on the practices central to the build-up of the crisis, first, because those practices provide a better illustration of the relationship between specific and general practices and the significance of politico-epistemic domains; second, because the "riot" and "boycotting" practices are reasonably well known from empirical accounts of the crisis. One might also have devoted more attention to the cartoon crises outside of Denmark, telling the practice story from those vantage points. There were "local" crises in a number of other countries – most vocally probably in France and Sweden – and given that comparative analyses of press coverage of the crisis and its political reception have been offered,[61] one would hope that the practice perspective offered in this chapter would be applied to one or more of these. Finally, although the materiality of the communications environment was crucial to the process of "crisis becoming," as was arguably the visual character of the cartoons, these will not be extensively dealt with here.[62]

Events–practices I: printing–cartooning

The first practice we encounter is that of "publishing" itself, without which there would have been no cartoons and hence no crisis. Yet, even this seemingly descriptive practice shows a complicated relationship between specific and general practices. Crucially, the cartoons were widely seen as editorial cartoons, but *Jyllands-Posten*'s active soliciting actually runs counter to the normal practices through which editorial cartoons are produced. Editorial cartoonists pick their own subject, theme, and message for their drawings and editorial cartoons stand apart from other texts and images.[63] The specific practice through which the cartoons are procured differs in both respects: *Jyllands-Posten* requests a particular "thing" to be depicted and the cartoons are published with the text of the cultural editor-in-chief. The cartoons are not

---

[61] See Kunelius *et al.*, 2007 on Canada, China, Egypt, Finland, France, Germany, Israel, Norway, Pakistan, Russia, Sweden, the United Kingdom, and the United States, and Peterson, 2007 on the United States; Holm, 2006 on France, Germany, Spain, and the United Kingdom; Modood *et al.*, 2006 on the United Kingdom and the United States; and Balcı and Miş, 2008 on Turkey.

[62] For such accounts see Hansen, 2011; and Sakr, 2008.

[63] See Edwards, 1997; and Seymore-Ure, 2001.

"illustrations" either as such drawings are expected to be "illustrative of" – and hence loyal/secondary to – a written text.[64] The specific practice of soliciting the cartoons thus does not "belong" to an established general practice, but this disconnect between specific and general practice goes unnoticed in the debate. There is no evidence to suggest that there is an intentional "misfit perform-ance" where *Jyllands-Posten* is trying to pass off the cartoons as belonging to the genre of editorial cartooning. This genre constitution gains hold as the crisis unfolds, and it has no identifiable locus of agency. Nevertheless, the continued references to the cartoons as editorial has politico-epistemic consequences as it shifts the question from "why were these cartoons procured?" to "should they be published?" – a question that presumes that the cartoons would exist independently of *Jyllands-Posten*'s actions. Although one should be careful to attribute intentionality to *Jyllands-Posten* in this respect, there is an important way in which the editorial text is ambiguous as to the cartoons' epistemic status. On the one hand, the agency of solicitation is evident in the articulation of their procurement as a heroic act in defense of free speech. Here, the epistemic domains are those of political resistance and artistic freedom. But this heroic act also implies, on the other hand, that the cartoons were already in the world as repressed images prior to *Jyllands-Posten*'s solicitation: the latter uncovers something – satire of Islam – which is self-censored, but could have happened otherwise. This constitutes *Jyllands-Posten* as a (heroic) facilitator rather than an image-producer or provocateur. This politico-epistemic ambiguity has obvious implications for what the cartoons signify and what kind of agency they attribute to *Jyllands-Posten*.

The mismatch between the specific practice through which the cartoons were solicited and published and the general practice of editorial cartooning is important for how the cartoons became homogenized, radicalized, and decon-textualized. Because the cartoons were printed with Rose's texts, they lacked the individual frame, caption, title, and separation from other texts and images that characterize the conventional editorial cartoon. This facilitated a reading of the cartoons through Rose's text – and *Jyllands-Posten*'s editorial – and such a reading helped reinforce a homogenization and radicalization of the cartoons. The three cartoons that explicitly satirized *Jyllands-Posten*'s assignment and discourse were overshadowed by a construction of "the" cartoons as a homo-genous group, and the one deemed most offensive – Westergaard's drawing of a man with a bomb in his turban – became, as the crisis gained hold, the one that the others were read and radicalized through. Yet even Westergaard's drawing is ambiguous insofar as it is impossible to say with certainty which collective subject it signifies: "Muslims," "terrorists," "some Muslims"?[65] The fact that, five years after its publication, one still finds heated debates over its message is indicative of the cartoon's inherent ambiguity.[66] Yet while the cartoons became

---

[64] Hansen, 2011.   [65] Spiegelman, 2006, 48–49.   [66] Hansen, 2011.

homogenized and radicalized in part because of their tenuous relation to an established general practice, which made them less "resistant" to the texts that surrounded them, once the cartoons started to circulate beyond a Danish context, they lost their textual context and the audience for whom they were produced. Eugene Robinson, columnist at *The Washington Post*, described the cartoons as "lame and unsophisticated, crudely equating Islam's Prophet Muhammad – and thus, by clear implication, all of Islam – with terrorism and ignorance." This is one example of how the cartoons became decontextualized, particularly how the satirical cartoons aimed at *Jyllands-Posten* itself were lost.[67] From a politico-epistemic perspective it is also crucial that the decontextualization which happened as "the crisis" unfolded and the cartoons circulated was one that often attributed an intentionality and epistemic quality to the cartoons which is at odds with editorial cartooning itself. The editorial cartoon is considered a "fast read" and a "fast product" as editorial cartoonists might draw several cartoons a week – or, in some cases, a day.[68] As some of the twelve cartoonists explained, the process of drawing their "Muhammad cartoon" had been similar, and they had had no inkling that this would escalate to the level of an international crisis.

Events–practices II: meeting – requesting, refusing

The cartoons themselves cannot in short explain "the crisis." Taking a practice perspective, the first significant "doing" that pushes the issue in that direction was the eleven diplomats' request for a meeting with Prime Minister Anders Fogh Rasmussen, and his refusal. The specific practice of requesting this meeting draws upon the general practice of diplomacy, where diplomats routinely meet with their "hosts." What is unusual about this specific performance is that the request is made public before Fogh Rasmussen answers. According to standard diplomatic practice, most requests are handled without them reaching the spectacular public realm: either diplomats and hosts meet in private and the issue in question is "handled" outside of the public view or, if the meeting is announced to the public, it happens in such a way that both parties can constitute the meeting as successful. "As a diplomat" one understands that diplomats from other countries might be speaking to their domestic audiences in addition to audiences in the host country and it is thus part of diplomatic practice to seek to coordinate such performances. This element of the request implied that there was a certain gap between the specific practice and the general practice of diplomacy, as the move to "take diplomacy public" prior to the meeting was a break with standard routines and conventions. As a consequence, the situation was constituted as extraordinary. The "gap" between the specific request and general diplomatic practice is thus different from the

[67] Robinson, 2006.   [68] Seymour-Ure, 2001.

gap between *Jyllands-Posten*'s soliciting and the general practice of editorial cartooning: in the latter we found a practice that lacked a clear general practice, in the case of the meeting request a specific practice is performed as if it belongs to a general practice, although it broke with "routine" practices and expectations.

The public request is also a practice that communicates to different audiences at once. To the Danish Government, the message is that the situation is deemed extraordinary, and that the ambassadors are willing to perform in public; in this respect the request relies upon shared knowledge and routines even as it transgresses them. To the Danish Muslim community, the diplomats communicate that their countries are willing to articulate and represent "their" grievances, thereby discursively constituting "a" Danish Muslim subject that is ambiguously located between "the Danish" and "the Muslim." To other "Muslim" governments and "Muslims" world-wide, the diplomats communicate that "anti-Muslim" actions need to be resisted by "representatives" on the spot. And to the broader Danish public, the diplomats state that "it" should be cognizant of the practices through which "Muslims" are constituted as Other.

Taking the request public is an ambiguous performance of a general practice, but Fogh Rasmussen's refusal to meet is even more at odds with the conventions of diplomatic practices. To refuse a meeting is extremely unusual: a meeting might be very short and it might consist of nothing more than the recital of established positions, or of the handing over of protest notes, etc. But the very practice of meeting is deeply embedded in diplomatic practice not least because it draws upon the general practice of interstate recognition.[69] Yet, while refusing a meeting is a striking break from general diplomatic practice, the primary audience for whom Fogh Rasmussen was legitimating his refusal was the Danish public. "Meeting" has the status of an "anchoring practice" for diplomacy, and it is superior to the practice of reaching a substantial agreement. For a Danish audience not familiar with the conventions of this practice, the epistemic weight bestowed upon "meeting" and "substance" was different. Therefore, when speaking to the general Danish audience, Fogh Rasmussen could constitute the substance of the request as the reason he could not meet, whereas this performance would sit uneasily with a diplomatic audience. This constitution of "meeting" and "substance" also involves a "negotiation" of politico-epistemic terrains: "to meet" is to recognize those meeting regardless of the outcome; to see the terrain as one of "substance" presupposes irreconcilable – and unacceptable – views that cannot be overcome through dialogue. The refusal also has epistemic implications in a more concrete sense in that it generates criticism from former expert practitioners. Such criticism, most prominently raised in a December op-ed written by twenty-two former top ambassadors,

---

[69] Adler-Nissen, 2008.

who held that Fogh's decision had been a diplomatic blunder, effectively challenging his politico-epistemic competence.[70]

The shifting of the politico-epistemic domain from one of recognition to that of substance is underpinned by the fact that, according to Fogh Rasmussen, the October letter demanded that action be taken against *Jyllands-Posten*. Since this would be in clear violation, not just of Danish law, but also of Danish values and identity, a meeting cannot take place. Although Fogh Rasmussen quotes from the diplomats' letter, the letter in its entirety is not made available to the politicians on the Parliament's Foreign Policy Committee until February 1, 2006 and it is not until mid-February that it is publicly available to the media. That is not because the Government deliberately hides it, but rather because there is widespread support for Fogh Rasmussen's position – and trust in his ability to quote correctly.[71] When the letter is released, it turns out that it is more ambiguous in its wording than Fogh Rasmussen has indicated, and a "translation debate" ensues. The letter begins by pointing to an "on-going smearing campaign in Danish public circles and media against Islam and Muslims," giving four examples including the Muhammad cartoons. The key and closing passage states that "[w]e deplore these statements and publications and urge Your Excellency's government to take all those responsible to task under law of the land." It is this passage Fogh Rasmussen interprets as demanding his interference with *Jyllands-Posten*'s freedom of speech. Yet, as critics later point out, "to take all those responsible ... under law of the land" is not an established legal expression and might be read to the effect that Fogh Rasmussen is encouraged to do what its possible under the laws already in place.[72] In this interpretation the letter is calling for a political rather than a legal stance on the publication of the cartoons and on the general public debate on Islam and immigration.

Fogh Rasmussen's refusal has two implications for the subsequent debate: it situates the cartoons within a legal politico-epistemic domain and it reinforces the constitution of a Muslim subject. The "Muslim" diplomats' request has of course invoked a Muslim subject insofar as it lists the grievances that this subject faces; this subject is also constituted through the diplomats' claim to be able to speak on its behalf. Yet, there is also a certain slippage between "the Muslim" and the diplomats, who after all sign the letter on behalf of their states

---

[70] See Davidsen-Nielsen *et al.*, 2005; and Wæver, 2006. *Jyllands-Posten*'s response was that the twenty-two former ambassadors had become accustomed to interacting with dictatorial regimes and this meant that they were "hardly the most trustworthy spokespeople for a free and critical press" (Diplomats Astray, December 21, 2005. Translation L. H.). Here the twenty-two ambassadors' invocation of authority as experts, practitioners, and "diplomats" is rejected in a counterdiscourse that constitutes "diplomacy" as an elite activity that blinds rather than facilitates an understanding of liberal politics.

[71] Emborg, 2006.   [72] Hundsbæk *et al.*, 2006.

rather than a collective religious subject. As events unfold, the diplomats become known simply as "Muslim" and Fogh Rasmussen's constitution of the issue as one of "free speech" casts them as illiberal, non-Western, and non-democratic. Much of the media discourse on the crisis is also invoking a standard colonial construction of the non-Western subject as an underachieving student of civilization. Turkey, who is one of the signatories, is for instance asked to do more to demonstrate that it has the democratic conviction that is required to enter the European Union, a long-term Turkish objective. This constitution of the diplomats as in need of further liberal education was vocally challenged by Maie Sarraf, the signatory on behalf of the Palestinian General Delegation: "Listen, does he [Fogh Rasmussen] think I'm stupid. I have a law degree. I studied at a British University. I know what a government can and cannot do. He doesn't have to lecture me."[73]

Events–practices III: legalization and religification

In hindsight, we might see Fogh Rasmussen's refusal to meet with the diplomats as unsuccessful insofar as the cartoon case escalates over the months that follow, but it is successful in terms of constituting a politico-epistemic domain: Fogh Rasmussen refuses not only the meeting itself, but any attempt to compromise the freedom of speech, a position that is widely supported within Denmark. As a specific practice, Fogh Rasmussen's repeated response that any aggrieved party must go to the courts performs a general practice of legalizing that, in Foucault's words, grounds power in the "juridico-discursive."[74] "The law" is one that claims a rule-bound regularity, where all are equal in front of the judge and legislator, and where the subject is an obedient one. For Fogh Rasmussen to invoke the practice of legalization is to claim that there is a neutral institution that will provide objective arbitration on the question whether the cartoons are "offensive" or not.[75] The extent to which this move is successful is indicated by the fact that when Fogh Rasmussen finally speaks on the cartoons in late January 2006, he does so in his "personal capacity," not in his "political" capacity as prime minister. As a performance this invocation of a split between practices undertaken as "a person" and as "a politician" indicates a split in politico-epistemic domains as well. For one thing, it seeks to establish a domain where Fogh Rasmussen could speak "in a personal manner," a claim which is difficult to sustain in something as high-profiled as the cartoon crisis. It also seeks to provide a space from which Fogh Rasmussen

---

[73] Quoted in El-Gourfti, Hundsbæk, and Thomsen, 2006, 3. Translation L.H.

[74] Foucault, 1978, 82–85.

[75] By mid-March 2006 the Director of Public Prosecutions makes the verdict that there are insufficient grounds for prosecuting *Jyllands-Posten*. The verdict analyzes each cartoon and holds that the editorial text must be considered as well (Rigsadvokaten, 2006).

can speak without compromising his previous position. And most importantly, perhaps, it claims a politico-epistemic domain that is a-political and ethical–normative. The boundary between these domains is not, of course, given outside of discursive practice, and in Danish parliamentary politics – which is characterized by a very high level of party discipline – "independent voting" is allowed only on "ethical–normative questions" said to concern "one's conscience," historically questions of reproductive health, life–death criteria, abortion, and adoption. It is hard to see an immediate link between these issues and those of the cartoon crisis and we might therefore identify instability between Fogh Rasmussen's specific practice and the general practice of "conscience-based" decision-making.

The performance out of the politico-epistemic domain of the political and into that of individual conscience is also evidenced in Fogh Rasmussen's statement that he would never deliberately treat religious figures in a way that hurt "the feelings" of those who believe.[76] This resonated more broadly with discussions of the cartoons through the specter of "religious feelings," where many of those who criticized *Jyllands-Posten* – and the government's handling of the case – pointed to the need they had to take "religious feelings" into consideration.[77] From a practice perspective, we might identify this as a specific practice that "religified" the issue. In terms of the politico-epistemic domain, bringing in religion *and* feelings had important consequences for the subjectivities of "Muslims" and "Danes." One discourse constituted Christians not as devoid of religious feelings, but as capable of controlling them, institutionally as well as personally. As was frequently pointed out, the United States was a "religious society," too. The "Muslim" subject, by contrast, was not similarly capable of controlling emotions or locating them within the private sphere where they belong. Others took issue with this representation of Muslim difference holding that "Muslims," like "Christians," should be treated with respect for what they held divine. Some of this debate concerned whether there was a Muslim ban on depicting Muhammad. While this discourse was sympathetic to "Muslim" grievances it also involved a reading of the crisis through the politico-epistemic domain of religious emotionality rather than that of the political. The latter domain had in fact been more strongly invoked by the eleven diplomats' letter that pointed to the cartoons as examples of a broader anti-Muslim campaign. Yet while the cartoons were described as "demeaning," there was no mention of a general ban on depiction.

Events–practices IV: allied responses

As we get to the events of late January and early February – when the crisis becomes "a crisis" – we find two politico-epistemic domains pitched against each other: the juridico–discursive of the free-speech camp and the normative–respect of the

---

[76] Larsen, 2007, 57.   [77] See also Wæver, 2006; and Rostbøll, 2009.

religious sensibilities camp.[78] As the United Kingdom, the European Union, and the United States enter the discussion, the cartoons are homogenized and constituted as offensive by the UK and US governments. Since getting into office in 2001, Fogh Rasmussen had promoted a neoconservative discourse reminiscent of that of the Bush Administration, and Denmark had been a staunch supporter of the Coalition of the Willing, with troops in Afghanistan and Iraq. The unwillingness of the Bush and Blair Administrations to support Fogh Rasmussen's discourse was evident in statements such as that of Jack Straw, British Foreign Secretary, who held that "there is freedom of speech, we all respect that, but there is not any obligation to insult or to be gratuitously inflammatory," and "I believe that the republication of these cartoons has been unnecessary, it has been insensitive, it has been disrespectful and it has been wrong."[79] Although Straw's condemnation is strictly speaking directed at the republication of the cartoons – in fact, he said he had "no comment about their original publication" – his assessment was heard in Denmark as implicating the original publication as well. Similar views were expressed by the Bush Administration, with Department of State spokesman, Sean McCormack, describing the images as "offensive." Such quotes were seen by most outside of the Danish Government as a break with the general practice of "alliance solidarity." If we think of this as "a practice withheld," this was a serious issue, not only because a "dis-practice of solidarity," particularly in the case of major allies is serious *per se*, but because Fogh Rasmussen had made the practice of shared values crucial to the alliance as such. For the Bush and Blair Administrations to declare the cartoons offensive was thus to challenge Fogh Rasmussen's constitution of what liberalism and "being the West" entailed.

Coming back to the debate in the first section about whether the cartoon crisis had negative consequences for Danish "soft power," the strength of the practice perspective might be to draw attention to how the government tries to perform across the gap between the specific practice of the UK and US governments and the general practice of alliance solidarity. That something was not quite "routine" is evidenced by the repeated specific discursive practices through which representatives of the government and the Ministry of Foreign Affairs seek to perform the situation as "normal" and the allies as "supportive." We find repeated references to the significance of Secretary of State Condoleezza Rice speaking to the Minister of Foreign Affairs on February 4, to Bush phoning Fogh Rasmussen on February 7, and to the Danish ambassador meeting with Vice-President Cheney between February 7 and 10. These are all specific practices performed to shore up the gap in the general practices of diplomacy and alliance support. In the years that follow we find government performances that "work" temporally along two dimensions: they normalize relations after the crisis, but they also perform "into the past" through an interpretation of alliance support as having been decisive during the crisis itself.

---

[78] Larsen, 2007.   [79] Jack Straw quoted in Tryhorn, 2006.

In the words of, for example, the Danish Permanent Secretary of State for Foreign Affairs, Ulrik Federspiel: "International support for Denmark, in particular from the US and the EU, was essential in stabilising the situation."[80] There were also specific practice performances that went beyond those of "normal" diplomatic conduct and into that of friendship. Most noteworthy in this respect is Fogh Rasmussen's public performance of a bond between him and President Bush. Danish media covers, for instance, Fogh Rasmussen's visits to Bush's ranch in Crawford, Texas, with photos of the two men mountain biking, smiling, and doing exactly the kinds of activities that good friends do. Two years after the cartoon crisis, a large front-page interview in *Politiken* causes quite a stir as Fogh Rasmussen states that Abu Ghraib and Guantanamo have been bumps in the road on the way to democracy and human rights worldwide, and that he and Bush are fighting for a larger cause.[81] In response to the waning support for Bush among the US public, Fogh replies that theirs is a personal friendship in which they could celebrate birthdays together, not one based on polls.

Conclusion

This chapter has offered one version of what adopting an international practices perspective might imply. Bringing poststructuralism and practice together, it has argued that one might study the unfolding of foreign policy events, particularly those of crisis, by tracing particular practices and the way in which these perform, or seek to perform, general ones. I suggested that such specific and general practice performances always take place within politico-epistemic domains and that these domains are important because they tell us which kinds of knowledge and authority are required to speak on a given issue, as well as more concretely what types of questions can and should be asked. This framework is derived from a general poststructuralist understanding of discourses as simultaneously unstable and structured, which implies that specific practices are never going to exhaust or perform general practice in full, even when performed successfully. The development of the theoretical framework and the analysis of the cartoon crisis have been focused on constructing a poststructuralist-practice perspective building on the general framework laid out in Chapter 1, rather than on a discussion of where poststructuralism falls short "prior to practice." One should thus move with caution to a grand conclusion as what we can deduce on this issue. That said, I find that taking practice to poststructuralism has been a valuable "exercise" that has facilitated a better incorporation of "doings" that are not exclusively textual. Such a framework might allow for a more dynamic form of analysis and a closer interrogation of the space between texts and "doings." Were I to identify one issue which still needs

---

[80] Federspiel, 2007, 15.   [81] Fogh quoted in Børsting and Seidelin, 2008.

further work, it might be how to integrate the materiality and non-discursive practices more explicitly into the framework. The materiality of communication technology was, for instance, an important background condition in the study of the cartoon crisis, but it was not directly brought out in the analysis.

As noted at the beginning of this chapter, I have been particularly concerned with developing a perspective particularly suited to the study of foreign policy crises which I assumed would provide us with further knowledge of what happens when routines break down. As important studies of international practice that draw on Bourdieu have stressed, the significance of background knowledge and practices as routines need little justification. This is why I thought there might be a valuable "division of labor" between this literature and the perspective I offer here. Clearly, practice perspectives as a whole must be able to incorporate and allow for empirical variation in the way in which cases involve routine or not-so-routine performances. Using the Muhammad cartoon crisis as an inspirational inductive platform from which to build my framework and for showing its subsequent applicability, I identified a series of intersecting – and competing – practices as well as multiple forms of relations between specific and general practices. Although they lacked an actual general practice, specific practices were performed in ways that contravened routine understandings of what the general practice entailed and retrospectively closed a gap that audiences had identified as politically problematic. These are all instances that point to instabilities in how specific practices perform "their" general practice, yet I could surely have identified more "loyal" or unproblematized routine performances had I interviewed diplomats from the Ministry of Foreign Affairs. My conclusion is not therefore that the practice analysis I have offered would be the same across all "practitioners" or possible sites of analysis.

Whether my theoretical framework is "applicable," or valuable, for other types of cases, particularly those of a less spectacular kind than the cartoon crisis, is a good question. I would assume that it is, and that it has particular strengths in dealing with events that rise to the level of public contestation, but an affirmative answer would have to await future studies.

References

Adler, Emanuel, 2008. The Spread of Security Communities: Communities of Practice, Self-Restraint, and NATO's Post-Cold War Evolution. *European Journal of International Relations* 14 (2): 195–230.

Adler-Nissen, Rebecca, 2008. The Diplomacy of Opting Out: A Bourdieudian Approach to National Integration Strategies. *Journal of Common Market Studies* 46 (3): 663–684.

Andreasen, Uffe, 2008. Reflections on Public Diplomacy after the Danish Cartoon Crises: From Crisis Management to Normal Public Diplomacy Work. *The Hague Journal of Diplomacy* 3 (2): 201–207.

Balcı, Ali and Nebi Mis, 2008. Turkey's Role in the Alliance of Civilizations: A New Perspective in Turkish Foreign Policy? *Turkish Studies* 9 (3): 387–406.

Barnes, Barry, 2001. Practice as Collective Action. In *The Practice Turn in Contemporary Theory*, edited by Theodore R. Schatzki, Karin Knorr Cetina, and Eike von Savigny, 17–28. New York: Routledge.

Børsting, Mikael and Matias Seidelin, 2008. Fogh: George Bush og Jeg Kæmper for en Større Sag. *Politiken*, February 28, 2008, pp. 1–2.

Breitenbauch, Henrik Ø. and Anders Wivel, 2004. Understanding National IR Disciplines Outside the United States: Political Culture and the Construction of International Relations in Denmark. *Journal of International Relations and Development* 7 (4): 414–443.

Davidsen-Nielsen, David, Stéphanie Surrugue, Tanja Parker Astrup, and Rasmus Emborg, 2005. Danske Ambassadører i Skarp Kritik af Fogh. *Politiken*, December 20, 2005, section 1, p. 1.

Der Derian, James, 1992. *Antidiplomacy: Spies, Terror, Speed, and War.* Oxford: Blackwell.

Edwards, Janis L., 1997. *Political Cartoons in the 1998 Presidential Campaign – Image, Metaphor, and Narrative.* New York: Garland Publishing.

El-Gourfti, Fikré, Thomas Hundsbæk, and Claus Blok Thomsen, 2006. Muhammedsag: Ikke Ligefrem en Genistreg. *Politiken*, February 12, 2006, section 4, pp. 1 and 3.

Emborg, Rasmus, 2006. Muhammed-Tegningerne: Analyse: Politiske Vagthunde uden Tænder. *Politiken*, February 25, 2006, section F, p. 3.

Etzioni, Amitai, 2006. The Global Importance of Illiberal Moderates. *Cambridge Review of International Affairs* 19 (3): 369–385.

Federspiel, Ulrik, 2007. The International Situation and Danish Foreign Policy 2006. In *Danish Foreign Policy Yearbook 2007*, edited by Nanna Hvidt and Hans Mouritzen, 13–30. Copenhagen: Danish Institute for International Studies.

Fierke, Karin M., 2007. *Critical Approaches to International Security.* Cambridge: Polity Press.

Foucault, Michel, 1970. *The Order of Things: An Archaeology of the Human Sciences.* New York: Vintage Books.

1972. *The Archaeology of Knowledge.* London: Tavistock Publications.

1975. *Discipline and Punish: The Birth of the Prison.* Harmondsworth: Penguin Books.

1978. *The History of Sexuality.* Volume 1, *An Introduction.* New York: Vintage Books.

Gregersen, Niels Henrik, 2009. On Taboos: The Danish Cartoon Crisis 2005–2008. *Theology Update* 48 (1): 79–96.

Hansen, Lene, 2006. *Security as Practice: Discourse Analysis and the Bosnian War.* London: Routledge.

2011. Theorizing the Image for Security Studies: Visual Securitization and the Muhammad Cartoon Crisis. *European Journal of International Relations* 17 (1): 51–74.

Holm, Ulla, 2006. Muhammed-Tegningerne – Debatter om Liberale Værdier i Europæiske Lande. *Den Ny Verden* 39 (2): 21–29.

Hove, Søren, 2007. Aktuelle Politiske Tendenser i Saudi-Arabien og Golfstaterne og deres Regionale Betydning. In *Nye Kolde Krige i Mellemøsten: USA's Mellemøststrategi, Situationen i Golfen og Forandringer i den Arabiske Offentlighed*, edited by Lars Erslev Andersen, Søren Hove, and Morten Valbjørn, 61–79. Odense: Syddansk Universitetsforlag.

Hundsbæk, Thomas, Mathias Seidelin, Tanja Parker Astrup, Fikré El-Gourfti, Adam Hannestad, and Claus Blok Thomsen, 2006. Profetsagen: Da Fogh Undervurderede Muhammed. *Politiken*, February 19, 2006, section 4, p. 1.

Klausen, Jytte, 2009. *The Cartoons that Shook the World*. New Haven: Yale University Press.

Kunelius, Risto, Elisabeth Eide, Oliver Hahn, and Roland Schröder, eds., 2007. *Reading the Mohammed Cartoons Controversy: An International Analysis of Press Discourses on Free Speech and Political Spin*. Bochum: Projektverlag.

Laclau, Ernesto and Chantal Mouffe, 1985. *Hegemony and Socialist Strategy: Towards a Radical Democratic Politics*. London: Verso.

Larsen, Henrik, 2007. The Cartoon Crisis in Danish Foreign Policy: A New Balance between the EU and the US? In *Danish Foreign Policy Yearbook 2007*, edited by Nanna Hvidt, and Hans Mouritzen, 51–85. Copenhagen: Danish Institute for International Studies.

Lægaard, Sune, 2007. The Cartoon Controversy: Offense, Identity, Oppression? *Political Studies* 55 (3): 481–498.

Modood, Tariq, Randall Hansen, Erik Bleich, Brendan O'Leary, and Joseph H. Carens, 2006. The Danish Cartoon Affair: Free Speech, Racism, Islamism, and Integration. *International Migration* 44 (5): 4–62.

Mouritzen, Hans, 2006. The Nordic–Baltic Area: Divisive Geopolitics at Work. *Cambridge Review of International Affairs* 19 (3): 495–511.

Møller, Bjørn, 2006. Diplomati i Lyset af Muhammed-Krisen. *Den Ny Verden* 39 (2): 85–94.

Neumann, Iver B., 2002. Returning Practice to the Linguistic Turn: The Case of Diplomacy. *Millennium* 31 (3): 627–651.

———. 2005. To Be a Diplomat. *International Studies Perspectives* 6 (1): 72–93.

———. 2008. The Body of the Diplomat. *European Journal of International Relations* 14 (4): 671–695.

Petersen, Nikolaj, 1977. Adaptation as a Framework for the Analysis of Foreign Policy Behavior. *Cooperation and Conflict* 12 (4): 221–250.

———. 2006. Handlerummet for Dansk Udenrigspolitik efter Muhammed-Krisen. *Den Ny Verden* 39 (2): 31–60.

Peterson, Mark Allen, 2007. Making Global News: "Freedom of Speech" and "Muslim Rage" in US Journalism. *Contemporary Islam: Dynamics of Muslim Life* 1 (3): 247–264.

Pouliot, Vincent, 2008. The Logic of Practicality: A Theory of Practice of Security Communities. *International Organization* 62 (2): 257–288.

Rasmussen, Mikkel Vedby, 2006. Dette er Ikke en Krise: Alliancer, Globalisering og Karikaturkrisen. *Militært Tidsskrift* 135 (2): 196–204.

Rigsadvokaten, 2006. *Afgørelse om Eventuel Strafforfølgning i Sagen om Jyllands-Postens Artikel "Muhammeds Ansigt."* March 15, 2006. Available at www.rigsadvokaten.dk/ref.aspx?id=889. Accessed November 29, 2010.

Robinson, Eugene, 2006. Prophetic Provocation. *The Washington Post*, February 7, 2006.

Rostbøll, Christian F., 2009. Autonomy, Respect, and Arrogance in the Danish Cartoon Controversy. *Political Theory* 37 (5): 623–648.

Rytkønen, Helle, 2007. Drawing the Line: The Cartoons Controversy in the US. In *Danish Foreign Policy Yearbook 2007*, edited by Nanna Hvidt and Hans Mouritzen, 86–109. Copenhagen: Danish Institute for International Studies.

Sakr, Naomi, 2008. Diversity and Diaspora: Arab Communities and Satellite Communication in Europe. *Global Media and Communication* 4 (3): 277–300.

Saurette, Paul, 2006. You Dissin' Me? Humiliation and Post-9/11 Global Politics. *Review of International Studies* 32 (3): 495–522.

Schatzki, Theodore R., 2001. Introduction: Practice Theory. In *The Practice Turn in Contemporary Theory*, edited by Theodore R. Schatzki, Karin Knorr Cetina, and Eike von Savigny, 1–14. New York: Routledge.

Seymour-Ure, Colin, 2001. What Future for the British Political Cartoon? *Journalism Studies* 2 (3): 333–355.

Spiegelman, Art, 2006. Drawing Blood: Outrageous Cartoons and the Art of Outrage. *Harper's Magazine* 312 (1873): 43–52.

Swidler, Ann, 2001. What Anchors Cultural Practices. In *The Practice Turn in Contemporary Theory*, edited by Theodore R. Schatzki, Karin Knorr Cetina, and Eike von Savigny, 83–101. New York: Routledge.

Tryhorn, Chris, 2006. Jack Straw Praises UK Media's "Sensitivity" over Cartoons. *The Guardian*, February 3, 2006. Available at www.guardian.co.uk/media/2006/feb/03/pressandpublishing.religion5. Accessed November 29, 2010.

Williams, Michael C., 2007. *Culture and Security: Symbolic Power and the Politics of International Security.* New York: Routledge.

Wæver, Ole, 2004. Discursive Approaches. In *European Integration Theory*, edited by Antje Wiener, and Thomas Diez, 197–216. Oxford: Oxford University Press.

2006. Gadens Diplomati. *Weekendavisen*, February 17, 2006.

12 Privatization in practice: power and capital in the field of global security

RITA ABRAHAMSEN AND MICHAEL C. WILLIAMS

The study of international security has traditionally been dominated by a focus on states, their militaries, and their interactions. Traced historically, this reflects a powerful set of practices surrounding modern state formation, including the increasing centralization and identification of security with the state, the concentration of coercive power in the hands of public authorities, and the emergence of a clear distinction between security inside the state and security between states. Over the past three centuries, these practices have become so deeply ingrained that the idea of the state's monopoly of legitimate violence, and of security as a quintessentially public (and national) good, is almost taken for granted in the modern political imagination, and its eventual achievement has become part of near-teleological visions of state formation and development in the West and beyond.[1]

The recent rebirth of private security[2] seems at first sight to reverse this trajectory, and in this chapter we examine how the ordinary unfolding of security practices have generated and contributed to the emergence of a transnational commercial security sector that is in turn transforming practices of security at a global level. Foregrounding practices, we explore the multiple levels at which aspects of contemporary security are being reconfigured by the tremendous expansion in the activities of private security companies (PSCs) in non-militarized, everyday security activities. We argue that the growth and influence of the private security sector in security governance arises from shifts in social practices that cross traditional "levels of analysis" between the individual, national, and international, and also cut across divides between economics and security. These transformations are giving rise to new structures that link global and local security in novel ways, with significant impacts on the provision of security and the distribution of power in societies across the globe.

Grasping these processes requires an expansive vision of security practices, since it involves a complex set of transformations in subjectivities of private citizens (particularly their relationship to security); domestic politics and

---

[1] See Slansky, 2006; Thomson, 1994; and Avant, 2005. [2] Johnston, 1992.

policies within states; organizational and technological evolution within rapidly growing PSCs; and economic activities and practices such as neo-liberal state restructuring and free trade. These interlinked transformations in what we might call the "practices of community" in relation to security have been central to the emergence of new communities of practice that have enabled and empowered private security actors in various ways, and allowed them to emerge as significant and competent performers in a variety of different settings across the globe. These new communities of practice span the public–private and global–local divides, and mark new relations of power and structures of security provision. This is not, in other words, a straightforward privatization of security, but a complex re-articulation of relations between public and private, global and local security actors, where the categories of public and private, global and local continue to have effects on security practices even as they are being transformed.

To unravel these developments and relationships, we draw on Bourdieu's concepts of power, field, and capital. Viewing security as a field of practice constituted by a relationship between the public and the private that reflects shifting forms and distributions of capital, we argue that the growth of private security can be understood as both a result and a reflection of its increasing acquisition of forms of capital and as part of a reconfiguration of the security field. Transformations in practices of security are not just a matter of shifting norms or material capabilities – they are forms of power that provide private actors with new possibilities in the security field that change their relations with public actors, and that play powerful roles in its globalization. Close attention to security practices also shows that these new structures cannot be classified as either public or private, global or local, but draws attention to the manner in which transformations in practices at the individual and national levels generate changes in practices at the global and transnational levels.

We illustrate our argument with reference to South Africa, a country which as a percentage of gross domestic product (GDP) has the largest private security sector in the world. The growth and trajectory of South Africa's private security sector has been highly controversial and deeply politicized, and the integration of global private security companies into public–private policing partnerships shows the extent to which global and local practices are interwoven in contemporary security provision. South Africa's experience also highlights the extent to which these new communities of practice, while embedded in legitimated social structures and global norms and discourses, can lead to new exclusions and may conflict with other practices of community.

The social practices of security

The past thirty years have seen an explosion in private security services such as guarding, surveillance, and risk analysis. Private security officers now outnumber public police by a ratio of almost two to one in the United Kingdom, almost three to one in the United States, and five to one in Hong Kong; in some developing countries, the number may be as high as ten to one.[3] Globally, the commercial security market is valued at US$ 139 billion, and its expansion is forecast to continue at an annual rate of 8 percent for the foreseeable future.[4] Around the world, increasing numbers of corporations, governments, NGOs, and individuals have come to rely to varying degrees on private providers for their day-to-day security, and the past decade has witnessed the emergence of a global commercial security industry and transnational PSCs. The world's largest PSC, Group4Securicor (G4S), had an annual turnover of approximately $9 billion in 2008, and ranks as one of the 100 largest corporations in the United Kingdom by market capitalization. Operating in 110 countries, G4S has 585,000 employees, making it the largest employer on the London Stock Exchange and, according to some sources, the largest private employer on the African continent.[5] Other leading companies, such as Securitas and Prosegur, also span continents, and have come to play key roles in security provision for individuals, corporations, and communities.

While the rise of the privatized military is generally traced to the end of the Cold War and the politics of superpower retrenchment, capturing the growth of commercial security requires engagement with a broader array of shifts in social practices at the individual, national, and international levels since it is these changes that have allowed PSCs to play expanded and recognized roles as competent performers in security. Here, Bourdieu's theory of practice, and especially his concepts of capital and field, proves particularly useful.[6] For Bourdieu, the operation of power can be unraveled by examining the relationship of actors to specific types of what he terms "capital."[7] Capital takes three main forms: economic, cultural, and symbolic. As John Thompson summarizes it: "there are many different forms of capital: not only 'economic capital' in the strict sense (i.e. material wealth in the form of money, stocks and shares, etc.), but also 'cultural capital' (i.e. knowledge, skill and other cultural acquisitions, as exemplified by educational or technical qualifications), 'symbolic capital' (i.e. accumulated prestige or honor) and so on."[8] In practice, these three forms of capital are often entwined. One of Bourdieu's most important insights, however, is that there is no direct relationship between the possession of a particular form of capital and effective action or power within any given domain. This is

---

[3] Mancini, 2005.   [4] *Securitas Annual Report*, 2007, p. 13.   [5] See G4S, 2008 and n.d.

[6] For other explorations of how Bourdieu's ideas can be used in IR, see Pouliot, 2008 and 2010.

[7] These sections draw in part on Williams, 2007. Within criminology, insightful attempts to apply Bourdieu to new security networks are developed in Dupont, 2004 and 2006; see also Leander, 2005.

[8] Thompson, 1991, 14.

because capital is not a seamlessly transferable or fungible capacity, but is only realized – that is, has practical effects – within a specific sphere of activity.

Bourdieu calls these spheres of activity "fields." Different fields are characterized, constituted, and dominated by specific forms, distributions, and relations of capital – of what is valued and recognized within a field, and thus provides power within it. Since a specific field is structured by the operation and distribution of particular forms of capital, the ability to move in that field (to be a competent performer, and to be recognized as such) is tied to an agent's possession of the relevant forms of capital. Neither the distribution of capital nor its valorization within or between fields is fixed. Indeed fields are characterized by both struggles over the distribution of currently recognized forms of capital and by struggles to change the social relationship by changing the structures of valorization within the field. While some forms of capital may retain their value both within and across fields at particular points in time, they by no means do so easily, fixedly, or universally, and the structures of a field are continual arenas of struggle and power.

Seen from this perspective, the most obvious aspect of security privatization involves the accumulation of economic capital and material resources by PSCs. Historically, these resources have remained very limited in comparison to the resources of the state, and seen in the round they continue to be so. Yet the worldwide predominance of neo-liberal modes of governance has stimulated a process of privatization and outsourcing of public sector security functions previously regarded as the proper domain of the state, including prisons, prisoner transport, immigration control, and airport security.[9] The growth of private security, in general, and of large providers, in particular, is closely connected to these shifts in governance which have led to a proliferation of market opportunities and substantial, longer-term contracts from privatization and outsourcing.[10] Often, the considerable expansion both numerically and functionally of private security actors has been abetted by state advocacy of public–private partnerships (PPPs) in many areas of public policy, and the rise of private actors should not be seen as an automatic diminution in the power of the state. Instead, as David Garland has indicated, in these new arrangements the private can often be seen as a "third sector" of security provision, operating alongside the policing and punitive institutions of the state, and arising out of state policies.[11] As a result of these shifts in governance, private security has increasingly carved out a recognized role as providing a "service" that can be bought and sold on a free market.

[9] See O'Malley and Palmer, 1996; Jones and Newburn, 1998; and Quinlan, Thomas, and Gautreaux, 2001. After the events of September 11, 2001, the United States returned airport security to the public sector. Private companies continue to play this role in Europe, under public supervision; see Verkuil, 2007.

[10] See Button, 2002; Johnston, 1992; Johnston and Shearing, 2003; and Wakefield, 2003.

[11] Garland, 2001.

The latter point indicates how shifts in economic capacities alone are not enough to explain the power and influence of contemporary global private security. Equally important is the acquisition of symbolic and cultural capital. Cultural capital takes many forms, but it can broadly be understood as recognized status or authority, whether deriving from personal charisma or social background (class, for example), or conferred by institutional membership or organizational leadership. Symbolic capital is grounded in symbolic systems, pre-eminently language. But it also arises from abstract forms such as knowledge and status systems and the capital generated by their possession. Cultural and symbolic forms of capital are linked to specific forms of power. Most broadly, Bourdieu holds that cultural and symbolic power is a power that is recognized; in his formulation: "I contend that a power or capital becomes symbolic, and exerts a specific effect of domination, which I call symbolic power or symbolic violence, when it is known and recognized . . . , that is, when it is the object of an act of knowledge and recognition."[12]

The acquisition of cultural and symbolic capital is at the core of the increasingly recognized competence of private security actors, a status itself connected to wider social practices involving the commodification and technification of security, which have seen a delinking of security from public visions of welfare and security, making it a "service" or a commodity to be bought and sold in a competitive market place. Here, shifts in individual and national practices have been crucial, creating forms of symbolic and cultural capital underpinning extensive security privatization. An insightful starting point for unpacking the complex set of interlinked social transformations in the practices of crime and punishment that underpin these developments can be found in what Garland has termed the "crisis of penal modernism": a widespread skepticism toward rehabilitative approaches to criminality, accompanied by the rise of more punitive attitudes stressing the importance of incarceration and the tightening of parole provisions.[13] Since the 1970s, this increasingly punitive approach to crime has reflected profound changes in predominant understandings of criminality. While in the 1970s "welfarist" understandings of criminality as a product of deprivation or deviance predominated, this was gradually challenged by the ascendance of "economic" views of criminal behavior stressing rational calculation and opportunity structures as key variables. As a result, the welfarist component of public authorities' responses to crime have been overlain with techniques of crime control based on efficiency, surveillance, and spatial design, a process that has further encouraged and legitimated the expanded role of private actors. As security has become less tightly identified with the direct and exclusive authority of state officials and instead seen as a service that can be bought and sold on a free market, it has been in a specific way depoliticized and partially transformed from a political problem requiring

---

[12] Bourdieu, 1990, 111.   [13] Garland, 2001, 53–73.

welfarist social policy and state intervention to a technical problem amenable to private solution.

In this more market-oriented and individualized vision of security, consumers are to a degree responsible for their own security, in terms of both their behavior and of making provisions for their own protection.[14] The prevalence of risk-based thinking and security technologies is also revealing in this context. Risk is not simply a synonym for danger; it is a particular way of thinking about and responding to potential dangers. Risk is preventative, not restorative. Primarily actuarial and calculative, it works by designing and controlling spaces, through the collection of statistics and the production of categories of danger, and by surveillance. Risk is, therefore, a way of approaching security that can be deployed by private actors just as effectively as by public ones. It is also broadly universalizable – in principle applicable regardless of local conceptions of order and justice. Thus, as security has been considered increasingly as a matter of risk mentalities, of design, planning, and prevention, rather than as an issue of reactive policing and public policy, the capacity of private actors to claim expertise – to acquire cultural and symbolic capital and to exercise power – has increased.

While it is often recognized that domestically these transformations have resulted in a more "pluralized" or "hybrid" security provision,[15] it is less frequently noted that they have also provided the conditions for the emergence of new transnational security actors. Empowered by the importation of neo-liberal logics and by large-scale domestic security markets, PSCs have become well-resourced, corporate structures possessing the material, organizational, and ideational capacities to operate on increasingly global scales. Commodification constitutes security as a technique and a form of expert knowledge that, while specialized, is by no means the sole purview of public (or national) authorities, and gives PSCs the possibility to become recognized and competent performers in the technical and managerial dimensions of security provision, as well as in broader forms of risk analysis and intelligence.

The commodification of security as a "service" also enables PSCs to draw upon powerful market logics in the expansion and transnationalization of their activities. As neo-liberal political and economic structures have become increasingly widespread, this cultural capital is not restricted to a specific jurisdiction. In principle, it is extendable across borders, and as providers of a legitimately traded service/commodity, private security actors are able to connect their activities to the broader structures of market liberalism and free trade. Tellingly, the World Trade Organization (WTO) now includes private security in the General Agreement on Trade in Services (GATS), thus providing a strong incentive for member states to allow free and fair competition in security

[14] See O'Malley and Palmer, 1996; and Loader, 1999.
[15] See Johnston, 1992; Jones and Newburn, 1998; and Wood and Dupont, 2006.

services. Similarly, the European Union has also sought to promote free trade in security services across Europe as part of its Services Directive. While security remains the prerogative of the state in many areas of policing, the capacity to cast security as a politically neutral service legitimately provided by the private sector allows global private security firms to draw upon logics of free trade to facilitate their entry into new markets, even where this is resisted by the host state.

In sum, at the heart of the globalization of private security are transformations in security practices, shifts in "background knowledge" that make the turn to private security strategies and "competent" providers seem increasingly rational, reasonable, and even mundane. These transformations cannot be located solely at the individual, state, or international levels, but are the consequences of interrelated social practices that cut across these divisions. Economic globalization and the neo-liberal restructuring of the state has combined with shifts in moral logics of criminality, economistic understandings of criminal behavior, and specific forms of depoliticization to make the current situation possible. One of the benefits of a practice approach is that it allows these domains and dynamics to be connected and explored as part of an interacting field.

A further advantage of seeing these processes from the perspective of Bourdieu's concept of capital is that capital is only realized in a field – something that is particularly significant in the security field, with its traditionally tight connections to state sovereignty and public authority. While capacities may have been developed by PSCs (and can in general, abstract terms be identified in terms of amounts of financial capital or socially recognized forms of expertise, for instance), no automatic relationship exists between the possession of a capacity (material resources, for example) and effective capacity. Such capacities do not translate automatically into power and effective action, much less the domination of security practices.

In fact, in security as in other domains of practice, the increasing accumulation of a given form of capital in the absence of other forms may paradoxically disempower actors while empowering competitors in the field. In the area of military privatization, for instance, the increasing material capacity of private military firms such as Executive Outcomes in the 1990s (enhanced weaponry, transport capacities, and even air support) certainly marked an increase in their material capacities and power. However, it also contributed to increased alarm about the company and its activities and a reassertion of the legitimacy of state actors and claims about their necessary and legitimate dominance in the security domain. The increase in material capital thus led, paradoxically, to a decrease in the effective capacity of the company to operate: a paradox that is the result of the operation of the field and the relative lack of symbolic and cultural capital possessed by this type of private military firm. Power in a specific field is practical, not arithmetic, and it depends on the forms and distribution of relevant capital.

The symbolic capital of the public

To understand the security field, it is necessary to stress its specific relational structure, to see how it is structured by the relation between public and private, not by their straightforward opposition or their seamless cooperation. In other words, while it is analytically helpful to see the public and private as structuring oppositions constituting the field, it is equally important to note how in practice public and private are already always interpenetrating in the constitution of both public and private security actors, and how this fact impacts security as a field of practice. By this, we do not just mean that private actors function in a setting that also includes public agents (military, paramilitary, police), but also that the positions of these actors have to be seen in the context of their relative possession of the multiple forms of capital operating in the field. As such, an analysis of the security field requires not only the location of shifting material capacities, but also an excavation of the deep historical roots of the security field and its connections to the conceptual and institutional structures of modern understandings of politics and sovereignty. Recognizing these connections is by no means a purely academic exercise; on the contrary, it is essential to an appreciation of the distribution of capital in security practice, and hence to who gets secured, and how.

The growing role of private security is not a simple question of privatization, and the transfer of previously public functions to private actors, but is instead a re-articulation of the relationships between the public and the private, the global and the local within the security field. The security field remains structured in important ways by its connections to public authorities and conceptions of the public good. The idea that security is a public good is an almost inescapable aspect of modern politics. Indeed, one could claim that within the dominant traditions of modern political thought it is almost impossible not to think of security in this way. It is not our intention here to engage in the numerous political and theoretical debates that arise from this understanding of security. Instead, our point is a rather simple one: that the centrality of security as a public good – and its opposition or contrast to security as a private good – in modern conceptions of politics is one of the defining oppositions constituting the field of security. It is also a source of power within that field. Most obviously, it is a key aspect of the institutional and material power of modern police forces, which generate political support and material resources on the basis of their recognized role as agents and guardians of the public good of security. It also underpins the unique universal jurisdictional reach of the police – their right to go anywhere – that so clearly distinguishes them from private security.[16] Equally, it links the agencies of state security directly with the operation of the judiciary, and through this to the powerful idea of the rule of

---

[16] Jones and Newburn, 1998.

law, of a legal (and security) order applying equally to all. Finally, of course, it is part of the ability in *extremis* to mobilize other coercive agencies of the state, including the military and intelligence services, to secure the public good.

More broadly, as Ian Loader and Neil Walker have argued at length, the idea of security as a public good represents an important part of the "structure of feeling" of citizens of modern polities.[17] One need perhaps not go so far as Loader and Walker in their declaration that the public good of security is *the* constitutive feature of societies capable of providing a full range of other public goods to recognize that this claim – and the corresponding charge that this principle is under threat from processes of security privatization – is not just a value or an abstract philosophic principle; it is also a symbolic resource, a form of capital that represents considerable power within the security field. This symbolic capital is crucial in the operation of public authorities and in their relationship to other actors in the security field. At the most straightforward level, the linking of the private and the foreign provides state actors with the capacity to link the public-ness of security to the defense of sovereignty. Globalized security privatization can thus potentially be cast as an issue of national security, enhancing the power of state actors who draw upon their institutional positions and their symbolic power as the representatives of national public security to define themselves and the provision of security in general in opposition to the impact of global private security, and to limit its influence.

To an important extent, therefore, the field of security is defined by a relational opposition to the private, and thus to the idea of private security and the influence of private economic capital on the provision of security. At the same time, however, the modern liberal state justifies and legitimizes its role precisely on the basis of the security of the individual and, in many cases, of property. In other words, we do not have a "state" pole that stands self-sufficiently in contrast to a "private" pole; while it may be useful to use these two concepts as abstract parameters of the field, in actuality we have a field in which the public–private relationship and its tension is intrinsic to the place of the state in the security field. In terms of power, this means that the position and symbolic capital of the state is not one-dimensional and linear: it is already implicated in a tension-filled relation to the private.

Moreover, public security agencies and logics are today embedded in global structures that can significantly impact their relationship to security privatization and their ability to mobilize the symbolic and cultural capital provided by an exclusionary sovereignty. The spread of these global norms means that all states operate in a context where, to admittedly differing degrees, they are subject to internationally dominant understandings of how security is best provided, including the legitimacy of the "service" of private security. The

---

[17] Loader and Walker, 2007.

increasing power of property rights via the extension of (often neo-) liberal economic ideas and structures has provided a global dimension to the public–private relationship, allowing private security to counter sovereigntist claims concerning the necessary monopoly of state security by linking it to the rights of individuals and propertyholders legitimately to provide for their own security by means of their own choosing, transnational or otherwise. This has chimed perfectly with processes of commodification, whereby security can be portrayed as a service just like any other, legitimately flowing across borders in a liberal world economy. The result is that a pure logic of "state" security, in which decisions about the provision of internal security are completely divorced from transnational influence, is increasingly rare. As part of this (essentially liberal) process, the individual's right to security, and the question of how best to provide for it, is implicated in global norms about legitimate sovereignty and security provision.

The forms of capital possessed by private and public actors thus exist in a dynamic tension. Each is also subject to reversals that are crucial in the operation of the security field as a whole. The state's claim to the public good of security, for instance, can be eroded or reversed if the state fails in this task, or is perceived as doing so. In this way, its source of symbolic power can paradoxically become a resource for others to challenge its monopoly – to assert that in the light of this failure it is necessary to legitimate the entrance of other – e.g. private – actors into the security field, even if this is only to support the state's limited abilities, or to exercise a partial right to self-protection in the absence (or perceived absence) of adequate public protection. In other cases, the state has often actively encouraged this process. This is not a zero-sum devaluation of its position, but it has contributed to the creation of actors with symbolic capital that they can deploy in the field.

Transformations and security practice in South Africa

Developments in the security sector in South Africa provide telling illustrations of how these various transformations affect and constitute new communities of practice that span the global–local, public–private divides.[18] Today, South Africa has more than 6,392 PSCs, employing 375,315 active security officers,[19] but the most rapid expansion took place in the immediate post-transition period. By the end of apartheid in 1994, there were three times as many private security personnel as public police officers, and from 1997 to 2000 the number of private security officers grew from 115,000 to 166,000.[20] South Africa's security market thus became one of the fastest-growing in the world,

---

[18] This section draws on several fieldwork visits to South Africa and Cape Town in the period 2002–2006.
[19] Private Security Industry Regulatory Authority, 2009, 10.
[20] Shaw and Shearing, 1998; additional data provided by a South African PSC.

experiencing annual growth rates of 30 percent in the mid-1990s and undergoing a substantial consolidation.[21] The rapid expansion of the market
attracted the attention of transnational PSCs looking for profitable acquisitions
and opportunities and, according to one report, foreign investors poured about
R187 million into the private security industry in 2000–2001.[22]

This massive growth of the private security sector and the entrance of foreign
firms soon became a source of considerable political controversy. As the relative
balance between public policing and private security tipped in favor of the private,
in terms of both personnel and firepower, the underresourced police forces at
times jealously guarded their status and role *vis-à-vis* a highly capitalized private
sector that sported not only new patrol vehicles, but frequently also the very latest
in surveillance and communications technologies. Police and politicians alike
questioned private security's "real" commitment to the reduction of crime,
pointing to the obvious connection between commercial success and the continuation and fear of crime. While the idea of companies "profiting from crime" was
antithetical to the worldview of many ANC politicians, the police regarded it as an
affront to their professional obligation to "protect life and property," regardless
of ability to pay. In addition, the fact that a largely white-owned sector employed
a predominantly low-paid, black labor force to guard white wealth, combined
with the fact that many of South Africa's PSCs were owned and managed by
former officers of the apartheid state's oppressive apparatuses, gave rise to fears
and allegations that the sector harbored right-wing sympathies, and that private
militias were being formed by security companies.[23] Private security was accordingly seen as an obstacle, and even a potential threat, to South Africa's fledgling
democracy.

Equally significantly for our case here, suspicions were voiced that foreign
involvement in the sector might be used to destabilize the new political order. In
1995, for example, the Deputy Minister of Intelligence Services, Joe Nhlanhla,
expressed concern that "third force elements see the private security industry as
a haven from where to continue their third force activities of destabilization."[24]
Similar opinions were voiced by the Coordinator for Intelligence, Linda Mti,
who maintained that "the connection that some of the actors in the private
security companies have with foreign intelligence services and the similarity of
objectives informed by their past co-operation in the Cold War era ... makes
them free agents to be exploited for espionage activities."[25] As the Chairman of
the Parliamentary Committee on Safety and Security summed it up: "This is a
very sensitive industry."[26]

[21] Credit Suisse/First Boston, 2001, 7.   [22] FDI, 2001.
[23] Irish, 1999; Schönteich, 1999; and Hough, 2002.   [24] Hough, 2002.
[25] Quoted in Hough, 2002, 5.
[26] Cauvin, 2001. Although country-specific in their details, these concerns are by no means
unique to South Africa.

These suspicions found a telling expression in October 2001, when the Parliamentary Committee on Safety and Security proposed to ban foreign ownership in the private security sector on grounds that it constituted a threat to national security.[27] The proposal brought a swift reaction that illustrates the forms of capital employed within South Africa's security field, as well as the extent to which this community of practice spans the public–private and the global–local. The global private security firms quickly mounted a campaign – coordinated through a South African lobbying and public relations firm – to counter the proposed Bill. As a spokesman for Securicor Gray said: "We made use of as many networks as we could in our determination to get our message across to the government in a firm but non-confrontational manner."[28] This, according to one of the individuals central to the formulation of the strategy, involved mobilizing international as well as domestic networks.[29] The latter included members of the political opposition, while the key international actors were the diplomatic representatives of the foreign companies' states of origin – the United Kingdom and Denmark, in particular. Their key argument was that the proposed regulation represented a restriction on trade in services, with the British High Commission stating that "we are concerned" and opining that "the proposed law could violate a 1998 trade agreement between the countries."[30] Moreover, it was argued that the legislation would be taken as a clear sign that South Africa was breaching liberal economic principles, and that foreign investment in all sectors (not merely security) was neither welcome nor secure in the country. As a director of BusinessMap, a Johannesburg-based investor intelligence consultancy, made the connection: "The suddenness of the announcement increases uncertainty for foreign investors in all sectors."[31]

In this campaign, the PSCs drew significant symbolic capital from the commodification of security. Tellingly, for example, their strategy was directed not only – or even primarily – toward the Parliamentary Committee, but focused instead on the office of the President and the Finance Minister (both of whom were out of the country on official business when the legislative proposal was announced), and the Minister of Trade – with the latter assuring the companies through a spokesman that he "thinks there are other ways to meet national security concerns ... and he will take up the matter this week with the minister of safety and security."[32] The campaign was remarkably successful, with the proposed legislation dropping from sight in a matter of days, reportedly quashed primarily by the Minister of Finance, Trevor

---

[27] See Abrahamsen and Williams, 2006; and Cauvin, 2001.
[28] FDI, 2001. Securicor Gray was at the time owned by the UK company Securicor, which later merged with Group4 to form G4S.
[29] Interview with a Securicor Gray official, Pretoria, April 2003. [30] Cauvin, 2001.
[31] FDI, 2001. [32] Cauvin, 2001.

Manuel.[33] As the Chairperson of the Safety and Security Committee sub-sequently reflected, "we were persuaded by the big companies to drop the ban."[34]

This incident illustrates key connections between shifting security practices, power, and the globalization of commercial security. The ability of global PSCs to present their activities as a service and to link their operations to the authority of market principles (and sanctions) played a crucial role. Principles of free trade linked to a specifically depoliticized vision of security successfully trumped concerns for national security and calls for the protection of domestic industry. By embedding security privatization in broader global norms connected to processes of commodification and responsibilization, the home states of the foreign companies were able to intercede on their behalf by using commercial arguments and forms of market-norm coercion, skirting the much more sensitive and difficult ground of "national security" policy. The symbolic power of the public had thus been re-articulated in light of the growing capital of both private and global actors to claim security as a service like any other.

Significantly, however, while this particular attempt to legislate the industry failed, the result has not been a general supplanting of the public by the private, or the national by the global. Over time, the South African private security sector has been subject to increasing state oversight and regulation. This regulation, particularly through mechanisms and bodies that involve the direct participation of those being regulated, marks a process of normalization and legitimation, one that to varying degrees integrates private actors into public decision-making institutions and processes. Partly as a result of regulation, there is now an increased acceptance of private security, including global firms, in South Africa, and the private is increasingly integrated into public–private policing partnerships. In the words of the South African Police Service (SAPS), there is a need for "the police, the public, elected officials, government, business and other agencies to work in partnership to address crime and community safety."[35] The Department of Community Safety has similarly concluded that the "SA Police Service can no longer be seen as the sole agency responsible for fighting crime ... other sectors of society with a force multiplying capacity must be called on to support the SA Police Service in their efforts."[36] As part of this

[33] Allegedly, Manuel first heard of the proposal when on a trip to Japan to encourage foreign investment. Key individuals behind the campaign also argued, probably with some justification, that the legislation reflected the interests of elements of the domestic security industry that saw an opportunity to see off competition and potentially pick up foreign-owned companies at distressed prices. Interviews, Cape Town and Pretoria, April 2003; and Abrahamsen and Williams, 2006.
[34] Interview with Mululeki George, MP, Chairperson, Safety and Security Committee, Cape Town, April 2003.
[35] Quoted in Berg, 2004, 227.   [36] Department of Community Safety, 2004, 6.

transformation, some tasks have been specifically assigned as "private" – all police stations across South Africa are now, for example, guarded by PSCs in recognition that commercial guards are cheaper than police officers – while much day-to-day policing has been reframed as a partnership with a multiplicity of private actors and local communities. Shifting security practices should not, therefore, be seen as simple processes of privatization, although there is no doubt they have contributed substantially to the power of private actors. Instead, they involve a re-articulation of the relationship between the public and private where the state retains a key role.

The manner in which the various transformations in security practices come together to produce and structure specific fields can be seen in the activities of the Cape Town Central City Improvement District (CCID). The CCID is an initiative of the Cape Town Partnership, a not-for-profit company founded in 1999 by the City Council and the local business community. The main aim of the Partnership is to reverse urban decay and prevent capital flight from the city center to surrounding suburbs and business parks. As part of this effort, the CCID was established in November 2000, after the majority of property owners, or ratepayers, in the area agreed to the payment of an additional levy on their council bill. Today, the CCID collects about R15 million annually from the 1,200 ratepayers, of which approximately 51 percent is allocated to security. The remainder is spent on the CCID's other three areas of responsibility – cleaning (22 percent), marketing (11 percent), and social development (3 percent, a recent decline from 8 percent), while 13 percent is allocated for administration.

The CCID is in effect a large-scale partnership policing effort aimed at making central Cape Town safe and secure; an international city and a first-class tourist destination.[37] To accomplish this goal, the world's largest PSC, G4S, has been contracted as the main security provider. At the start of the initiative, the CCID security force consisted of only seven officers, but it has since expanded to a total of six patrol vehicles, ten horse mounted officers, and sixty foot patrol officers providing a twenty-four-hour (often armed) security presence in the city center. At night, the city is patrolled by forty officers, supported by six vehicles. As a result, the presence of security personnel in the city has increased noticeably, and CCID vehicles and foot patrols are frequently encountered throughout Cape Town's relatively compact city center.

To a significant extent, the security of central Cape Town has been devolved to the largest security company in the world. Importantly, the CCID is different from the more long-standing practice of private guarding of "public private spaces"[38] such as shopping centers – here, a private company is involved in policing the public space of the city. The visibility of G4S' mounted, foot, and mobile patrols far exceeds that of the police in Cape Town. Both the City Police and the SAPS concentrate their efforts in the poorer areas of town, where crime

---

[37] CCID Cape Town, n.d.   [38] Shearing and Stenning, 1981.

rates are highest, and the City Police has dedicated only two mobile patrols to the city center. Moreover, the police do not conduct foot patrols. Yet, it would be incorrect to perceive the police as absent from Cape Town's security arrangement. G4S officers are closely networked with the police, especially the City Police, but also the SAPS, often in novel and surprising ways. The CCID/G4S branded patrol vehicles, for example, include a City Police officer, but there are no police markings on the car. The CCID security patrols are also linked to the City Police control room by radio. Furthermore, G4S operates the Strategic Surveillance Unit (SSU), the control room that supervises Cape Town's 170 closed-circuit television cameras. The SSU is manned by around fifty G4S officers, reinforced by eight City Police officers, and is in direct contact with the SAPS as well as the City Police, thus facilitating mobile response to incidents. G4S also participates in weekly sector policing forums to identify potential problems, share information, and coordinate the provision of security with the SAPS and the City Police. The company also provides support to police operations within the CCID – for example, by providing perimeter security when police are searching a building or an area. Because of this extensive and close collaboration (seen also in the approximately fifteen other City Improvement Districts (CIDs) in and around Cape Town), G4S managers in interviews often characterized the CIDs as a "paradigm shift" in the provision of security.

The CCID constitutes a new community of practice that spans the public–private, global–local divides. Within this community, a global PSC is recognized as a crucial component and a competent performer, whose material and symbolic capital is, in turn, linked in important ways to global discourses and practices. Market principles and economic capital exercise a particularly powerful influence, and the power of G4S derives in large part from the company acting as the agent of the city's property owners, and it is widely seen as entirely legitimate that ratepayers fund and directly participate in overseeing a system with security at its core.[39] The practitioners of security go well beyond state agents, even as the participation of those agents is essential to new security practices. The CCID is a contractual community between rate-payers, businesses, and the City Council, and security is regarded as a service like any other, to be bought from the best-qualified provider. The commodification of security enables the CCID to present itself as a consumer (as opposed to a client) of security, actively making choices about security provision within a marketplace where public authorities are only one possible provider. The influence of transnational policing models of community policing and partnership, spearheaded by international advisors and financed by development budgets, has further encouraged this development and underlines the presence

---

[39] This is not to say that the arrangements are without political opposition or public concern, as we discuss on p. 326.

of the global in the local.[40] In this sense, the CIDs are in part a consequence of the shift towards neo-liberal policies, but they also reflect a more marketized approach to civic management.[41] Within this marketplace, the CCIDs' choice of G4S was directly related to the company's extensive organizational and financial resources, its expertise, technical and managerial capabilities, as well as its global reputation and brand recognition. In short, the company's possession of material, symbolic, and cultural capital allowed it to establish a central position within South Africa's security sector.

At the same time, the security field remains in important ways structured by the symbolic capital of the public. The CCID is far from entirely private; the City Council makes up one-third of the Cape Town Partnership, and the public police play an important role in security provision. In this way, G4S derives considerable legitimacy precisely from its connection to the symbolic capital of the public and its incorporation into "hybrid" security assemblages. Put differently, its legality and relationship to law and order maintenance bestows considerable symbolic and cultural capital on private security, but not necessarily at the expense of the state. Indeed, in Cape Town – and, arguably, in South Africa more generally – it seems that PSCs have to an important extent helped secure the authority of the state by allowing for the presence of a much larger security force than the state alone could have afforded, thus providing important material and symbolic resources for combating post-transition insecurity, urban blight, and capital flight. In brief, the utilization of private security resources has made it easier for the government to claim that it is "doing something about crime."[42] In this way, the public has to a significant extent been able to mobilize the economic capital of the private sector to strengthen its own symbolic position, both nationally and internationally.

Approached from the perspective of practice, the CCID appears as a new community of security practice, where private actors have been empowered by the capital derived from transformations in broader social processes. Yet the effects of these new communities of practice are by no means neutral: they are also part of shifts in social power and can lead to new exclusions, where new communities of practice conflict with existing practices of community. In the CCID, those who pay are also able to play a powerful role in determining the security agenda, or to speak on behalf of or represent the "community." In Cape

---

[40] On the influence of international policing models in South Africa, see Dixon, 2007; and van der Spuy, 2000.

[41] Miraftab, 2007.

[42] The exact achievements of the CCID in terms of crime reduction are difficult to assess, due to a lack of local statistics and independent evaluations. Some claim a 60 percent drop in crime, particularly in the most common forms of offence, such as pickpocketing, mugging, and theft from cars. Research in 2002 showed that 52 percent of respondents felt safe in the city center, compared to only 17 percent only two years earlier. Urban capital flight also appears to have been reversed. See Palmary, 2002; Sylvester, 2002; and Smith, 2007.

Town this has had significant implications in terms of who gets secured, and how, and has led to a focus on "cleaning up the city." There are more than faint echoes of the American neoconservative "broken windows" thesis in the public discourse of the CCID.[43] In the words of the Provincial Development Council of the Western Cape: "In order to become a 'world class city' ... we must vanquish 'crime and grime' ... and remove the 'undesirable elements.'"[44] While this has resulted in an impressive twenty-four-hour cleaning service, it has also generated a security effort focused on "order maintenance" and on reducing what are often described as "minor nuisances" like beggars, vagrants, informal parking assistants, and street children. G4S officers are instructed to "move along" beggars congregating at intersections. For "undesirable elements," such as street children and vagrants, the CCID has accordingly meant increased harassment and more frequent arrest. Street children are regarded as a special problem, allegedly perceived by Capetonians and tourists alike as both a nuisance and as responsible for the majority of petty crime.[45] G4S officers frequently transport street children to so-called safe houses, in order to get them off the street, in full knowledge that they will be back the next day. A number of by-laws have also been passed to facilitate the clean-up of Cape Town, including prohibition of begging which inhibits or obstructs the public, begging within 6 meters of an automatic teller machine/cash point, as well as washing and drying clothes on city streets.[46]

For sections of the population in Cape Town, the altered politics of protection brought about by the CCID is thus experienced as an increasing restriction of access, as a combination of public by-laws and private enforcement serves to prevent the poor and the homeless from utilizing the city's public spaces, where they frequently make their living through various forms of informal trading. The comparison to the apartheid era is obvious, but now these dividing practices are continued through the mobilization of "community" and PPPs, and the incorporation of active, responsible citizens of all races. And, unlike apartheid proper, it is sustained by global transformations in economics and social practices.

It would be both wrong and insincere to suggest that the CCID, the police, or the private security sector, are unaware of these issues. All actors are conscious of the potential divisiveness of "community" even as new public–private "communities of [security] practice" are reconfiguring the social landscape, and as different sections of the population make unequal use of available (including private) resources to improve their security. For the police, partnership policing is precisely a manner of extending their resources further, allowing more affluent communities to contribute to their own security while the police

---

[43] Wilson and Kelling, 2004.   [44] Quoted in Berg, 2004, 242.   [45] Sylvester, 2002.
[46] City of Cape Town, n.d. For a highly critical view of the CCID along these lines, see Samara, 2003.

claim to concentrate their efforts in less privileged areas. The Cape Town Partnership and its security provider, G4S, are also aware of the social implications and symbolic politics of its operations, and recognize that the causes of vagrancy and homelessness are social and political and cannot be solved by security measures alone. However, security practices have their own social and political implications, and the relationship between a commodified contractual security structure, PPPs, and principles of equal (and democratic) politics and policing entwine these emerging practices with questions of legitimacy that are among the most difficult and challenging in increasingly globalized political domains.

Conclusion

Bourdieu's theory of practice, with its stress on the complex relations between capital and field, provides one illustration of the theoretical agenda and possibilities opened up by foregrounding international practices. However, as our analysis shows, it also demonstrates some of the substantial challenges posed by such an agenda. Tracing the links between micro- and macro-processes often requires crossing disciplinary boundaries (such as those between criminology, sociology, and IR). This is not an easy task, intellectually or practically, and involves investments of time and a commitment to interdisciplinarity that (despite its oft-declared necessity) is frequently at odds with the structures and imperatives of modern social science and academic life. Perhaps even more challengingly, theories of practice often reflect their origins in highly localized domains of analysis, extended at most to the level of the nation-state. It is not an accident that such theories are particularly popular and most fully developed in anthropologically detailed research (as were many of Bourdieu's most incisive studies). Extending these frameworks to the international confronts problems of scale and depth. It is difficult to imagine the size of a research program and team that would be required to provide an analysis of international practices at the level of empirical detail and sophistication found in more focused sociological studies. Our analysis of global security privatization here is a case in point, forced as it is to bracket the concept of the *habitus* that Bourdieu sees as central, and treating social institutions in the developed and developing worlds (and mediating structures such as international trade institutions) at rather high levels of abstraction. To a large degree, these tradeoffs are inevitable, and hopefully worth the sacrifice, if some of the insights of practice theories are to better inform understandings of global processes. But they also exemplify the challenges faced by IR and virtually every other traditional social science discipline (including sociology and anthropology) in a globalizing world that fits increasingly few of the analytic or political categories, or institutional divisions of research labor, that continue to reflect their origins in the development of the modern nation-state.

The practices of security, and especially international security, have traditionally been seen as dominated by material power, coercion, and state-centrism. There is no doubt that material power and the capacity to mobilize and control coercion plays a crucial role at any level of security, from policing to war. But, as this chapter shows, to understand the dynamics of security privatization it is necessary to see it as operating in a field constituted not only by coercive or material power but also by competing forms of symbolic and cultural capital. This is especially important when considering the impact of private economic capital – the ability to buy security in a market – because security privatization cannot be seen simply as the increasing domination of the security field by private economic capital. On the contrary, the relationship between forms of capital is essential in understanding the security field, and the dynamics of security privatization. The impact of economic capital is realized in the security field only through a complex set of relations that often results in its revaluation, a limitation of its power as other actors seek to structure the field in such a way that the possession of economic power also becomes a partial weakness or liability, rather than a straightforward component of an actor's power.

Security privatization and the rise of global PSCs are connected to shifts at all three of the levels laid out by Adler and Pouliot in Chapter 1 in this volume: that is, in subjectivities, specific practices, and social orders. Individuals' decisions about providing (or not) for their security through commercial arrangements, shifting moral registers surrounding criminality, processes of responsibilization and security commodification, neo-liberal public policy initiatives, international economic structures, and security discourses have combined, as local or national shifts in different parts of the globe contribute to the development of transnationalized security practices where public and private agents are "fitted together" in diverse yet powerful ways. These new structures – or, as we call them elsewhere, "global security assemblages"[47] – are important sites of political struggle, with wider impacts on the distribution and operation of social and political power. Seeing security as a social practice allows us to connect these seemingly disparate dynamics, to demonstrate the connections between transformations in micro- and macro-practices in diverse and yet interrelated local and global domains, and thus better to explain the emergence of global actors and local effects which are part of increasingly significant transformations in global security provision.

References

Abrahamsen, Rita and Michael C. Williams, 2006. Privatisation, Globalisation, and the Politics of Protection in South Africa. In *The Politics of Protection: Sites of*

[47] Abrahamsen and Williams, 2011.

Insecurity and Political Agency, edited by Jef Huysmans, Andrew Dobson, and Raia Prokhovnik, 34–47. London: Routledge.

2011. *Security Beyond the State: Private Security in International Politics.* Cambridge: Cambridge University Press.

Avant, Deborah D., 2005. *The Market for Force: The Consequences of Privatizing Security.* Cambridge: Cambridge University Press.

Berg, Julie, 2004. Private Policing in South Africa: The Cape Town City Improvement District – Pluralisation in Practice. *Society in Transition* 35 (2): 224–250.

Bourdieu, Pierre, 1990. *In Other Words: Essays Towards a Reflexive Sociology.* Translated by Matthew Adamson. Stanford: Stanford University Press.

Button, Mark, 2002. *Private Policing.* London: Willan.

Cauvin, Henri E., 2001. "Homegrown Guards," *New York Times.* October 9, 2001, B3.

CCID Cape Town, n.d. Cape Town Partnership. Available at www.capetownpartnership.co.za/ccid/ccid-overview. Accessed November 29, 2010.

City of Cape Town, n.d. Bylaws. Available at www.capetown.gov.za/en/bylaws/Pages/Home.aspx. Accessed November 29, 2010.

Credit Suisse/First Boston, 2001. *Review of the South African Private Security Industry.* Boston: Credit Suisse/First Boston, February 7.

Department of Community Safety, 2004. Provincial Government Western Cape: Strategic Plan 2003/04 to 2005/06. Cape Town: Government Printer.

Dixon, Bill, 2007. Globalising the Local: A Genealogy of Sector Policing in South Africa. *International Relations* 21 (2): 163–182.

Dupont, Benoît, 2004. Security in the Age of Networks. *Policing and Society* 14 (1): 76–91.

2006. Power Struggles in the Field of Security: Implications for Democratic Transformation. In *Democracy, Society, and the Governance of Security,* edited by Jennifer Wood and Benoît Dupont, 86–110. Cambridge: Cambridge University Press.

FDI, 2001. South African Security Sector Wins Bill Reprieve. *FDI Magazine.* November 2, 2001.

G4S, 2008. G4S and UNI Sign Global Agreement. Available at www.g4s.com/en/Media Centre/News/2008/12/16/G4S and UNI sign global agreement. Accessed November 29, 2010.

n.d. Key Facts and Figures. Available at www.g4s.com/en/Media Centre/Key facts and figures. Accessed November 29, 2010.

Garland, David, 2001. *The Culture of Control: Crime and Social Order in Contemporary Society.* Oxford: Oxford University Press.

Hough, Mike, 2002. Private and Public Security in the RSA: Competition or Cooperation? *Strategic Review for Southern Africa* 24 (2): 78–96.

Irish, Jenny, 1999. *Policing for Profit: The Future of South Africa's Private Security Industry.* Pretoria: Institute for Security Studies.

Johnston, Les, 1992. *The Rebirth of Private Policing.* London: Routledge.

Johnston, Les and Clifford Shearing, 2003. *Governing Security: Explorations in Policing and Justice*. London: Routledge.

Jones, Trevor and Tim Newburn, 1998. *Private Security and Public Policing*. Oxford: Clarendon Press.

Leander, Anna, 2005. The Power to Construct International Security: On the Significance of Private Military Companies. *Millennium* 33 (3): 803–826.

Loader, Ian, 1999. Consumer Culture and the Commodification of Policing and Security. *Sociology* 33 (2): 373–392.

Loader, Ian and Neil Walker, 2007. *Civilizing Security*. Cambridge: Cambridge University Press.

Mancini, Francesco, 2005. *In Good Company? The Role of Business in Security Sector Reform*. London: Demos.

Miraftab, Faranak, 2007. Governing Post-Apartheid Spatiality: Implementing City Improvement Districts in Cape Town. *Antipode* 39 (4): 602–626.

O'Malley, Pat and Darren Palmer, 1996. Post-Keynesian Policing. *Economy and Society* 25 (2): 137–155.

Palmary, Ingrid, 2002. Shifting Agendas: Crime Prevention in the Major Cities. In *Crime Prevention Partnerships: Lessons from Practice*, edited by Eric Pelser, 27–46. Pretoria: Institute for Security Studies.

Pouliot, Vincent, 2008. The Logic of Practicality: A Theory of Practice of Security Communities. *International Organization* 62 (2): 257–288.

2010. *International Security in Practice: The Politics of NATO–Russia Diplomacy*. Cambridge: Cambridge University Press.

Private Security Industry Regulatory Authority, 2009. *Annual Report 2008/2009*. Pretoria: Private Security Industry Regulatory Authority.

Quinlan, J. Michael, Charles W. Thomas, and Sherril Gautreaux, 2001. The Privatization of Correctional Facilities. In *Privatizing Governmental Functions*, edited by Deborah Ballati, Chapter 10. New York: Law Journal Press.

Samara, Tony Roshan, 2003. State Security in Transition: The War on Crime in Post-Apartheid South Africa. *Social Identities* 9 (2): 277–312.

Schönteich, Martin, 1999. Fighting Crime with Private Muscle: The Private Sector and Crime Prevention. *African Security Review* 8 (5): 65–75.

Securitas, 2007. *Annual Report 2007*. Stockholm: Securitas.

Shaw, Mark and Clifford Shearing, 1998. Reshaping Security: An Examination of the Governance of Security in South Africa. *African Security Review* 7 (3): 3–12.

Shearing, Clifford D. and Phillip C. Stenning, 1981. Modern Private Security: Its Growth and Implications. In *Crime and Justice: An Annual Review of Research*, Vol. 3, edited by Michael Tonry and Noval Morris, 193–245. Chicago: University of Chicago Press.

Slansky, David, 2006. Private Police and Democracy. *American Criminal Law Review* 43 (89): 89–105.

Smith, Anna-Marie, 2007. "South Africa: Mother City as a Role Model," *Business Day* (Johannesburg). November 9, 2007.

Sylvester, Elliott, 2002. "It's Official: Cape Town is Clean and Safe," *Cape Argus*. March 6, 2002.

Thompson, John B., 1991. Editor's Introduction. In Pierre Bourdieu. *Language and Symbolic Power*, edited by John B. Thompson, 1–31. Cambridge: Cambridge University Press.

Thomson, Janice E., 1994. *Mercenaries, Pirates and Sovereigns: State-Building and Extraterritorial Violence in Early Modern Europe*. Princeton: Princeton University Press.

Van Der Spuy, Elrena, 2000. Foreign Donor Assistance and Policing Reform in South Africa. *Policing and Society* 10 (4): 343–436.

Verkuil, Paul R., 2007. *Outsourcing Sovereignty: Why Privatization of Government Function Threatens Democracy and What We Can Do about It*. Cambridge: Cambridge University Press.

Wakefield, Alison, 2003. *Selling Security: The Private Policing of Public Space*. London: Willan.

Williams, Michael C., 2007. *Culture and Security: Symbolic Power and the Politics of International Security*. New York: Routledge.

Wilson, James Q. and George L. Kelling, 2004. Broken Windows: The Police and Neighborhood Safety. In *Neoconservatism*, edited by Irwin Stelzer, 151–166. London: Atlantic Books.

Wood, Jennifer and Benoît Dupont, eds., 2006. *Democracy, Society, and the Governance of Security*. Cambridge: Cambridge University Press.

PART V

Conclusion

13 | *Practices of theory*

RAYMOND D. DUVALL AND ARJUN CHOWDHURY

Introduction: three questions

Practice makes perfect, or so the adage has it. But does that principle apply to the scholarly practices of theorizing international politics? Will the practice of centering practices as objects of analysis lead to an improved (if still imperfect) theoretic account? Will it better enable the practitioners of the discipline of International Relations (IR) to engage in productive intertheoretic or interparadigmatic dialogue and, in doing so, to transcend the oft-invoked binaries of material vs. ideational perspectives and agential vs. structural emphases? The contributors to this volume maintain that it will: if IR scholars were regularly to focus attention on "social doing" – on grounding theory in social–political life as it is performed in competent performances – they would be better able to converse across substantive domains, theoretic perspectives, and methodological approaches.

We respond as sympathetic critics. Specifically, we endorse the argument that a focus on practices holds appreciable potential as a conceptual framework for the analysis of the empirics of international politics. Placing practices at the center of analysis, making them a "conceptual focal point," we agree, should aid and enrich researchers' efforts to grasp the complexities of international social–political life, while also providing the basis for theoretically fruitful conversations that bridge the many divides that afflict the IR field. Focusing on practices, and the background knowledge that they embody, and through which they are socially meaningful, holds the potential to foster serious engagement between realists and liberals, for example, over the conditions of possibility for and limitations on stable patterns of cooperation among agents of state, as well as the production of interstate enmities. Rather than recapitulating meta-theoretic assumptions about the determinative (or plastic) role of anarchy – whether or not it is what states make of it – or conversely about the world-order-making role of transgovernmental networks and global civil society in addressing such core questions of the discipline, IR scholars' turn to practices – asking what is being *done* in producing interstate harmonies and/or enmities, what competent performances are involved – should go a long way

335

toward bridging paradigmatic divides. Similarly, the agent-centered analyses of many constructivists and the intertextual focus of some poststructuralists could reach a point of productive conversation about the materialization of discourse in practices of normalization of international social life. We believe and we hope that the partisans of the "isms" of the discipline can effectively mute much of the currently sterile war of scholarly position by turning away from the defense of respective meta-theoretic foundations and toward empirical atten- tion to the "doing" of international politics. Accordingly, we commend the editors of and the contributors to this volume for providing systematic exem- plification of a framework for focusing on practices.

At the same time, we are cautious and seek to offer a critique of the foregrounding of practices in IR. For one thing, we would be concerned if the advocacy of a focus on practice were to morph into a new variety of partisan- ship, and we are particularly skeptical of grander claims or implications to the effect that practices are a unique ontology (the editors use the phrase, "[p]ractices' broader ontology"), for reasons that we will attempt to make clear in the remainder of this chapter. Thus, in our view, the contribution of an analytical centering of practices can be substantial, even if more modest than the strong proponents of a field-wide adoption of the scholarly practice of doing so might have it. To realize the full potential that a focus on practices holds for organizing empirical analysis, however, scholars would be well advised, we argue, to address several theoretical issues that haunt this volume.

Our concerns draw heavily on theories of signification and subject formation and, as such, may appear to rest on poststructural meta-theoretic bases often understood as antithetical to the empirical analysis of practices. Despite that appearance and our admitted inclination to be suspicious of *any* claim to have identified *the* gluon that holds all of social life together, we intend our (sym- pathetic) criticism to be taken as an invitation for engagement, not grounds for "a new great debate." We, like the other contributors to this volume, fear that such a debate would divide on epistemological lines, and our comments would be rejected because of the particular meta-theoretical approaches on which they draw. It may also appear that we are bringing too wide a variety of conceptually challenging, and epistemologically contested, approaches to bear, possibly more than any scholar can be expected to reckon with in the course of an empirical research project. This is not our choice *per se* but, as we will argue, it stems from the decision to take practices as an object of analysis. Metaphorically speaking, the focus on practice opens a can of worms. We applaud the practice of doing so, but now the worms cannot be put back in or ignored as and when scholars choose in the pursuit of their research. Scholars seeking to analyze practices in international politics will of course delimit their projects as their conceptual apparatus and research puzzles demand. Our purpose, in this chapter, is to highlight what may be left on the table as a consequence.

The chapter is organized in four sections. In the first three we discuss seriatim three theoretical concerns thrown up by taking practices as objects of analysis in IR. First, we pose the question of "the subject" of practices, and discuss how that question is implicitly answered in terms of a particular theory of the subject, which privileges its pre-constituted being. We suggest that that theory limits the scope of what practices themselves are, and the effects they bring about. An alternative that expressly emphasizes the constitution of subjects would compel a rethinking of the current conceptualization of practices as "competent performances." In the second section, we take up the question of "meaning" and challenge the (again implicit) assumption that practices are to be understood as expressing and conveying a univocal meaning for the practitioner and the broader community of practice. Third, we raise the question of stability and change, and argue that the analysis of practices falls short of offering satisfying ways of theorizing change in international politics. Indeed, in being premised on pattern, regularity, and repetition, albeit with a bit of "wiggle room," the focus on practices generates an exaggerated sense of stability and can obscure both the social processes that generate change and the inherent instability of practices themselves. Throughout our discussion of these three questions, we seek to provide what we see as a complicated and nuanced, but prospectively appropriate, theoretical basis for realizing the potential of a centering of practices in the study of international politics; we illustrate our points with a few select examples from the chapters of the volume, and beyond. We conclude in a fourth section by discussing a methodological issue for any research program focusing on practices, and we propose how to resolve it.

Theorizing the subject

Interrogating practices in the study of international social–political life promises to bring attention back to the performers of the "competent performances" of statements, actions, and interactions. The "doing" is done by "doers" – or, in the terminology of this volume, "practitioners." As Emanuel Adler and Vincent Pouliot state in their framework Chapter 1, they "insist that agency is front and center in the interplay of practice, if only because it is practitioners who, ultimately, are the performers."[1] In this formulation, actors figure as agents not just in their rational, goal-oriented pursuits, but within a culturally and temporally bounded social context, and even, perhaps, as emotional beings (as in Chapter 3 by Bially Mattern). Insofar as the focus on practices is locating "front and center" these materially situated beings *doing* practices, then, one can safely say that analyzing practices in IR centers the subject, manifested in his or her "competent performances."

---

[1] Adler and Pouliot, Chapter 1 in this volume.

A practice is "competent" in the sense of resonating with existing understandings (background knowledge), against which it becomes socially meaningful. There are two implications of this conceptualization that, in their conjunction, set the pre-constituted subject as the assumed theoretic ground. At the level of consciousness, the subject is self-aware of her behavior according to social standards, an awareness that constitutes her as a competent subject. However, as several contributors acknowledge, conscious actions do not exhaust the universe of practices; many practices are performed almost absent-mindedly, out of habit, for example. They are nevertheless competent performances – that is to say, practices – to the extent that others in the community of practice recognize them as such. This leads to the second implication of practice for the theory of the subject, namely the importance of social recognition. A social being is recognized as a subject within a community when it performs a practice competently, whether consciously or absent-mindedly. Brunnée and Toope provide the example of legal obligation in Chapter 5, where a community of lawyers shares understandings about legal frameworks that may then operate without formal enforcement mechanisms.[2] Central to this process is "reciprocity," where reasons are given for a particular regulation that can then be accepted by those who live by it: practices are competent by virtue of being social.[3]

It is in the centering of the subject, in placing the agent "front and center" as "practitioner," that the focus on competent social practices can potentially lead to a significant analytical oversight. Practices are not just performances of subjects, the competencies through which they act in the world and do things. The social context of competent performances means that practices are also the means through which subjects are produced as such.[4] It is by engaging in social practices that beings become subjects; in that respect "there is no doer before the deed." Through particular kinds of performances (the deed), the doer is produced – a subject's social identities are established. These identities, performed competently, and often attended by markers such as professional certifications, enable recognition as a legitimate player in a social forum or game. To be recognized as a legitimate participant in World Bank forums, for example, an individual has to be conversant with, if not sympathetic to, neoclassical economic approaches.[5] If an individual espousing different views is faced by material difficulties such as an extended peer review process in having her voice heard, she may either leave the organization, or alter her views to fit the dominant consensus, in a version of groupthink.[6]

---

[2] Brunnée and Toope, Chapter 5 in this volume.   [3] *Ibid.*

[4] Judith Butler makes the crucial observation that to be a subject means both a process of creation ("becoming a subject") but also being "subjected" to a particular social structure. Individuals become subjects in delimited ways that always refer to broader social relations – by playing "roles," for example. Butler, 1997, 106–131.

[5] Sending and Neumann, Chapter 9 in this volume.   [6] Janis, 1983.

Groupthink highlights the always potentially troubled relationship between the subject and practices as competent performances. We point to it as illustrative, but over the next several pages we move well beyond it through reference to chapters in this volume in order, not simply to emphasize the problematic theorization that privileges the subject but more importantly to bring into doubt the very conceptualization of practices as competent performances which is part and parcel of a subject-centered theory. According to the notion of groupthink, agents often sacrifice their views of the best course of action in the performance of being team players, and this can inhibit openness to information or views that challenge the group's ideas, leading in some cases to decisions that counter the very purpose of the group. Such a dynamic of producing and performing collective subjects introduces two complications: first, that two facets of competence – the competent performances productive of the collective subject and the competent performances of that collective subject – may be in tension; and, second, there may exist a multiplicity and divergence of social contexts of competence productive of subjects.

With respect to the first, Sending and Neumann's Chapter 9 provides an excellent example.[7] The Performance Based Allocation System (PBA) is an index used by the World Bank to determine aid allocations aimed at spurring economic growth. Within the PBA, the most heavily weighted feature is "governance," now largely understood as legal and regulatory issues such as corruption. The PBA, however, abstracts from country-specific variables. As a consequence, a country can have desirable outcomes like a high growth rate while scoring low marks on the PBA if it has high levels of corruption, for example, or vice versa. This means either that the PBA has little causal efficacy in evaluating prospects for growth, or that the World Bank might, on a case-by-case basis, reward those anomalies that see high growth rates despite corruption to further boost the prospects of development. The practical alternatives would be either to scrap the PBA as an analytical tool or to allow conditional deviations from it. Neither of these alternatives is likely to be adopted; rather, a focus on a rules-based system of allocations has trumped other concerns, including even the Bank's remit to promote economic growth. In other words, in competently performing the outward appearance of objective and equal treatment of all states, productive of its subjectivity as an international organization (IO), the World Bank compromises the end for which it was instituted. Here the performances through which the Bank is produced as subject are in tension with – indeed, contradict – its reason for being, and hence its practices as subject.[8]

---

[7] Sending and Neumann, Chapter 9 in this volume.

[8] A similar point can be made of Stein's argument that even when NGO accountability renders their actions inefficient or ineffective, those practices are still necessary to "convince watching audiences" of their virtue. Stein, Chapter 4 in this volume.

This kind of situation compels the question of when and how practices should be conceptualized as incompetent performances, a question not addressed in this volume. However, such "incompetent practices" are consequential, and further, there are rich literatures that deal with their consequences. Anthropologists and sociologists, for example, have documented how acts of spectacular consumption or waste mark individuals as socially important.[9] The idea that seemingly excessive behavior is important in the production of self is hardly unknown in the IR literature: Thomas Schelling's famous story of the rich men throwing coins into the bay in San Francisco to outdo each other is an excellent example.[10]

Voeten's Chapter 10 provides an example. In the negotiations around the 1960 *Declaration on the Granting of Independence to Colonial Countries and Peoples*, Voeten argues, the USSR brought the resolution before the plenary session, continuing past efforts to publicize the issue, but it was the language drawn on by the decolonized countries that stressed liberal principles of human rights that was ultimately responsible for the affirmative votes from the Western powers. Despite advocating for the *Declaration*, Khrushchev chastised the Western powers for their "colonial behavior" and "exploitation," making it unlikely that the Western powers would actually support it.[11] It is easy to read the USSR's crude language as a mistaken, or botched, effort at advocacy – the "incompetence" was to make a statement which reduced the chances of achieving the ostensible objective of the practice of speaking. However, the issue of "incompetent performance" that we are raising is not so much a matter of engaging in practices that undermine their purpose. Rather, it is more in recognizing the ambiguity and tension surrounding the production of the Soviet subject in international politics. One could quite easily see the practices as productive (and performative) of the USSR as subject in relation to "the West," standing in tension with its agency *vis-à-vis* the colonized world.[12] This suggests revising Voeten's argument somewhat. Insofar as the USSR was pushing the concept of self-determination, it was productive of the subject position of the USSR as an opponent of Western powers. The practices in question, in this light, should be understood within the broader context of the production and performance of superpower rivalry, as well as the limited goals of passing the resolution.

[9] See, for example, Mauss, 1990; Bourdieu, 1984; and Bataille, 1989.
[10] Schelling, 1966, 119.   [11] Voeten, Chapter 10 in this volume.
[12] If one considers that Khrushchev's famous shoe-banging episode, which we will discuss further on p. 342, occurred on October 12, 1960, about three weeks after the statement Voeten cites, it becomes likely that the USSR had several other issues in mind. Voeten does not mention this incident. Benjamin Welles, "Khrushchev Bangs His Shoe on Desk; Khrushchev Adds Shoe-Waving To His Heckling Antics at UN," *New York Times*, October 13, 1960.

Voeten's Chapter 10 brings us to the second issue thrown up by the possibility of "incompetent performances" in relation to the implicit theorization of the subject underlying the study of international practices – that of understanding the social context within which practices are situated. Little in Chapter 7 makes the point that practices around the same event may be in accordance with different social contexts.[13] We would go further to suggest that the practices around an event, insofar as they constitute particular subjects empowered to act, are themselves areas of contestation. Again, practices in such contexts may drive us further afield from a comfortable conclusion of competence. Take, for example, an election in an environment where terrorism is a significant campaign issue. A candidate from a historically dovish party may wish not to be seen as "soft" on national security, and hardens her position accordingly. To win the election, the candidate must position herself as a credible voice on national security issues and, in this instance, that involves taking a hard line, both rhetorically and in terms of proposed policies. If her competitor plays the same game, there is very quickly a consensus on the policies towards terrorism that have little to do with the threat, *per se*, and more to do with making a claim to be the legitimate speaker (and eventually representative) on the issue of national security.[14] Here, while the event motivating the practices may be a terrorist act or threat, the practices may have little to do with that event. This makes it not only difficult to evaluate the "competence" of a practice, but indeed could cause us to question the utility of "competence" itself as a criterion for practices.

In the example of the election, we saw how the need to appear vigilant in dealing with terrorism may be detrimental to counterterrorist policy. However, the politicians in question are not consciously adopting "incompetent" strategies; they are being maneuvered into them as the consequence of their contest to appear to be a particular kind of subject. There are instances, however, where actors either reflexively or self-consciously act incompetently in order to establish their identity – or, more precisely, their identity itself is constituted by departing from what would constitute "competent performance." We might schematically term these types of practices "acting out," and "transgressing."[15] "Acting out," familiar to students of psychoanalysis and parents alike, is a

---

[13] He makes the argument that the international system and international society are governed by separate practices. Little, Chapter 7 in this volume.

[14] This is hardly a hypothetical example. On the broad argument that governments commit greater resources to observable anti-terrorist policies than is strictly necessary, see Mueller, 2006; and Lustick, 2006.

[15] Here we suggest that the psychoanalytical literature may offer valuable insights into exploring what Bially Mattern in Chapter 3 terms "emotional practices." Not only have emotions been a central object of analysis in this literature, approaching emotions from the perspective of subject-formation may provide a simpler and more elegant model for theorizing them.

reflexive action where the subject seeks to discharge some mental conflict, and consequently appears rebellious or even threatens the parental figures. In the analytical situation, the subject acts out because she is unable to remember or articulate what is upsetting her, and enacts the source of her distress on the target.[16] This manifests itself in a continuing struggle with existing norms and order.

"Transgressing" is a more self-conscious and actively subversive practice. Here, an agent engages in practices that subvert the identity she is expected to adopt. For example, gay activists have adopted the term "queer," previously a derogatory reference, as an identity in politically consequential ways.[17] In being queer, they reject the more mainstream LGBT appellation, and are able to have their own political space from which to speak. Equally, "queer" functions not just as a noun, but also as a verb, enabling queer activists to "queer" hetero-normative practices, such as broadening what should constitute marriage to include civil partnerships. The line between "acting out" and "transgressing" is not clear-cut. Consider Khrushchev banging on the table with his shoe at the United Nations in 1960, an action that came less than a month after the debate on self-determination. From his daughter's account, Khrushchev felt he was not being taken seriously during his protests over the U-2 incident, and the rejection of his disarmament plan, and decided to respond in similar coin: "dismissing him as a worthy opponent, capitalists thought of Khrushchev as a vaudeville character . . . very well then, he would become one." As he asseverated, banging on the table, "his watch fell off. Meanwhile, his shoes, made of durable Soviet leather in a special shoe atelier for the Soviet nomenclature, were too new and too tight, and he removed them. He bent down to pick up the watch and saw his empty shoes."[18]

The outcome was the subsequently legendary shoe-banging scene, still an iconic image of the Cold War. Khrushchev's performance was not premeditated, stemming as it did from his sense of irritation at the situation. However, in transgressing the norms of diplomatic practice, it made more or less the statement he intended: the USSR was not going to accept what it perceived as UN support of the so-called colonial powers.

Practices that take the form of "incompetent" performances are therefore consequential: they ground certain types of subjects, and they have important political effects – for example, signaling a refusal to abide by the existing rules. Of course, an objection may be raised to our emphasis on "incompetent" practices. Surely these are rare events, exceptions that mark the rule, and it is entirely justifiable for scholars to focus instead on iterated practices because these constitute the *stuff* of international politics. We resist this objection on

[16] Freud first noted this phenomenon in the famous case of Dora. Freud, 1989, 236.
[17] Butler 1990.
[18] Nina Khrushcheva, "The Case of Khrushchev's Shoe," *New Statesman*, October 2, 2000.

two grounds. In international politics, it is often the exceptions, like war, that are the most important objects of analysis. To leave "incompetent" or exceptional practices out of the universe of observations seems inappropriate for our discipline in particular. Also, if we do not take incompetent practices seriously, we will be unable to recognize those actors in international politics who are resisting or transgressing the existing rules. This would handicap the ability of scholars of international practices to understand change in the international system, a point which we shall expand on below. More perniciously, from a political perspective, a focus on competent practices is to ignore those who contest existing rules using decidedly "incompetent" practices. Anti-dam activists, for example, are often not recognized as legitimate participants in policies around dam projects and development, because their practices valorize local knowledge and values, not economic calculation. Yet, precisely through being "incompetent," these practices and their practitioners have forced major changes in the perceptions of the utility of dam projects.[19] We feel confident in asserting that IR scholars, and the contributors to this volume, in particular, have neither as an analytical nor political goal the silencing of already marginalized groups – ignoring their subjectivity; yet, this is potentially an implication and consequence of the understanding of practice as competent performance by subjects.

Theorizing meaning

The focus on practice gives, at least implicitly, a pride of place to meaning. In two ways, understanding practices in IR pivots around "meaning." Practices become such only against an existing context of meaning, or background knowledge.[20] And practices take form within a "community of practice," which gives them meaning as competence.[21] The emphasis on meaning seems intuitive: surely practices must mean something to their practitioners and audiences in order to be socially consequential and hence to be a candidate for a gluon of social life. Yet, just as was argued in the discussion of incompetent practices above, this may obscure rather than illuminate consequential events in international politics that involve misperception and/or misinterpretation. Fundamentally, we suggest, the meaning of practices may not necessarily be self-evident or transparent to their author or their recipient. This stems from

---

[19] In the famous case of the Narmada dam in India, the anti-dam movement led to a World Bank review, and the Bank ultimately pulled funding for the project in 1993 (albeit the Indian Government provided the money itself).
[20] See Adler and Pouliot, Chapter 1 in this volume; and Brunnée and Toope, Chapter 5 in this volume.
[21] See Stein, Chapter 4 in this volume; Little, Chapter 7 in this volume; Hansen, Chapter 11 in this volume; and Morgan, Chapter 6 in this volume.

the inherent instability of language, and the relationship between practices and language, which requires rigorous theorization.

As Hansen points out in Chapter 11, practices are "ambiguously situated between the sedimented and self-evident on the one hand, and the contested and unstable on the other."[22] Practices work to anchor a particular set of meanings that are then taken as self-evident and *prior to the practices themselves*. This is a form of retroactive or structural causality, which can be understood in the way Lacan theorized the relation between the imaginary and symbolic order.[23] The example Lacan used was of a worker in a strike.[24] An individual understood himself as a worker, and therefore participated in the strike. In this sense, the individual only participated because he was already a worker, in an already adversarial relationship between labor and capital. But, in another sense, the individual's participation in the strike is what constituted the individual as worker, and framed the dispute as an adversarial one rather than a collaborative relationship between labor and capital, for example. The adversarial labor–capital relationship at the level of political structure is a product of the material practice of the worker (striking), yet appears prior to him and driving his actions.

Yet, this adversarial relationship is neither self-evident, nor existing outside of the worker's actions. The employer may understand, or represent, the actions of the worker within a different frame, constituting them very differently as practices. Labor activism in Detroit between the world wars was framed by both sides as a matter of national security, not the class struggle: labor painted Henry Ford as a Nazi sympathizer; capital painted labor as in cahoots with communism.[25] The workers themselves may not understand their actions as being structured by an adversarial relationship between labor and capital: they may strike because of particular grievances, or be in solidarity with their peers even if they think the strike is a bad idea. In other words, the strike may be grounding quite different meanings than the class struggle.

What this suggests is that meaning is far more unstable than can be inferred from the practice itself: what needs theorization is the linguistic structure to which it refers. This structure, by the very nature of language, is fluid and contradictory. As Saussure suggested, signifiers derive their meaning in relation to other signifiers: a cat is a cat because it is not a bat, for example.[26] Yet, because the other signifiers are infinite in number, meaning is perpetually differentiated, and hard to fix finally, depending on which signifiers are in play at any time.[27]

---

[22] Hansen, Chapter 11 in this volume.

[23] On structural causality, see Althusser, 1970, 186–188. Lacan defined the relation between imaginary and symbolic as follows: "The symbolic function presents itself as a double movement within the subject: man makes an object of his action, but only in order to restore to this action in due time its place as a grounding." Lacan, 1977, 80.

[24] *Ibid.*, 81.   [25] Rupert, 1995.   [26] Saussure, 1959.

[27] A cat is not a bat, but it is also not a dog or a truck either. Derrida, 1982.

Any practice gains meaning not just from the particular signifier(s) to which it refers, but potentially also from the universe of signifiers which differentiate the "appropriate" signifier. In the above example, workers striking in Detroit may want the general public to understand them as standing up for the "rights" of "labor" against "capital," and, through the metonymy of these signifiers, for the rights of all hard-working Americans who work against a common adversary oppressing them in their place of work. But the general public may understand each signifier differently, creating a quite different metonymy. For "rights," they may understand the "entitlement" of a collectively bargained contract that guarantees relatively higher (and undeserved) wages; for "labor," they may understand a "union" that limits their own "right to work"; for "capital," they may understand the "American values" of free enterprise. The metonymy in this case becomes "the entitlements of union members that actively destabilize American values." Between sender (labor) and recipient (American public), the meaning of practices can be multiple and even contradictory.

Here we offer a very schematic theorization of the relationship between practices and signifiers, one that will hopefully assist scholars of practices. Practices can be understood as a form of enunciation, or what Foucault called a statement.[28] A statement is "not the text of discourse but its taking place."[29] That is, a practice enacts a certain discursive formation, or structure of signifiers. It does not just reflect or follow from that structure, as implied by the concept of *habitus* or background knowledge. Rather, it grounds that particular structure, brings it into existence, so to speak. The strike as practice is a statement that materializes the labor–capital struggle, bringing it into being. Yet, as the example suggests, this grounding is not univocal; insofar as the structure is constituted through signifiers that gain their meaning from being differentiated from other signifiers,[30] the possibility of polysemy is a structural necessity of practices.

In international politics, the polysemy and contradiction of practices is even more evident. This is partly because the international system is not as patterned by shared norms and understandings as a smaller-scale society. This creates the possibility that a specific action (or competent performance) refers to different signifiers in different contexts, and is therefore received differently – is, in that respect, socially constituted as different practices. Historically speaking, US policy-makers understood nationalist movements in the third world in relation to a system of signification in which "communist sympathizers" were meaningful subjects. While many African leaders called themselves socialists and advocated policies such as nationalization and centralized planning, they were

---

[28] Foucault, 1972.   [29] Agamben, 1999, 139.

[30] As Foucault puts it, "it is not enough to say a sentence, it is not even enough to say it in a particular relation to a field of objects or in a particular relation to a subject, for a statement to exist: it must be related to a whole adjacent field ... a statement always has borders peopled by other statements." Foucault, 1972, 97.

neither copying the Soviet model, nor necessarily allying with the Soviets. Indeed, leaders like Léopold Senghor of Senegal were critical of Soviet policies and differentiated "socialism" from "communism."[31] As Valentin Mudimbe has observed of African socialism, the significant term is "African," not "socialist," by which he means that African leaders were trying to carve out a distinct form of socialism, like Julius Nyerere of Tanzania's *Ujaama* socialism, where Nyerere argued that pre-colonial African traditions exemplified socialism.[32] For US policy-makers, however, the signifier "socialism" was not associated with "African traditions," but rather with "Soviet stooges." Practices such as nationalization had a quite different meaning in the two contexts, spurring US support of proxy wars across the continent, and US support of apartheid, staunchly anti-communist South Africa.

A further point can be made. The authors of this volume have generally suggested the necessity of a community within which practices become intelligible. However, practices that are understood differently can divide a community or create opposed communities as well. Consider the Rodney King incident. In 1991, four white Los Angeles police officers savagely beat a black man while the cameras were on, for which they were acquitted a year later. While the incident received much publicity, it was understood by many African-Americans as standard police behavior that was fortuitously captured by the cameras on this occasion. The trial was therefore an opportunity to punish the police for something they did routinely, and when the officers were acquitted there were riots in Los Angeles. The acquittal can be understood on one side as an exceptional, and excusable, reaction to an obvious threat (an intoxicated black man). On the other side, the acquittal was understood as legitimating the everyday experience of police brutality, to be responded to with violence of one's own.[33] The incident intensified the animosity between the police and the black community, in large part because they could not agree on the meaning of the incident.[34]

Our point is not that of relativism; rather, we are reiterating the central role of the ever-present instability of meaning in international politics – and correspondingly the loose boundaries of "communities of practice." For a parallel to the Rodney King incident in international politics, read the many cases of mutually exclusive claims to territory, which are reiterated through routinized practices such as drawing maps. A party in such a territorial dispute may represent a territory as its own on a map: India, for example, teaches schoolchildren that, for example, the territory of India includes the northern third of Kashmir, but the other – in this case, Pakistan – will not recognize that representation. Insofar as practices are understood as conveying meanings against

---

[31] Senghor, 1964, 46.   [32] Mudimbe, 1988, 95.

[33] See, for example, the lyrics of the hit song "Fuck tha Police" by N.W.A.

[34] Lyotard has called this type of disagreement a "differend," where two sides approach an issue from entirely opposite systems of signification that cannot coincide. Lyotard, 1988.

shared background knowledge, and within a community, these meanings can be different in different contexts – *the same performance is simultaneously different practices*. This does not mean that practices are inscrutable or unknowable. Rather, by theorizing their relationship to the signifiers they ground, and then tracing how those signifiers are understood through differentiation with other signifiers, we can understand how practices are often internally contradictory or constituted differently. These misunderstandings can be productive, in the sense that they can create separate communities around the same event, or even communities in conflict with each other.

Theorizing change

We suggested above that the focus on practices as competent performances might obscure important aspects of social activity in international politics, and that the unstable relationship of practices to the constitution of meaning in language should be explored, both theoretically and empirically. In this section, we will bring together the lines of critique of the previous two sections to suggest that the study of practices in IR may have great analytical potential, which the current theoretical approach risks overlooking. Arguably the most important area where the focus on practices can shed light is on how international politics, at the level of actors and the normative justifications for their actions, changes over time.

Presumably, a focus on everyday practice should provide the best purchase for understanding change because it reveals alterations of practices over time. Contributions to this volume illustrate well that analysts of practice can identify changes in how foreign policy is conducted, for example. Ripsman in Chapter 8 observes that in the period of bipartisanship opposition legislators in the United States were heavily involved in passing crucial foreign policy legislation such as the Marshall Plan and the ratification of NATO, because in some cases they had more influence on powerful committees than legislators from the ruling party.[35] This consensus did not follow from the balance of power (since, after the First World War, Woodrow Wilson did not reach out to opposition legislators, and they defeated his policy goals like the League of Nations), but from efforts on the part of the Roosevelt and first Truman Administrations. However, bipartisanship appears somewhat ad hoc as an explanation for policy coherence. Without diminishing its importance, one wonders whether this bipartisanship was itself not an artifact of something like a learning process: the US executive branch, wanting to avoid a repetition of Wilson's foreign policy blunders, reached out to the opposition.[36] Here, one might ask whether

---

[35] Ripsman, Chapter 8 in this volume.

[36] A self-conscious adaptive learning process seems an obvious implication of the fact, presented by Ripsman, that the Roosevelt and Truman Administrations pursued opposite staffing strategies than Wilson did. Ripsman, Chapter 8 in this volume.

and to what extent the focus on practices obscures the broader context in which practices occur. Specifically, can the theoretical approach to practice obscure two trajectories through which change can happen?

The first, which we call the diachronic, comes from ignoring precisely those transgressive actors that are most likely to bring change into the international system. As we suggested above, "incompetent" practices can mark a refusal to abide by the current rules, and can be the basis for a challenge to those rules – and, potentially, change in the rules themselves. Such practices, by deviating from the current order, also voice previously unthinkable possibilities. The rebelling slaves in French San Domingo claimed and won independence from France in 1804, and the resulting state, Haiti, has functioned as a sovereign state for the most part until the present.[37] But in the racialized international politics of the nineteenth century, the idea that a slave colony could be a sovereign state was unthinkable, so the United States and the Vatican did not grant diplomatic recognition to Haiti for decades and Haiti was not invited to the first hemispheric summit in 1826 in Panama.[38] From the standpoint of practices, the status of Haiti is almost a cipher: insofar as the practices of its officials in the performance of sovereignty were not socially recognized within the international community of the time, Haiti did not exist, despite engaging in otherwise recognizable activities of a state, such as invading Spanish Santo Domingo in 1804 and 1822.[39] Haiti is transgressive in the way we discussed and, as such, it both opened the possibility for change but also fell outside the socially legible, competent practices of the time. It is therefore interesting to note that none of the chapters in this volume sheds light on fundamental changes in the international system: revolutions from the Haitian to the Russian to the Chinese, decolonization itself (rather than a juridical act formalizing a process already in motion), or the end of the Cold War. Insofar as the authors theorize change, it is either of an incremental sort stemming from reflection within an already constituted community, as Stein analyzes in Chapter 4,[40] or change provides background conditions for a shift in practices, as Morgan's Chapter 6 on deterrence posits.[41] We would suggest that this is neither coincidence nor an artifact of the authors' choices. Rather, the theoretical orientation towards practices in IR may preclude an analysis of practices that appear incompetent or exceptional at the time. This downplays the transformative potential of actual practices across history.

---

[37] The United States occupied Haiti between 1919 and 1934.   [38] Trouillot, 1995, 95.

[39] Adler and Pouliot specify that practices "acquire concrete and workable theoretical and empirical meaning in the concept of *communities of practice*." Adler and Pouliot, Chapter 1 in this volume. Emphasis in the original.

[40] Stein, Chapter 4 in this volume.

[41] To wit, Morgan suggests that deterrence is a socially situated rather than a mechanical response to the threat of conflict, and as that context has changed, both the practices and community around deterrence have changed, too. Morgan, Chapter 6 in this volume.

Put otherwise, from a more structural perspective, the focus on competent practices serves to reify the existing order, because competence is always in relation to existing norms and mores. This seems to follow from the two explicit theoretical referents that the authors have provided: the Bourdieusian *habitus*; and pragmatism. First, the focus on Bourdieu's notion of *habitus* privileges a stable and iterable foundation to practice that is univocal within a particular community.[42] Bourdieu described *habitus* as:

> This immanent law, lex insita, laid down in each agent by his earliest upbringing, which is the precondition not only for the co-ordination of practices, but also for practices of co-ordination ... because they are the product of dispositions which, being the internalization of the same objective structures, are objectively concerted that the practices of the members of the same group or, in a differentiated society, the same class are endowed with an objective meaning that is at once unitary and systematic, transcending subjective intentions and conscious projects whether individual or collective.[43]

We would suggest that this univocality, the "objective meaning that is at once unitary and systematic," is not theoretically tenable, given the polysemy of language. Nor is it empirically viable, given the ways in which members of communities can multiply interpret seemingly straightforward signals. It is therefore important to grapple with approaches to signification, such as the ones we have highlighted, that explicitly theorize such polysemy and the possibility of inherent ambiguities and instabilities.

Second, Kratochwil's turn to pragmatism in Chapter 2 serves as a philosophical foundation for the focus on practices.[44] We agree with his steps towards explicating the necessity for a sophisticated theorization of what practices are. However, basing the theorization of practice on pragmatism can bracket the question of background knowledge in three senses. First, the meaning of background knowledge may be taken for granted; second, how background knowledge is itself contradictory or unstable, as Hansen puts it in Chapter 11, may be ignored;[45] third, how change would occur to background knowledge itself may be left untheorized. That said, we are not suggesting that pragmatism has no resources with which to understand background knowledge as a touchstone for practices: Charles Peirce, for example, suggested links between logic and signs.[46] From such a pragmatist perspective, interrogating the logic of practices would reduce the risk of reifying the "prejudices" from which analysis begins.[47]

---

[42] See Pouliot, 2008; and Adler and Pouliot, Chapter 1 in this volume.
[43] Bourdieu, 1977, 81. [44] Kratochwil, Chapter 2 in this volume.
[45] Hansen, Chapter 11 in this volume.
[46] He wrote that "Logic in its general sense, is ... only another name for semiotics (semeiotike), the quasi-necessary, or formal, doctrine of signs." Peirce, quoted in Derrida, 1976, 48.
[47] On prejudices as a starting point, see Kratochwil, Chapter 2 in this volume.

The second potentially overlooked trajectory of change, which we call the synchronic, comes from not theorizing the relationship between important signifiers and the practices that ground them. As we argued above, practices do not just reflect background knowledge; they serve as well to ground or enact a certain linguistic structure. The practice of giving every state a seat in the United Nations performs sovereignty. Yet, "sovereignty" itself has changed over time, and the UN practice can more properly be said to ground a certain sort of sovereignty.[48] Here, the study of practices can be of great analytical value in understanding these changes in sovereignty, which we illustrate through the example of the "Responsibility to Protect" paradigm.

In recent years, human rights activists have voiced dissatisfaction with the legal category of state sovereignty. Conceptualized as a right of non-interference, sovereignty allows rulers within a state to violate the rights of their subjects, while rendering illegal, in international law, an intervention that would address these excesses.[49] In international law, practices of intervention are illegal, because they violate the norm of sovereignty. In other words, the relationship between the practice (intervention) and the signifier ("sovereignty") renders the practice illegal in meaning. In 2001, the International Commission on Intervention and State Sovereignty (ICISS) suggested that sovereignty under international law be reconceptualized.[50] From a government's right of non-interference, sovereignty would become the responsibility of a government to protect the rights of its citizens. If the government failed in this responsibility, intervention would be both legitimate and legal. If this paradigm is adopted, the practice of intervention continues to operate in relation to the signifier "sovereignty," but now the meaning is transformed *through the change in practice*. It is the practices that change the signifier.

We term this "synchronic" because the signifier ("sovereignty") is the same before and after the Responsibility to Protect is formally instituted and interventions are embarked on in its name. But two significant changes would have taken place. First, the relationship between signifier and practice has changed, for sovereignty as "responsibility to protect" now renders interventions legal. Second, the practice can be said to change the signifier itself. An intervention, conducted under the aegis of the Responsibility to Protect, would concretize the legal and discursive shift in the signifier "sovereignty." Until such an intervention, recognized as legitimate by a significant part of the international community, the Responsibility to Protect cannot be said to have transformed the

---

[48] See Holsti, 2004; and Simpson, 2004.

[49] Hence, Anne-Marie Slaughter argues that intervention in Kosovo – and, by extension, Iraq – while illegal, was still legitimate. Anne-Marie Slaughter, "Good Reasons for Going Around the UN," *New York Times*, March 18, 2003, A33.

[50] See International Commission on Intervention and State Sovereignty, 2001; and Thakur, 2006.

meaning of sovereignty. This example indicates the promise (and, indeed, necessity) of analyzing practices in IR, but also suggests potential shortcomings of the current theoretical orientation, which invites bypassing a rigorous engagement with linguistic structure.

"Practical" problems of research

We have suggested that the study of practices in IR – a very positive development in its own right – can further benefit from a better theorization of three important themes, which we called, respectively, the subject, meaning, and change. In this conclusion, we lay out a challenging methodological issue facing the turn to practice, which we believe must be confronted if the turn is to realize its full potential as the basis for grounding interparadigmatic dialogue. We move away from the theoretical orientation we have used above to think here about method because we believe that it is as a means of accessing the empirical material in international politics that the study of practices holds greatest promise. As such, the study of practices can tell us much about the (changing) complexity of global social life and in that way bridge the chasm created by the "ism" wars. But before it can realize this promise, we need to ask how the universe of practices can be delimited to enable "practical" research projects.

We have argued that delimiting practices to "competent performances" risks precluding seemingly "incompetent" performances that ground subjects, practices whose meaning is contested or otherwise unstable, or transgressive performances that challenge the existing order. Insofar as this risks excluding from study truly consequential events, this is akin to studying the bathwater while ignoring the baby in the tub, or throwing her out of the tub. However, some might object that if our advice were to be followed it would put practices everywhere, and therefore, nowhere. Our argument, if accepted, might broaden the empirical scope of research projects beyond what is feasible. By making it "practically" impossible to study practices, we might appear double agents, fundamentally subverting the study of practices in IR under the guise of being sympathetic critics.

We mean neither to subvert the commitment to studying practices in IR, nor to explode the scope of the objects of analysis. As we hope to have made clear, the study of practices is extremely promising, and there are two relatively straightforward ways to delimit research projects. First, analysts can seek to understand practices in relationship to the practitioners as subjects. What are the subject-forming stakes of particular practices? And, conversely, why is an agent engaging in a particular practice? This is a process of reading backwards, from the practice to the practitioner, from which one can understand who the practitioner is, how she is produced through the practice, and what she understands herself to be and to be doing. Even exceptional or "incompetent" practices can be understood in this way. Khrushchev's shoe-banging, following the bellicose rhetoric of the USSR in the General Assembly, performs a particular subject-position, even when it compromises the purported goals of the enterprise.

Second, analysts can seek to understand practices in relationship to the signifiers they ground. How does a particular practice relate to the signifier it refers to: does it ground or subvert it? Now, it is certainly true that practices, as statements, refer to several signifiers, seemingly complicating this approach. But, insofar as practices are routinized, or iterable, they refer to specific signifiers over and over again. It is this process of repetition that enables analysts to decipher which signifiers are most significant for a particular practice. When the practice complicates or disrupts that repetition, it marks the potential for change. Also, the signifier, and its relation to other signifiers, can be inferred from the practice as performative act. Contrast two types of political advocacy for gay marriage. In the first, advocates suggest that allowing gay partners to marry will create wholesome families, thereby providing a better example of "family values" than current heterosexual families provide – with their high divorce rates, for example. In the second, advocates argue that allowing gay partners to marry will allow for more flexible family arrangements that subvert the hetero-normative nuclear family model.[51] "Family values" are a key signifier in both these efforts, but they mean different things. Analysts can work out the difference by examining the performative aspects of these statements in their associated practices. The first position, for example, often involves mobilizing church communities and using the children of gay couples as spokespeople; advocates of the second may use more transgressive practices that challenge such ideas of domesticity. *Both* may be visible in certain venues, like a Gay Pride parade.

Understanding practices in relation to the subject and the signifier is akin to a process of triangulation that eliminates much of the noise inherent to studying practices. It enables the analyst to take something that does not obviously lend itself to parsimony and derive its underlying structure, what Bourdieu called its "practical logic": "Practical logic – practical in both senses of the word – is able to organize the totality of an agent's thoughts, perceptions, and actions by means of a few generative principles, themselves reducible in the last analysis to a fundamental dichotomy."[52]

The practical logic, we suggest, can be teased out in analyzing the relation of practices to the subject and the signifier. But, given the nature of language, the "fundamental dichotomy" Bourdieu identifies is itself likely to be unstable and differentiated.[53]

---

[51] This argument is also used as a criticism of gay marriage.   [52] Bourdieu, 1977, 110.

[53] Bourdieu expects polysemy from the range of "universes of practice," a different source than language itself. *Ibid.*

If anything, trying to identify the structure or practical logic of practices will make the research project more parsimonious and streamlined, and avoid two risks in particular. First, the focus on a bounded set of practices may unnecessarily localize events in history, and miss the broader context within which a particular event or dispute is situated. As we suggested above, considering Khrushchev's shoe-banging incident would support a somewhat different interpretation of the Soviet approach to the decolonization resolution. It becomes important, therefore, to identify the signifiers and subjects that transcend a particular event-practice, as Hansen nicely defines it in Chapter 11, for such analysis to contribute to a broader historical picture.

Second, in hands less skillful than those of the contributors to the volume, the study of practices can easily become an analysis of minutiae in international politics. There is much to be said for minutiae, and as Ripsman correctly points out in Chapter 8, the stress on parsimony of theories like realism may blind us to consequential political phenomena.[54] Yet, the contributors are also correct to try to delimit the study of practices. While we have raised questions about the way they have done it (by limiting practices to "competent performances"), we agree that this is an important step for any research project. To the degree that it effectively navigates between the attractions of delimiting practices to competent performances, on the one hand, and engaging in the analysis of the unstable relationship of practices to the subject and meaning, on the other, we believe that the study of practices in IR holds a substantial possibility for fostering intertheoretic dialogue and transcending repetition of the binaries of structure–agency and material–discursive that have afflicted the discipline.

References

Agamben, Giorgio, 1999. *Remnants of Auschwitz: The Witness and the Archive.* Translated by Daniel Heller-Roazen. New York: Zone.

Althusser, Louis, 1970. *Reading Capital.* Translated by Ben Brewster. New York: Verso.

Bataille, George, 1989. *The Accursed Share.* Vol. 1, *Consumption.* Translated by Robert Hurley. New York: Zone.

Bourdieu, Pierre, 1977. *Outline of a Theory of Practice.* New York: Cambridge University Press.

  1984. *Distinction: A Social Critique of the Judgment of Taste.* Cambridge, MA: Harvard University Press.

Butler, Judith, 1990. *Gender Trouble: Feminism and the Subversion of Identity.* New York: Routledge.

  1997. *The Psychic Life of Power: Theories of Subjection.* Stanford: Stanford University Press.

---

[54] Ripsman, Chapter 8 in this volume.

Derrida, Jacques, 1976. *Of Grammatology.* Baltimore: Johns Hopkins University Press.

———. 1982. Differance. In *Margins of Philosophy,* translated by Alan Bass, 1–27. Chicago: University of Chicago Press.

Foucault, Michel, 1972. *The Archaeology of Knowledge.* Translated by A. M. Sheridan Smith. New York: Pantheon.

Freud, Sigmund, 1989. Fragment of an Analysis of a Case of Hysteria. In *The Freud Reader,* edited by Peter Gay, 172–239. New York: W.W. Norton.

Holsti, Kalevi, 2004. *Taming the Sovereigns: Institutional Change in International Politics.* New York: Cambridge University Press.

International Commission on Intervention and State Sovereignty, 2001. *The Responsibility to Protect.* Ottawa, Canada: Centre for International Development.

Janis, Irving, 1983. *Groupthink: Psychological Studies of Policy Decisions and Fiascos.* Boston: Houghton-Mifflin.

Lacan, Jacques, 1977. The Function and Field of Speech and Language in Psychoanalysis. In *Écrits,* translated by Alan Sheridan, 33–125. London: Routledge.

Lustick, Ian, 2006. *Trapped in the War on Terror.* Philadelphia: University of Pennsylvania Press.

Lyotard, Jean-François, 1988. *The Differend: Phrases in Dispute.* Translated by Georges Van Den Abbeele. Minneapolis: University of Minnesota Press.

Mauss, Marcel, 1990. *The Gift: The Form and Reason for Exchange in Archaic Societies.* Translated by W. D. Halls. New York: Routledge.

Mudimbe, V. Y., 1988. *The Invention of Africa: Gnosis, Philosophy, and the Order of Knowledge.* Bloomington: Indiana University Press.

Mueller, John, 2006. *Overblown: How Politicians and the Terrorism Industry Inflate National Security Threats, and Why We Believe Them.* New York: Free Press.

Pouliot, Vincent, 2008. The Logic of Practicality: A Theory of Practice of Security Communities. *International Organization* 62 (2): 257–288.

Rupert, Mark, 1995. *Producing Hegemony: The Politics of Mass Production and American Global Power.* New York: Cambridge University Press.

Saussure, Ferdinand de, 1959. *Course in General Linguistics.* New York: McGraw-Hill.

Schelling, Thomas, 1966. *Arms and Influence.* New Haven: Yale University Press.

Senghor, Léopold, 1964. *On African Socialism.* Translated by Mercer Cook. London: Pall Mall.

Simpson, Gerry, 2004. *Great Powers and Outlaw States: Unequal Sovereigns in the International Legal Order.* New York: Cambridge University Press.

Thakur, Ramesh, 2006. *The United Nations, Peace, and Security: From Collective Security to the Responsibility to Protect.* New York: Cambridge University Press.

Trouillot, Michel-Rolph, 1995. *Silencing the Past: Power and the Production of History.* Boston: Beacon.

Index

Cambridge Studies in International Relations